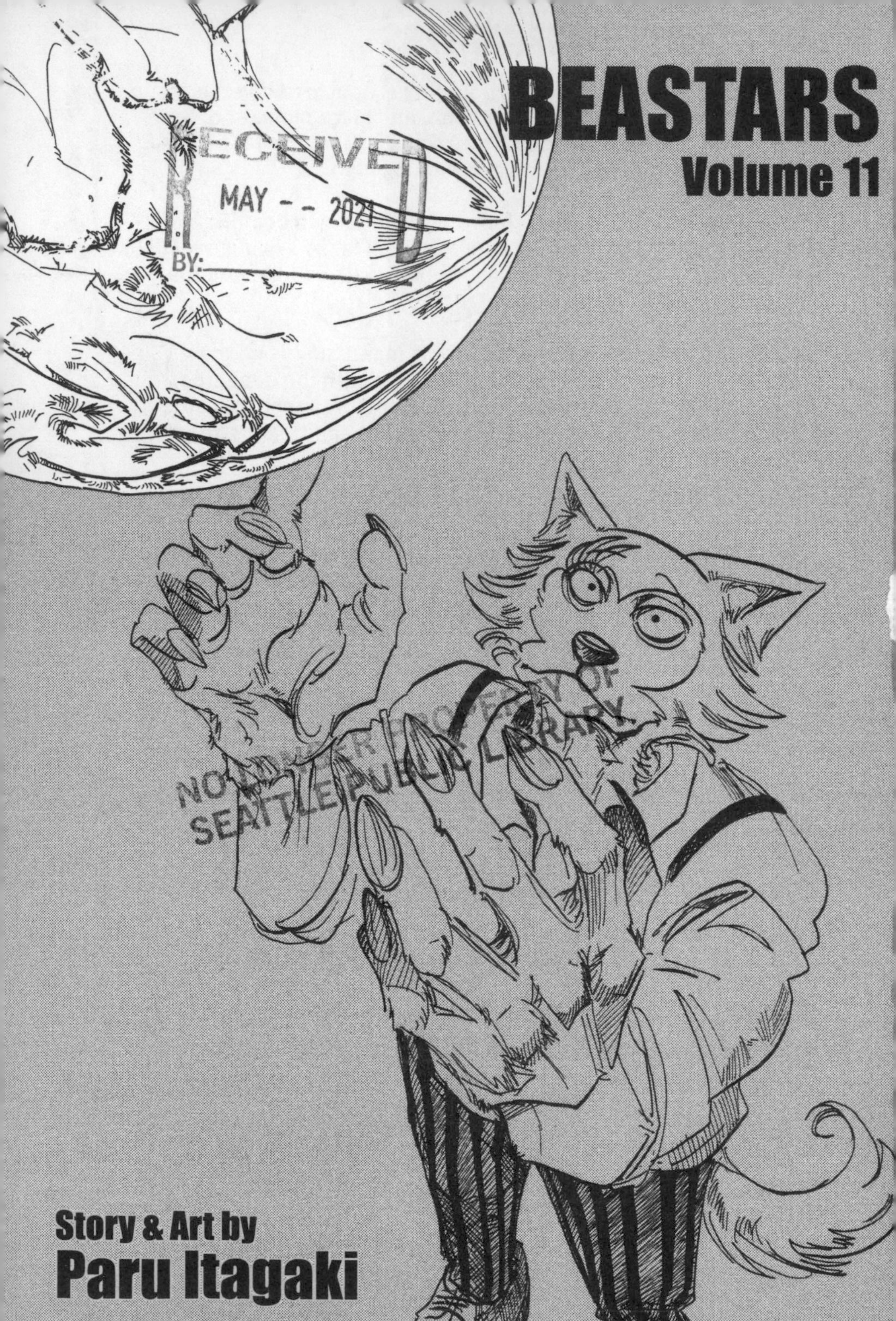

BEASTARS

Volume 11

Story & Art by

Paru Itagaki

STORY & CAST OF CHARACTERS

Plot Treatment... BEASTARS

Cherryton Academy is an integrated boarding school for a diverse group of carnivores and herbivores. Recently Tem, an alpaca member of the Drama Club, was slain and devoured on campus. Since then tensions between predators and prey have been running high...

Legoshi continues to train for his showdown with brown bear Riz, who murdered his friend Tem. In preparation, Legoshi takes a living being's life by eating an insect. This act floods his body with vitality, and his shaved fur grows back virtually overnight.

Legoshi finally sees Haru again at school. He makes up his mind to punish Riz for her sake, then finds himself alone with the dangerous bear in the boys' locker room. Riz wants to get rid of Legoshi because he knows Riz is the murderer. The two begin a life-and-death struggle, but are forced to stop fighting when a janitor appears. They vow to finish their duel on New Year's Eve...

Legoshi sneaks into the black market to see Louis, disguising himself as a female wolf so the Shishi-gumi lion gang won't recognize him. He finds Louis drinking at a bar, and tells him the truth about Riz. Legoshi then asks Louis to witness their duel, but Louis refuses. New Year's Eve is only three days away... The final showdown between Legoshi and Riz is fast approaching!

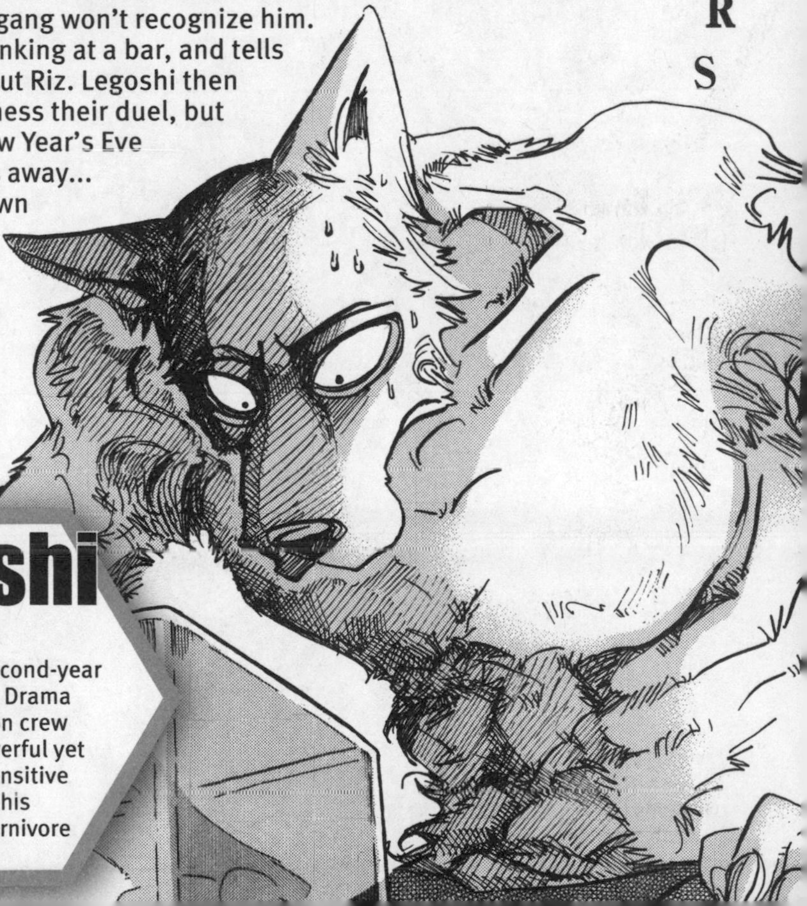

Legoshi

- ★Gray wolf ♂
- ★High school second-year
- ★Member of the Drama Club production crew
- ★Physically powerful yet emotionally sensitive
- ★Struggles with his identity as a carnivore

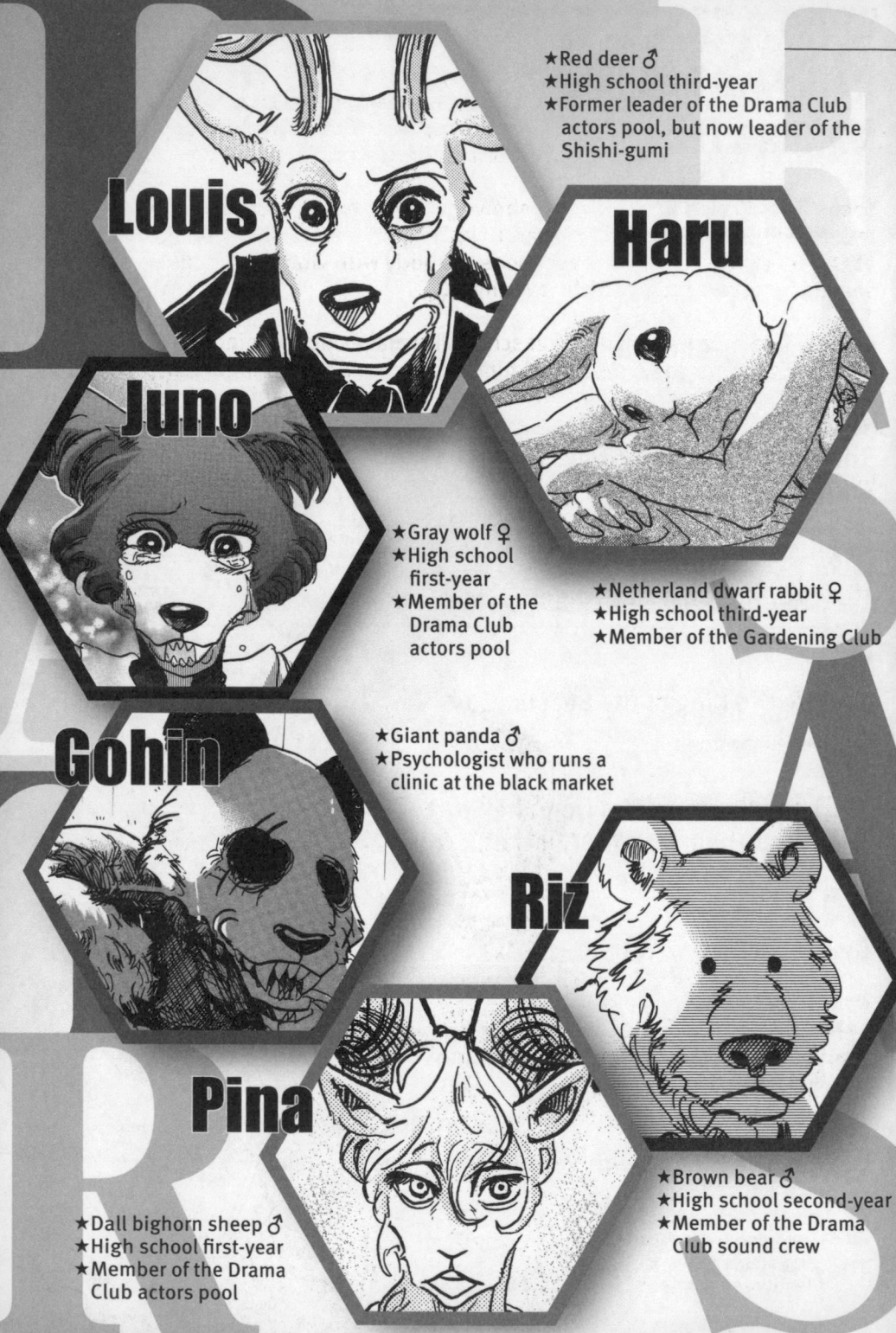

Louis

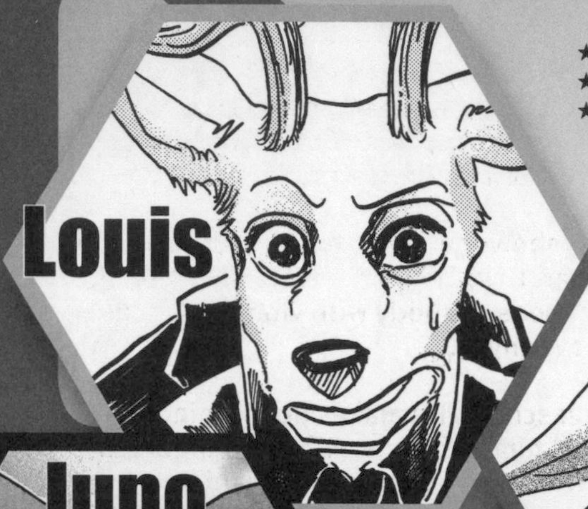

★Red deer ♂
★High school third-year
★Former leader of the Drama Club actors pool, but now leader of the Shishi-gumi

Haru

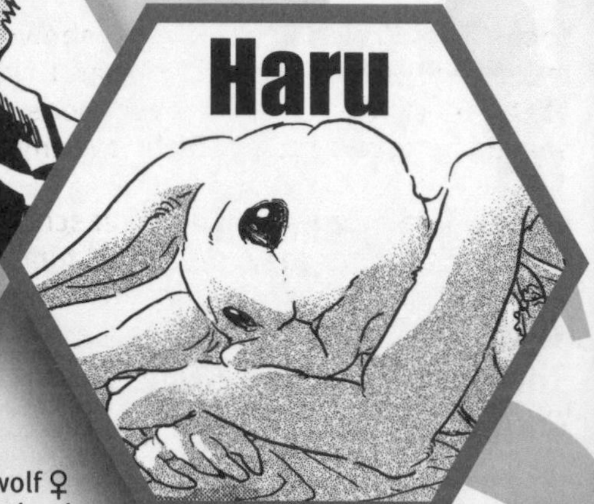

★Netherland dwarf rabbit ♀
★High school third-year
★Member of the Gardening Club

Juno

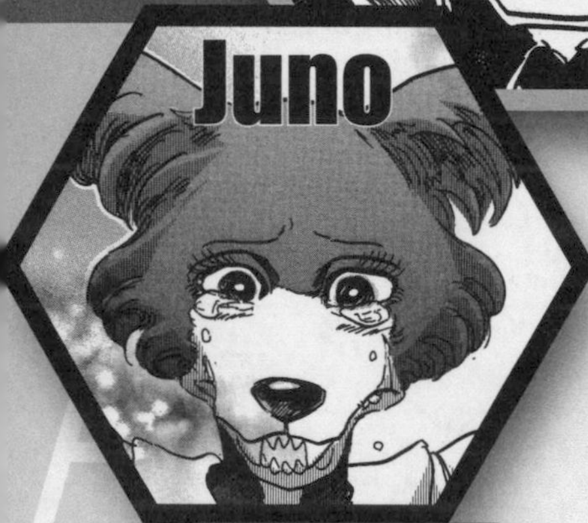

★Gray wolf ♀
★High school first-year
★Member of the Drama Club actors pool

Gohin

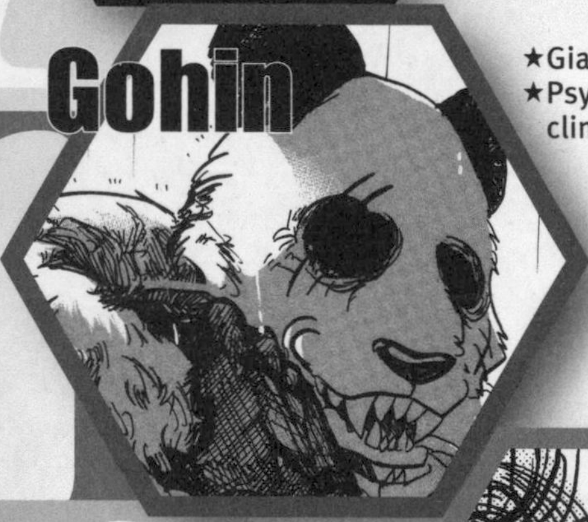

★Giant panda ♂
★Psychologist who runs a clinic at the black market

Riz

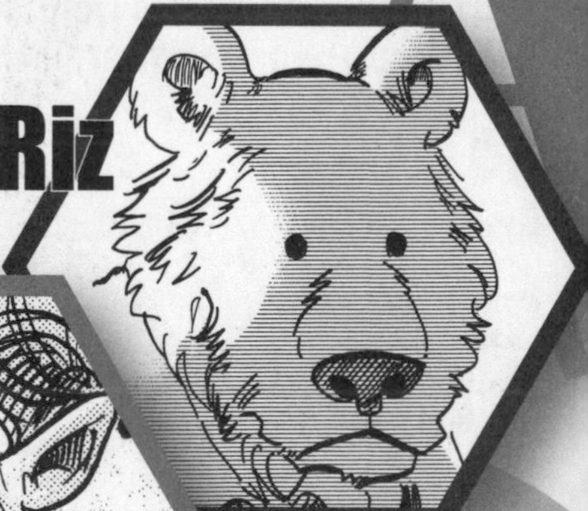

★Brown bear ♂
★High school second-year
★Member of the Drama Club sound crew

Pina

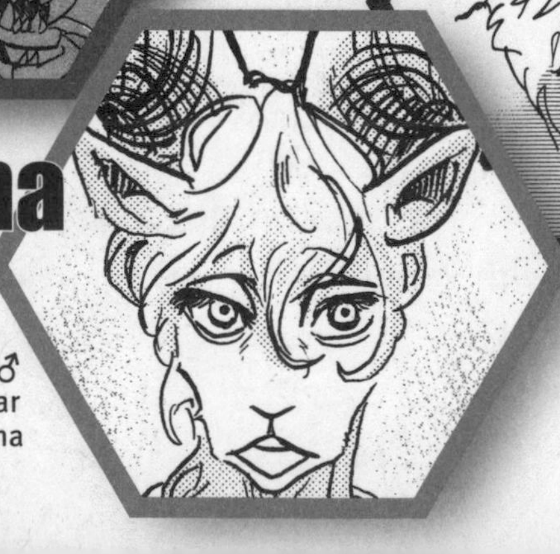

★Dall bighorn sheep ♂
★High school first-year
★Member of the Drama Club actors pool

BEASTARS
Volume 11
CONTENTS

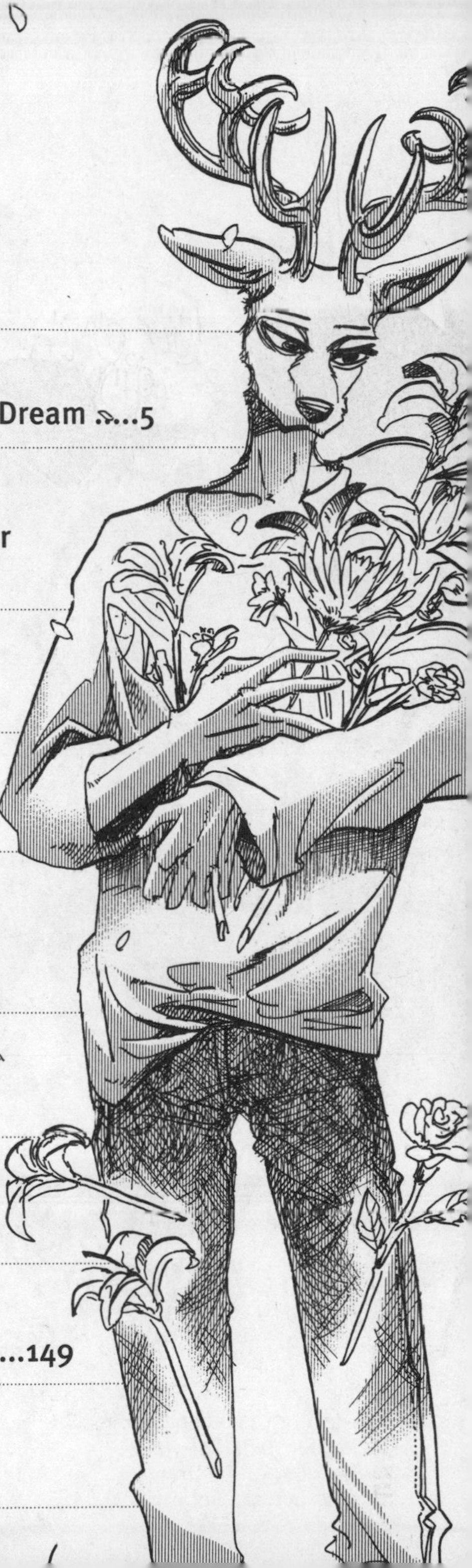

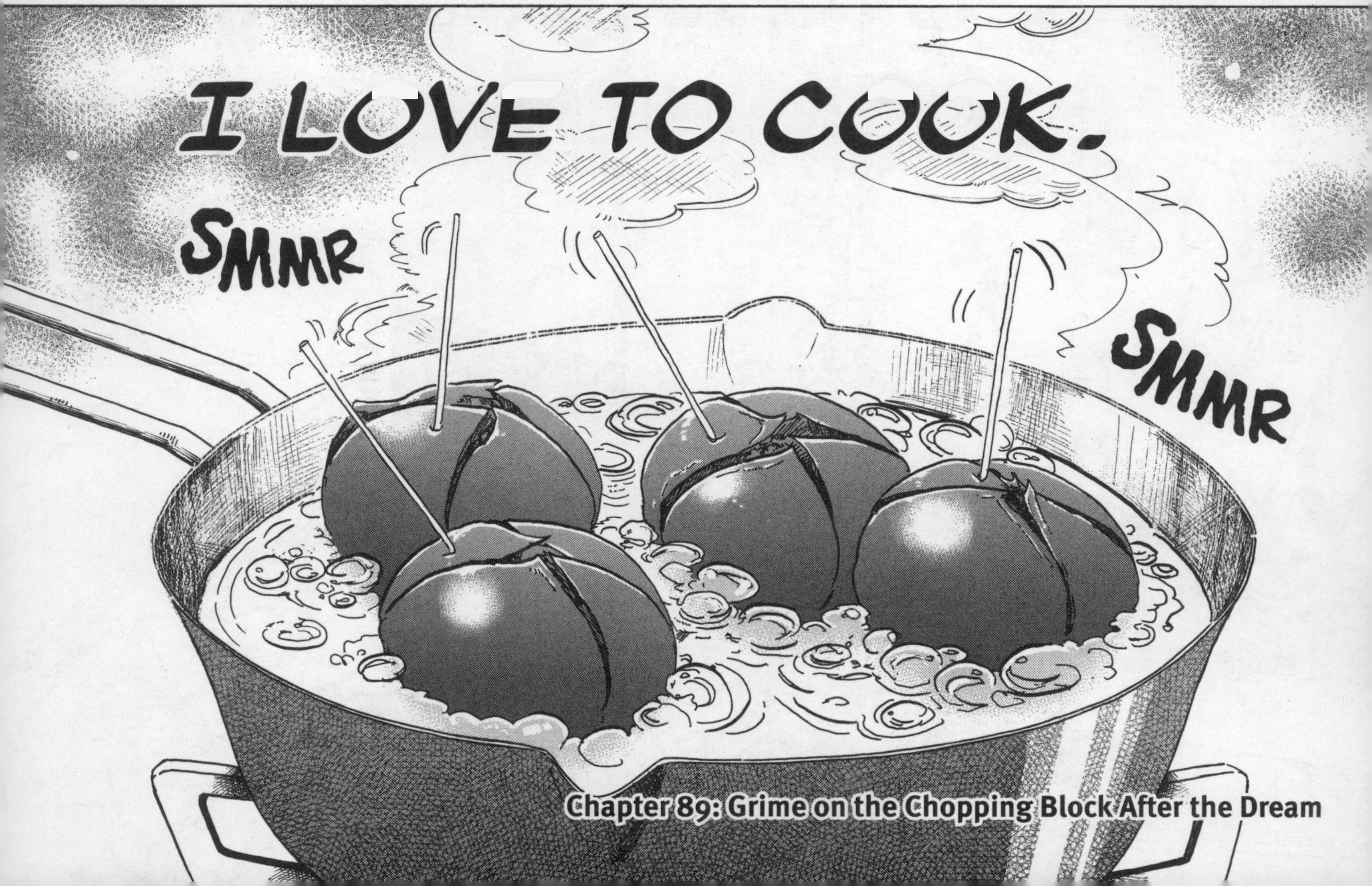
I LOVE TO COOK.
SMMR
SMMR
Chapter 89: Grime on the Chopping Block After the Dream

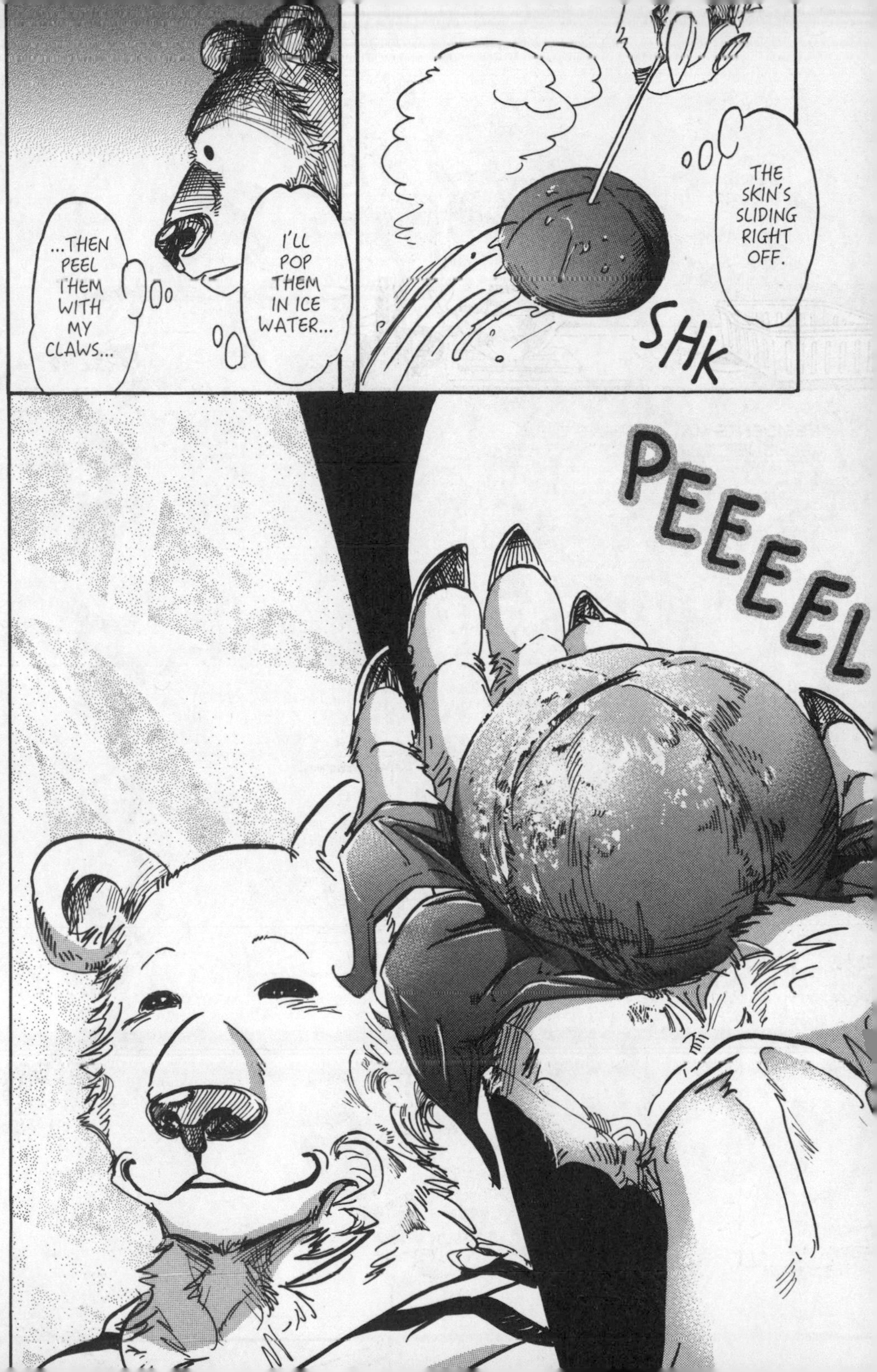
THE SKIN'S SLIDING RIGHT OFF.
SHK
I'LL POP THEM IN ICE WATER...
...THEN PEEL THEM WITH MY CLAWS...
PEEEEL

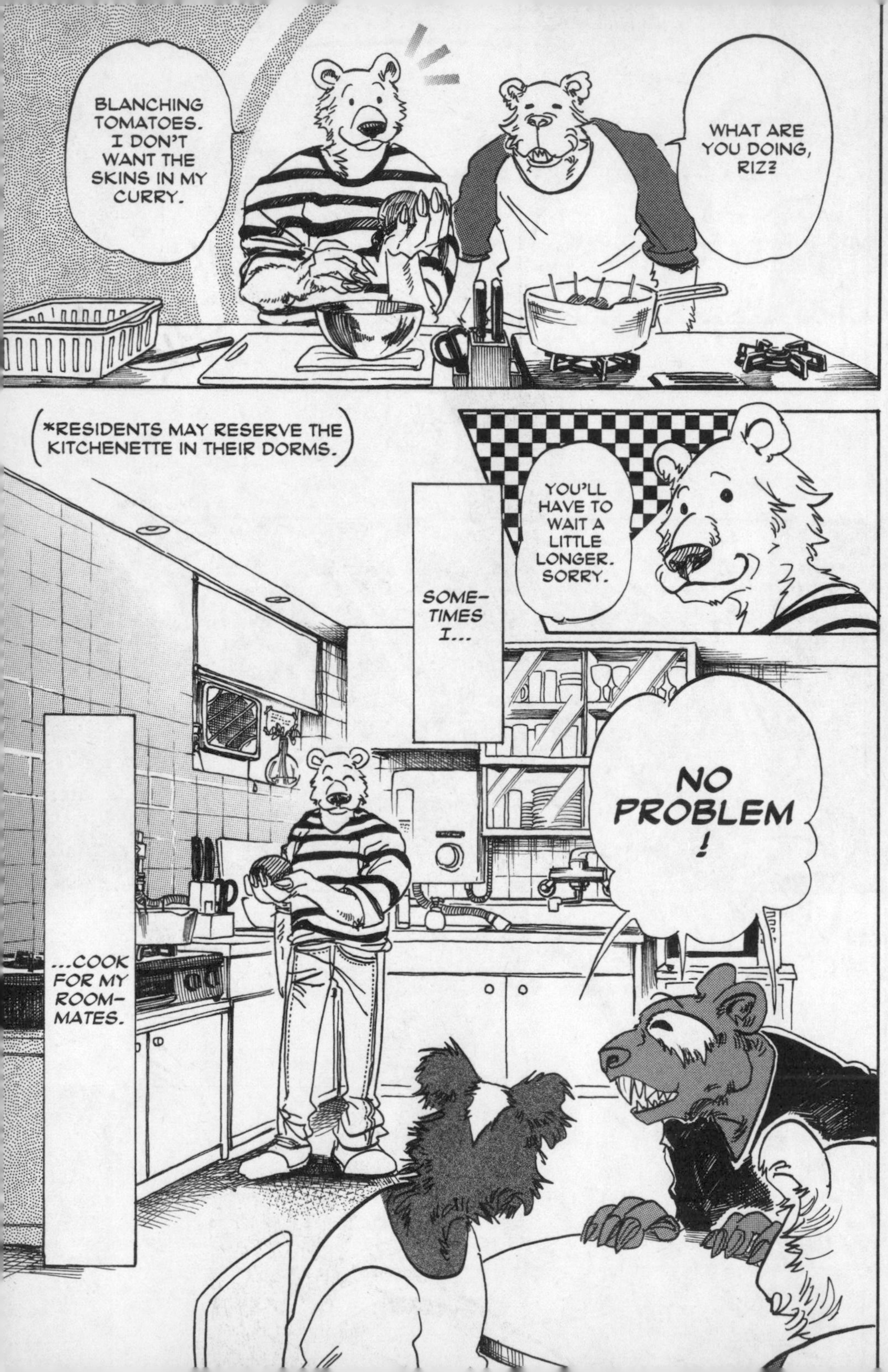
WHAT ARE YOU DOING, RIZ?
BLANCHING TOMATOES. I DON'T WANT THE SKINS IN MY CURRY.
YOU'LL HAVE TO WAIT A LITTLE LONGER. SORRY.
NO PROBLEM!
SOME-TIMES I...
*RESIDENTS MAY RESERVE THE KITCHENETTE IN THEIR DORMS.
...COOK FOR MY ROOM-MATES.

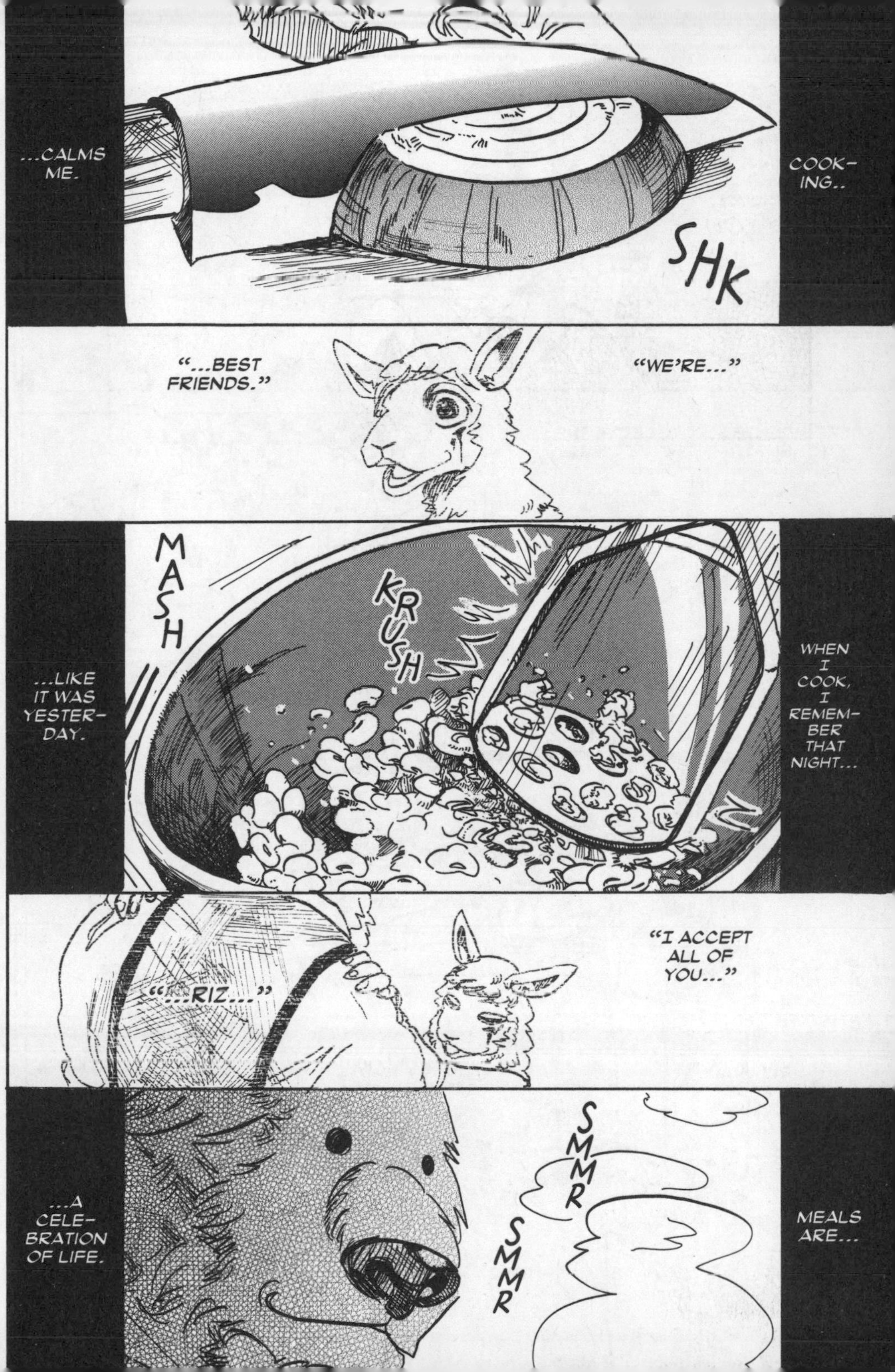
COOKING..
SHK
...CALMS ME.
"WE'RE..."
"...BEST FRIENDS."
WHEN I COOK, I REMEMBER THAT NIGHT...
KRUSH
MASH
...LIKE IT WAS YESTERDAY.
"I ACCEPT ALL OF YOU..."
"...RIZ..."
MEALS ARE...
SMMR
SMMR
...A CELEBRATION OF LIFE.

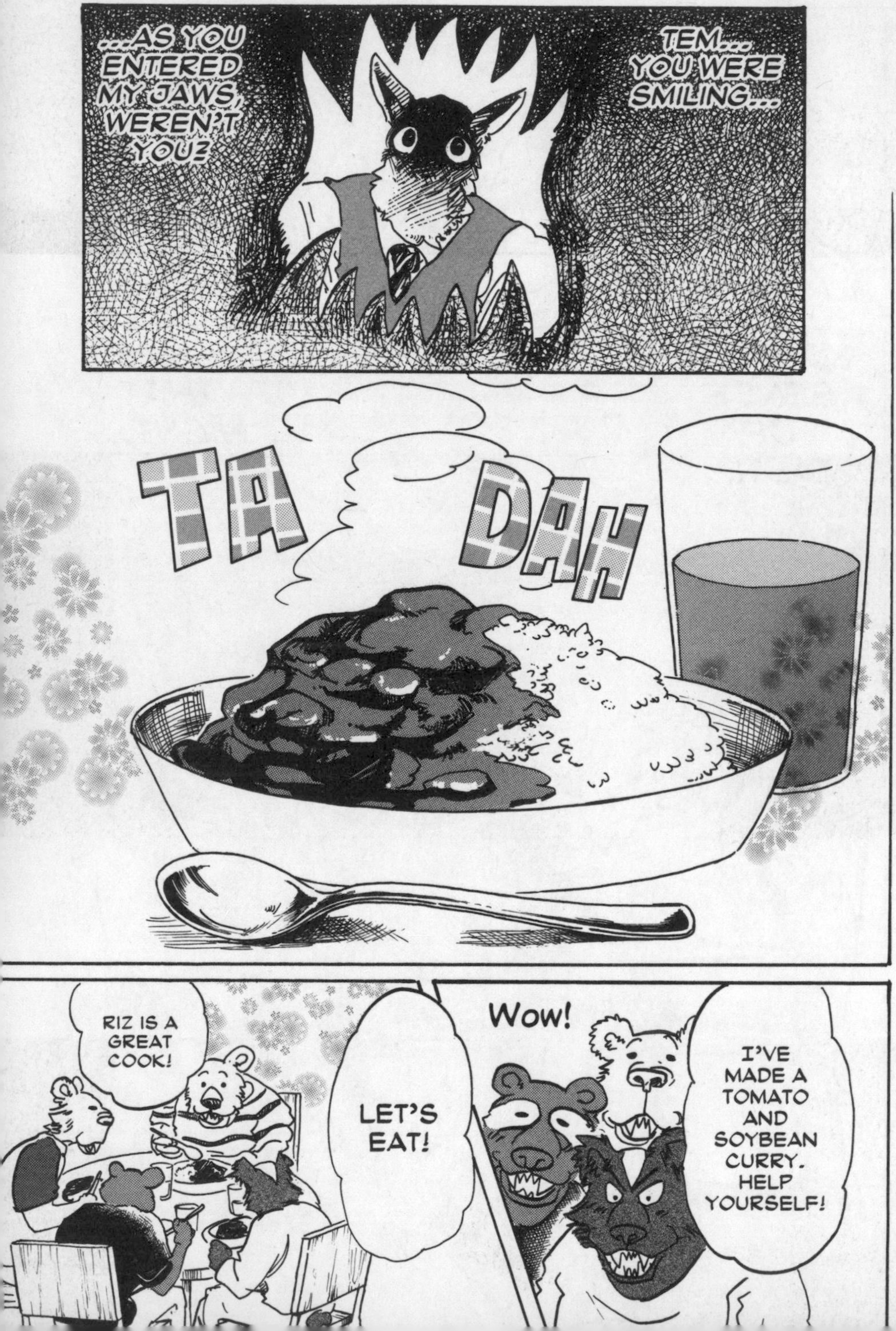
TEM... YOU WERE SMILING...
...AS YOU ENTERED MY JAWS, WEREN'T YOU?
TA DAH
I'VE MADE A TOMATO AND SOYBEAN CURRY. HELP YOURSELF!
Wow!
LET'S EAT!
RIZ IS A GREAT COOK!

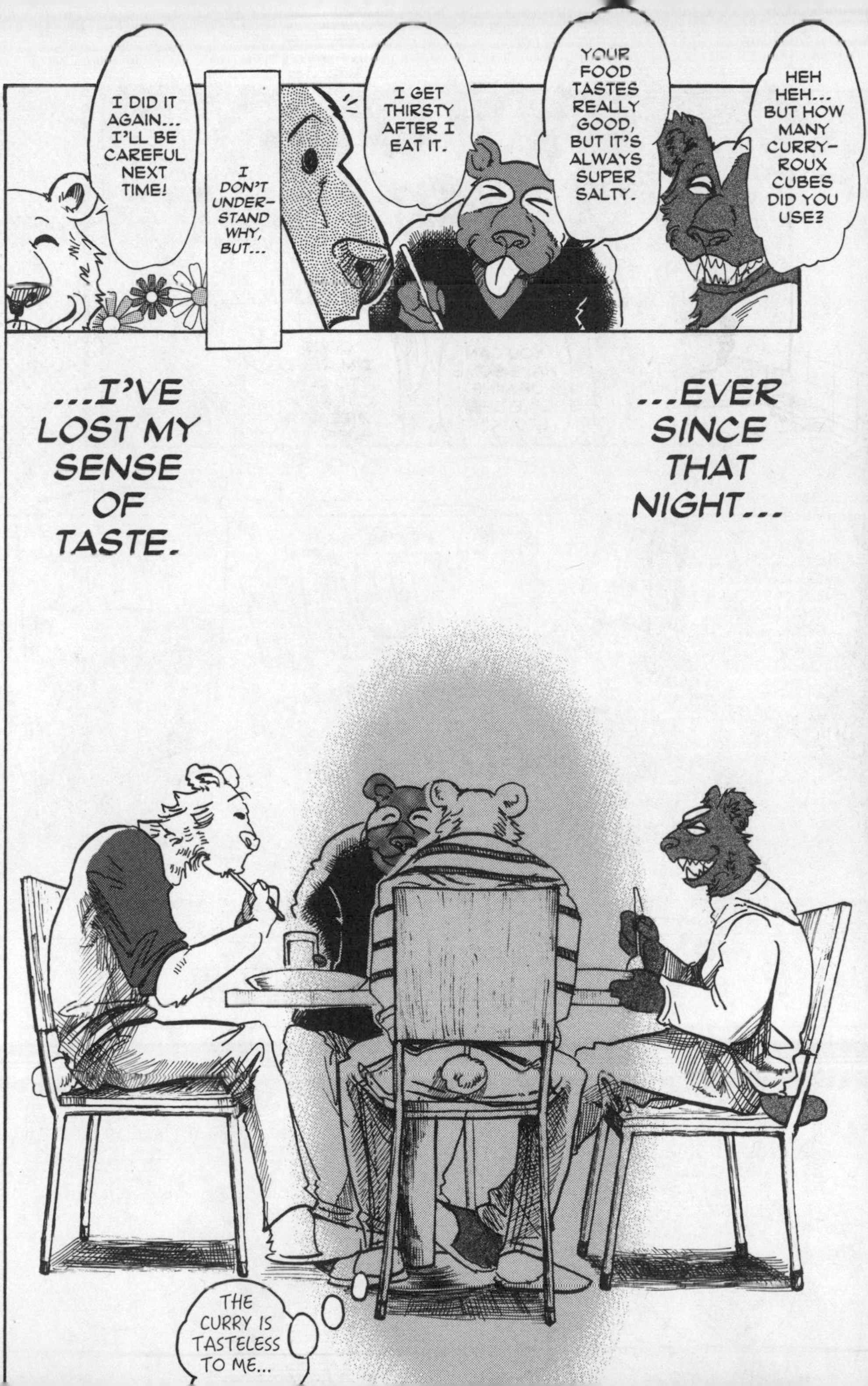
HEH HEH... BUT HOW MANY CURRY-ROUX CUBES DID YOU USE?
YOUR FOOD TASTES REALLY GOOD, BUT IT'S ALWAYS SUPER SALTY.
I GET THIRSTY AFTER I EAT IT.
I DON'T UNDERSTAND WHY, BUT...
I DID IT AGAIN... I'LL BE CAREFUL NEXT TIME!
...EVER SINCE THAT NIGHT...
...I'VE LOST MY SENSE OF TASTE.
THE CURRY IS TASTELESS TO ME...

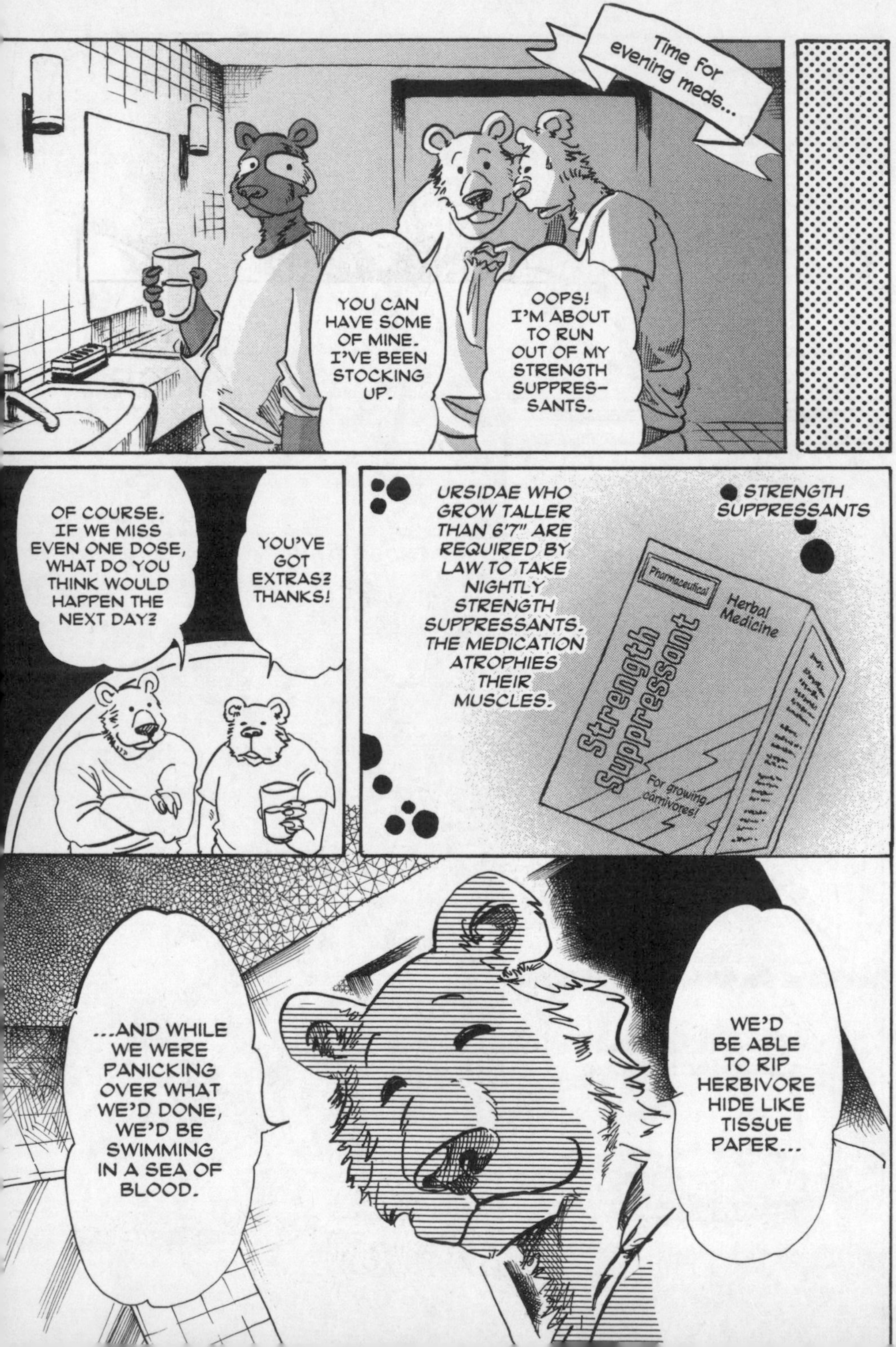
Time for evening meds...
OOPS! I'M ABOUT TO RUN OUT OF MY STRENGTH SUPPRESSANTS.
YOU CAN HAVE SOME OF MINE. I'VE BEEN STOCKING UP.
STRENGTH SUPPRESSANTS
URSIDAE WHO GROW TALLER THAN 6'7" ARE REQUIRED BY LAW TO TAKE NIGHTLY STRENGTH SUPPRESSANTS. THE MEDICATION ATROPHIES THEIR MUSCLES.
Pharmaceutical
Herbal Medicine
Strength Suppressant
For growing carnivores!
YOU'VE GOT EXTRAS? THANKS!
OF COURSE. IF WE MISS EVEN ONE DOSE, WHAT DO YOU THINK WOULD HAPPEN THE NEXT DAY?
WE'D BE ABLE TO RIP HERBIVORE HIDE LIKE TISSUE PAPER...
...AND WHILE WE WERE PANICKING OVER WHAT WE'D DONE, WE'D BE SWIMMING IN A SEA OF BLOOD.

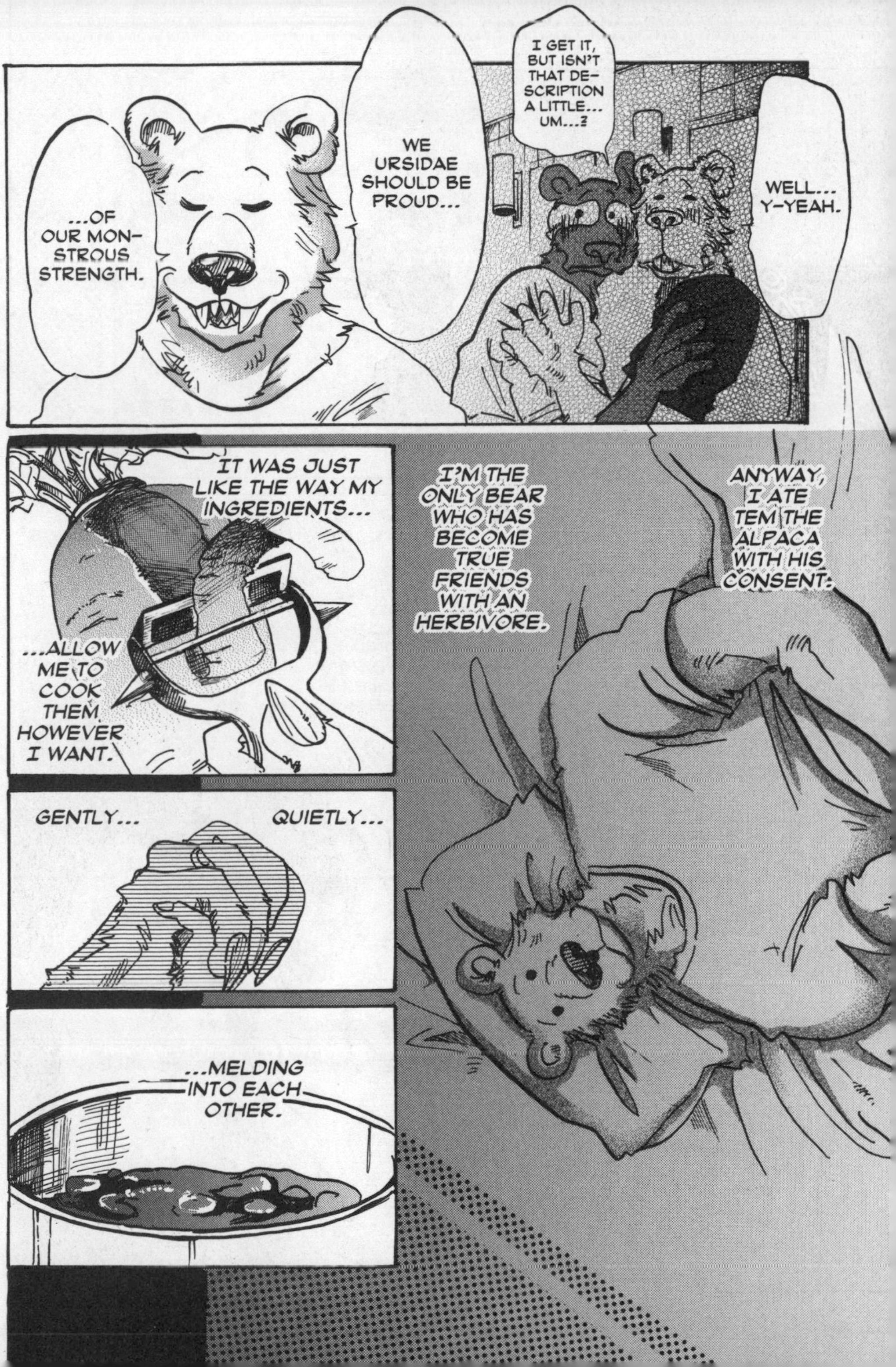
WELL... Y-YEAH.
I GET IT, BUT ISN'T THAT DE-SCRIPTION A LITTLE... UM...?
WE URSIDAE SHOULD BE PROUD...
...OF OUR MON-STROUS STRENGTH.
ANYWAY, I ATE TEM THE ALPACA WITH HIS CONSENT.
I'M THE ONLY BEAR WHO HAS BECOME TRUE FRIENDS WITH AN HERBIVORE.
IT WAS JUST LIKE THE WAY MY INGREDIENTS...
...ALLOW ME TO COOK THEM HOWEVER I WANT.
QUIETLY...
GENTLY...
...MELDING INTO EACH OTHER.

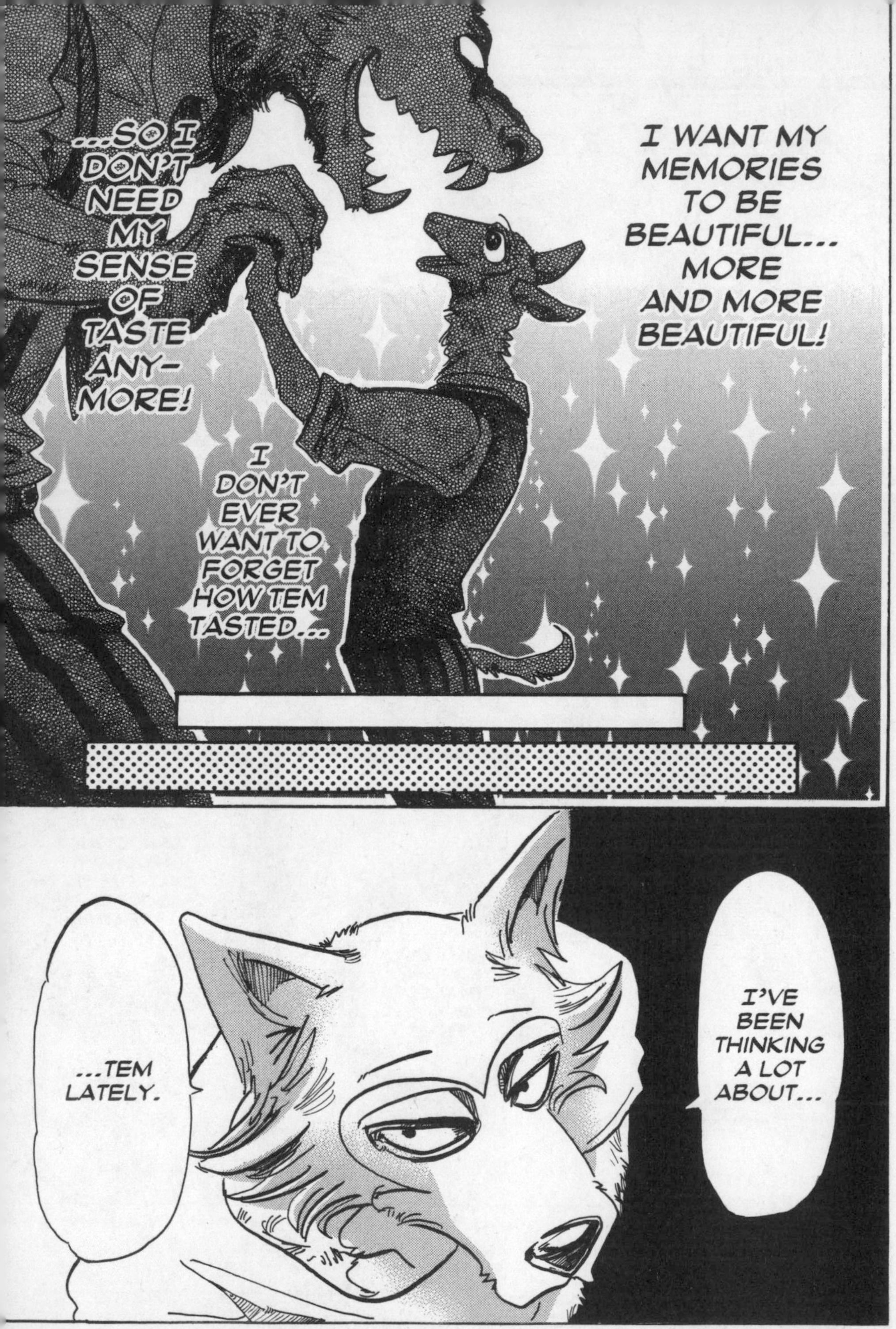
I WANT MY MEMORIES TO BE BEAUTIFUL... MORE AND MORE BEAUTIFUL!
I DON'T EVER WANT TO FORGET HOW TEM TASTED...
...SO I DON'T NEED MY SENSE OF TASTE ANY-MORE!
I'VE BEEN THINKING A LOT ABOUT...
...TEM LATELY.

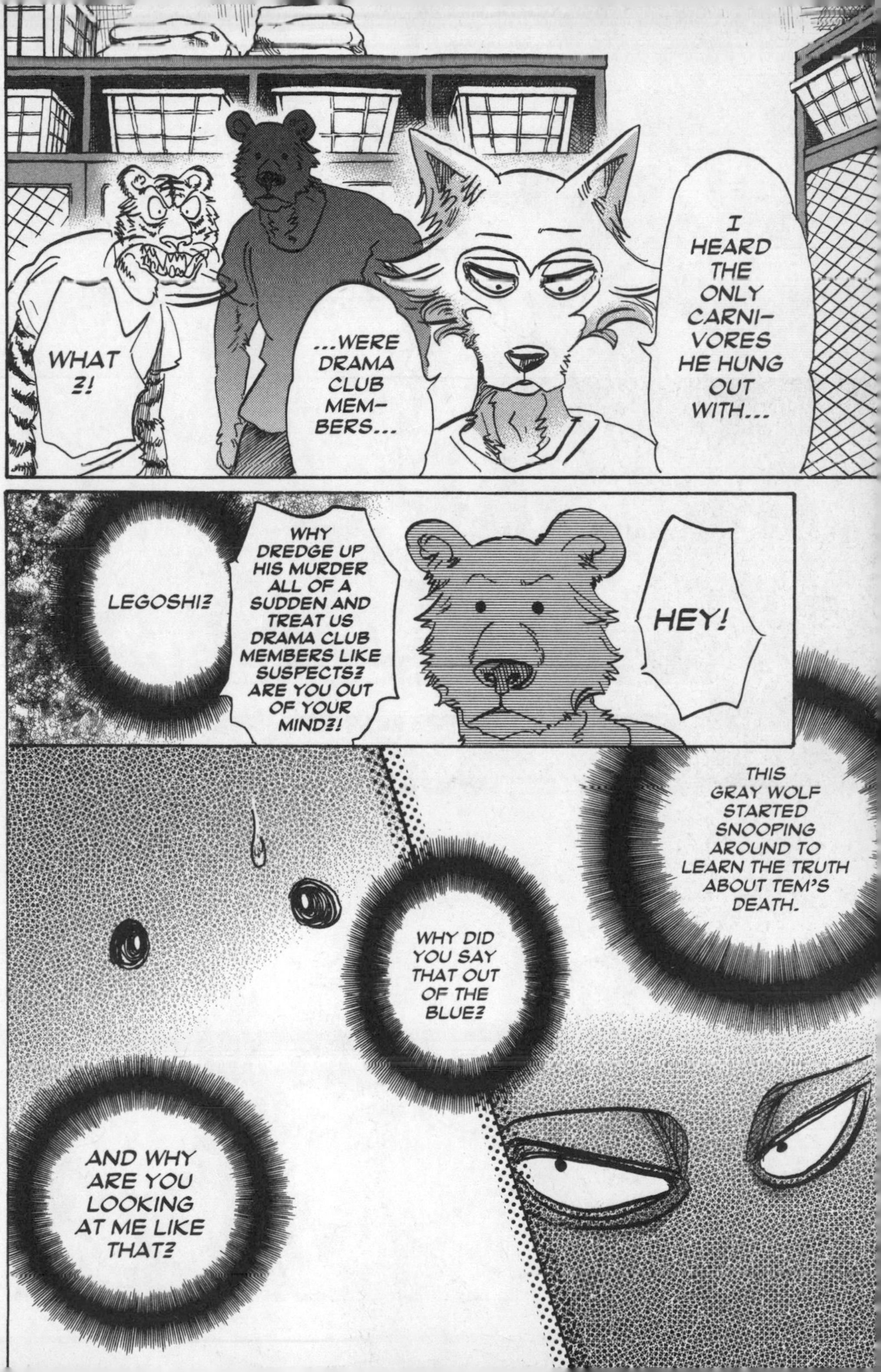
I HEARD THE ONLY CARNIVORES HE HUNG OUT WITH...
...WERE DRAMA CLUB MEMBERS...
WHAT?!
HEY!
WHY DREDGE UP HIS MURDER ALL OF A SUDDEN AND TREAT US DRAMA CLUB MEMBERS LIKE SUSPECTS? ARE YOU OUT OF YOUR MIND?!
LEGOSHI?
THIS GRAY WOLF STARTED SNOOPING AROUND TO LEARN THE TRUTH ABOUT TEM'S DEATH.
WHY DID YOU SAY THAT OUT OF THE BLUE?
AND WHY ARE YOU LOOKING AT ME LIKE THAT?

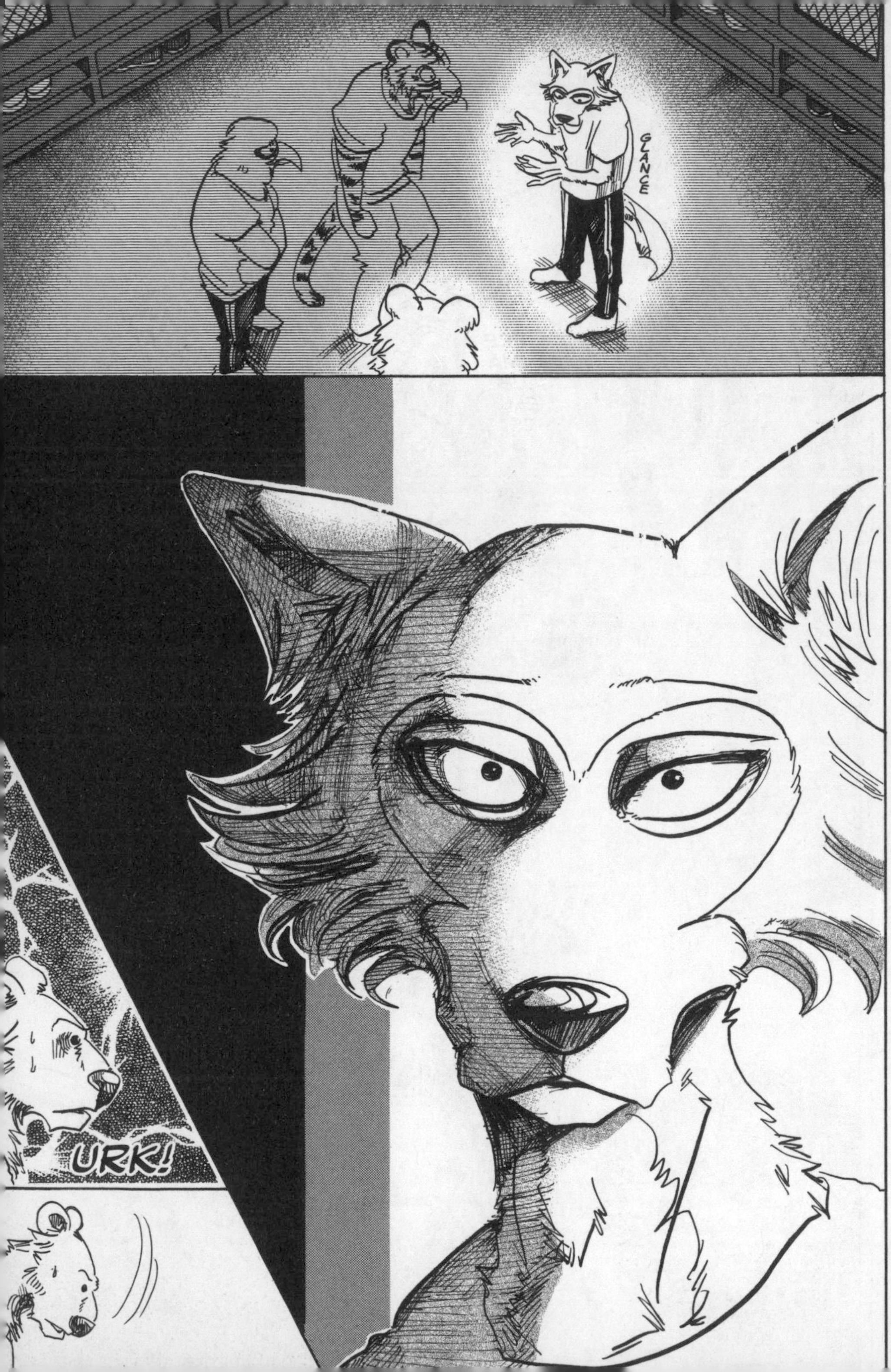
GLANCE
URK!

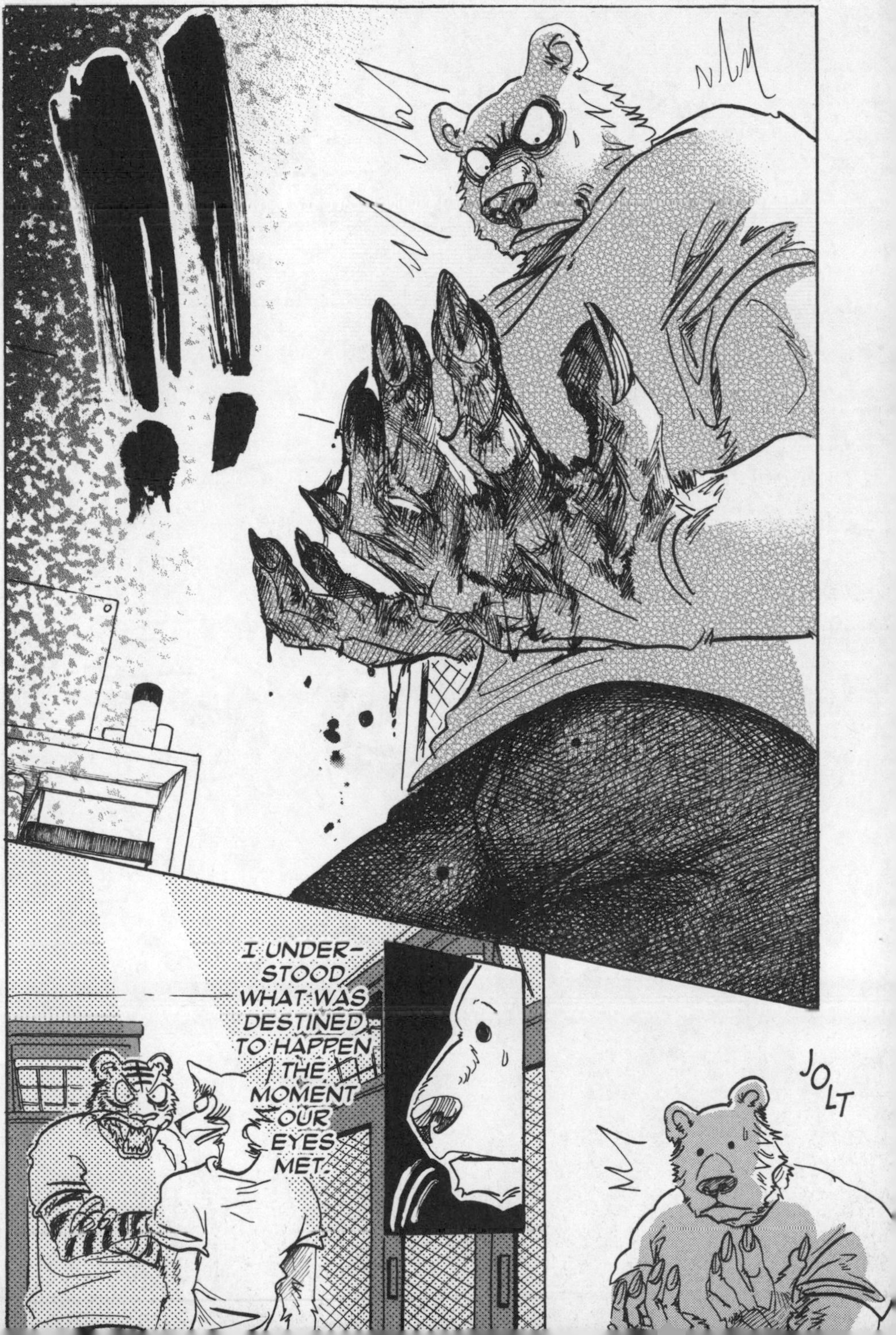
I UNDER-STOOD WHAT WAS DESTINED TO HAPPEN THE MOMENT OUR EYES MET.
JOLT

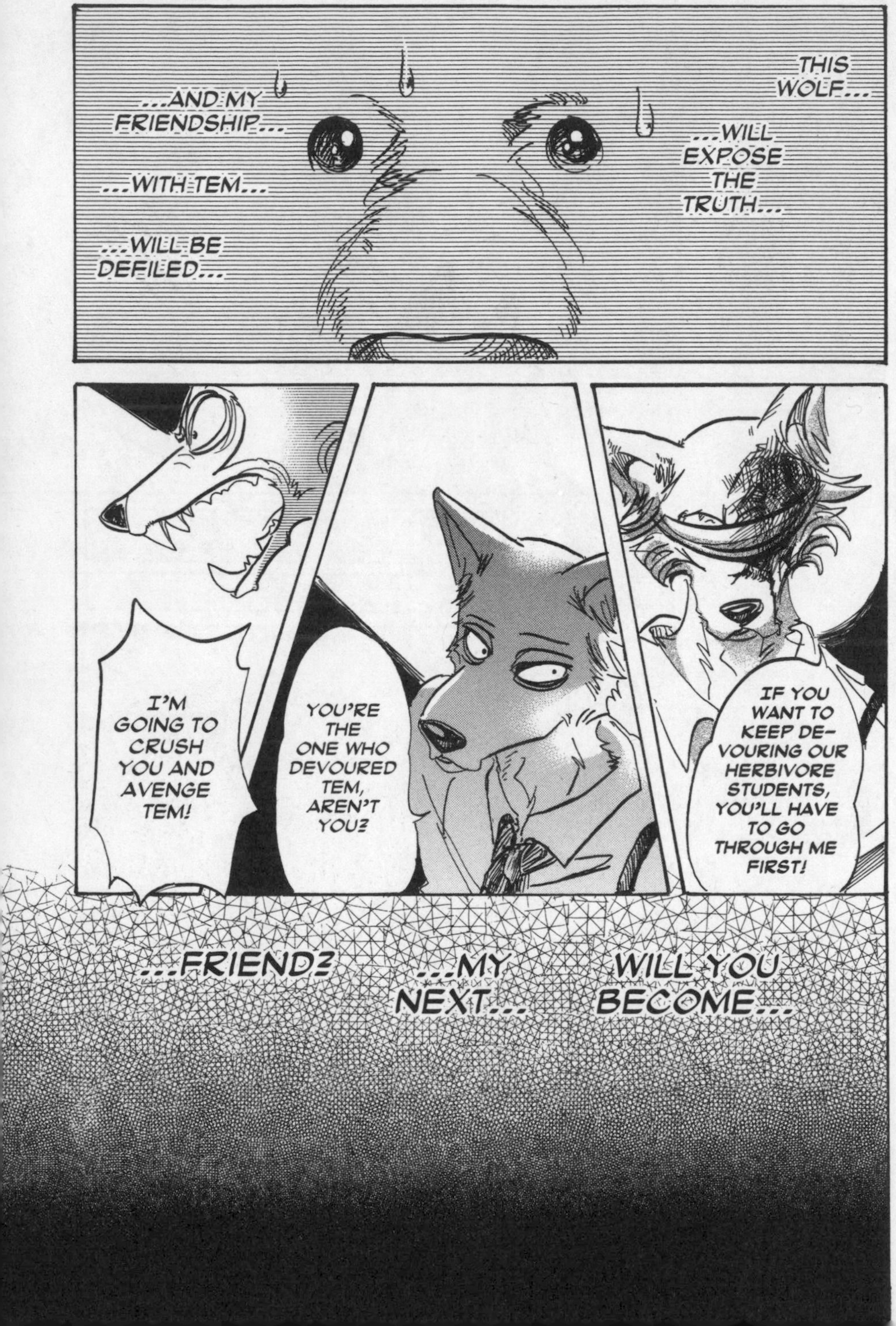
THIS WOLF...
...WILL EXPOSE THE TRUTH...
...AND MY FRIENDSHIP...
...WITH TEM...
...WILL BE DEFILED...
IF YOU WANT TO KEEP DE-VOURING OUR HERBIVORE STUDENTS, YOU'LL HAVE TO GO THROUGH ME FIRST!
YOU'RE THE ONE WHO DEVOURED TEM, AREN'T YOU?
I'M GOING TO CRUSH YOU AND AVENGE TEM!
WILL YOU BECOME...
...MY NEXT...
...FRIEND?

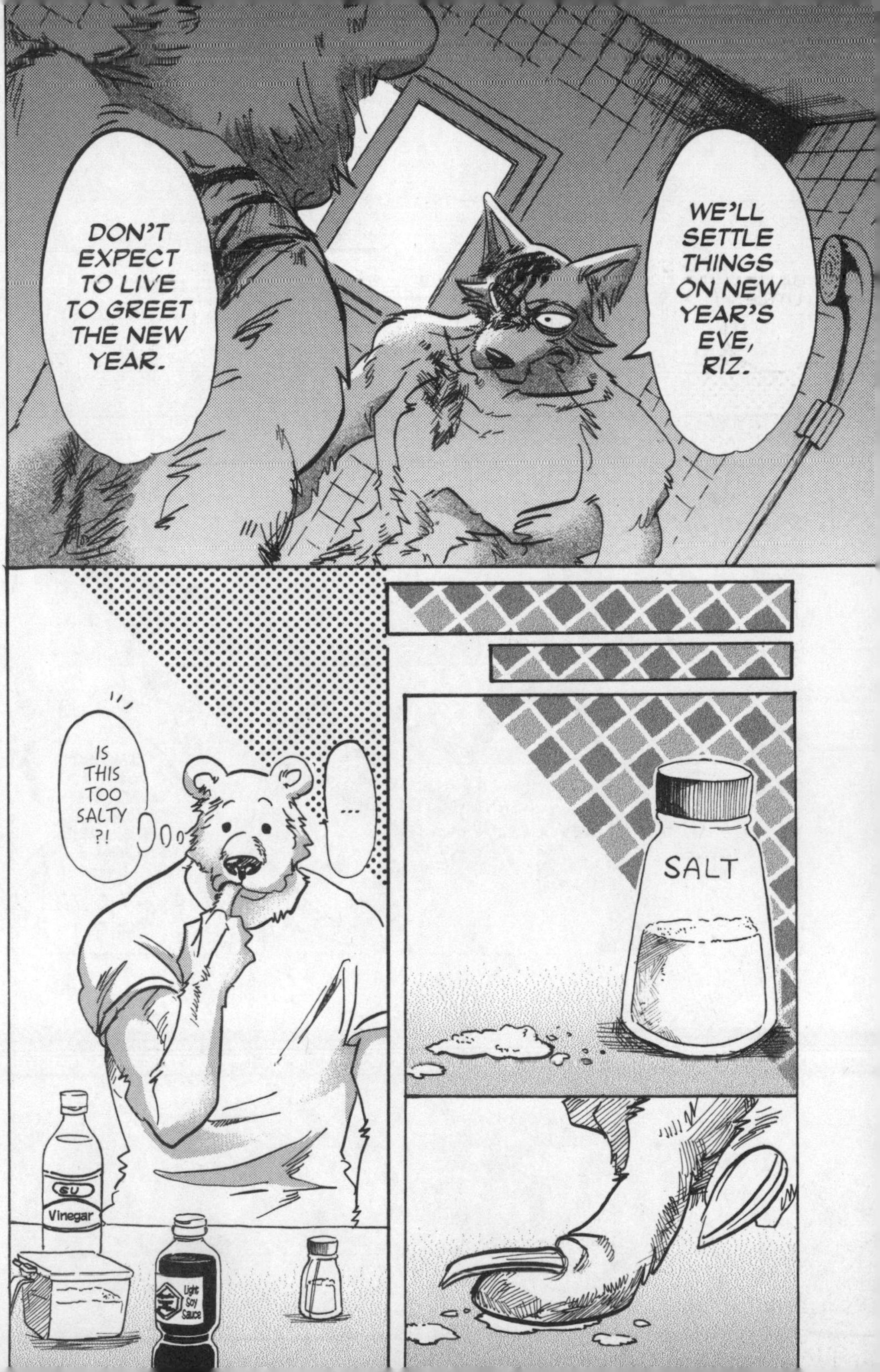
WE'LL SETTLE THINGS ON NEW YEAR'S EVE, RIZ.
DON'T EXPECT TO LIVE TO GREET THE NEW YEAR.
SALT
...
IS THIS TOO SALTY?!
SU
Vinegar
Light Soy Sauce

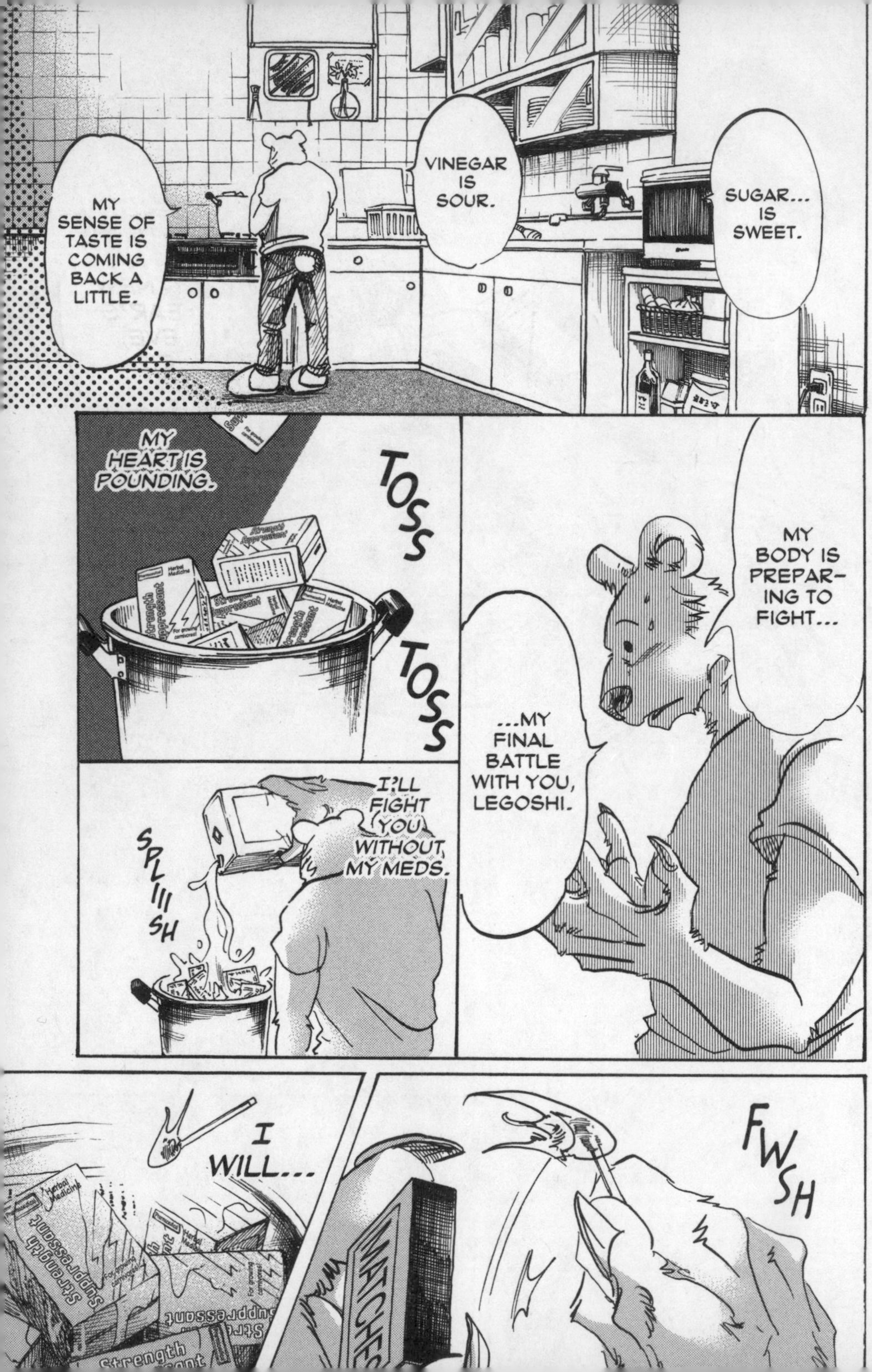
SUGAR... IS SWEET.
VINEGAR IS SOUR.
MY SENSE OF TASTE IS COMING BACK A LITTLE.
MY BODY IS PREPAR-ING TO FIGHT...
...MY FINAL BATTLE WITH YOU, LEGOSHI.
MY HEART IS POUNDING.
TOSS
TOSS
I'LL FIGHT YOU WITHOUT MY MEDS.
SPLIIIISH
FWSH
I WILL...

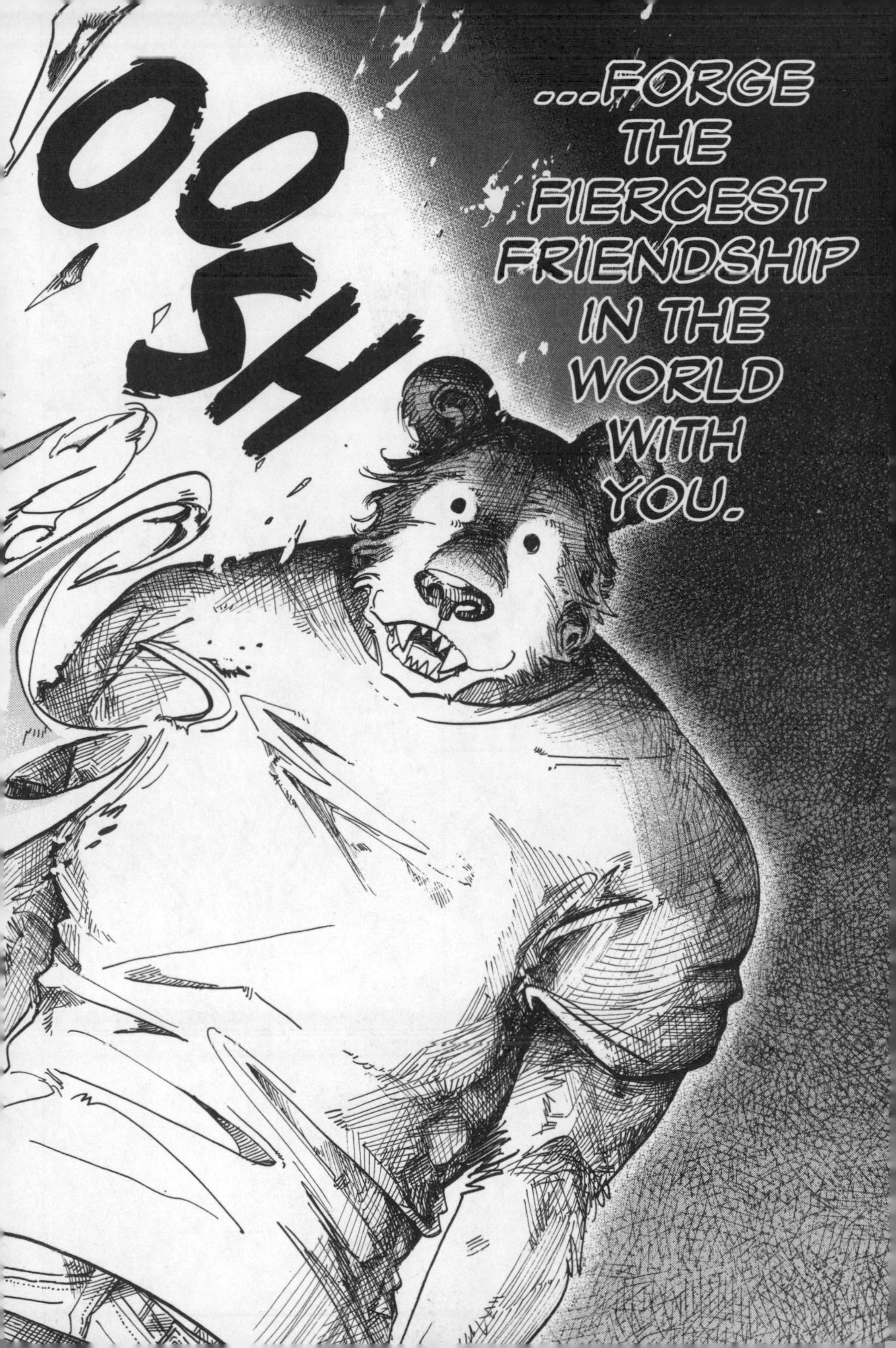
...FORGE THE FIERCEST FRIENDSHIP IN THE WORLD WITH YOU.
OOSH

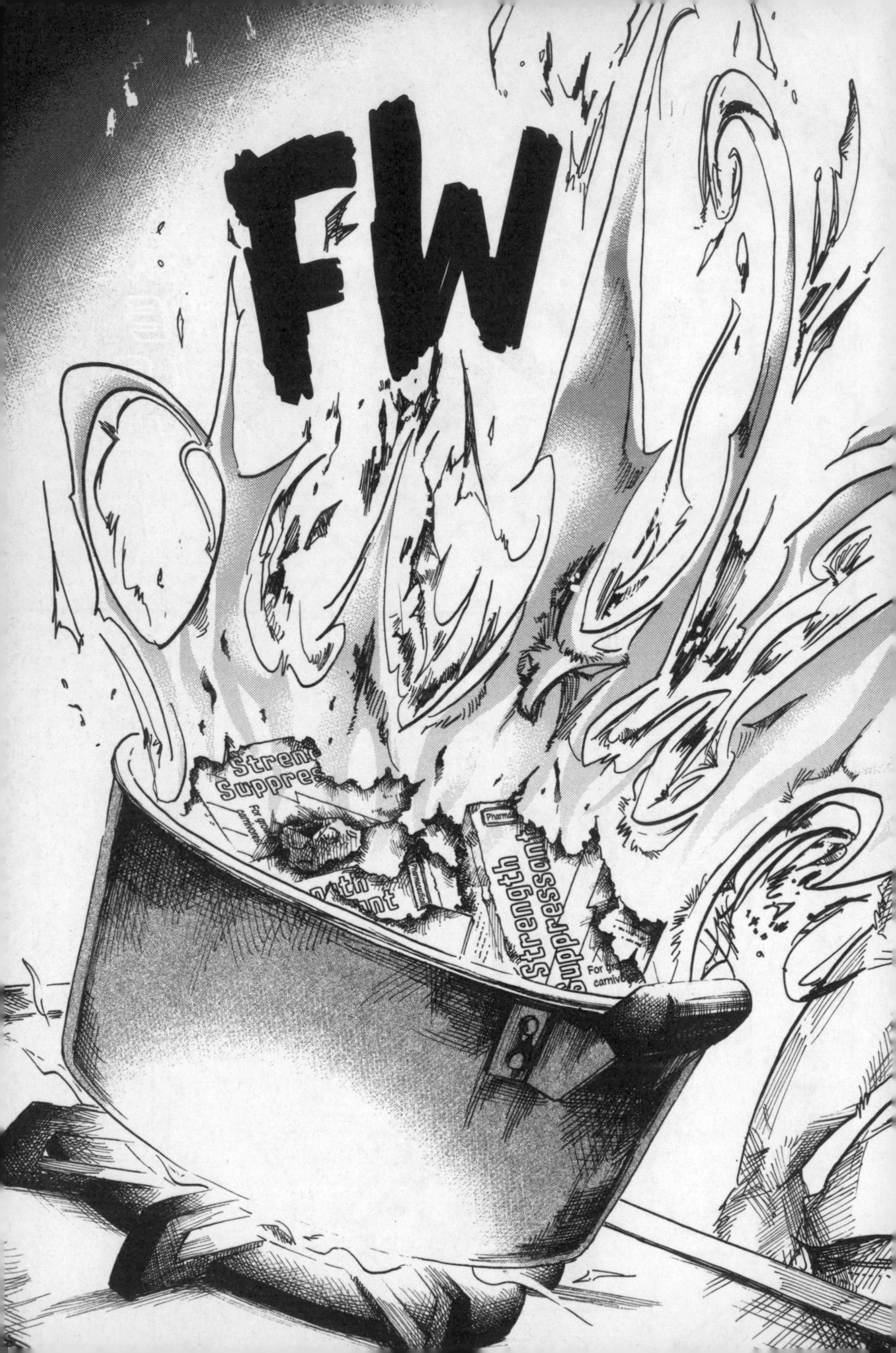
FW
Strength Suppressant

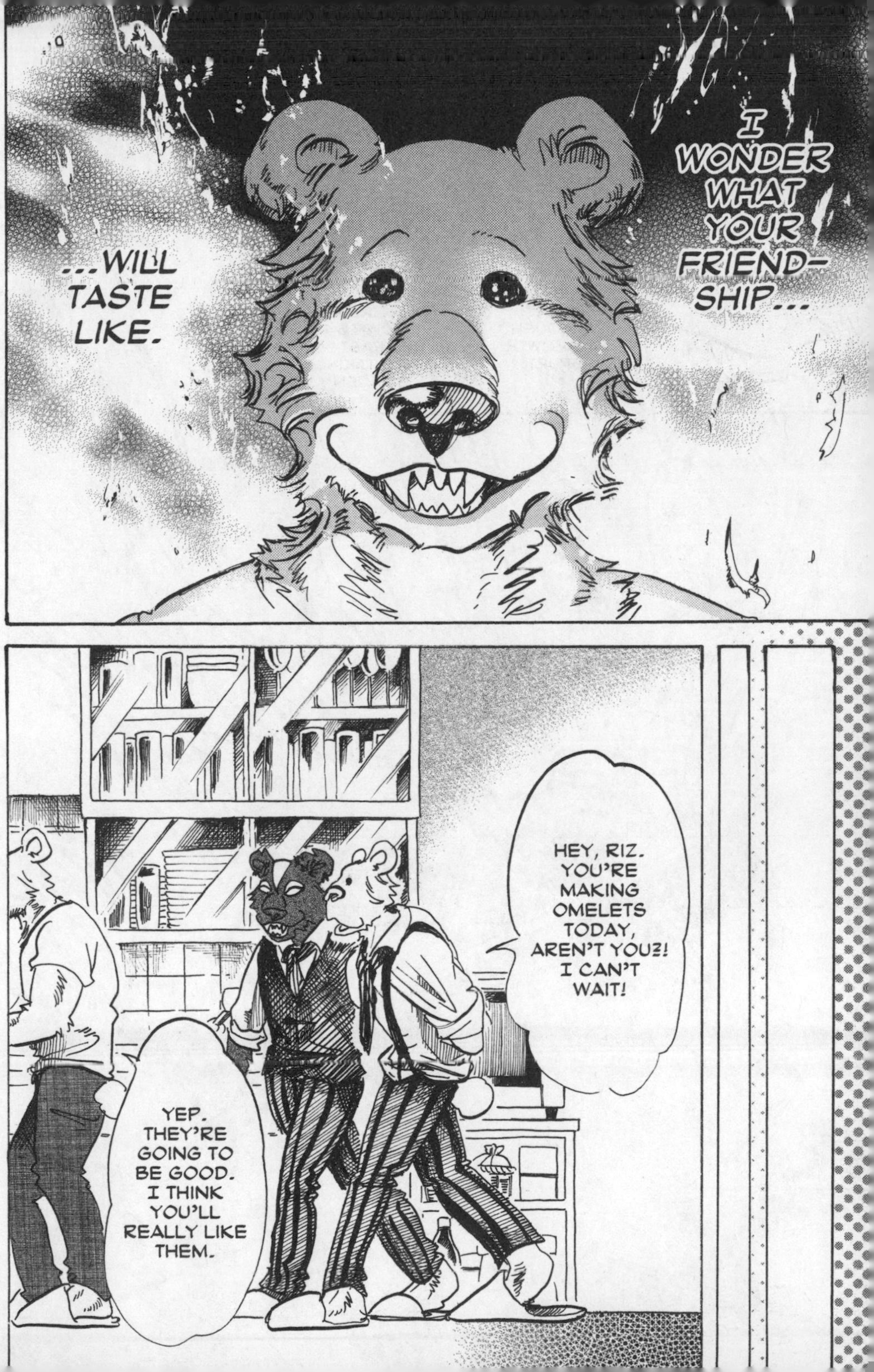
I WONDER WHAT YOUR FRIEND-SHIP...
...WILL TASTE LIKE.
HEY, RIZ. YOU'RE MAKING OMELETS TODAY, AREN'T YOU?! I CAN'T WAIT!
YEP. THEY'RE GOING TO BE GOOD. I THINK YOU'LL REALLY LIKE THEM.

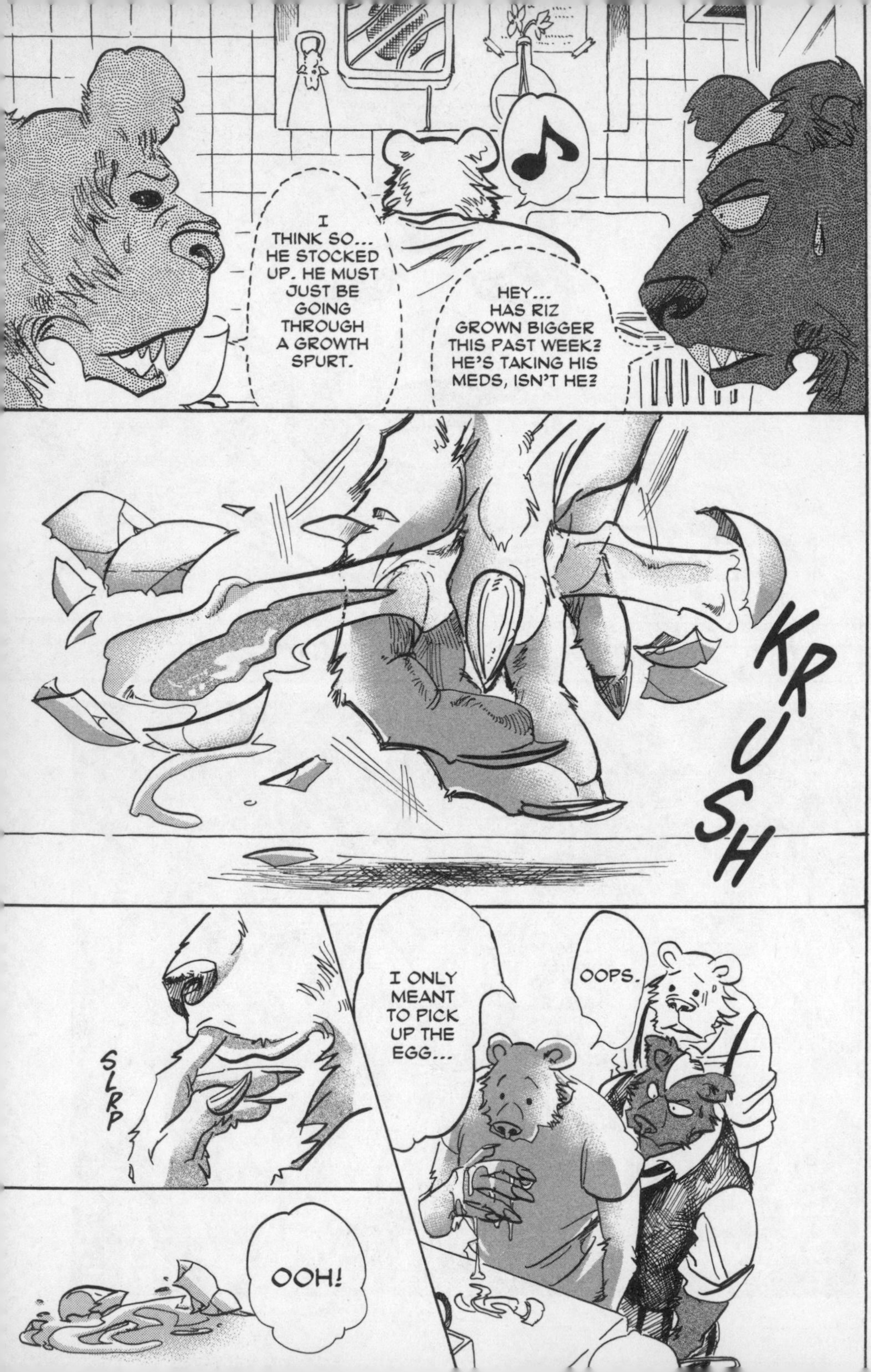
HEY... HAS RIZ GROWN BIGGER THIS PAST WEEK? HE'S TAKING HIS MEDS, ISN'T HE?
I THINK SO... HE STOCKED UP. HE MUST JUST BE GOING THROUGH A GROWTH SPURT.
KRUSH
OOPS.
I ONLY MEANT TO PICK UP THE EGG...
SLRP
OOH!

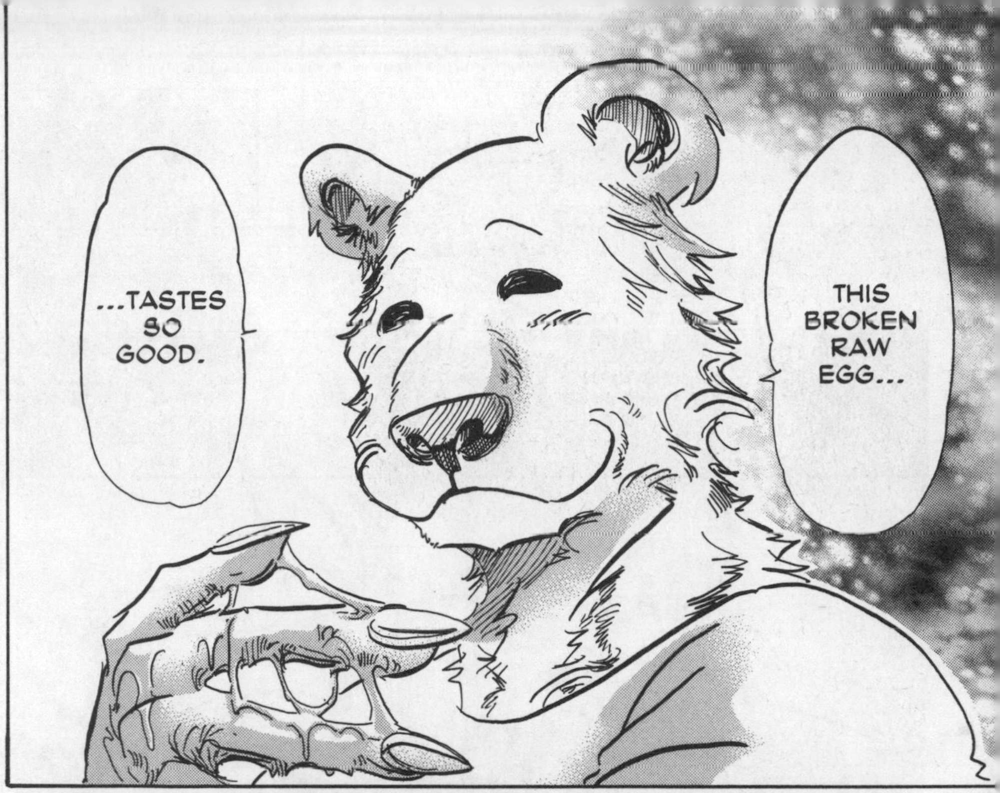
THIS BROKEN RAW EGG...
...TASTES SO GOOD.

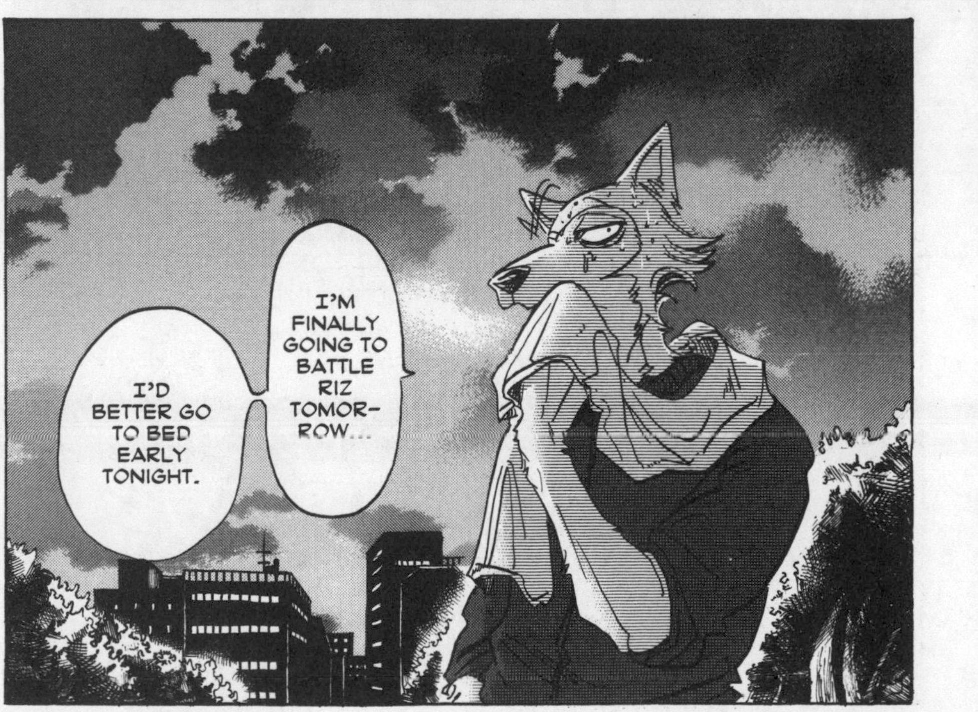
I'M FINALLY GOING TO BATTLE RIZ TOMOR-ROW...
I'D BETTER GO TO BED EARLY TONIGHT.

Chapter 90:
The Old Year Passes Away, the New Year Enters the Soul

NEW YEAR'S EVE

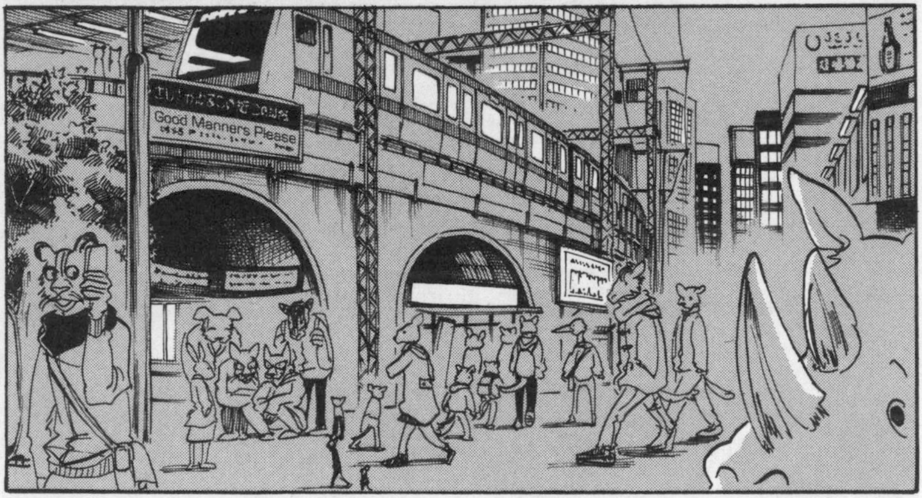
Good Manners Please

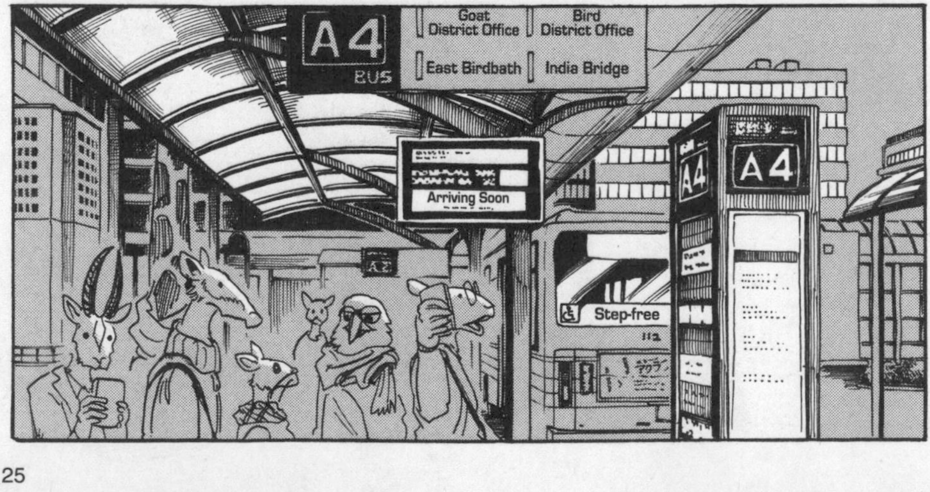
Goat District Office
Bird District Office
East Birdbath
India Bridge
A4
BUS
A4
Arriving Soon
Step-free

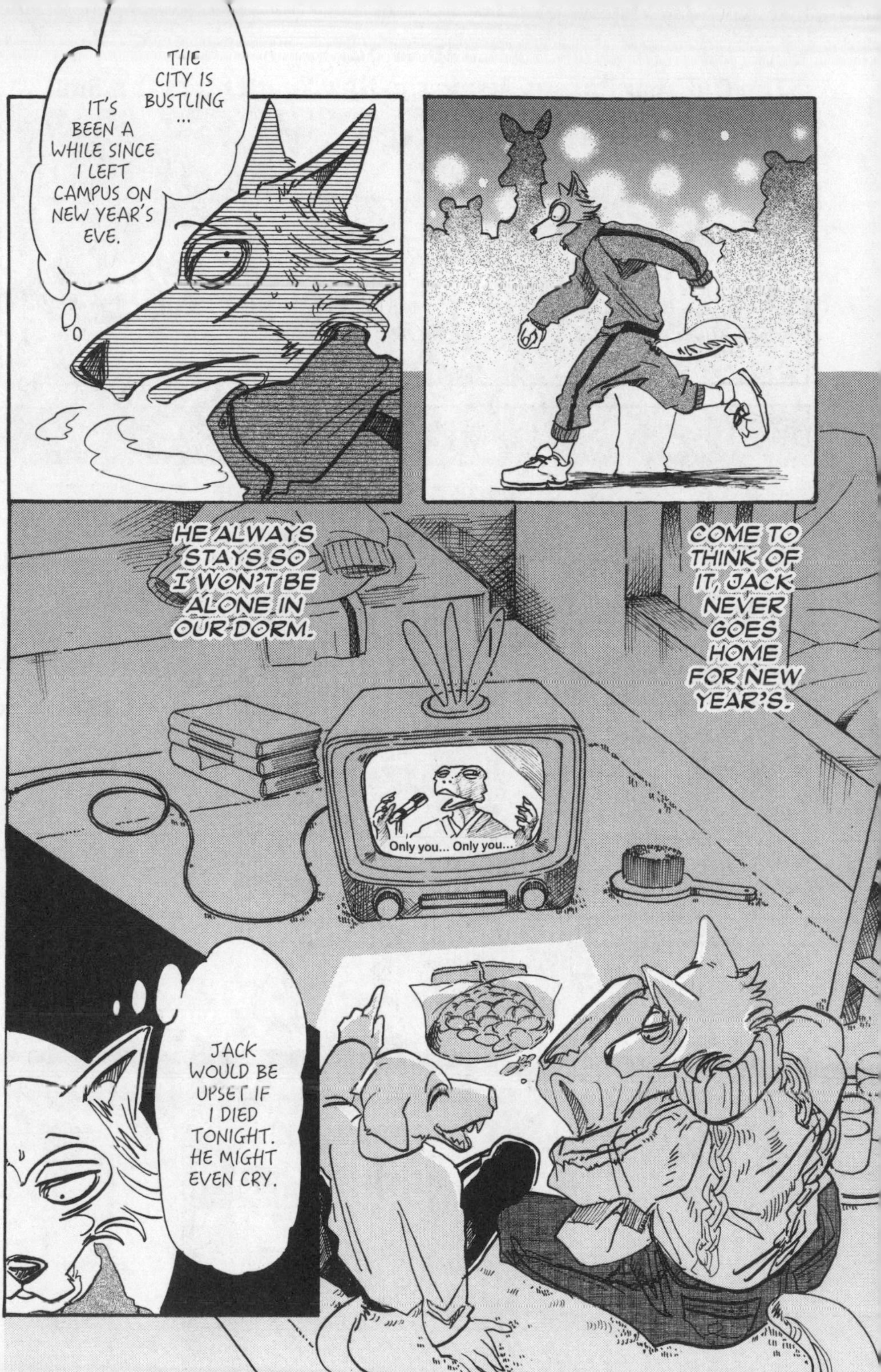
THE CITY IS BUSTLING ...
IT'S BEEN A WHILE SINCE I LEFT CAMPUS ON NEW YEAR'S EVE.
COME TO THINK OF IT, JACK NEVER GOES HOME FOR NEW YEAR'S.
HE ALWAYS STAYS SO I WON'T BE ALONE IN OUR DORM.
Only you... Only you...
JACK WOULD BE UPSET IF I DIED TONIGHT. HE MIGHT EVEN CRY.

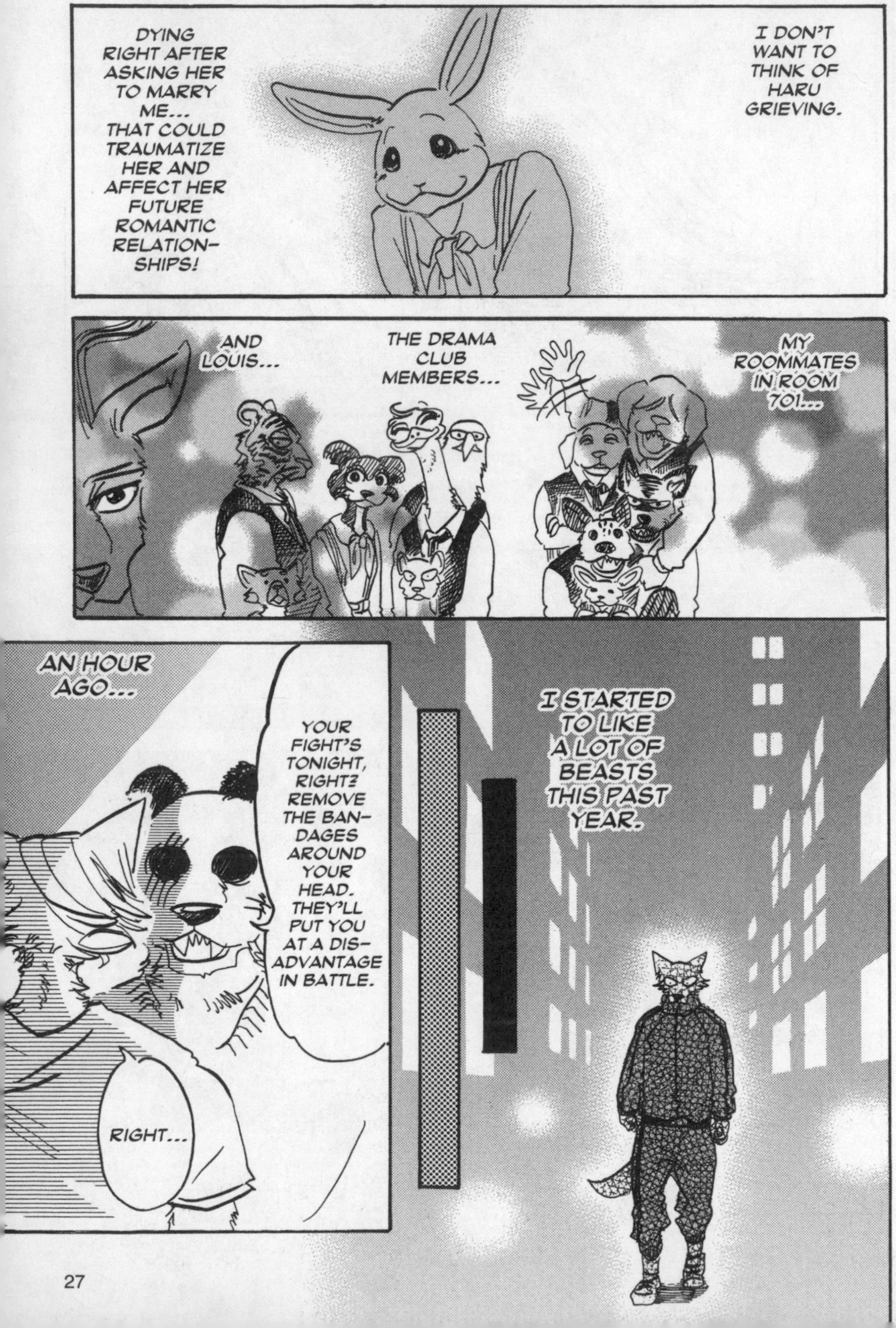
I DON'T WANT TO THINK OF HARU GRIEVING.
DYING RIGHT AFTER ASKING HER TO MARRY ME... THAT COULD TRAUMATIZE HER AND AFFECT HER FUTURE ROMANTIC RELATION-SHIPS!
MY ROOMMATES IN ROOM 701...
THE DRAMA CLUB MEMBERS...
AND LOUIS...
I STARTED TO LIKE A LOT OF BEASTS THIS PAST YEAR.
AN HOUR AGO...
YOUR FIGHT'S TONIGHT, RIGHT? REMOVE THE BAN-DAGES AROUND YOUR HEAD. THEY'LL PUT YOU AT A DIS-ADVANTAGE IN BATTLE.
RIGHT...

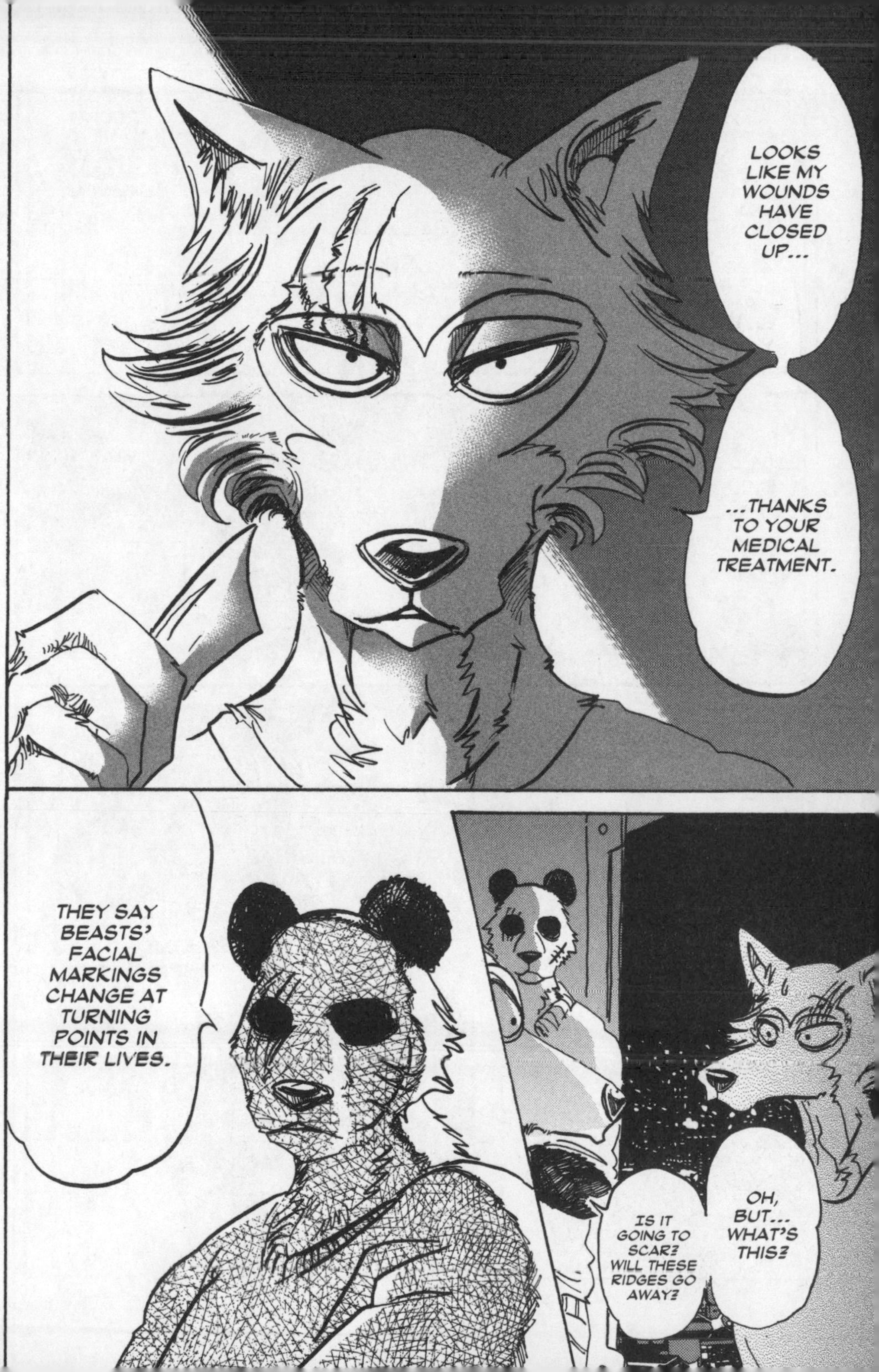
LOOKS LIKE MY WOUNDS HAVE CLOSED UP...
...THANKS TO YOUR MEDICAL TREATMENT.
OH, BUT... WHAT'S THIS?
IS IT GOING TO SCAR? WILL THESE RIDGES GO AWAY?
THEY SAY BEASTS' FACIAL MARKINGS CHANGE AT TURNING POINTS IN THEIR LIVES.

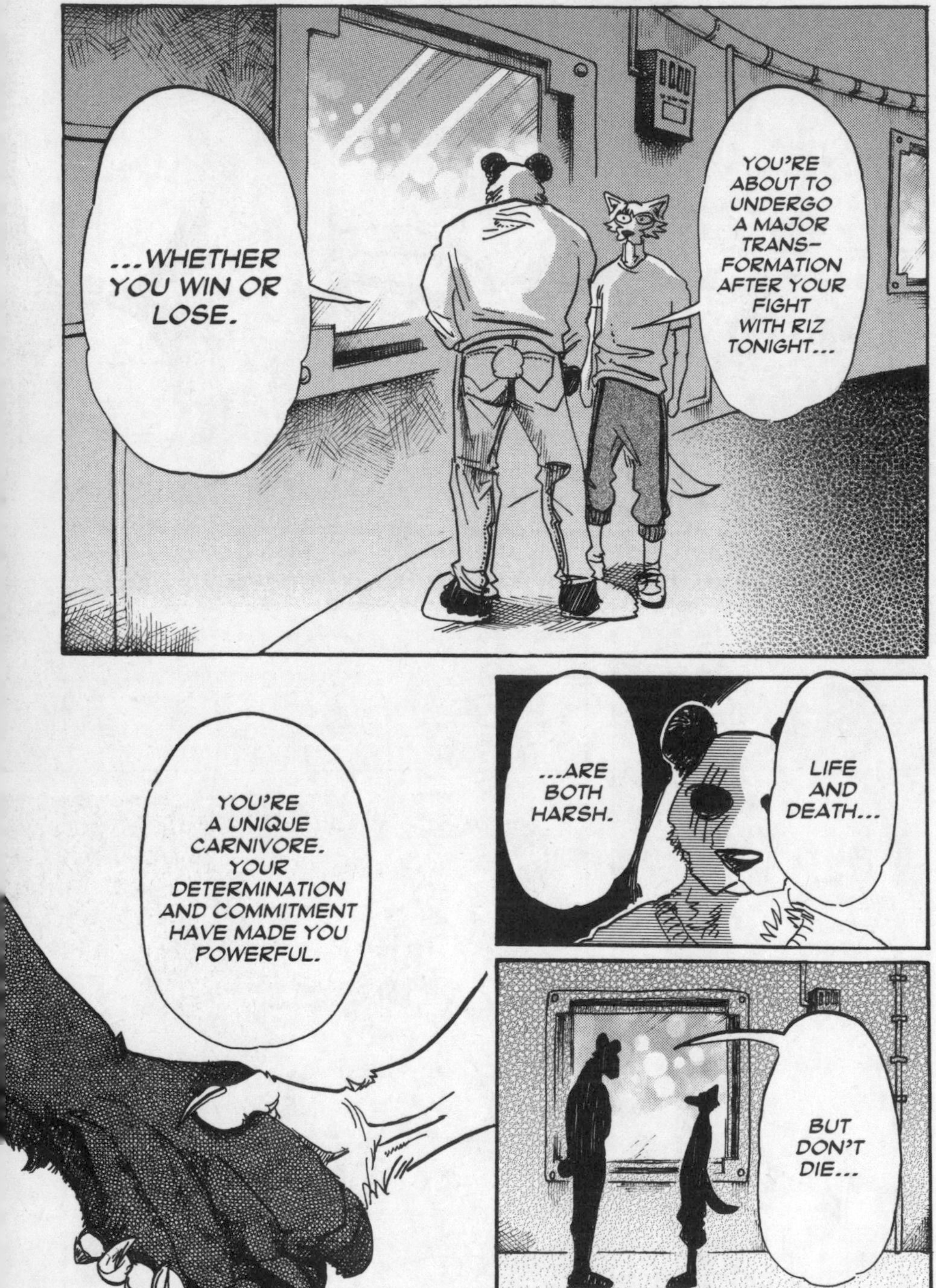
YOU'RE ABOUT TO UNDERGO A MAJOR TRANS-FORMATION AFTER YOUR FIGHT WITH RIZ TONIGHT...
...WHETHER YOU WIN OR LOSE.
LIFE AND DEATH...
...ARE BOTH HARSH.
BUT DON'T DIE...
YOU'RE A UNIQUE CARNIVORE. YOUR DETERMINATION AND COMMITMENT HAVE MADE YOU POWERFUL.

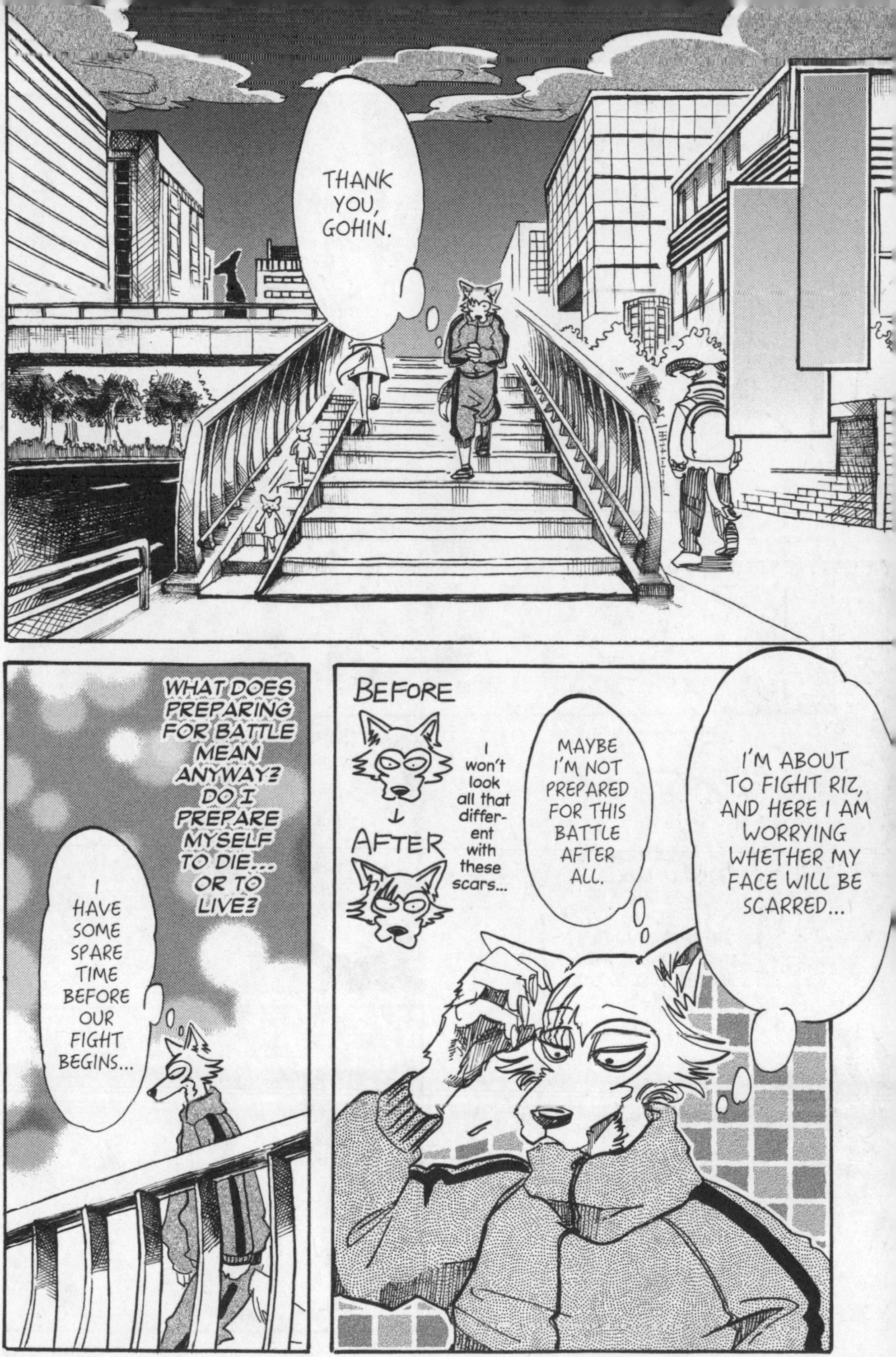
THANK YOU, GOHIN.
I'M ABOUT TO FIGHT RIZ, AND HERE I AM WORRYING WHETHER MY FACE WILL BE SCARRED...
MAYBE I'M NOT PREPARED FOR THIS BATTLE AFTER ALL.
BEFORE
AFTER
I won't look all that differ-ent with these scars...
WHAT DOES PREPARING FOR BATTLE MEAN ANYWAY? DO I PREPARE MYSELF TO DIE... OR TO LIVE?
I HAVE SOME SPARE TIME BEFORE OUR FIGHT BEGINS...

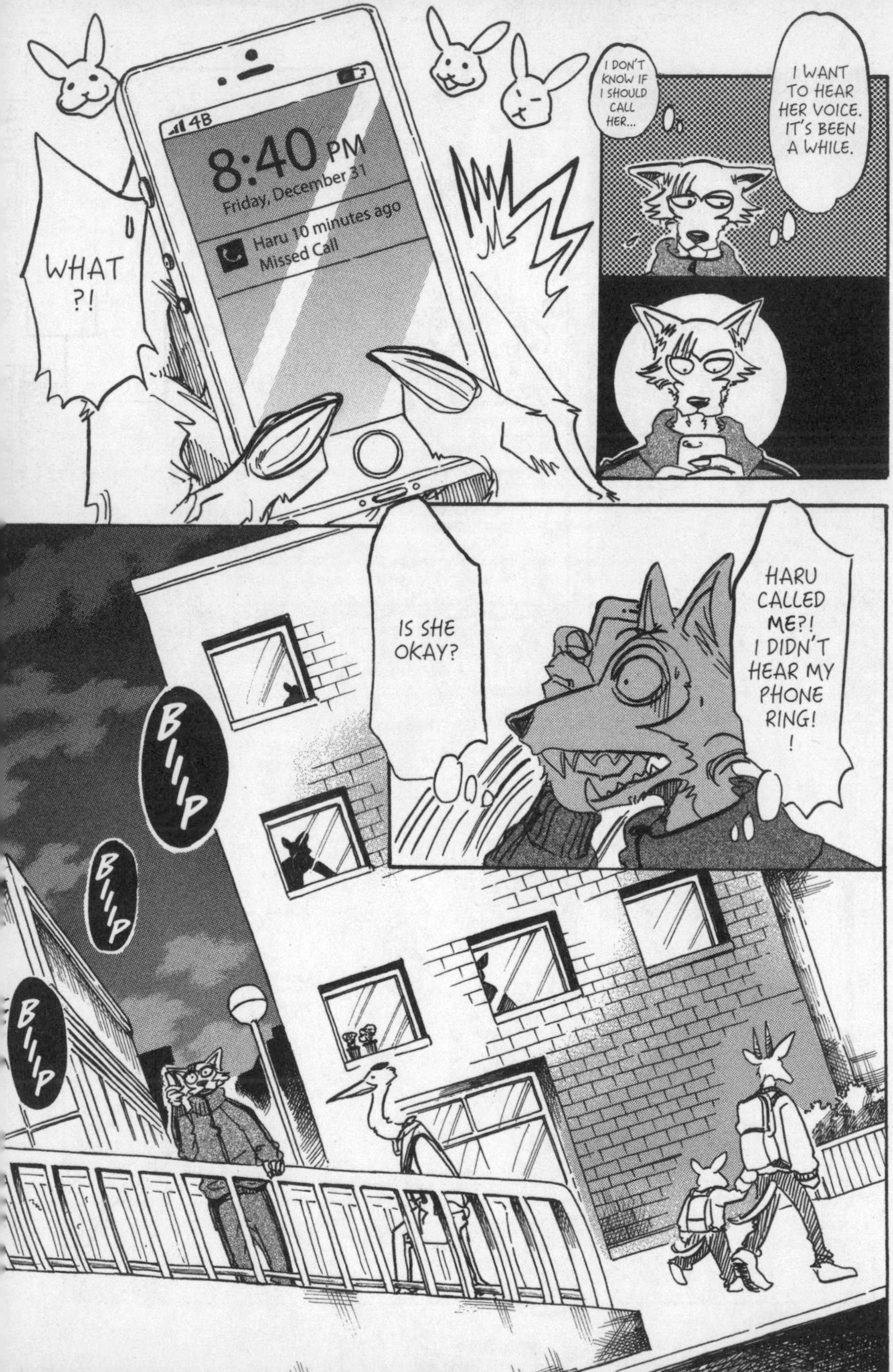
I WANT TO HEAR HER VOICE. IT'S BEEN A WHILE.
I DON'T KNOW IF I SHOULD CALL HER...
4B
8:40 PM
Friday, December 31
Haru 10 minutes ago
Missed Call
WHAT ?!
HARU CALLED ME?! I DIDN'T HEAR MY PHONE RING! !
IS SHE OKAY?
BIIIP
BIIIP
BIIIP

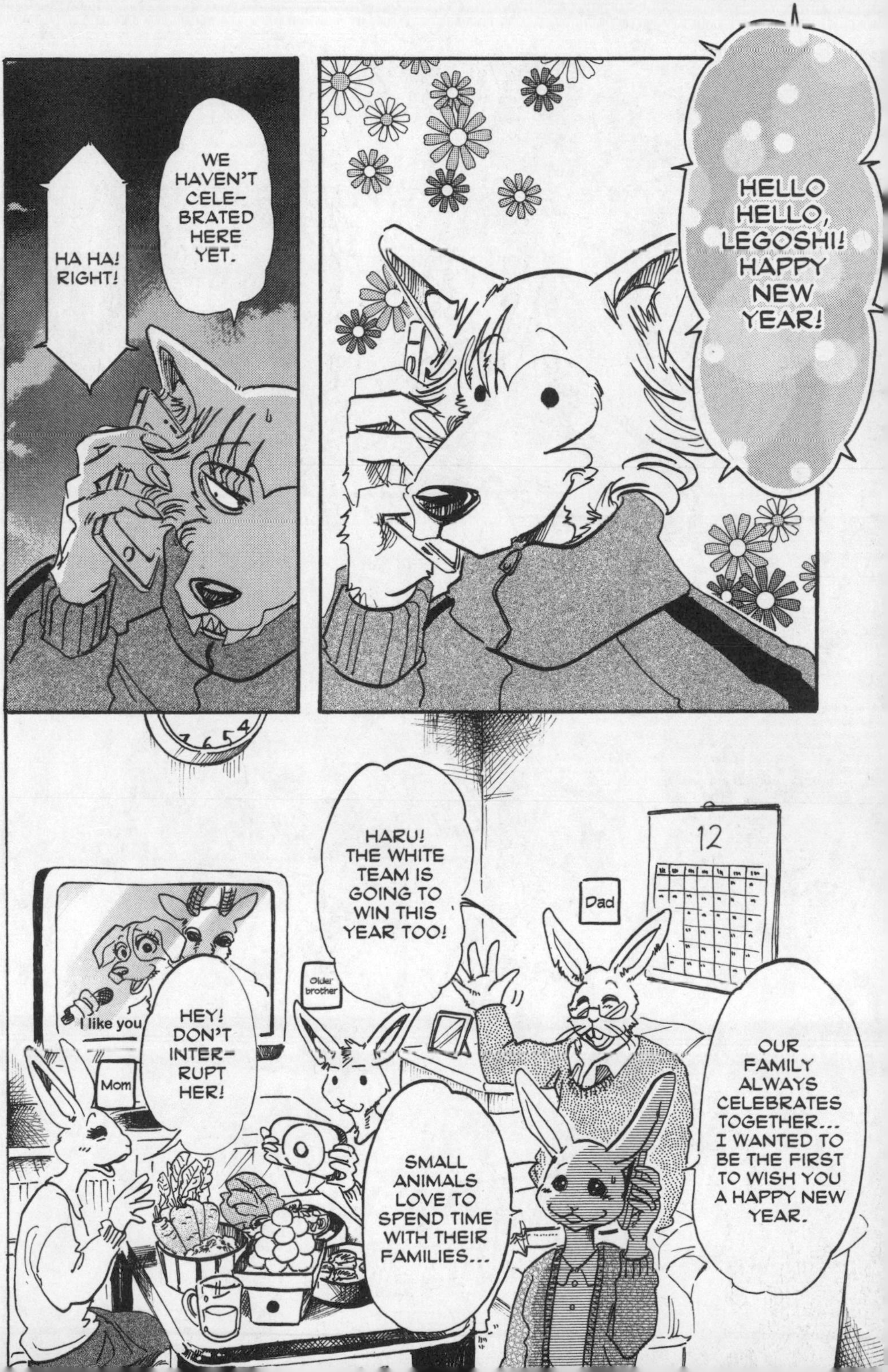
HELLO HELLO, LEGOSHI! HAPPY NEW YEAR!
WE HAVEN'T CELE-BRATED HERE YET.
HA HA! RIGHT!
12
Dad
HARU! THE WHITE TEAM IS GOING TO WIN THIS YEAR TOO!
OUR FAMILY ALWAYS CELEBRATES TOGETHER... I WANTED TO BE THE FIRST TO WISH YOU A HAPPY NEW YEAR.
SMALL ANIMALS LOVE TO SPEND TIME WITH THEIR FAMILIES...
Older brother
HEY! DON'T INTER-RUPT HER!
Mom
I like you

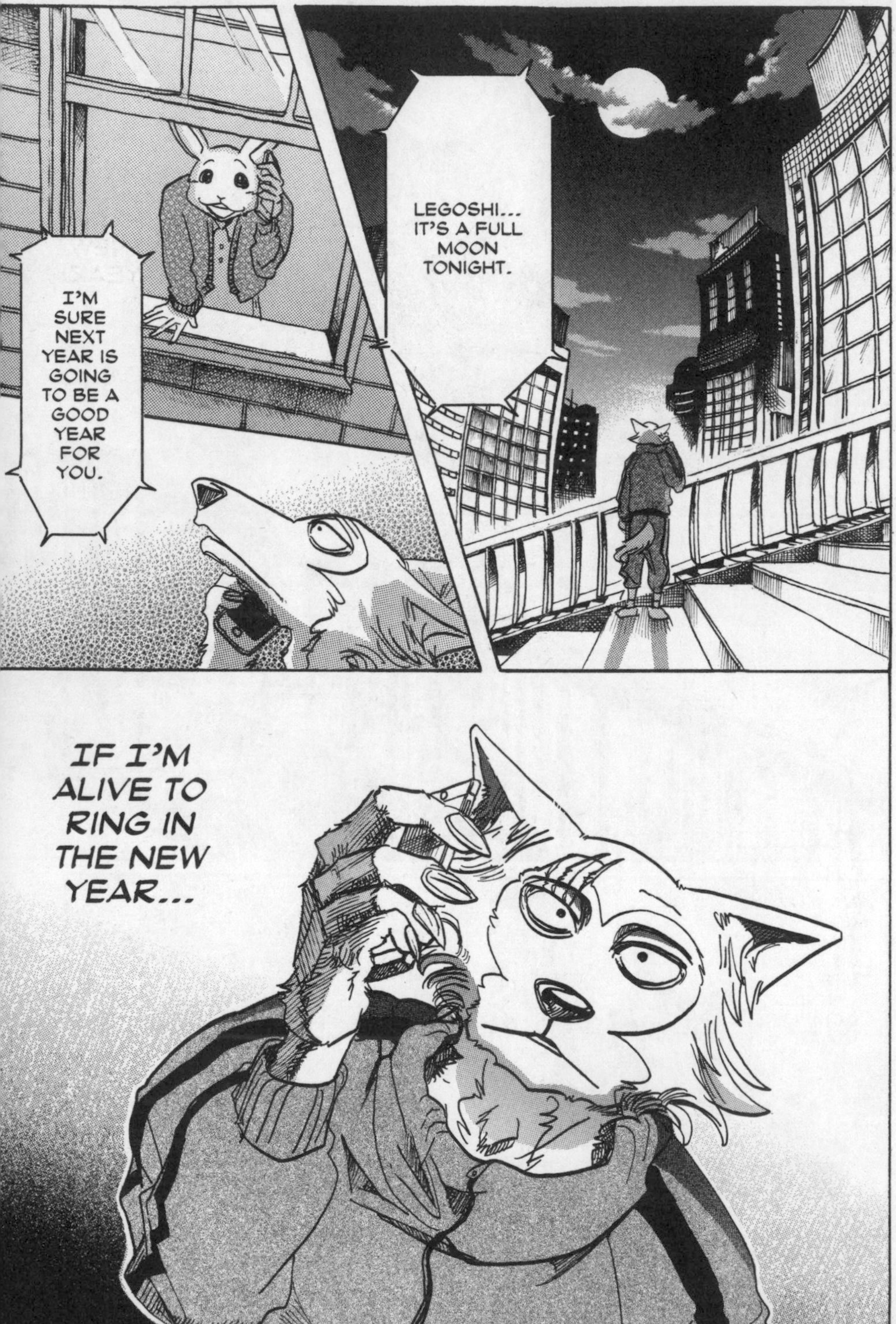
LEGOSHI... IT'S A FULL MOON TONIGHT.
I'M SURE NEXT YEAR IS GOING TO BE A GOOD YEAR FOR YOU.
IF I'M ALIVE TO RING IN THE NEW YEAR...

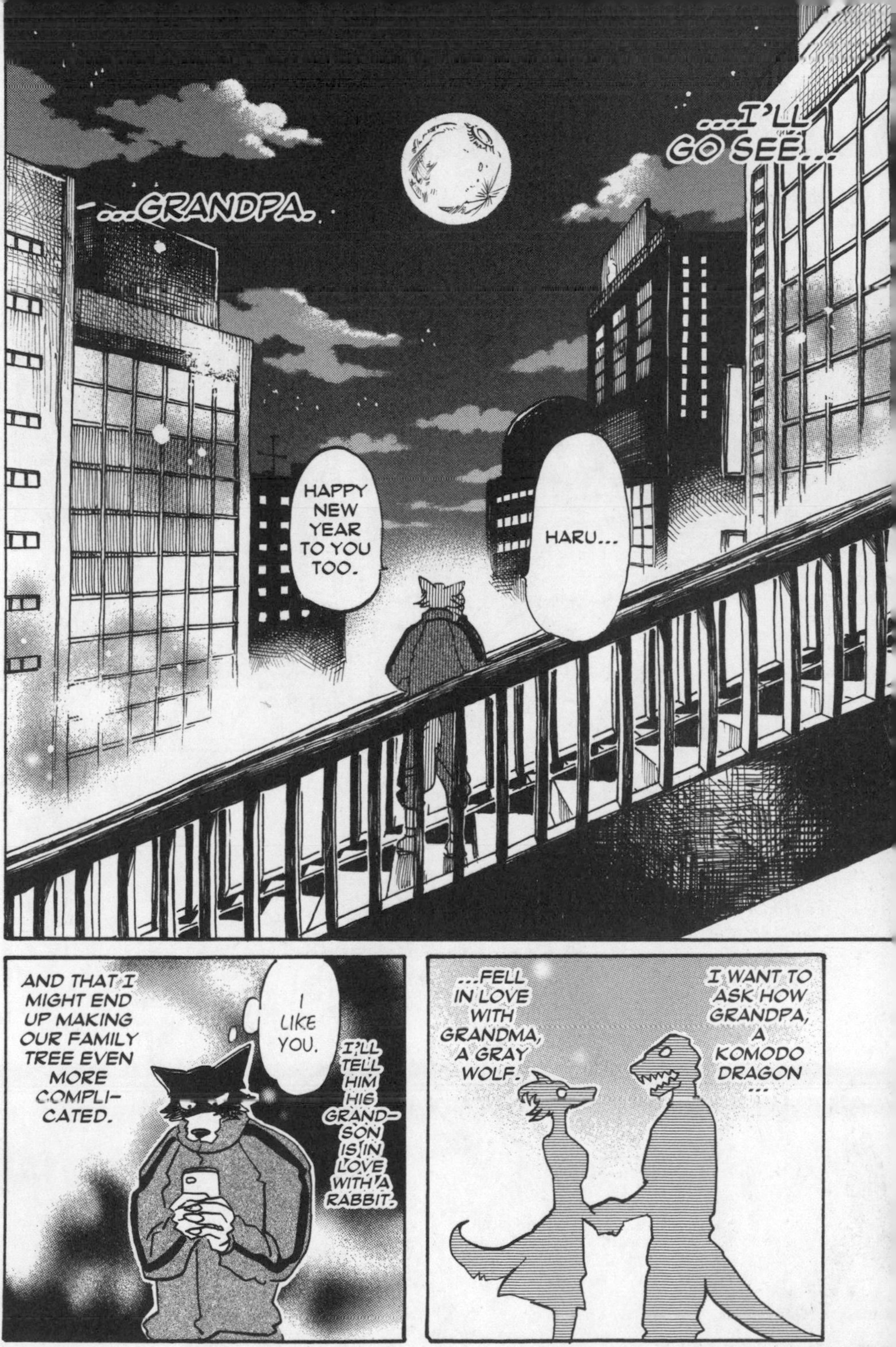
...I'LL GO SEE...
...GRANDPA.
HARU...
HAPPY NEW YEAR TO YOU TOO.
I WANT TO ASK HOW GRANDPA, A KOMODO DRAGON...
...FELL IN LOVE WITH GRANDMA, A GRAY WOLF.
I LIKE YOU.
I'LL TELL HIM HIS GRANDSON IS IN LOVE WITH A RABBIT.
AND THAT I MIGHT END UP MAKING OUR FAMILY TREE EVEN MORE COMPLICATED.

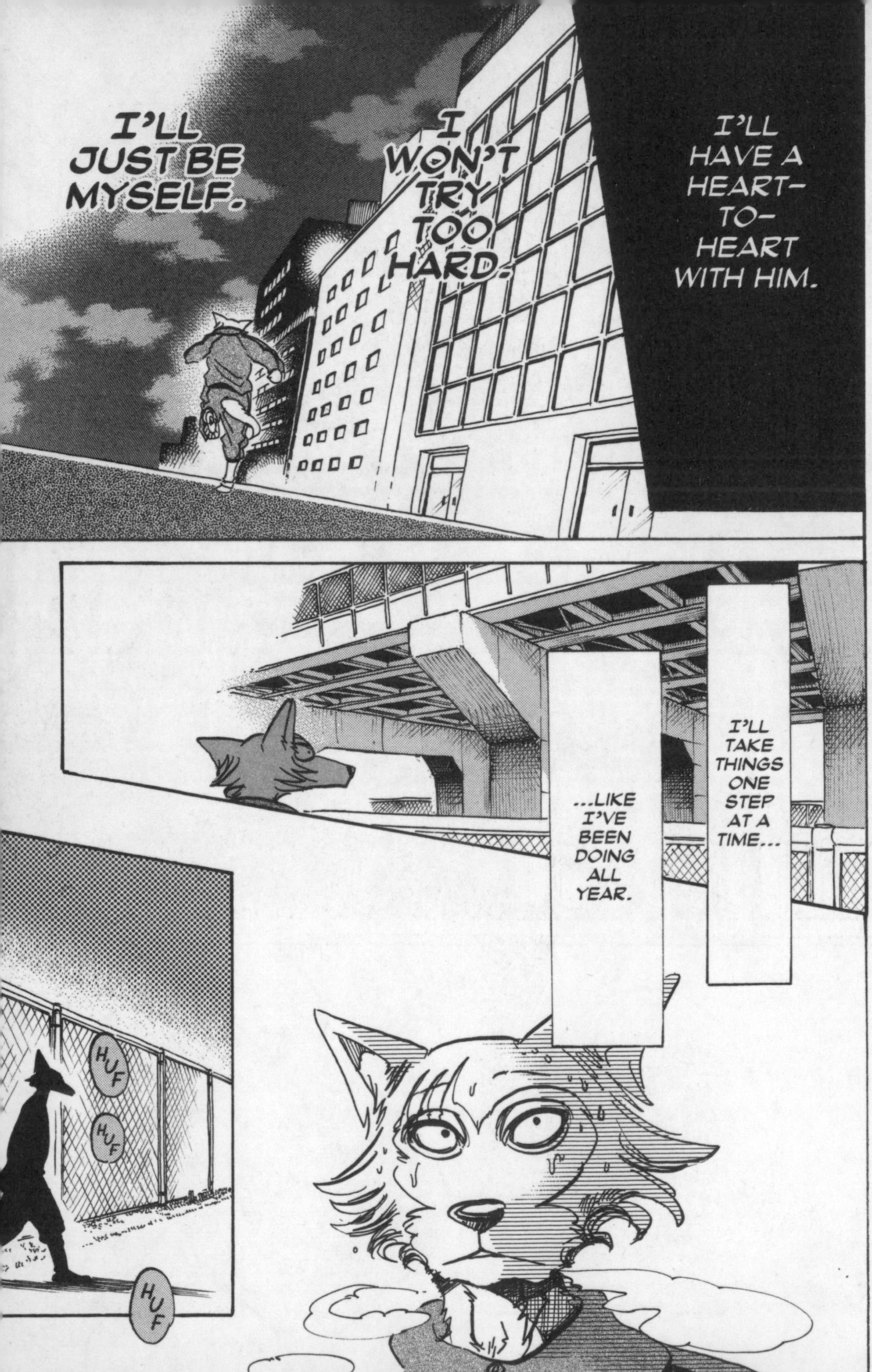
I'LL HAVE A HEART-TO-HEART WITH HIM.
I WON'T TRY TOO HARD.
I'LL JUST BE MYSELF.
I'LL TAKE THINGS ONE STEP AT A TIME...
...LIKE I'VE BEEN DOING ALL YEAR.
HUF
HUF
HUF

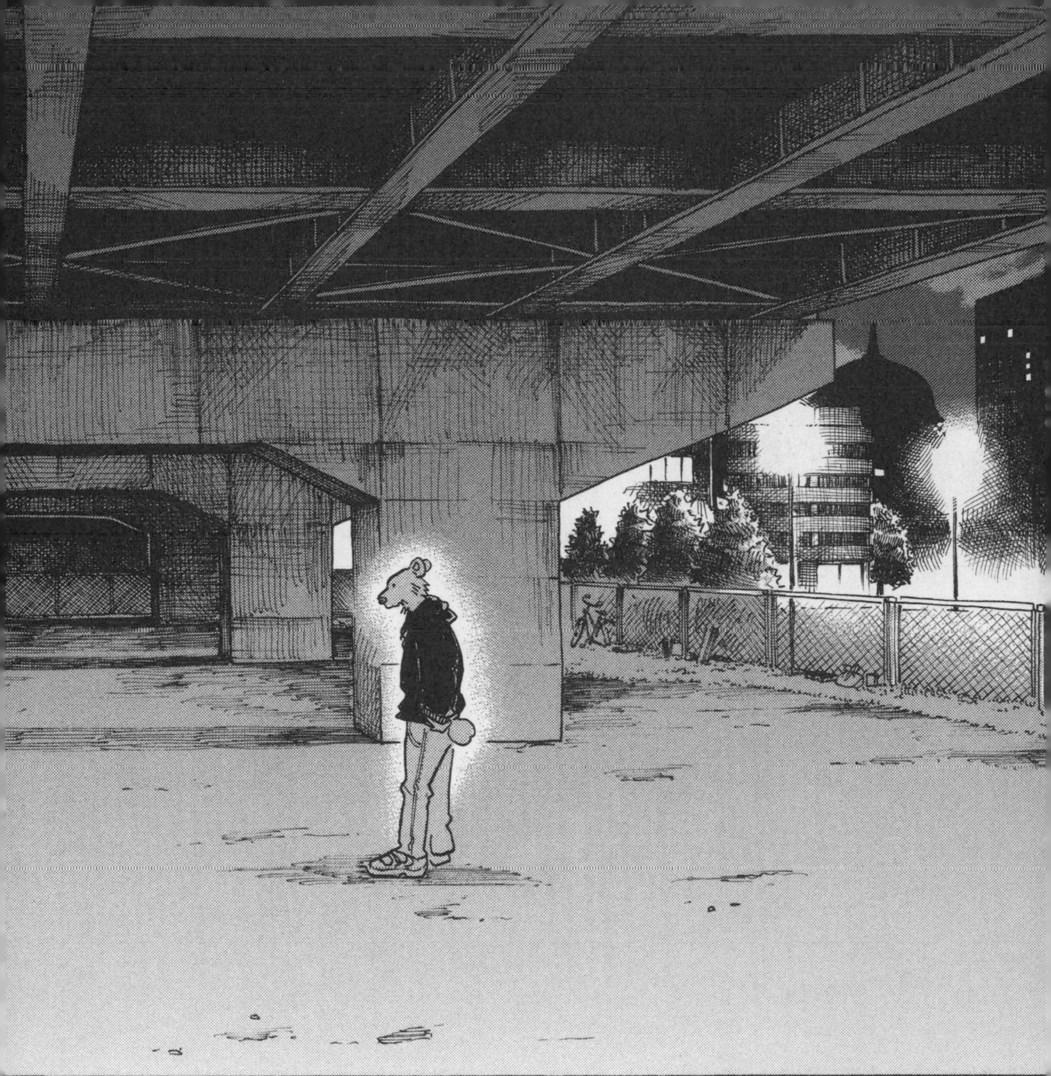

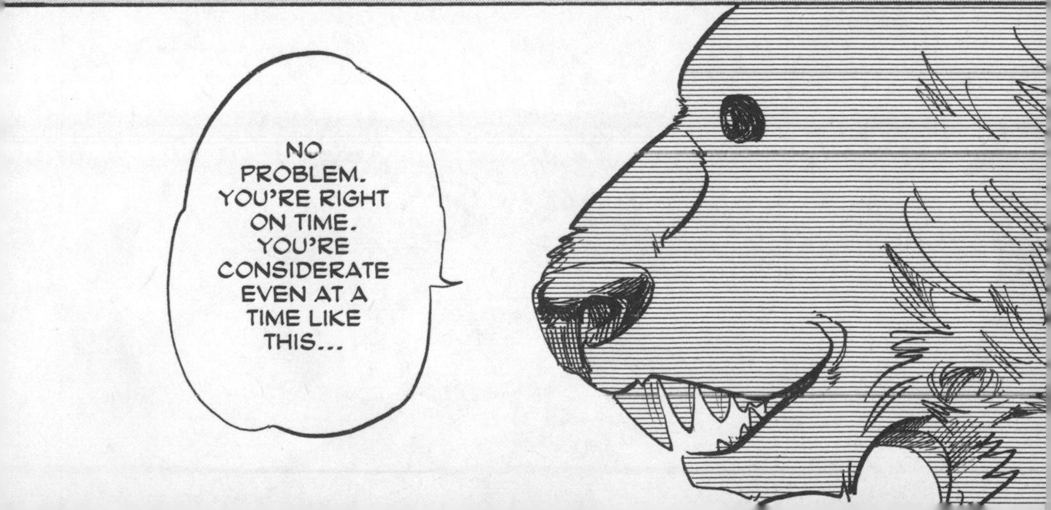
NO PROBLEM. YOU'RE RIGHT ON TIME. YOU'RE CONSIDERATE EVEN AT A TIME LIKE THIS...

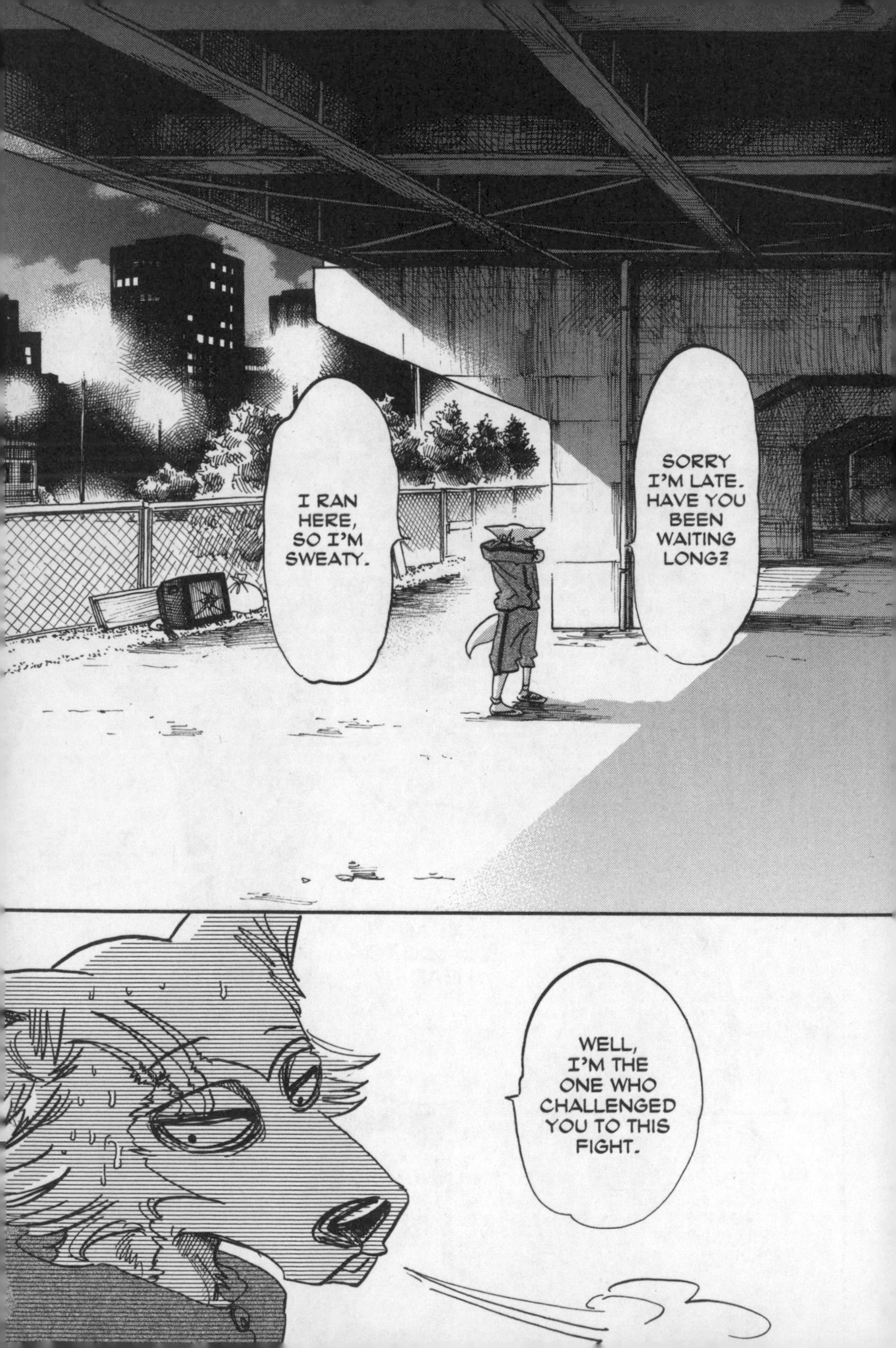
SORRY I'M LATE. HAVE YOU BEEN WAITING LONG?
I RAN HERE, SO I'M SWEATY.
WELL, I'M THE ONE WHO CHALLENGED YOU TO THIS FIGHT.

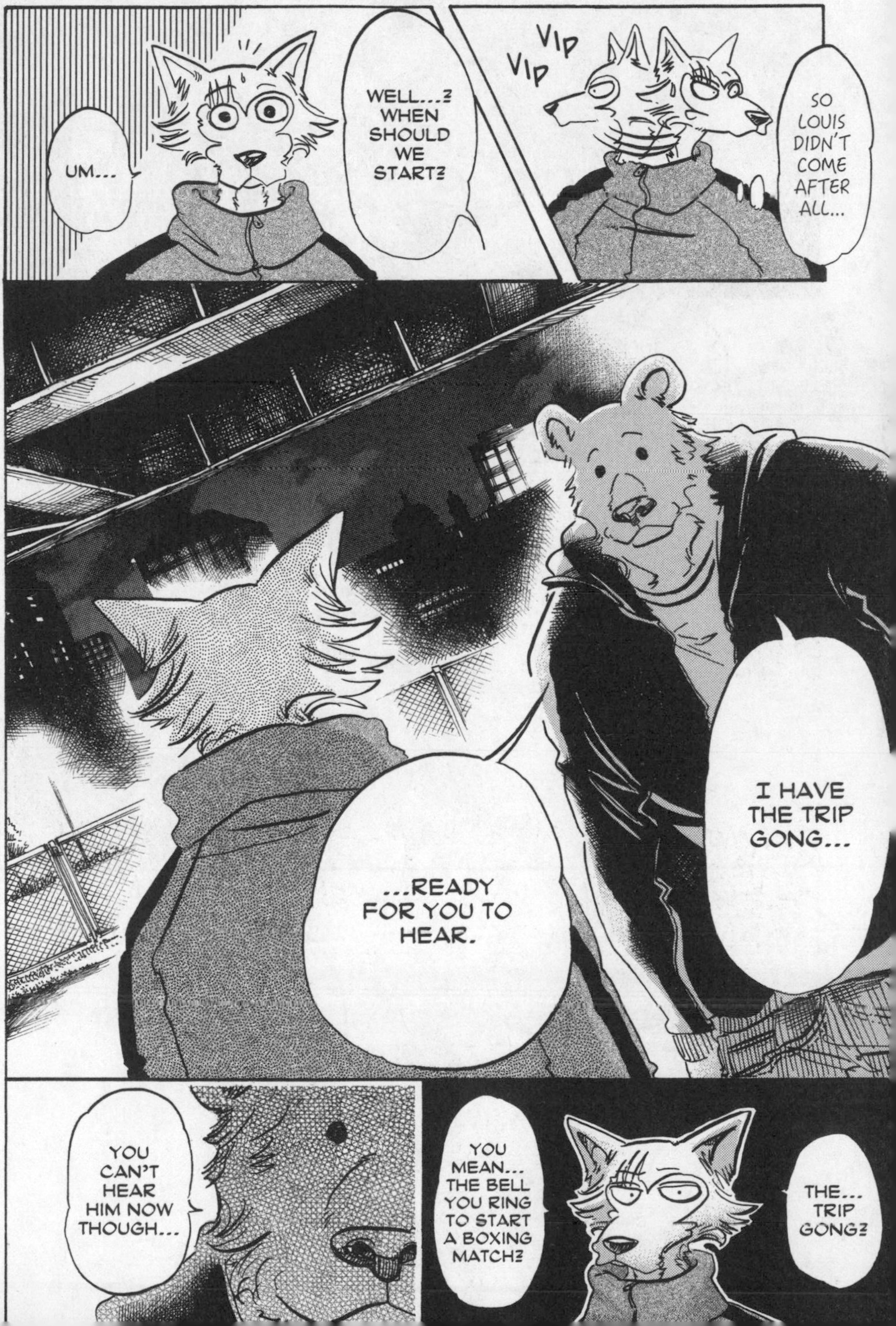
SO LOUIS DIDN'T COME AFTER ALL...
VIP VIP
WELL...? WHEN SHOULD WE START?
UM...
I HAVE THE TRIP GONG...
...READY FOR YOU TO HEAR.
THE... TRIP GONG?
YOU MEAN... THE BELL YOU RING TO START A BOXING MATCH?
YOU CAN'T HEAR HIM NOW THOUGH...

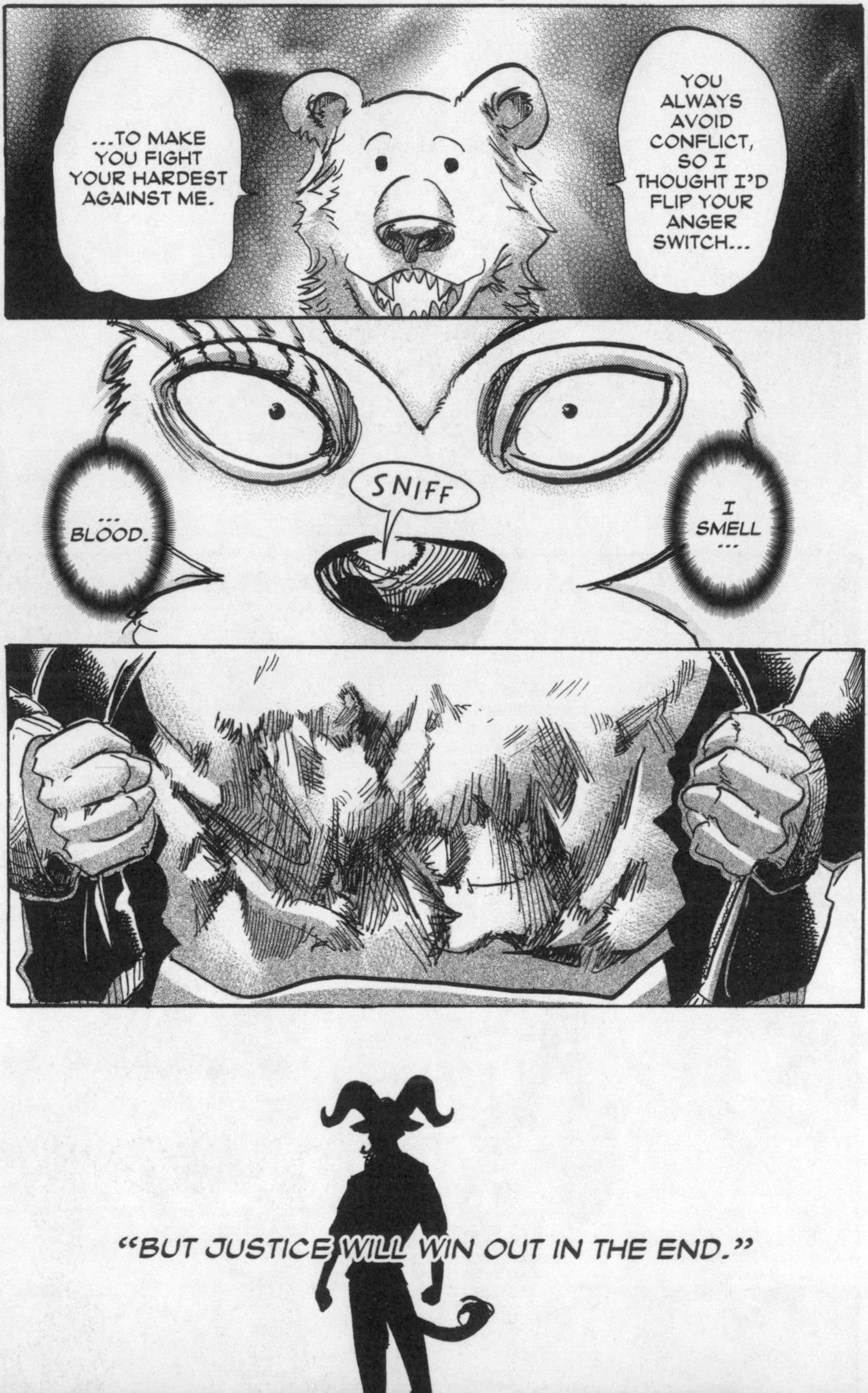
YOU ALWAYS AVOID CONFLICT, SO I THOUGHT I'D FLIP YOUR ANGER SWITCH...
...TO MAKE YOU FIGHT YOUR HARDEST AGAINST ME.
SNIFF
I SMELL ...
... BLOOD.
"BUT JUSTICE WILL WIN OUT IN THE END."

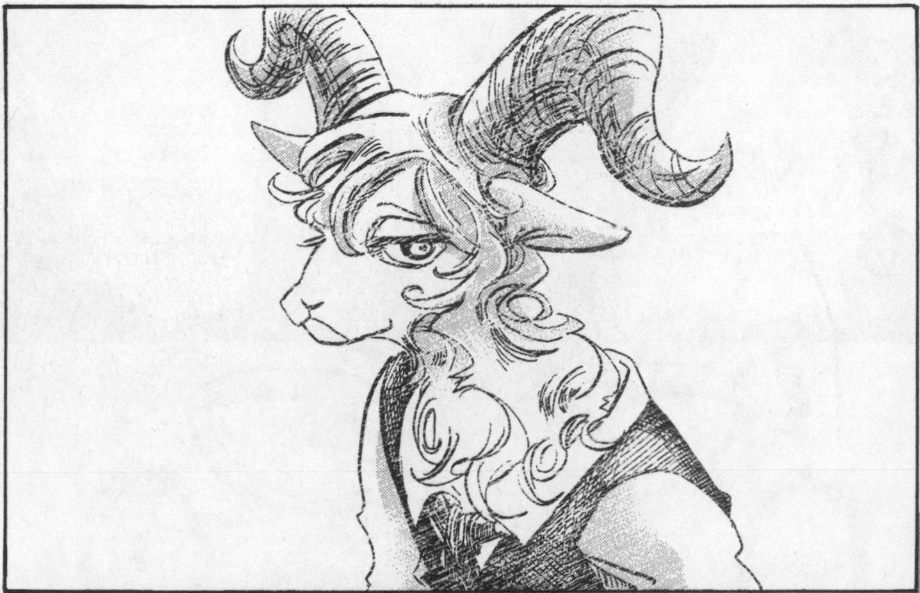
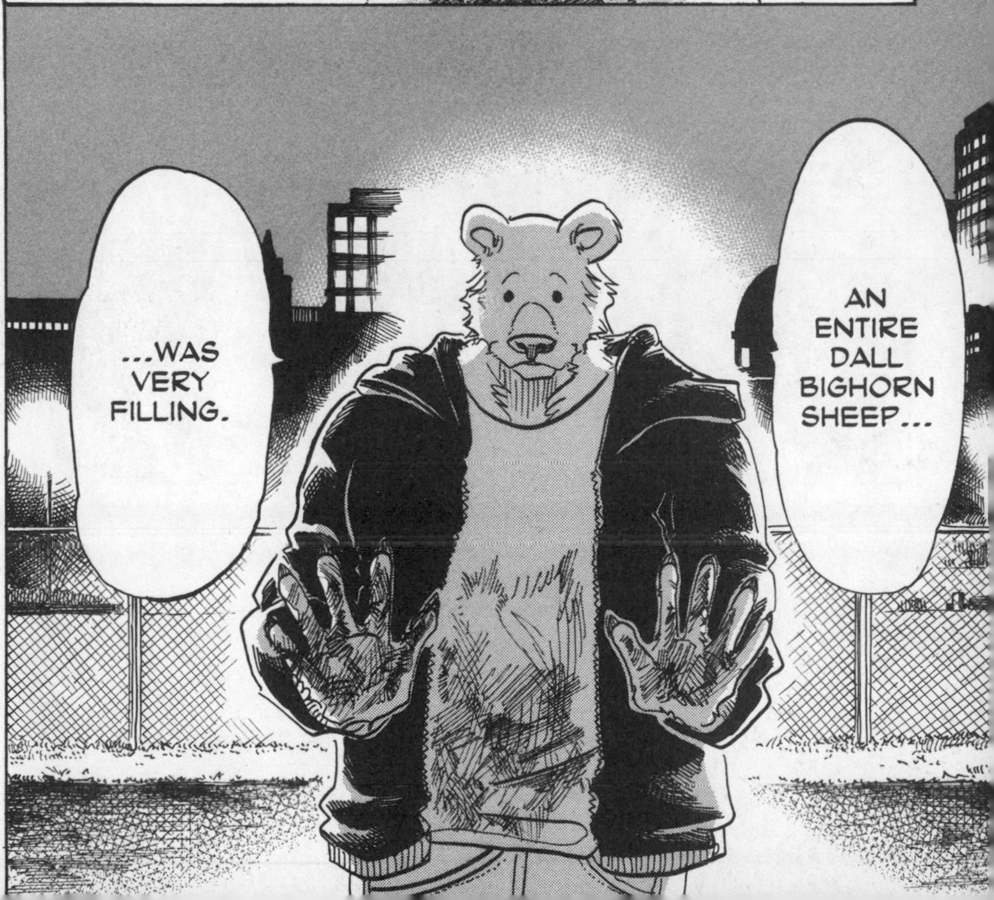
AN ENTIRE DALL BIGHORN SHEEP...
...WAS VERY FILLING.

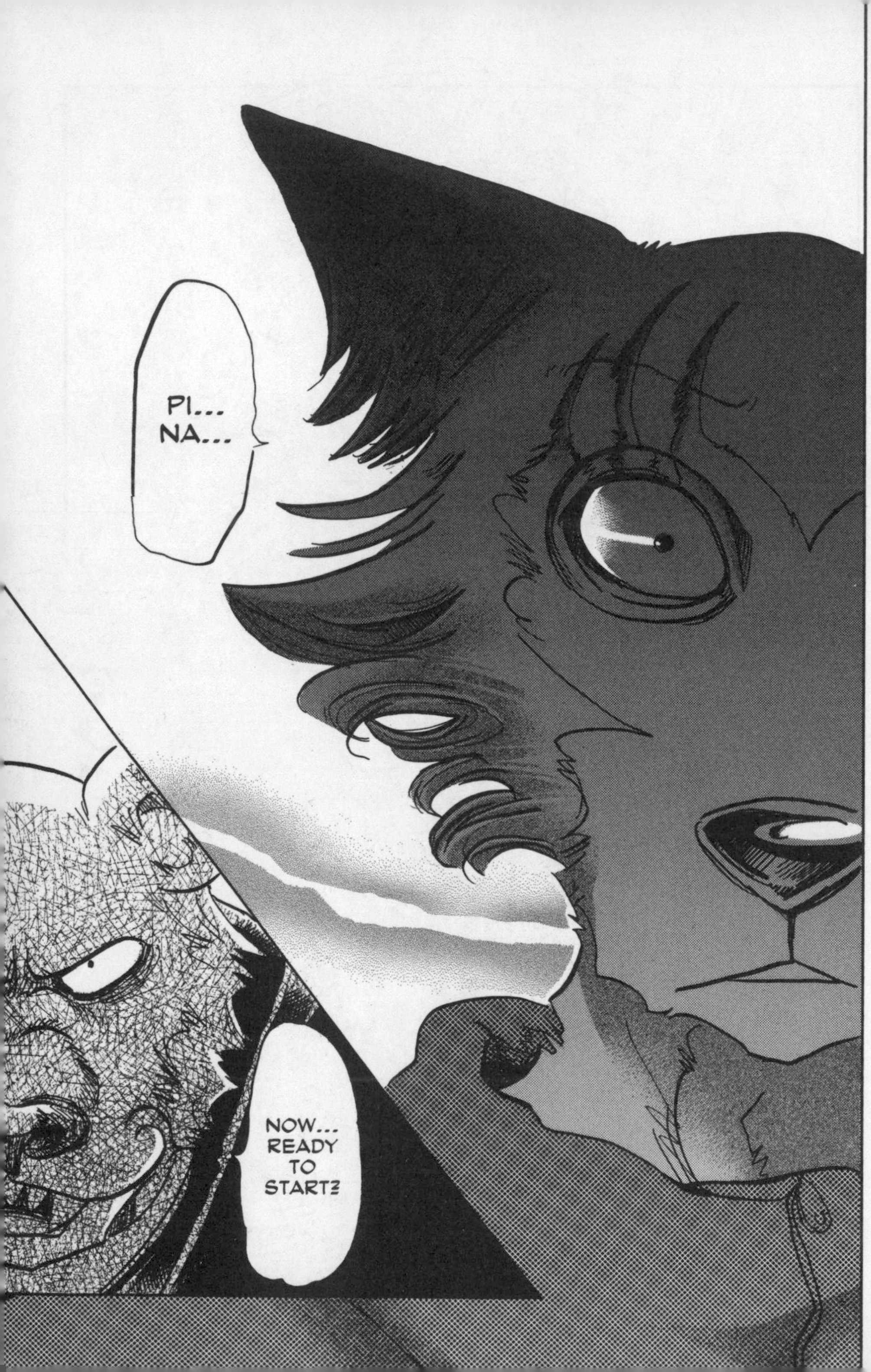
PI...
NA...
NOW...
READY
TO
START?

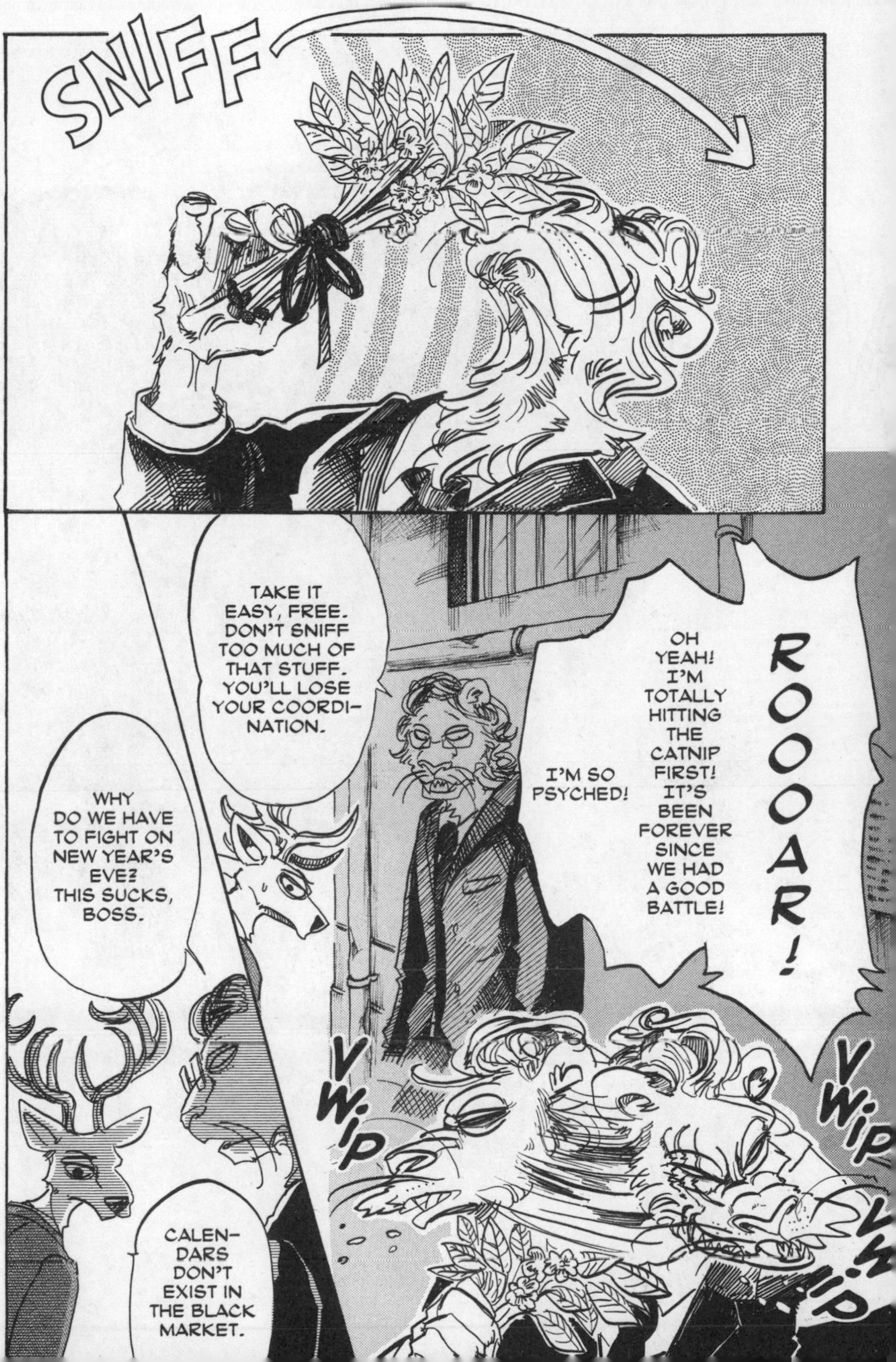
SNIFF
ROOOAR!
OH YEAH! I'M TOTALLY HITTING THE CATNIP FIRST! IT'S BEEN FOREVER SINCE WE HAD A GOOD BATTLE!
I'M SO PSYCHED!
TAKE IT EASY, FREE. DON'T SNIFF TOO MUCH OF THAT STUFF. YOU'LL LOSE YOUR COORDI-NATION.
WHY DO WE HAVE TO FIGHT ON NEW YEAR'S EVE? THIS SUCKS, BOSS.
VWIP
VWIP
VWIP
CALEN-DARS DON'T EXIST IN THE BLACK MARKET.

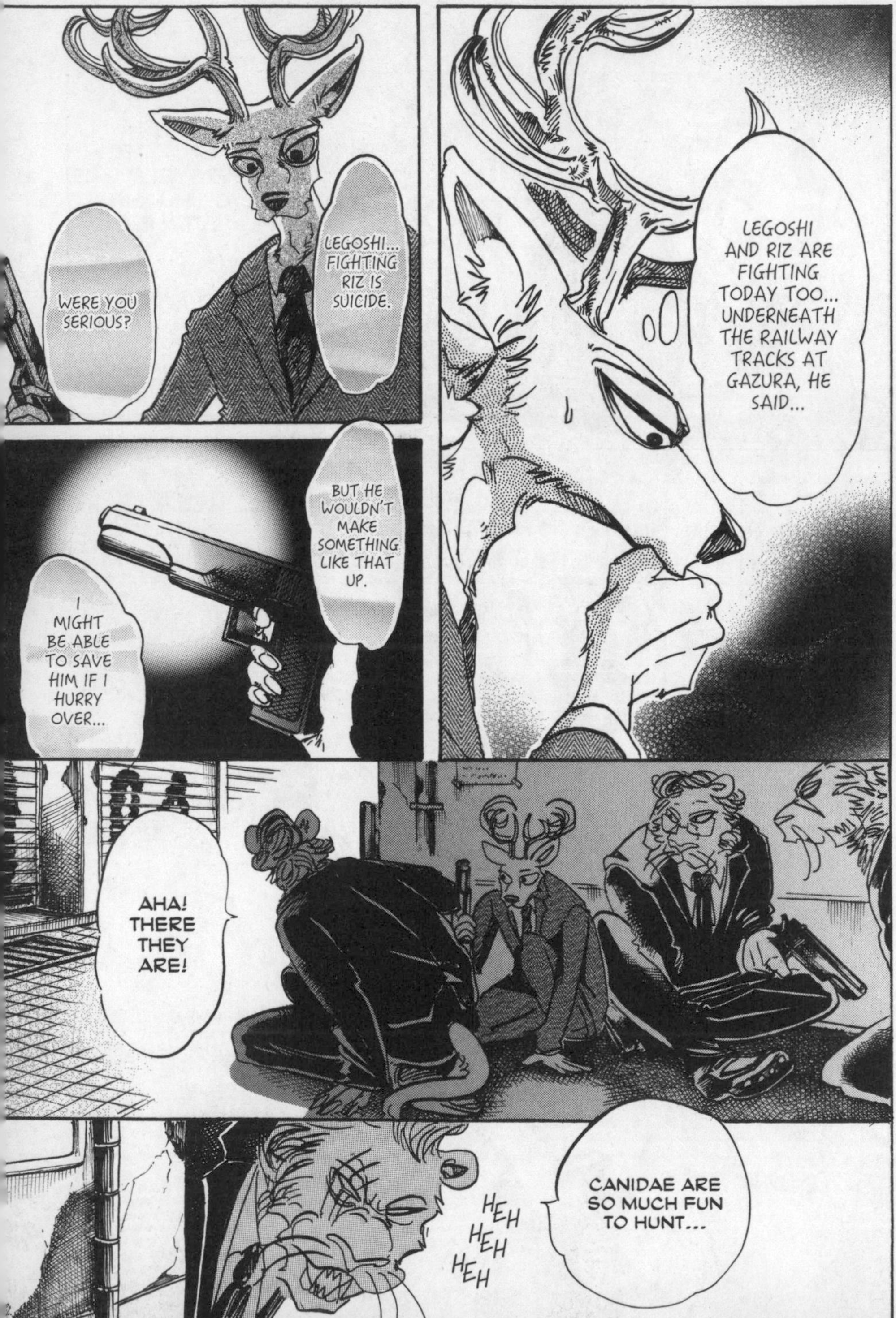
LEGOSHI AND RIZ ARE FIGHTING TODAY TOO... UNDERNEATH THE RAILWAY TRACKS AT GAZURA, HE SAID...
LEGOSHI... FIGHTING RIZ IS SUICIDE.
WERE YOU SERIOUS?
BUT HE WOULDN'T MAKE SOMETHING LIKE THAT UP.
I MIGHT BE ABLE TO SAVE HIM IF I HURRY OVER...
AHA! THERE THEY ARE!
CANIDAE ARE SO MUCH FUN TO HUNT...
HEH HEH HEH

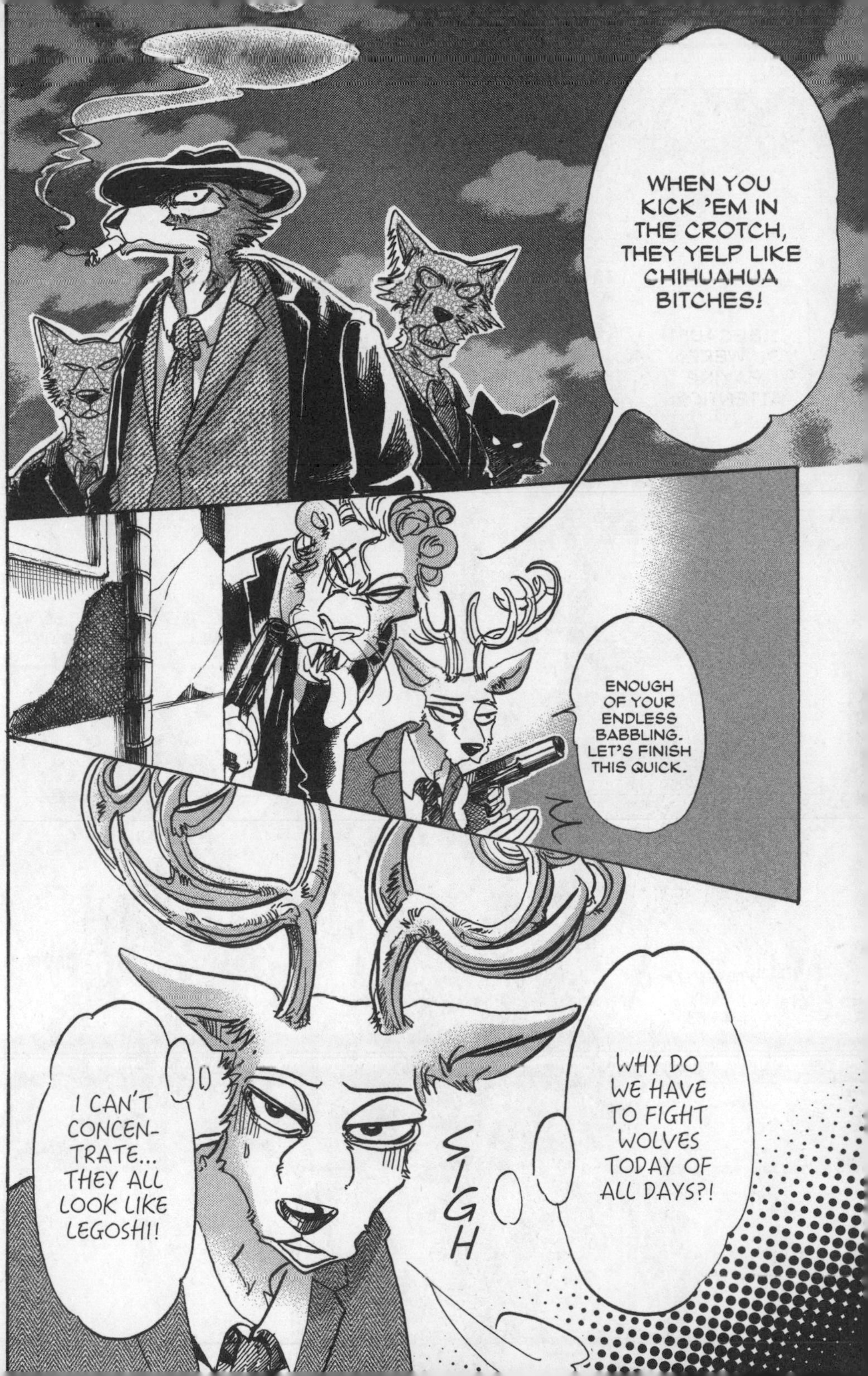
WHEN YOU KICK 'EM IN THE CROTCH, THEY YELP LIKE CHIHUAHUA BITCHES!
ENOUGH OF YOUR ENDLESS BABBLING. LET'S FINISH THIS QUICK.
WHY DO WE HAVE TO FIGHT WOLVES TODAY OF ALL DAYS?!
SIGH
I CAN'T CONCEN-TRATE... THEY ALL LOOK LIKE LEGOSHI!

Chapter 91: Howls of the Guardian Angel

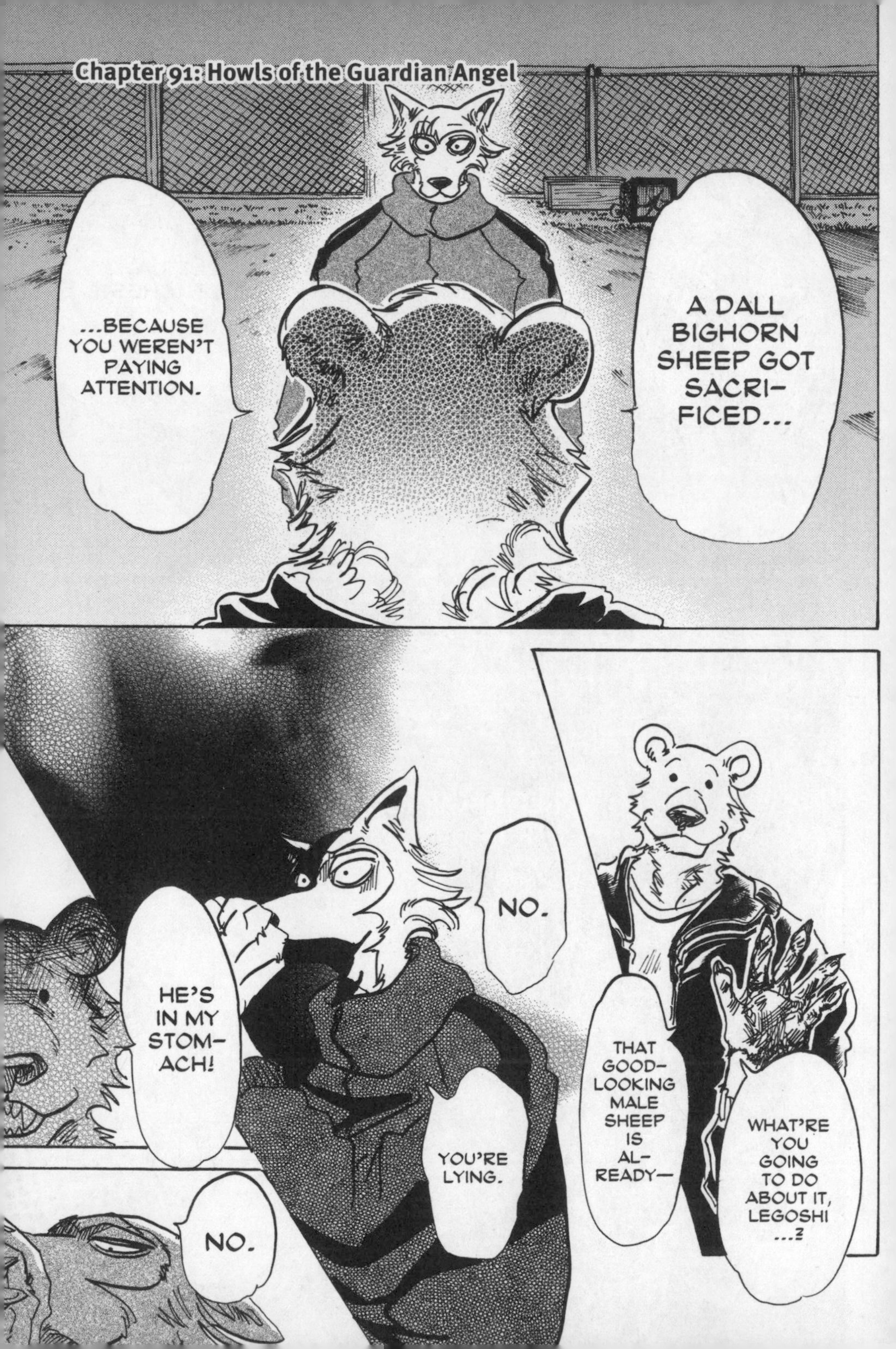
A DALL BIGHORN SHEEP GOT SACRIFICED...
...BECAUSE YOU WEREN'T PAYING ATTENTION.
WHAT'RE YOU GOING TO DO ABOUT IT, LEGOSHI...?
THAT GOOD-LOOKING MALE SHEEP IS ALREADY—
NO.
HE'S IN MY STOMACH!
YOU'RE LYING.
NO.

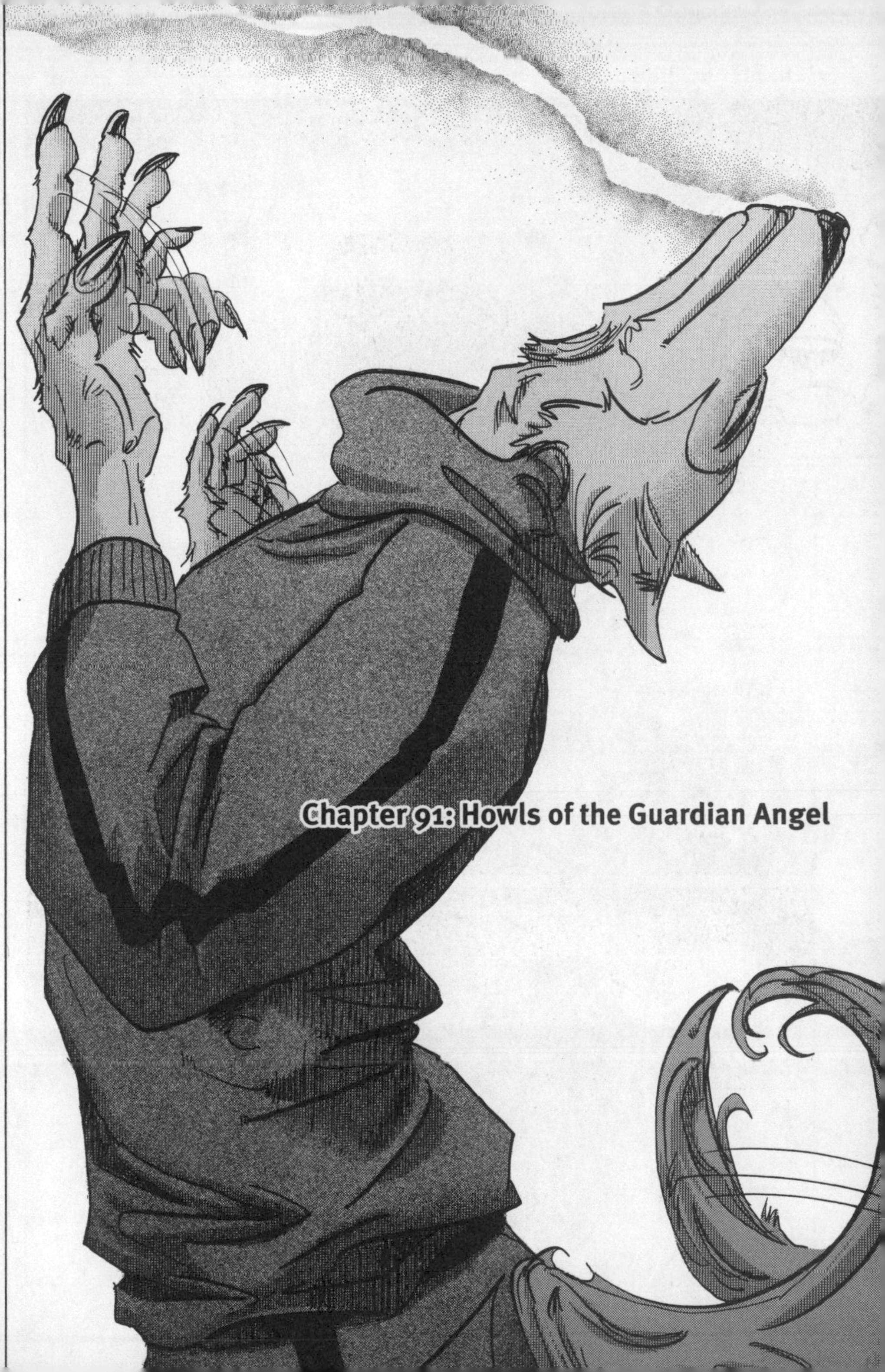

Chapter 91: Howls of the Guardian Angel

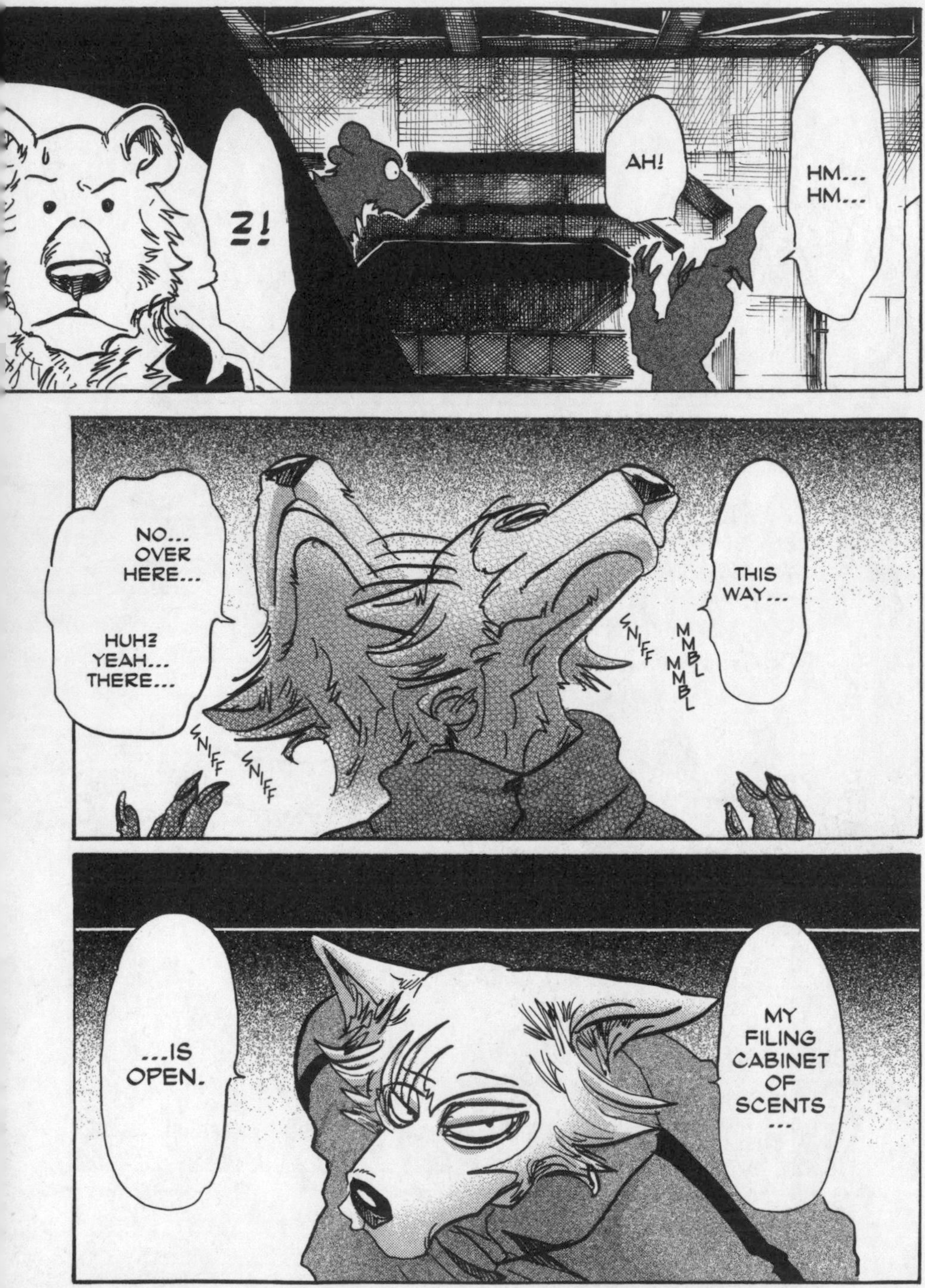
HM... HM...
AH!
!?
THIS WAY...
MMBL MMBL
SNIFF
NO... OVER HERE...
HUH? YEAH... THERE...
SNIFF SNIFF
MY FILING CABINET OF SCENTS...
...IS OPEN.

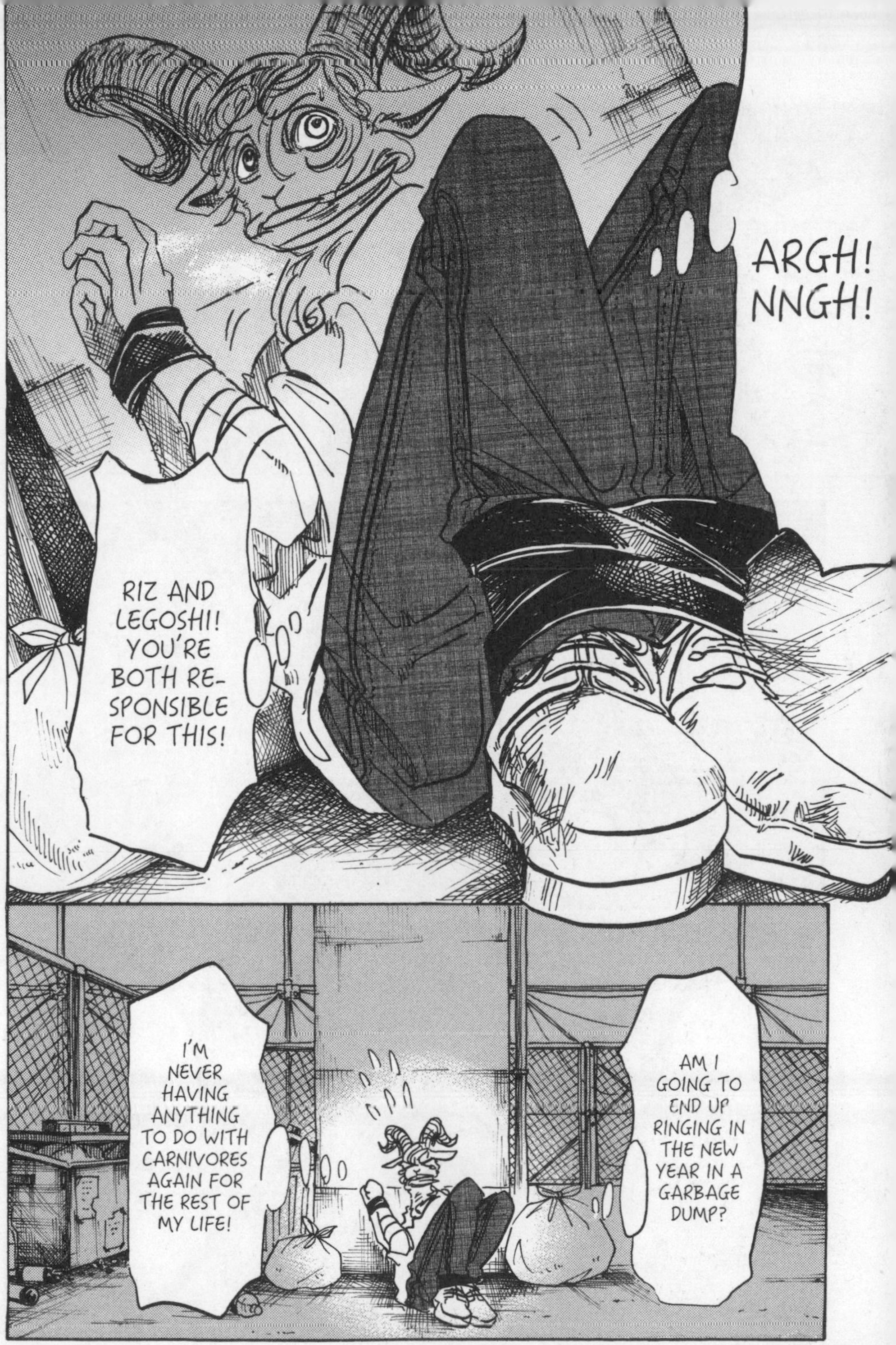
ARGH! NNGH!
RIZ AND LEGOSHI! YOU'RE BOTH RE-SPONSIBLE FOR THIS!
AM I GOING TO END UP RINGING IN THE NEW YEAR IN A GARBAGE DUMP?
I'M NEVER HAVING ANYTHING TO DO WITH CARNIVORES AGAIN FOR THE REST OF MY LIFE!

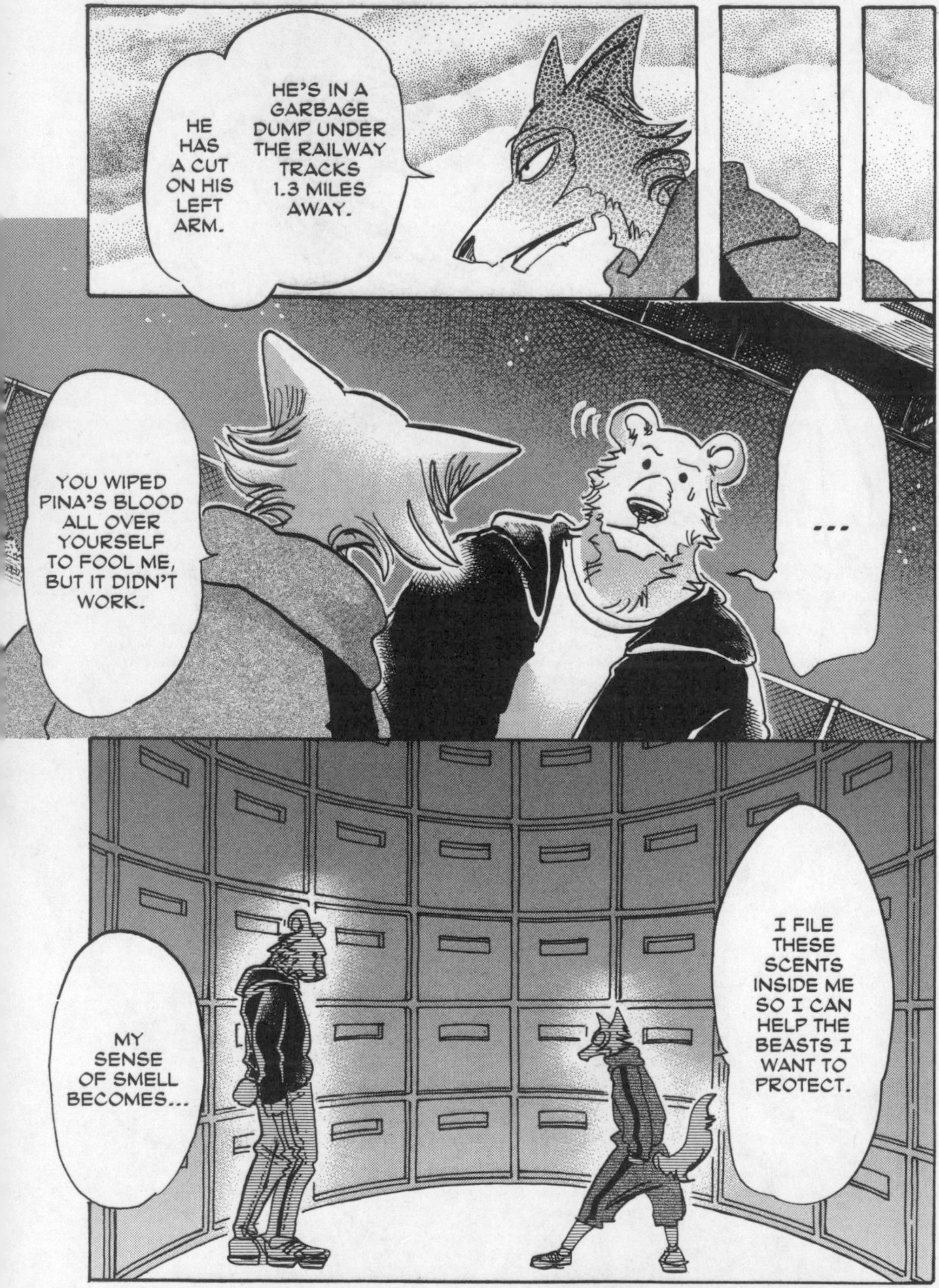
HE'S IN A GARBAGE DUMP UNDER THE RAILWAY TRACKS 1.3 MILES AWAY.
HE HAS A CUT ON HIS LEFT ARM.
...
YOU WIPED PINA'S BLOOD ALL OVER YOURSELF TO FOOL ME, BUT IT DIDN'T WORK.
I FILE THESE SCENTS INSIDE ME SO I CAN HELP THE BEASTS I WANT TO PROTECT.
MY SENSE OF SMELL BECOMES...

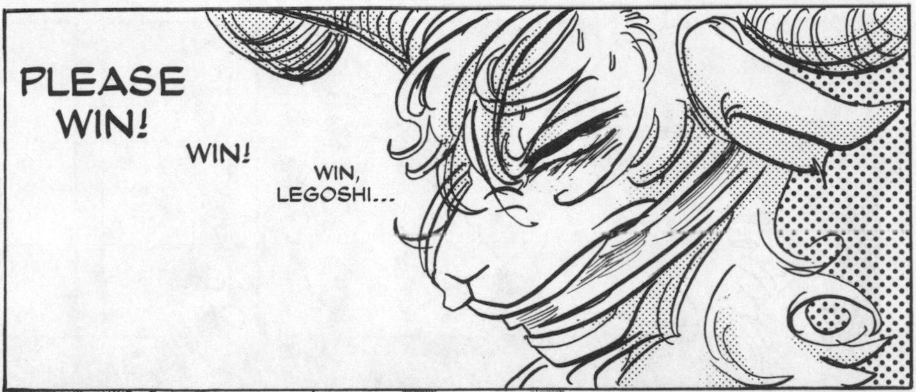
PLEASE WIN!
WIN!
WIN, LEGOSHI...
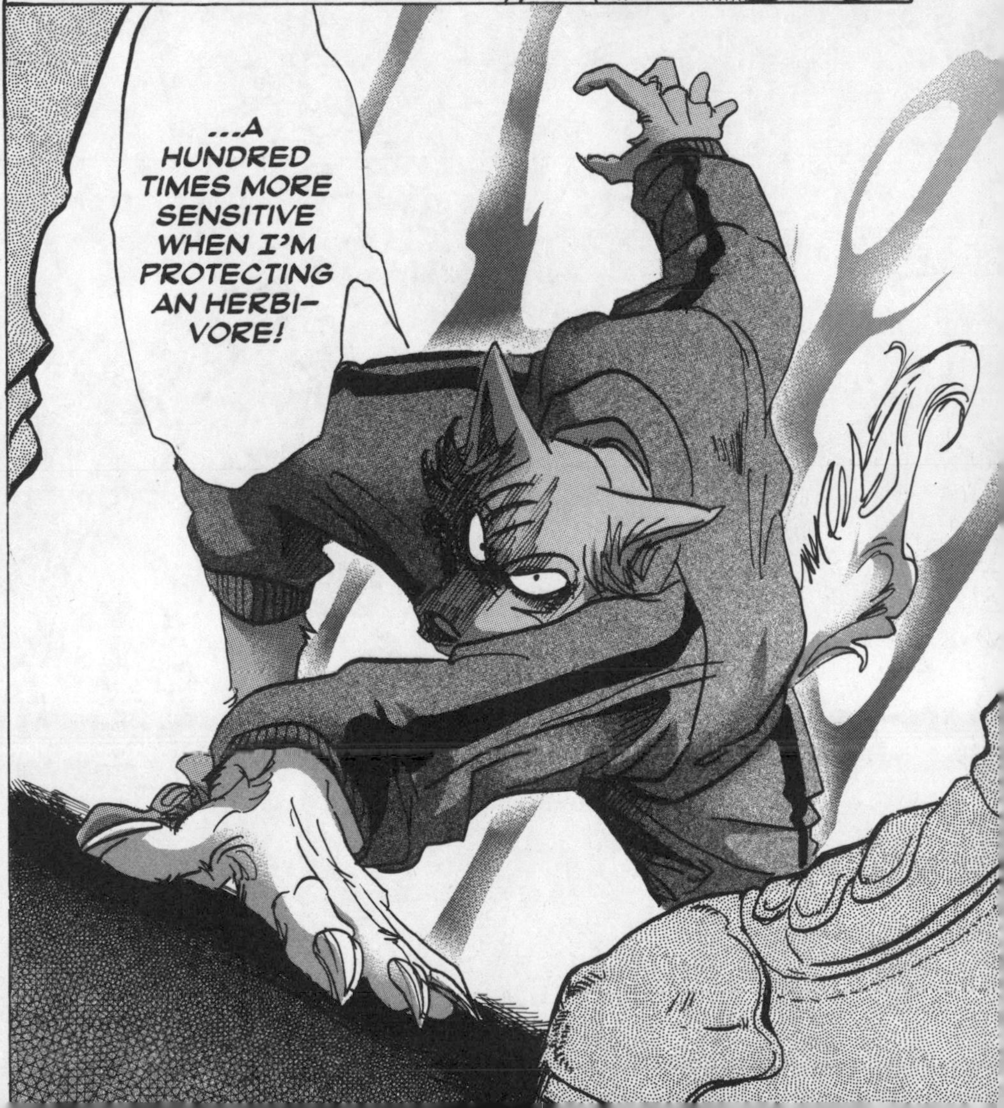
...A HUNDRED TIMES MORE SENSITIVE WHEN I'M PROTECTING AN HERBI-VORE!

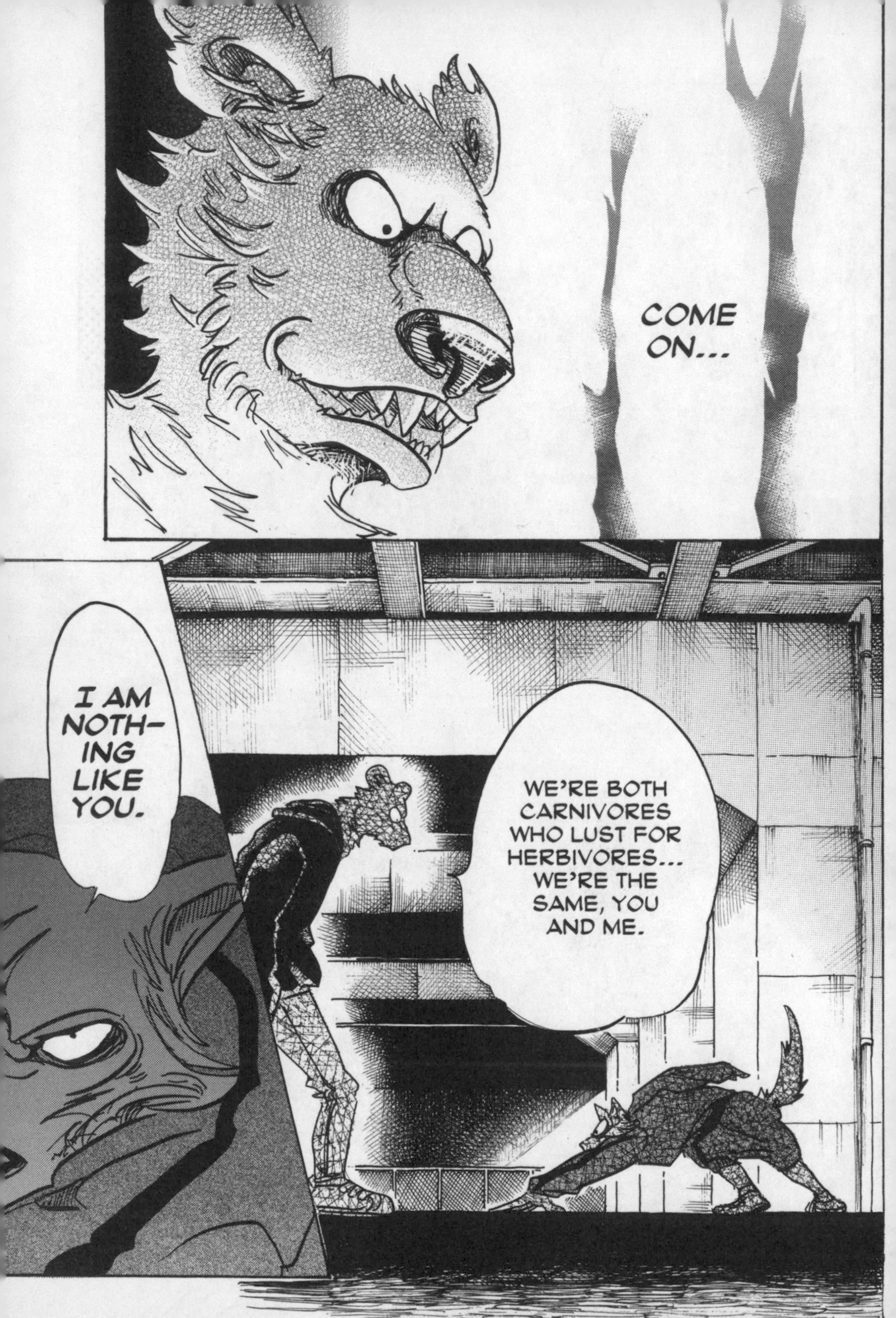
COME ON...
WE'RE BOTH CARNIVORES WHO LUST FOR HERBIVORES... WE'RE THE SAME, YOU AND ME.
I AM NOTHING LIKE YOU.

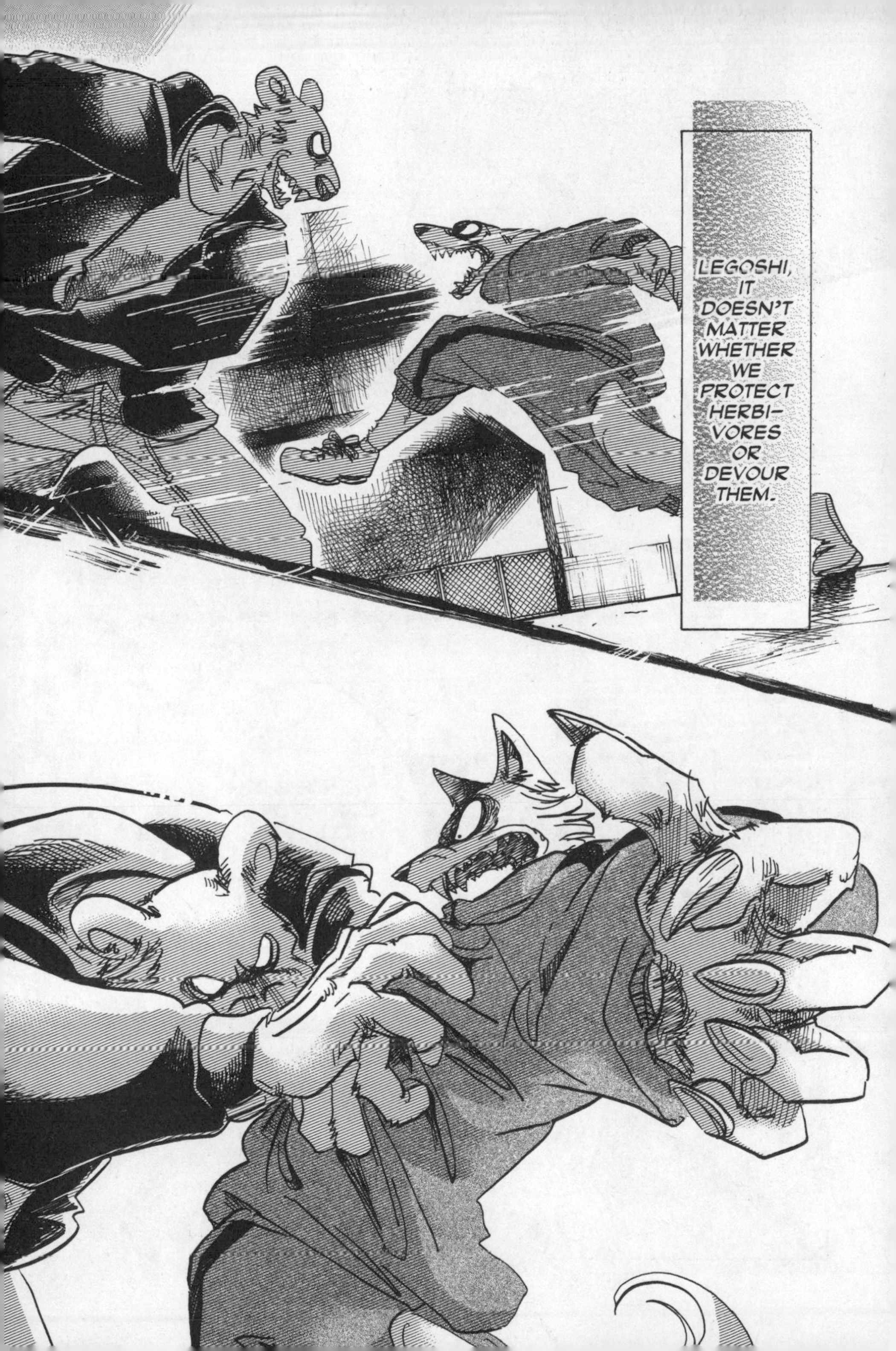
LEGOSHI, IT DOESN'T MATTER WHETHER WE PROTECT HERBI-VORES OR DEVOUR THEM.

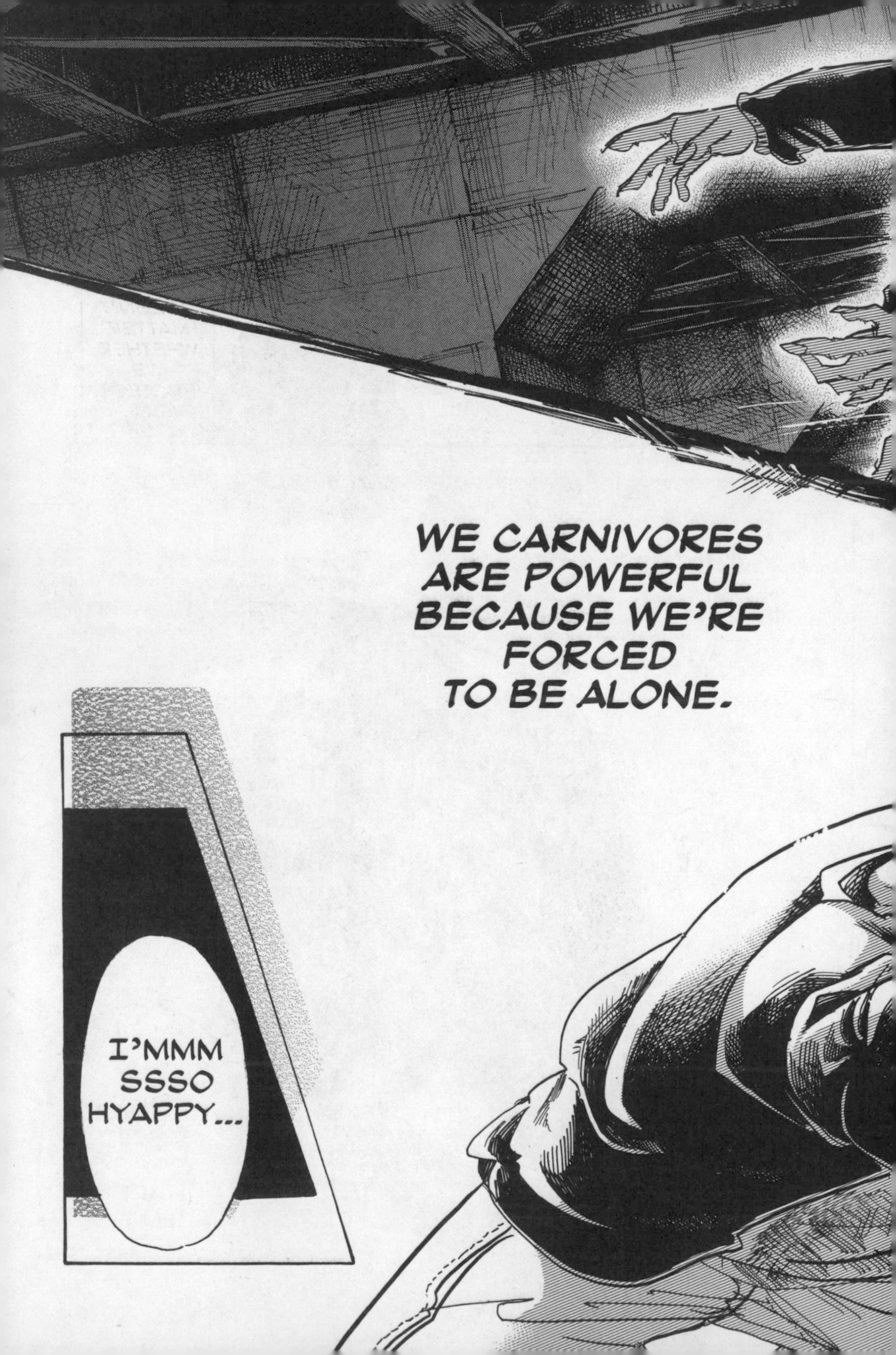
WE CARNIVORES ARE POWERFUL BECAUSE WE'RE FORCED TO BE ALONE.
I'MMM SSSO HYAPPY...

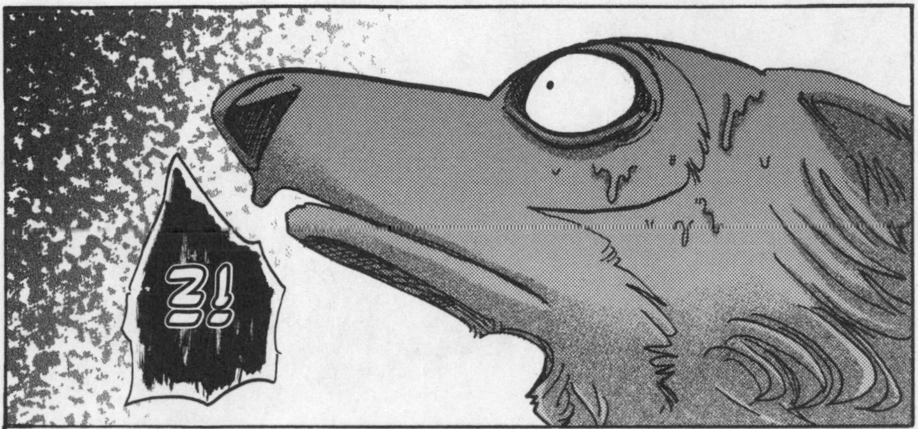
!?

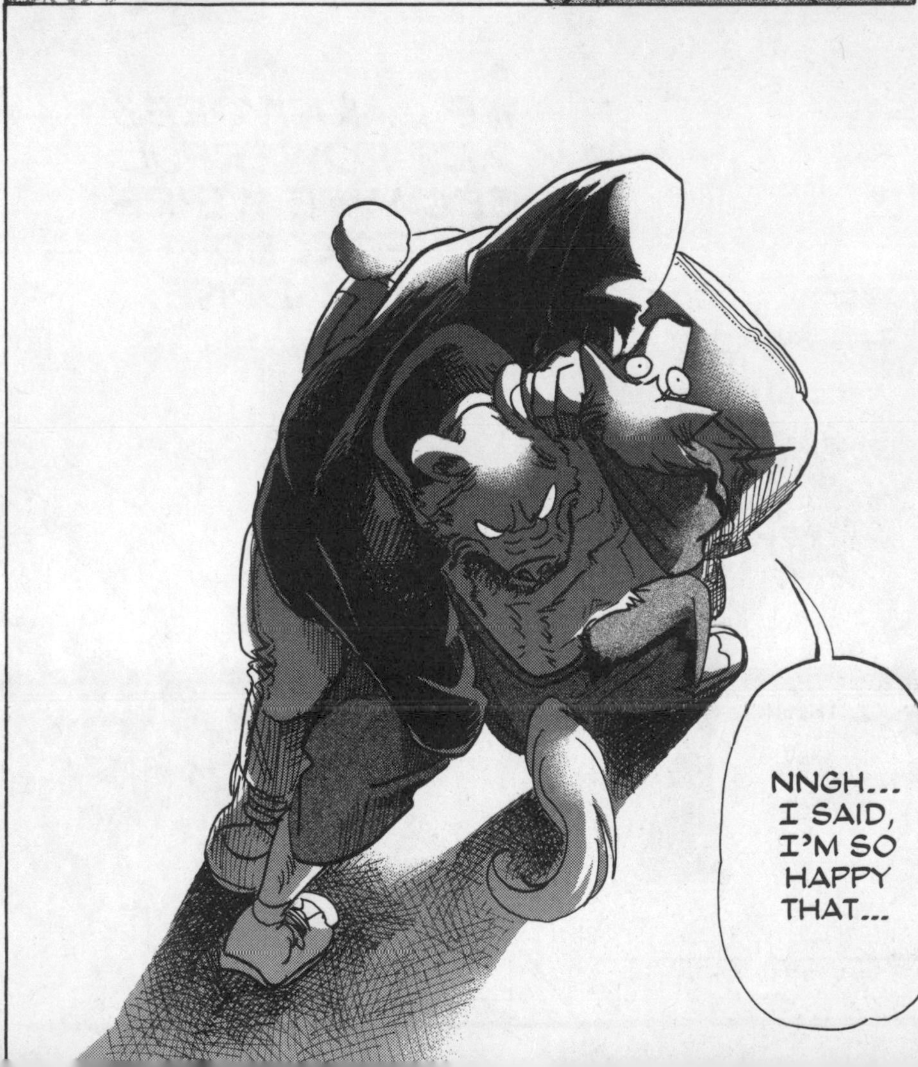
NNGH... I SAID, I'M SO HAPPY THAT...

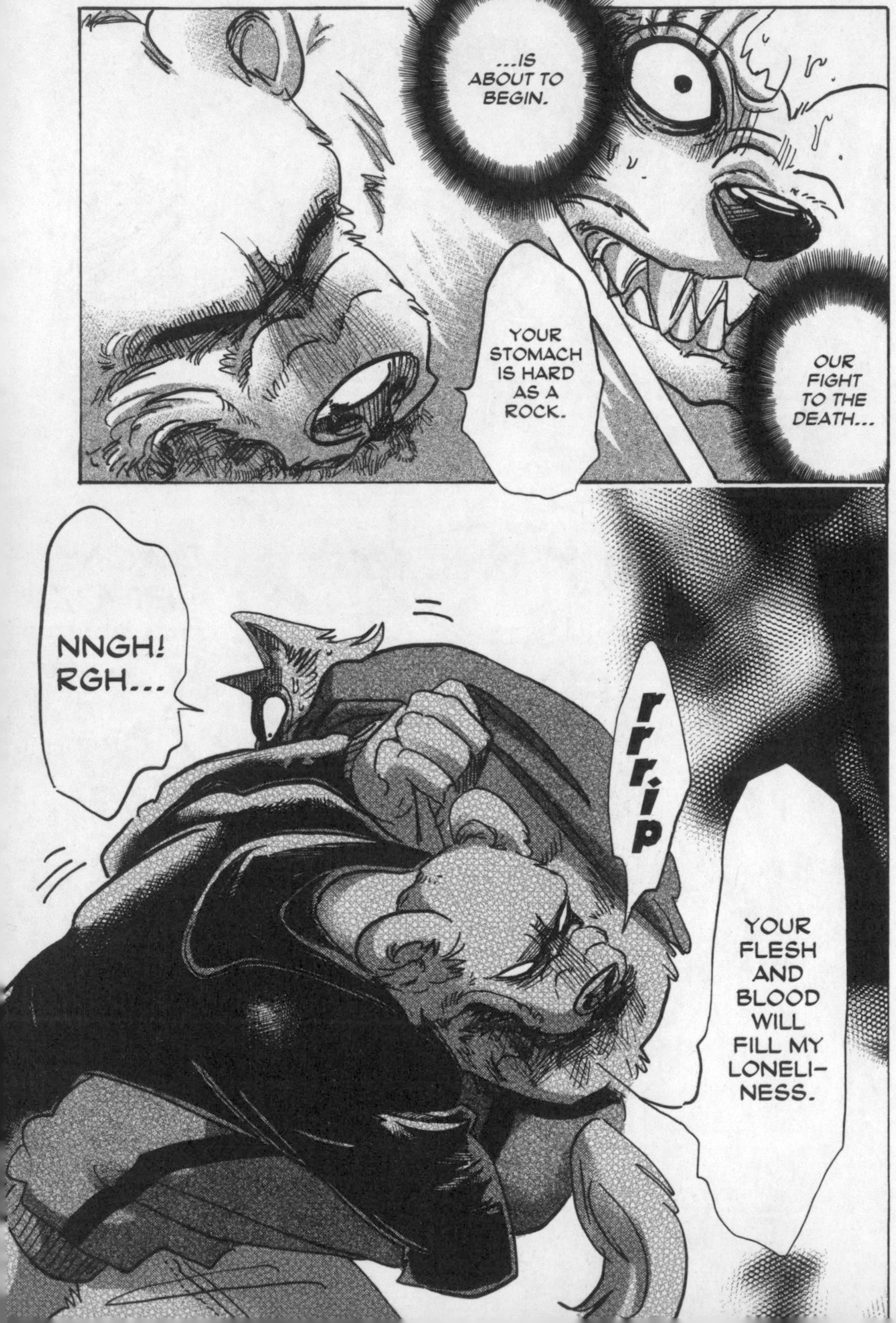
OUR FIGHT TO THE DEATH...
...IS ABOUT TO BEGIN.
YOUR STOMACH IS HARD AS A ROCK.
YOUR FLESH AND BLOOD WILL FILL MY LONELI-NESS.
rrrip
NNGH! RGH...

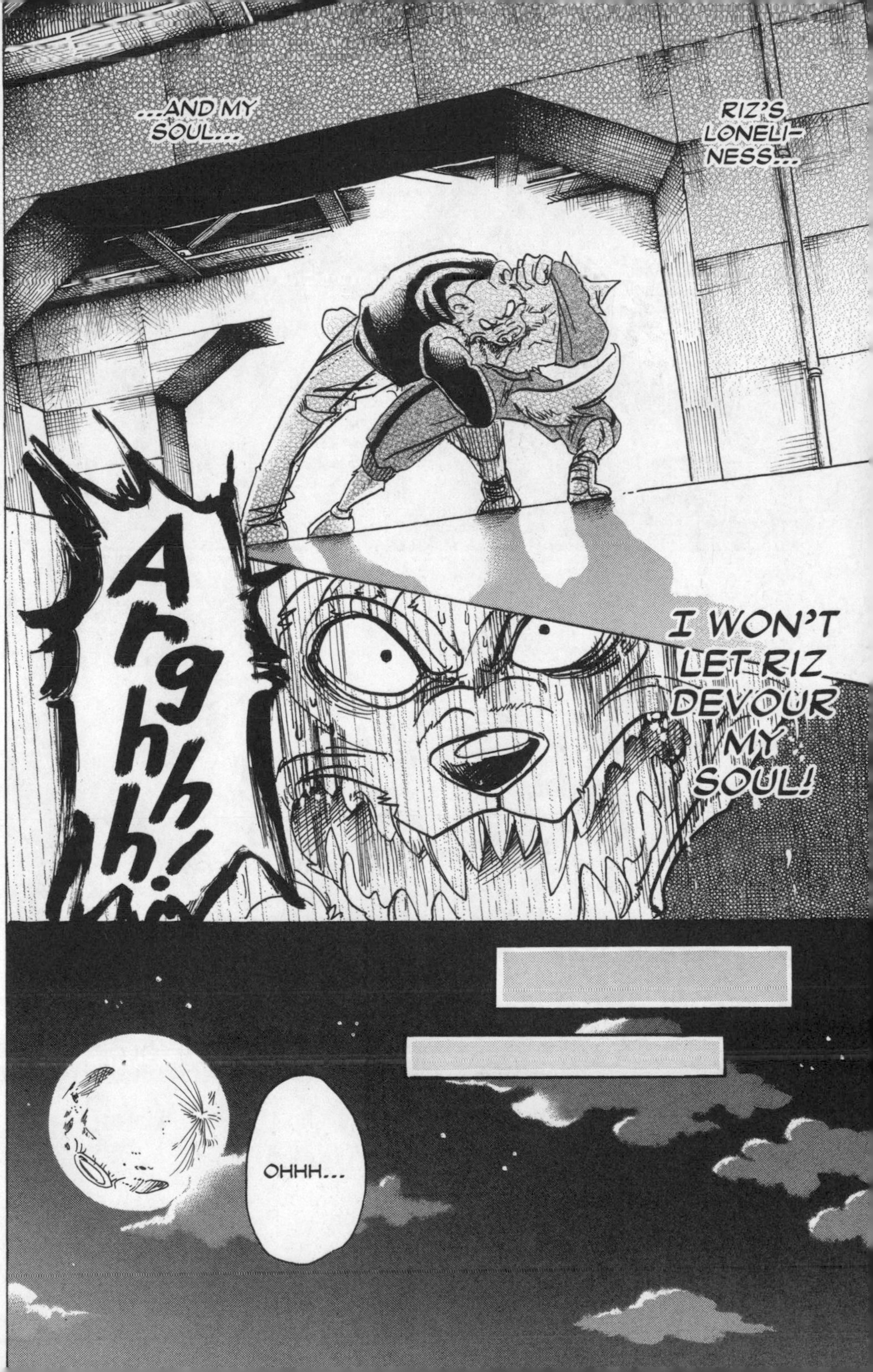
RIZ'S LONELI-NESS...
...AND MY SOUL...
I WON'T LET RIZ DEVOUR MY SOUL!
Arghhh!!
OHHH...

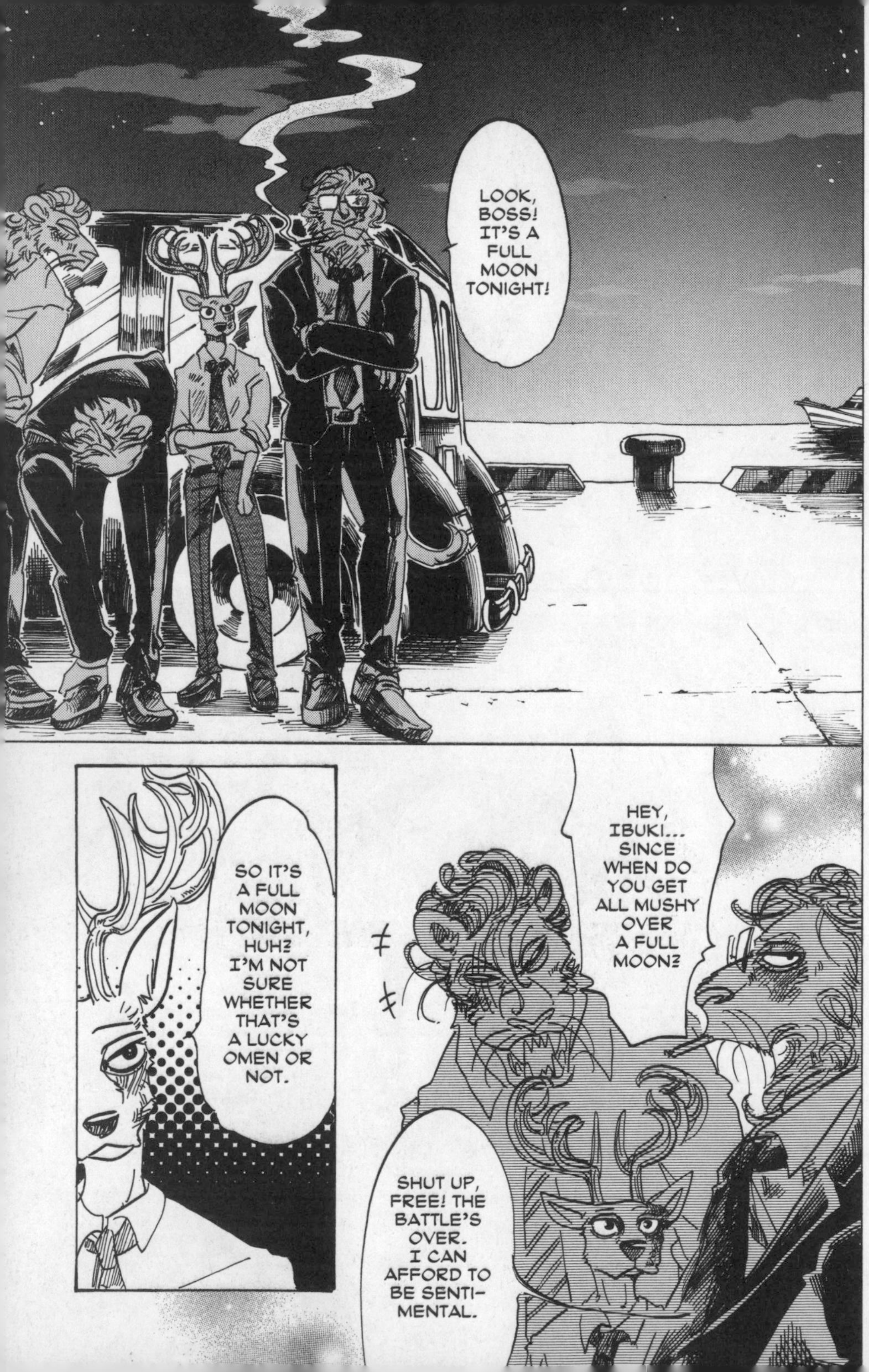
LOOK, BOSS! IT'S A FULL MOON TONIGHT!
SO IT'S A FULL MOON TONIGHT, HUH? I'M NOT SURE WHETHER THAT'S A LUCKY OMEN OR NOT.
HEY, IBUKI... SINCE WHEN DO YOU GET ALL MUSHY OVER A FULL MOON?
SHUT UP, FREE! THE BATTLE'S OVER. I CAN AFFORD TO BE SENTI-MENTAL.

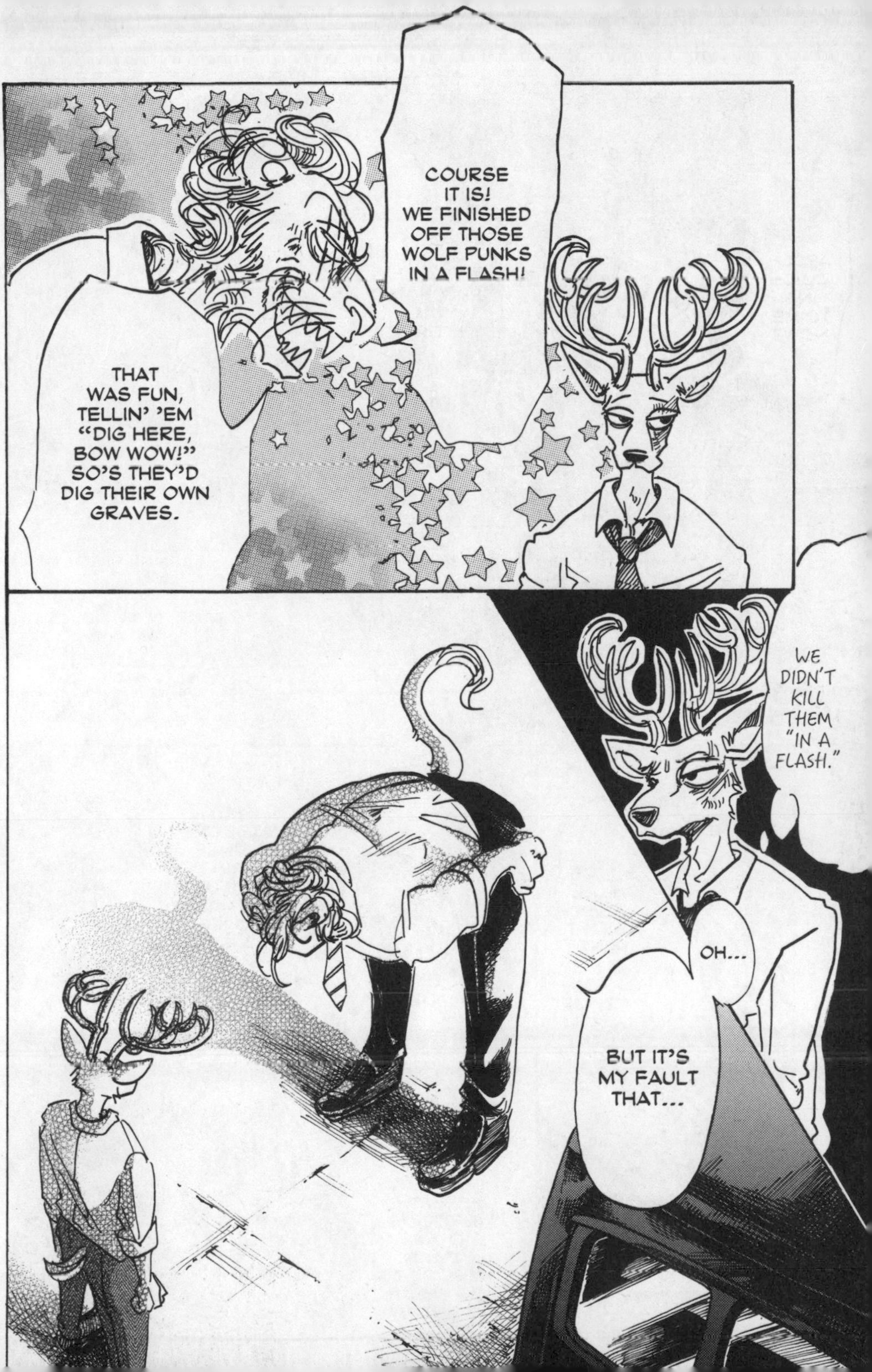
COURSE IT IS! WE FINISHED OFF THOSE WOLF PUNKS IN A FLASH!
THAT WAS FUN, TELLIN' 'EM "DIG HERE, BOW WOW!" SO'S THEY'D DIG THEIR OWN GRAVES.
WE DIDN'T KILL THEM "IN A FLASH."
OH...
BUT IT'S MY FAULT THAT...

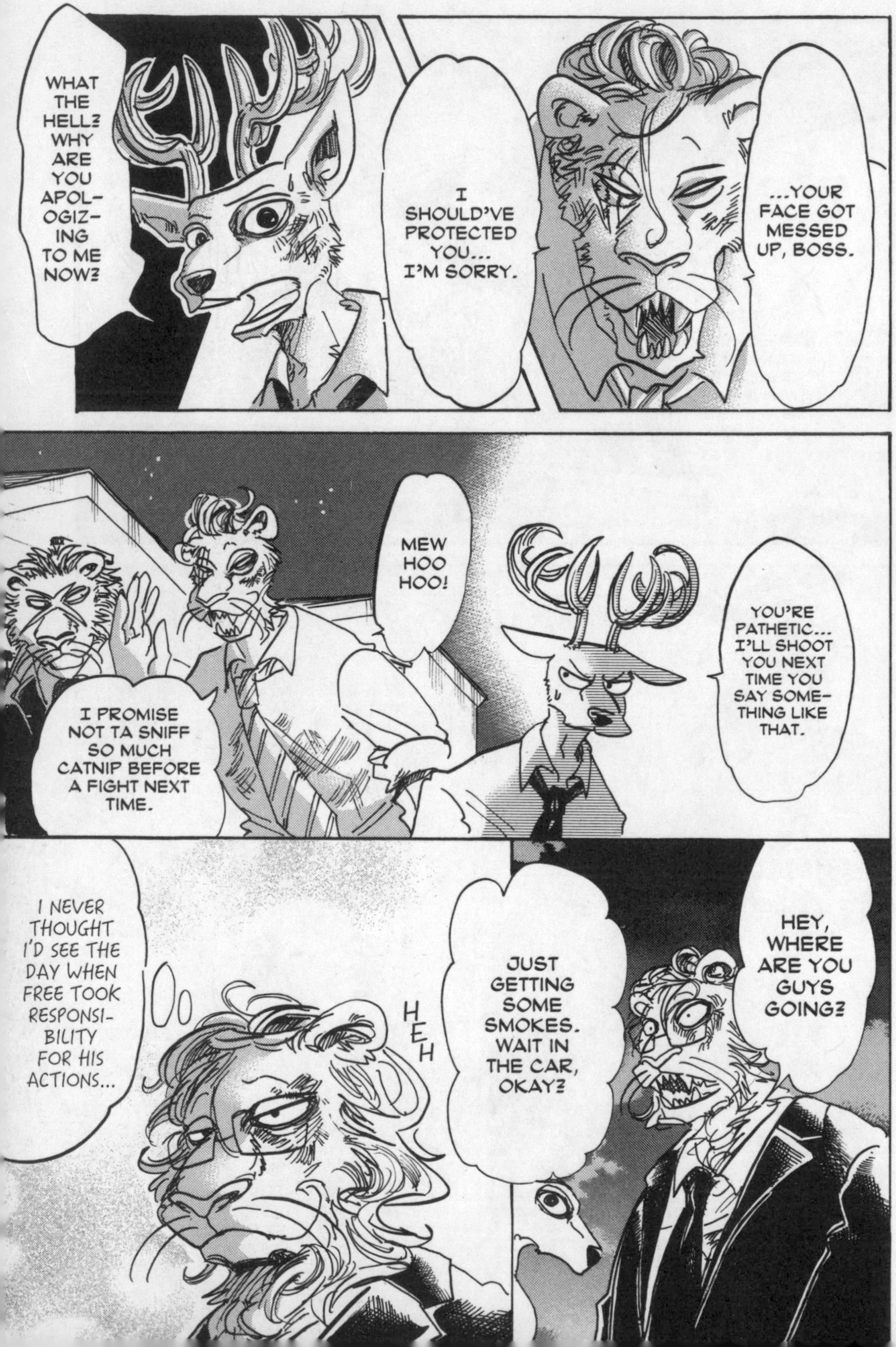
...YOUR FACE GOT MESSED UP, BOSS.
I SHOULD'VE PROTECTED YOU... I'M SORRY.
WHAT THE HELL? WHY ARE YOU APOLOGIZING TO ME NOW?
YOU'RE PATHETIC... I'LL SHOOT YOU NEXT TIME YOU SAY SOMETHING LIKE THAT.
MEW HOO HOO!
I PROMISE NOT TA SNIFF SO MUCH CATNIP BEFORE A FIGHT NEXT TIME.
HEY, WHERE ARE YOU GUYS GOING?
JUST GETTING SOME SMOKES. WAIT IN THE CAR, OKAY?
HEH
I NEVER THOUGHT I'D SEE THE DAY WHEN FREE TOOK RESPONSIBILITY FOR HIS ACTIONS...

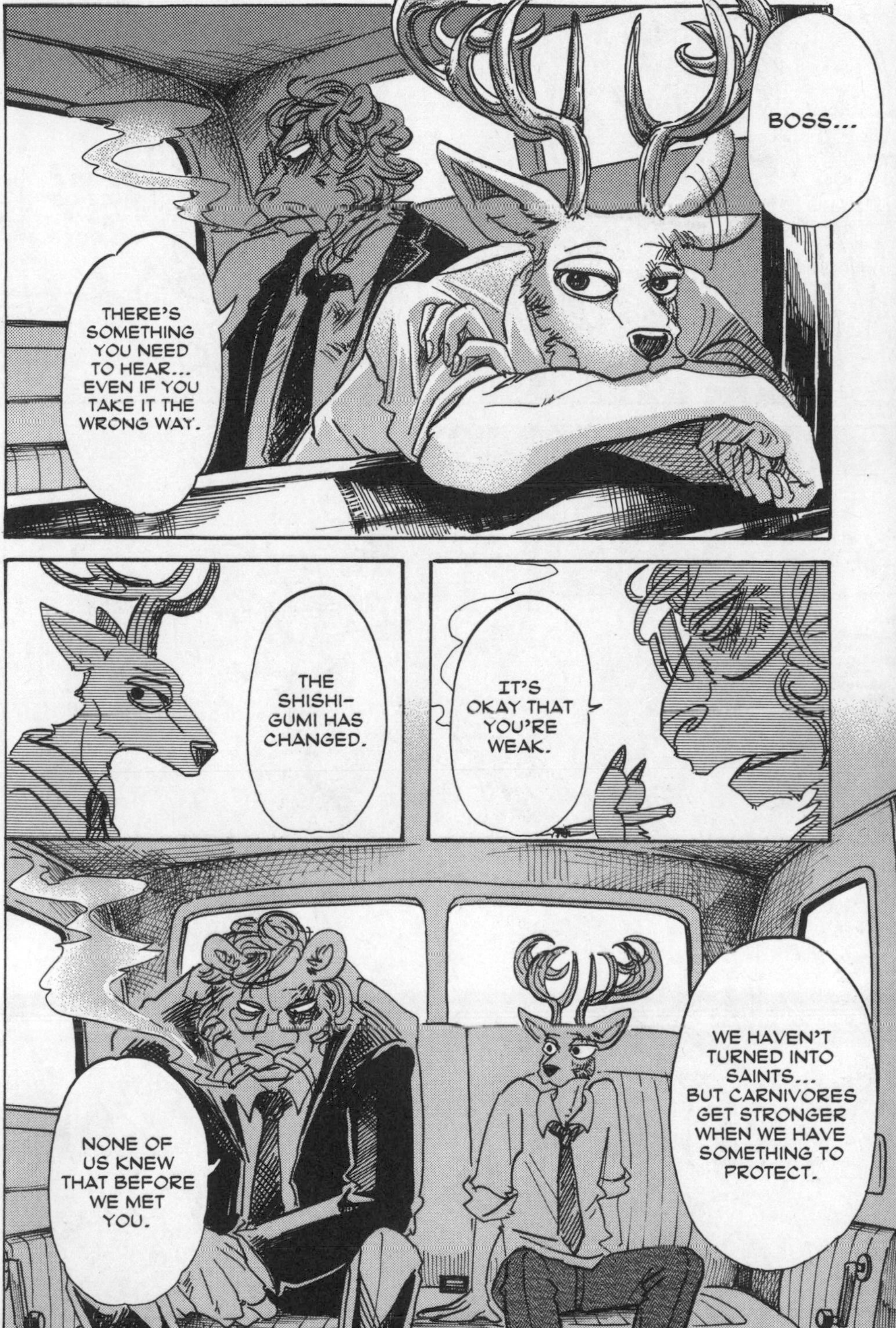
BOSS...
THERE'S SOMETHING YOU NEED TO HEAR... EVEN IF YOU TAKE IT THE WRONG WAY.
IT'S OKAY THAT YOU'RE WEAK.
THE SHISHI-GUMI HAS CHANGED.
WE HAVEN'T TURNED INTO SAINTS... BUT CARNIVORES GET STRONGER WHEN WE HAVE SOMETHING TO PROTECT.
NONE OF US KNEW THAT BEFORE WE MET YOU.

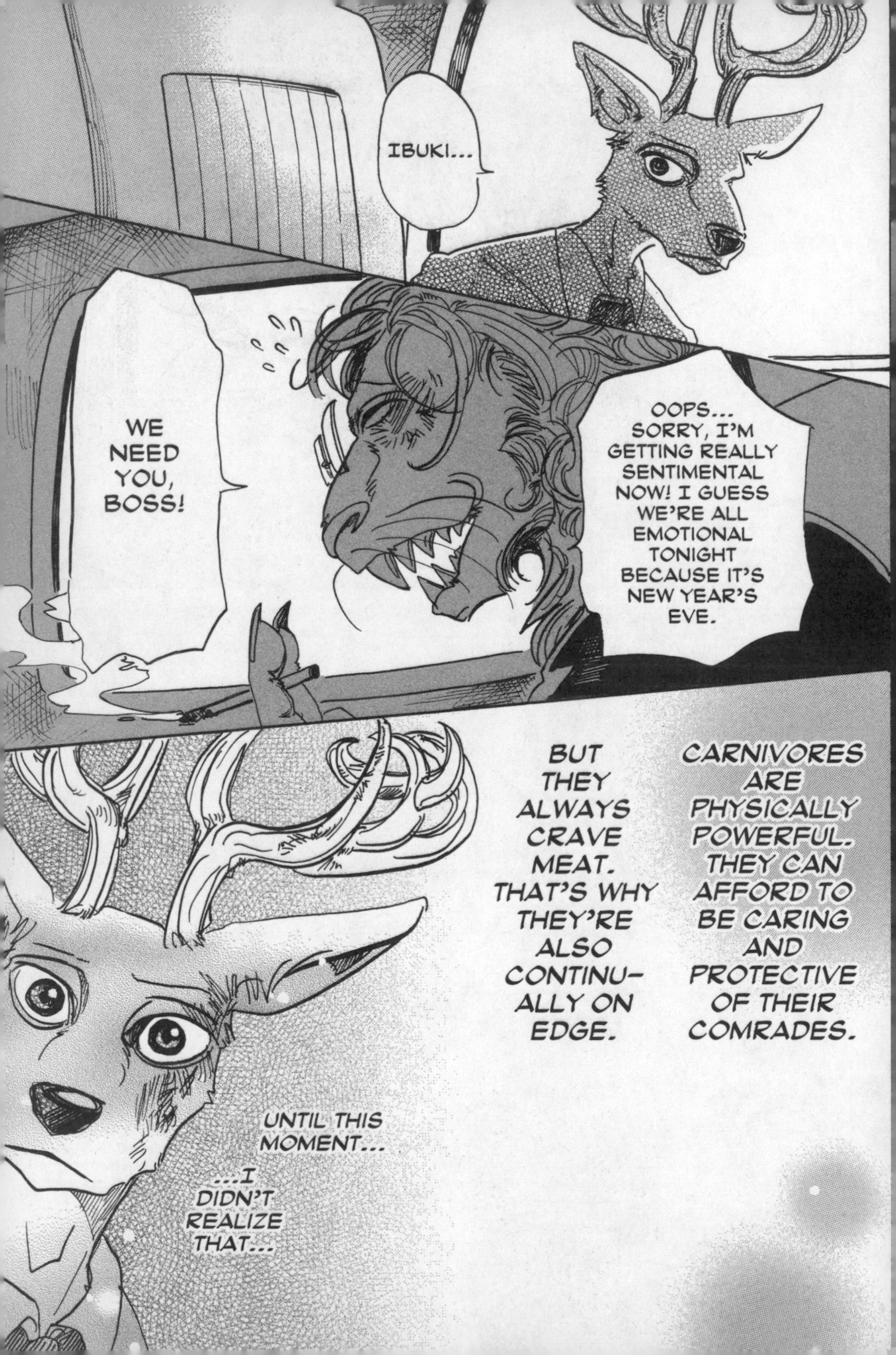
IBUKI...
WE NEED YOU, BOSS!
OOPS... SORRY, I'M GETTING REALLY SENTIMENTAL NOW! I GUESS WE'RE ALL EMOTIONAL TONIGHT BECAUSE IT'S NEW YEAR'S EVE.
CARNIVORES ARE PHYSICALLY POWERFUL. THEY CAN AFFORD TO BE CARING AND PROTECTIVE OF THEIR COMRADES.
BUT THEY ALWAYS CRAVE MEAT. THAT'S WHY THEY'RE ALSO CONTINU-ALLY ON EDGE.
UNTIL THIS MOMENT...
...I DIDN'T REALIZE THAT...

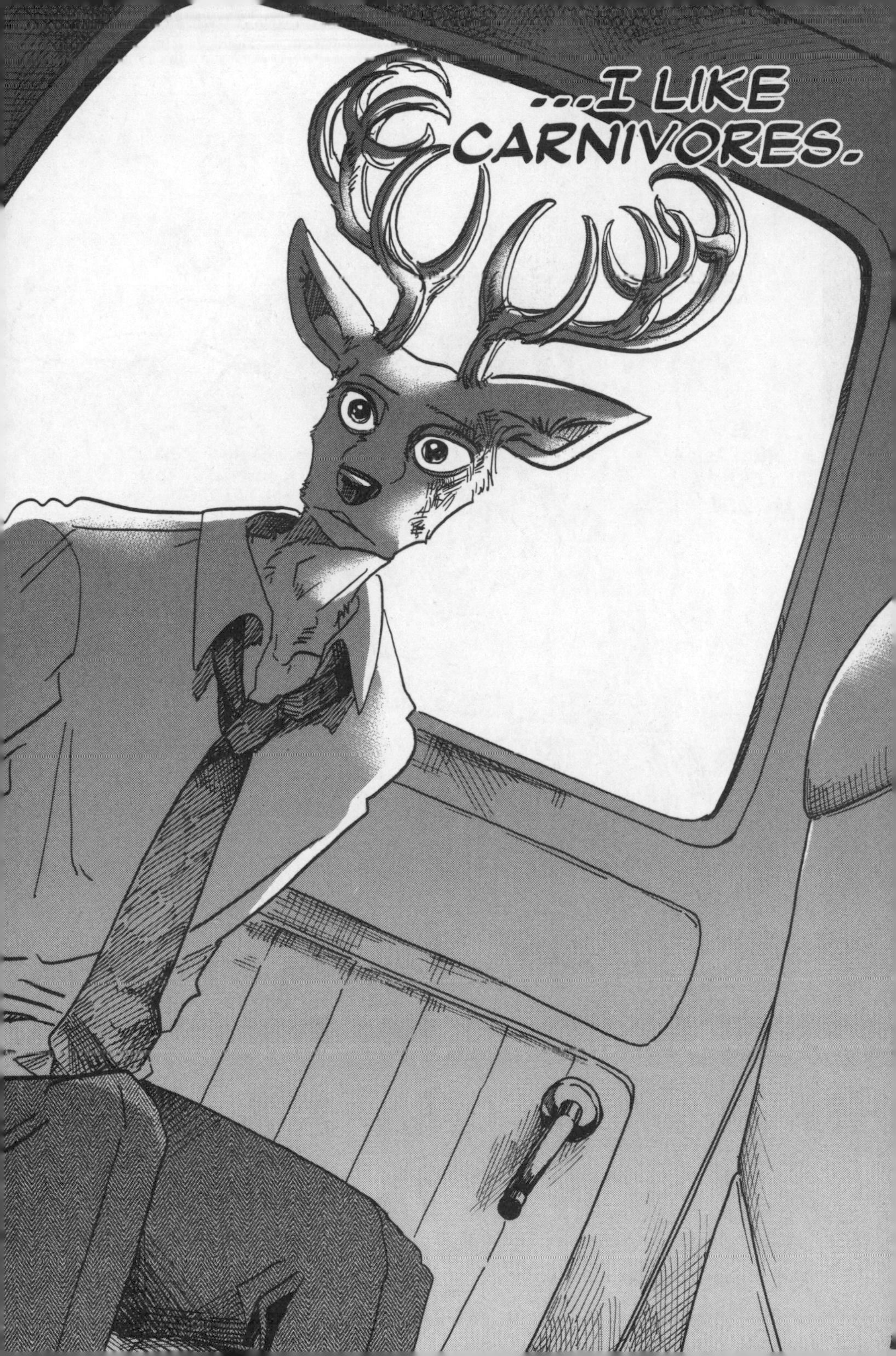
...I LIKE CARNIVORES.

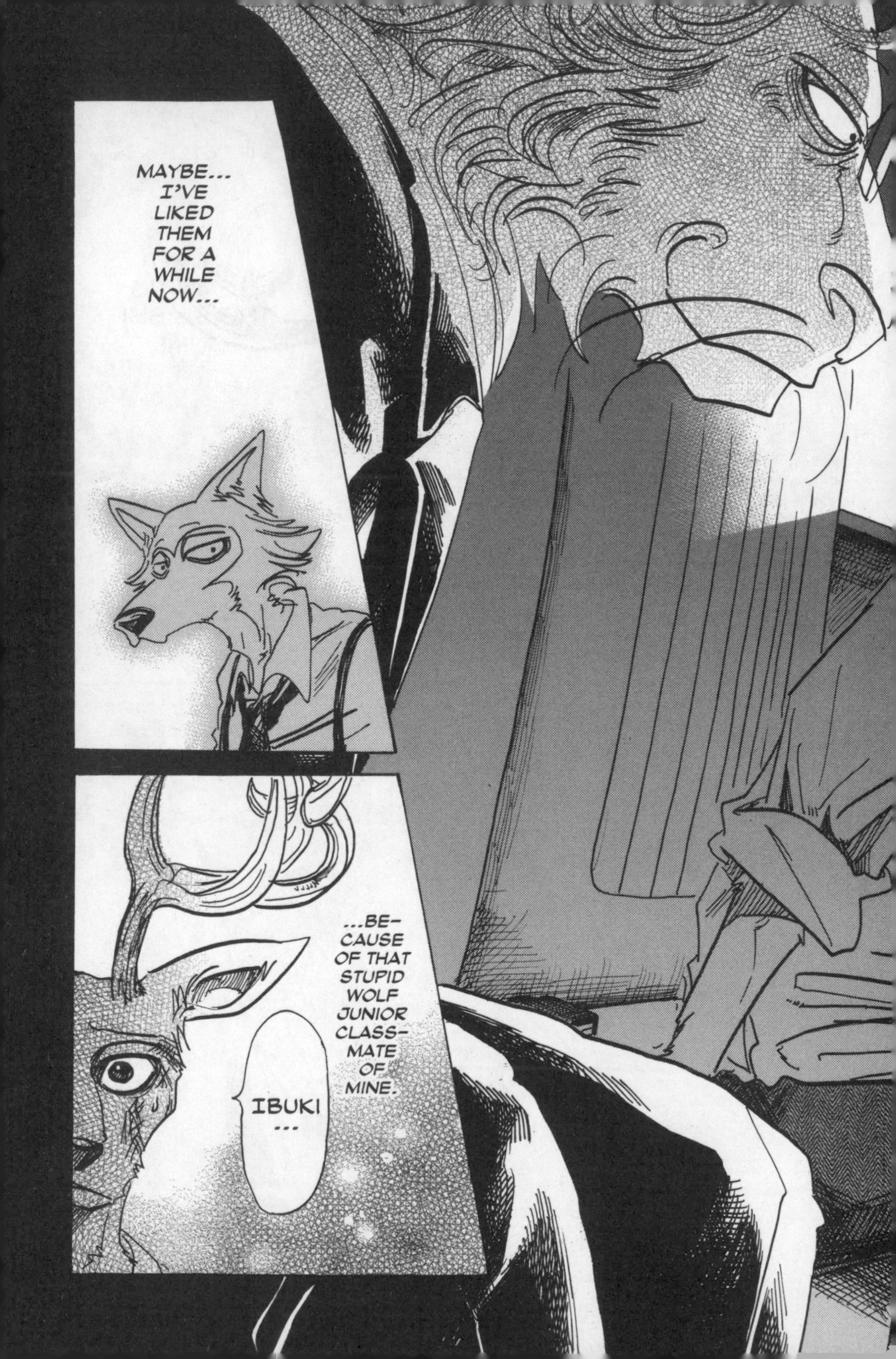
MAYBE... I'VE LIKED THEM FOR A WHILE NOW...
...BE-CAUSE OF THAT STUPID WOLF JUNIOR CLASS-MATE OF MINE.
IBUKI ...

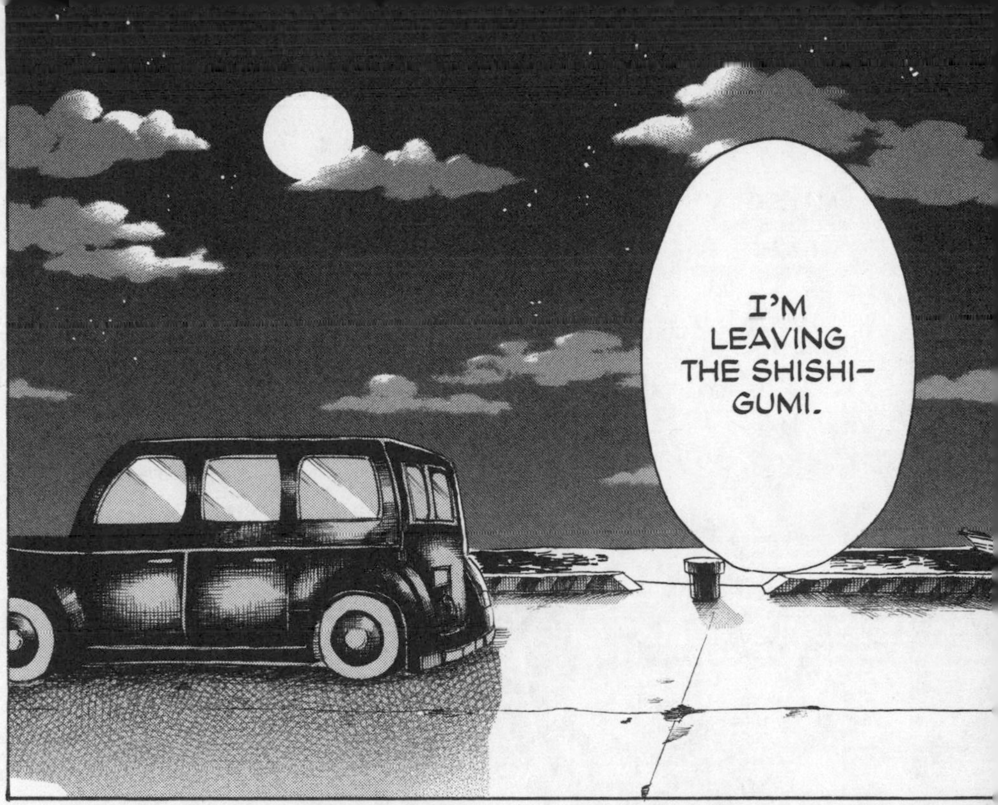
I'M LEAVING THE SHISHI-GUMI.
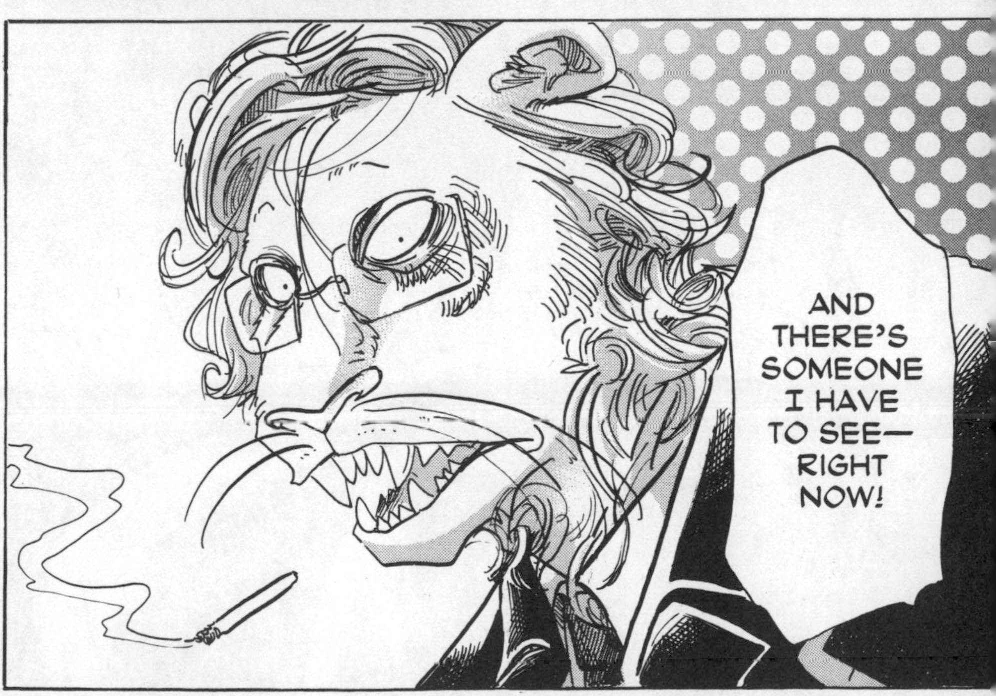
AND THERE'S SOMEONE I HAVE TO SEE— RIGHT NOW!

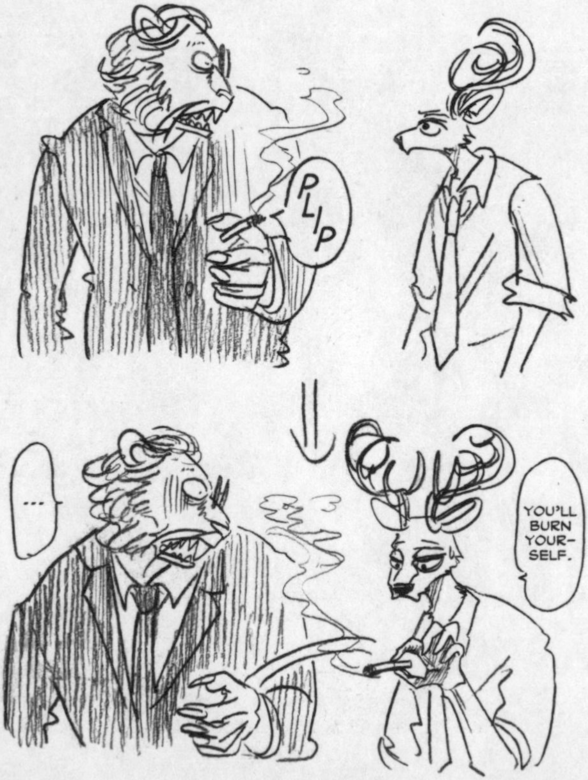
PLIP
YOU'LL BURN YOUR-SELF.
...

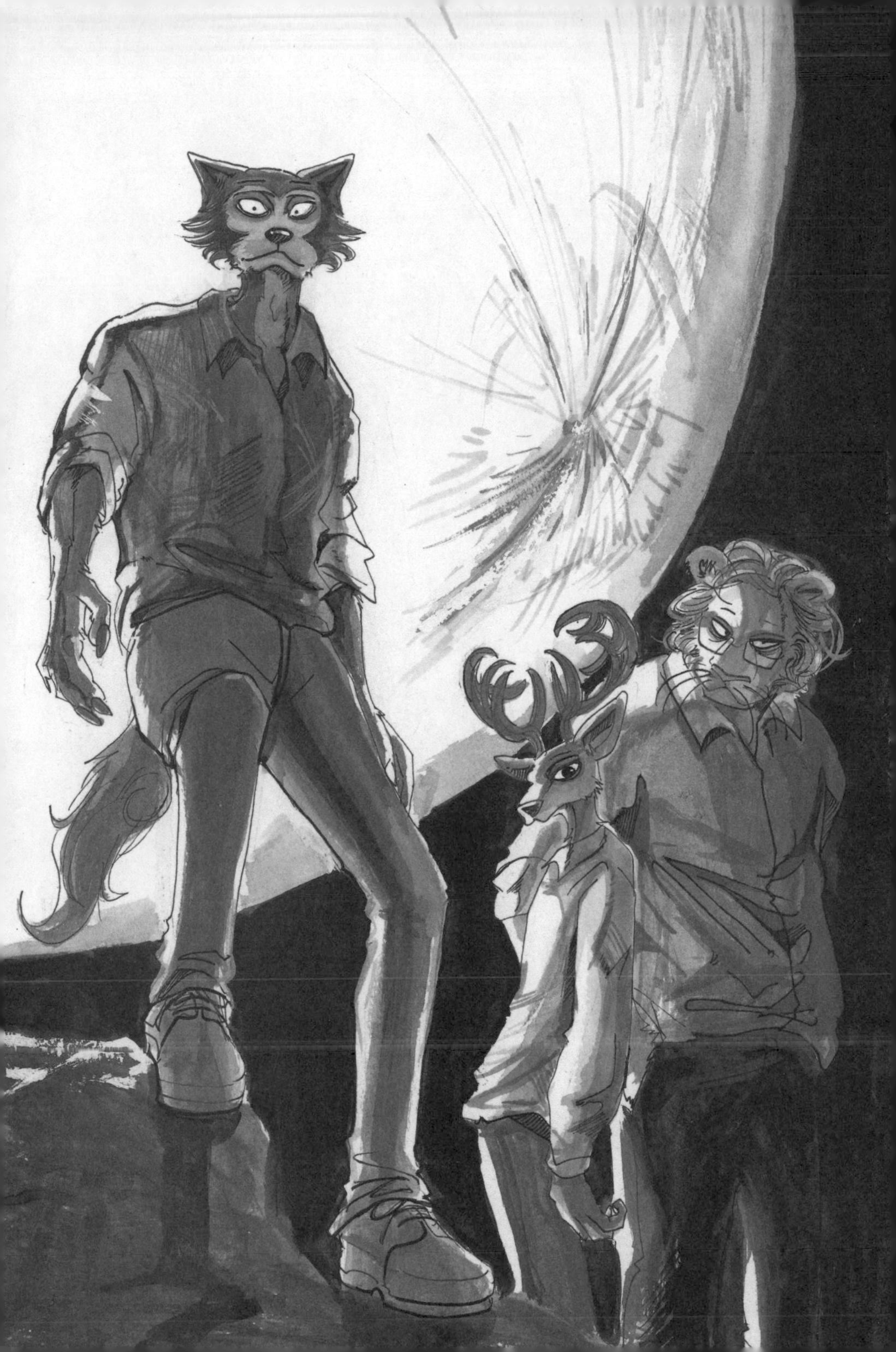

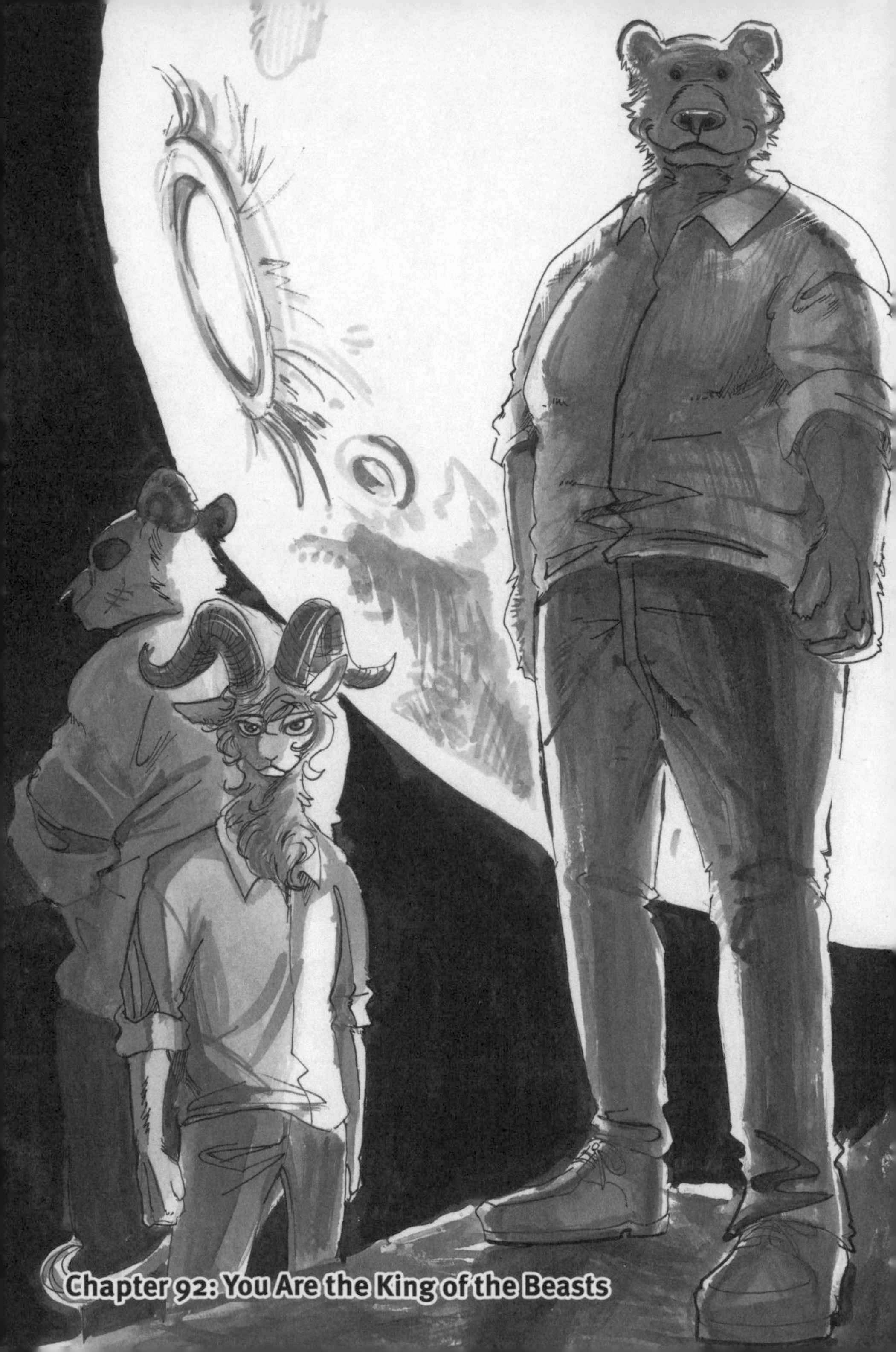

Chapter 92: You Are the King of the Beasts

BEASTARS
Vol. 11

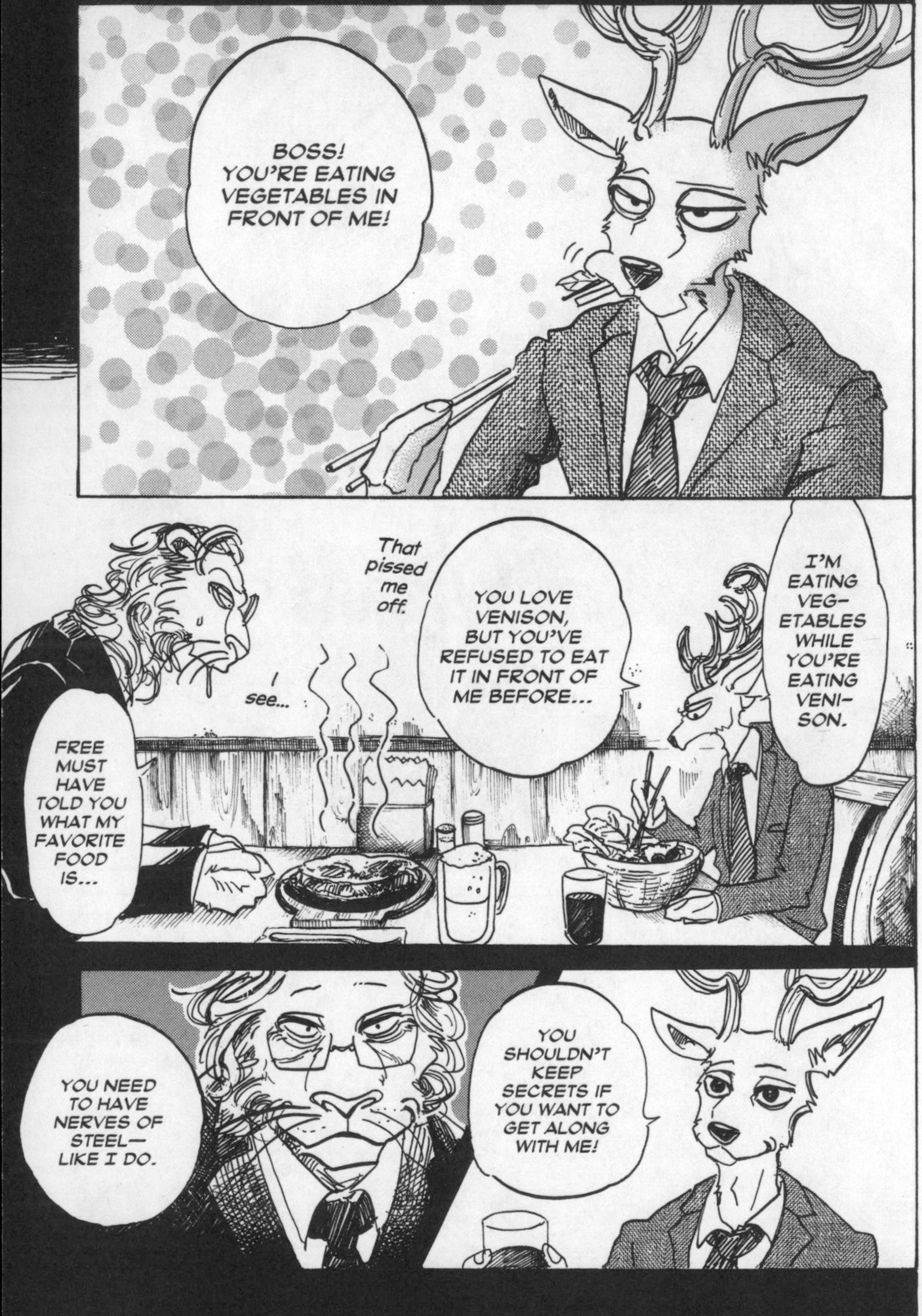
BOSS! YOU'RE EATING VEGETABLES IN FRONT OF ME!
I'M EATING VEG-ETABLES WHILE YOU'RE EATING VENI-SON.
YOU LOVE VENISON, BUT YOU'VE REFUSED TO EAT IT IN FRONT OF ME BEFORE...
That pissed me off.
I see...
FREE MUST HAVE TOLD YOU WHAT MY FAVORITE FOOD IS...
YOU SHOULDN'T KEEP SECRETS IF YOU WANT TO GET ALONG WITH ME!
YOU NEED TO HAVE NERVES OF STEEL— LIKE I DO.

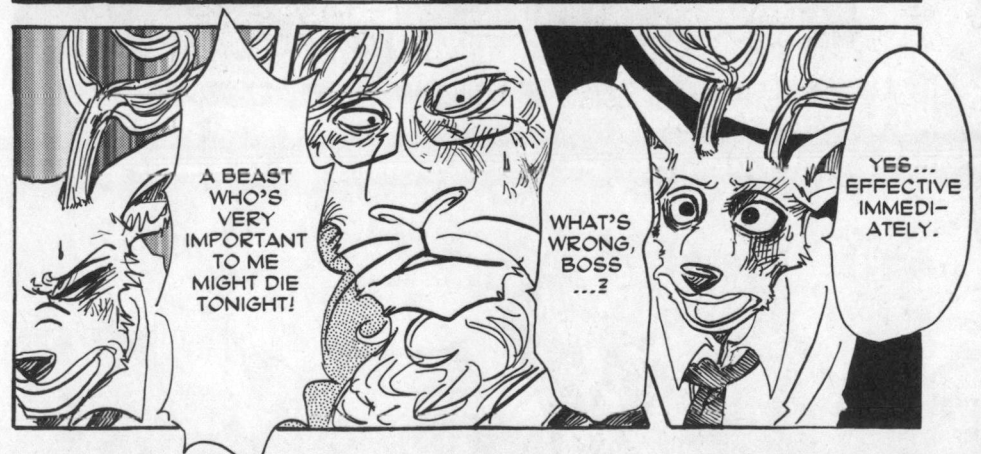

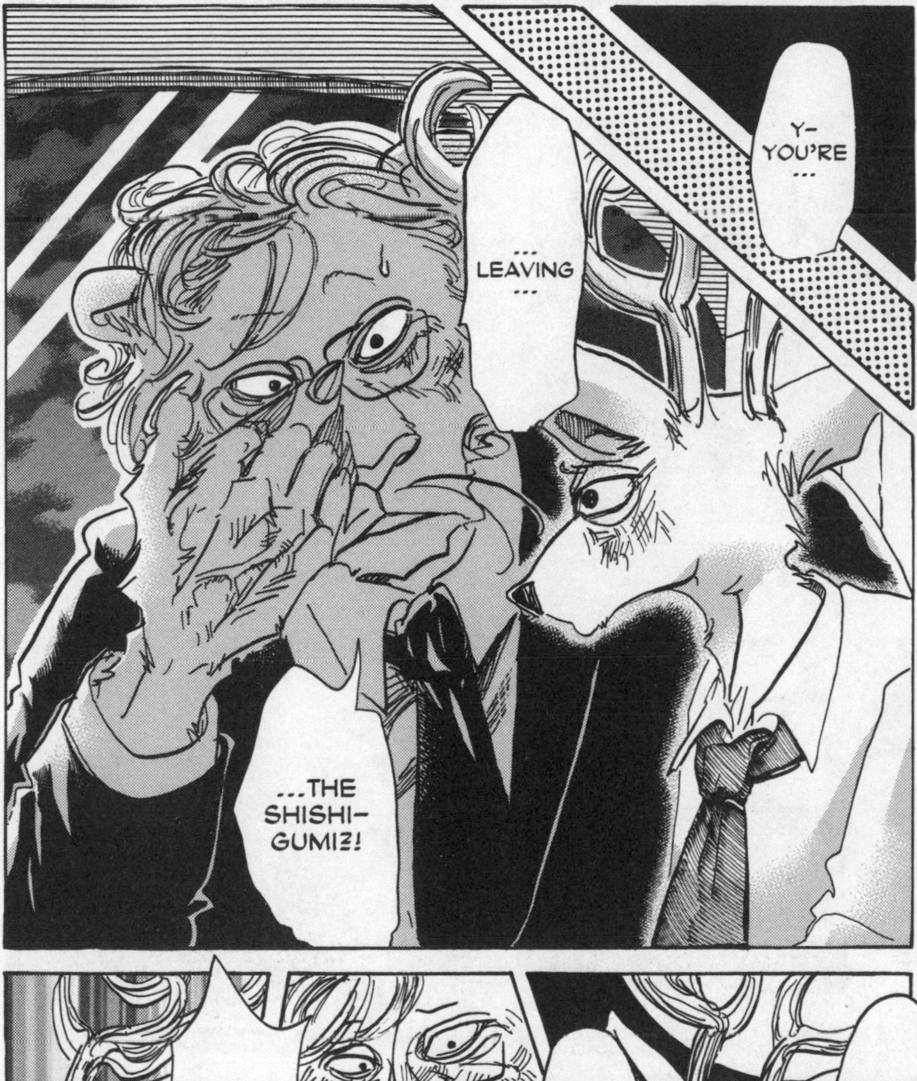
Y-YOU'RE...
...LEAVING...
...THE SHISHI-GUMI?!
YES... EFFECTIVE IMMEDIATELY.
WHAT'S WRONG, BOSS...?
A BEAST WHO'S VERY IMPORTANT TO ME MIGHT DIE TONIGHT!

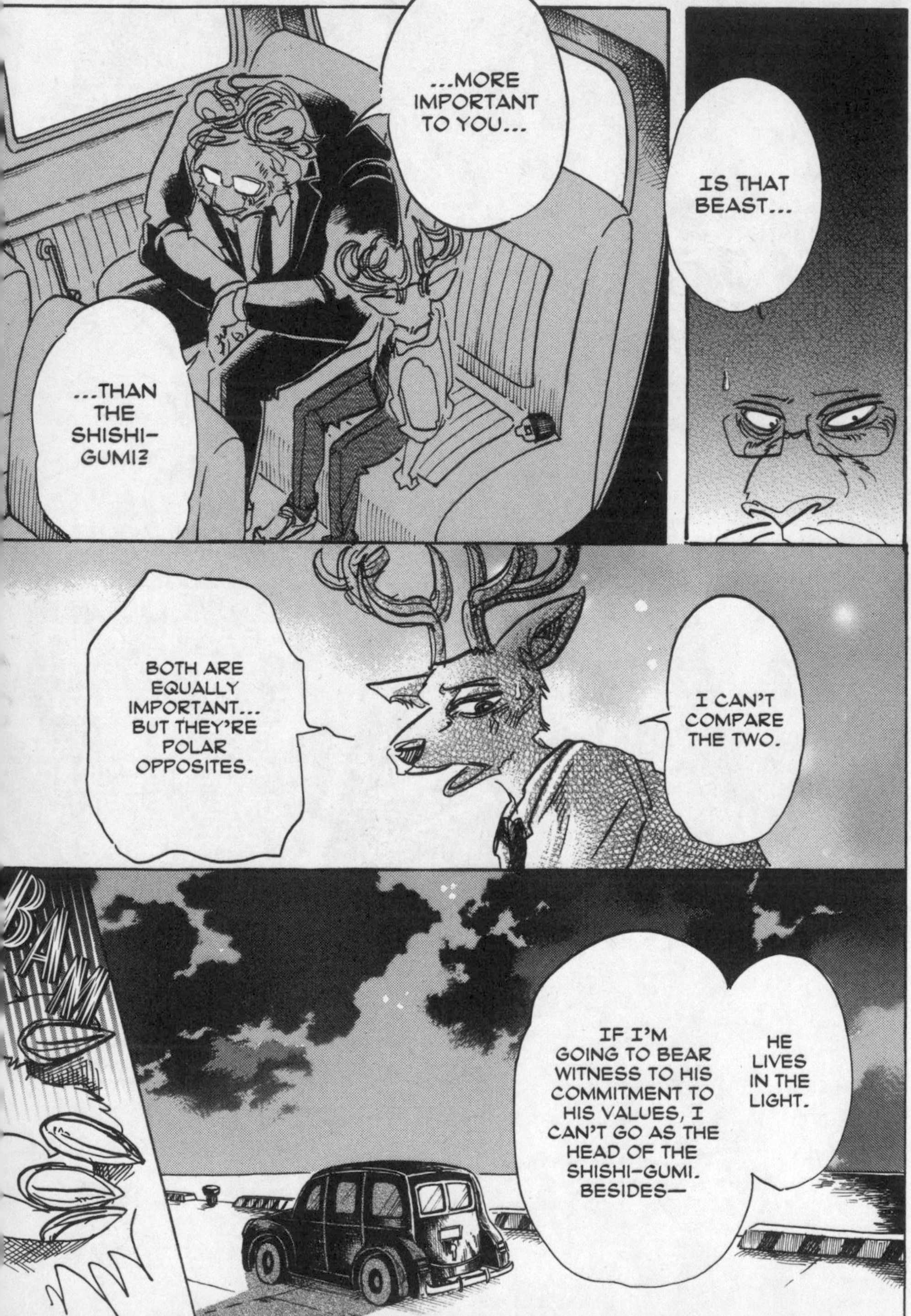
IS THAT BEAST...
...MORE IMPORTANT TO YOU...
...THAN THE SHISHI-GUMI?
I CAN'T COMPARE THE TWO.
BOTH ARE EQUALLY IMPORTANT... BUT THEY'RE POLAR OPPOSITES.
HE LIVES IN THE LIGHT.
IF I'M GOING TO BEAR WITNESS TO HIS COMMITMENT TO HIS VALUES, I CAN'T GO AS THE HEAD OF THE SHISHI-GUMI. BESIDES—
BAM

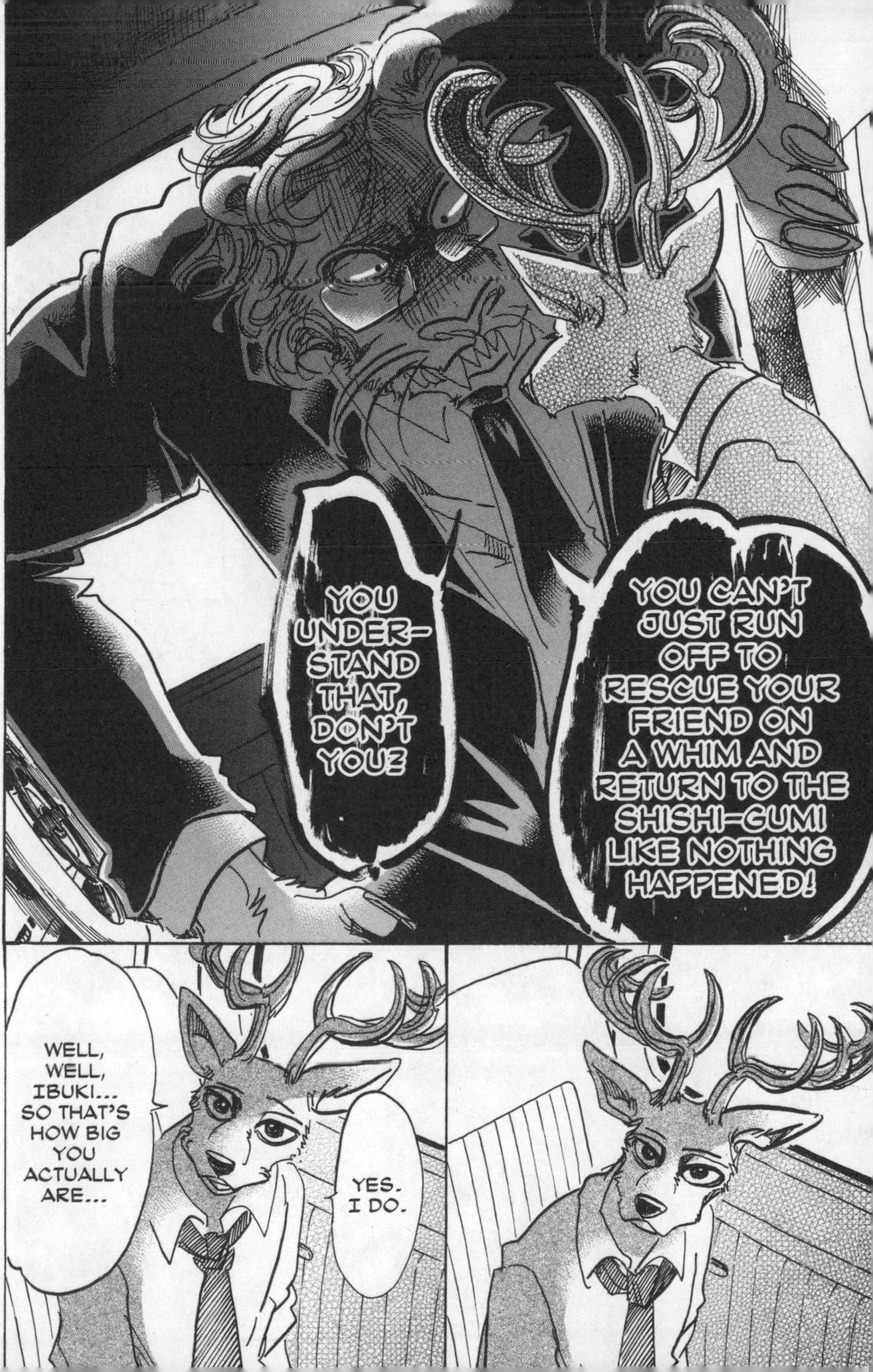
YOU CAN'T JUST RUN OFF TO RESCUE YOUR FRIEND ON A WHIM AND RETURN TO THE SHISHI-GUMI LIKE NOTHING HAPPENED!
YOU UNDER-STAND THAT, DON'T YOU?
YES. I DO.
WELL, WELL, IBUKI... SO THAT'S HOW BIG YOU ACTUALLY ARE...

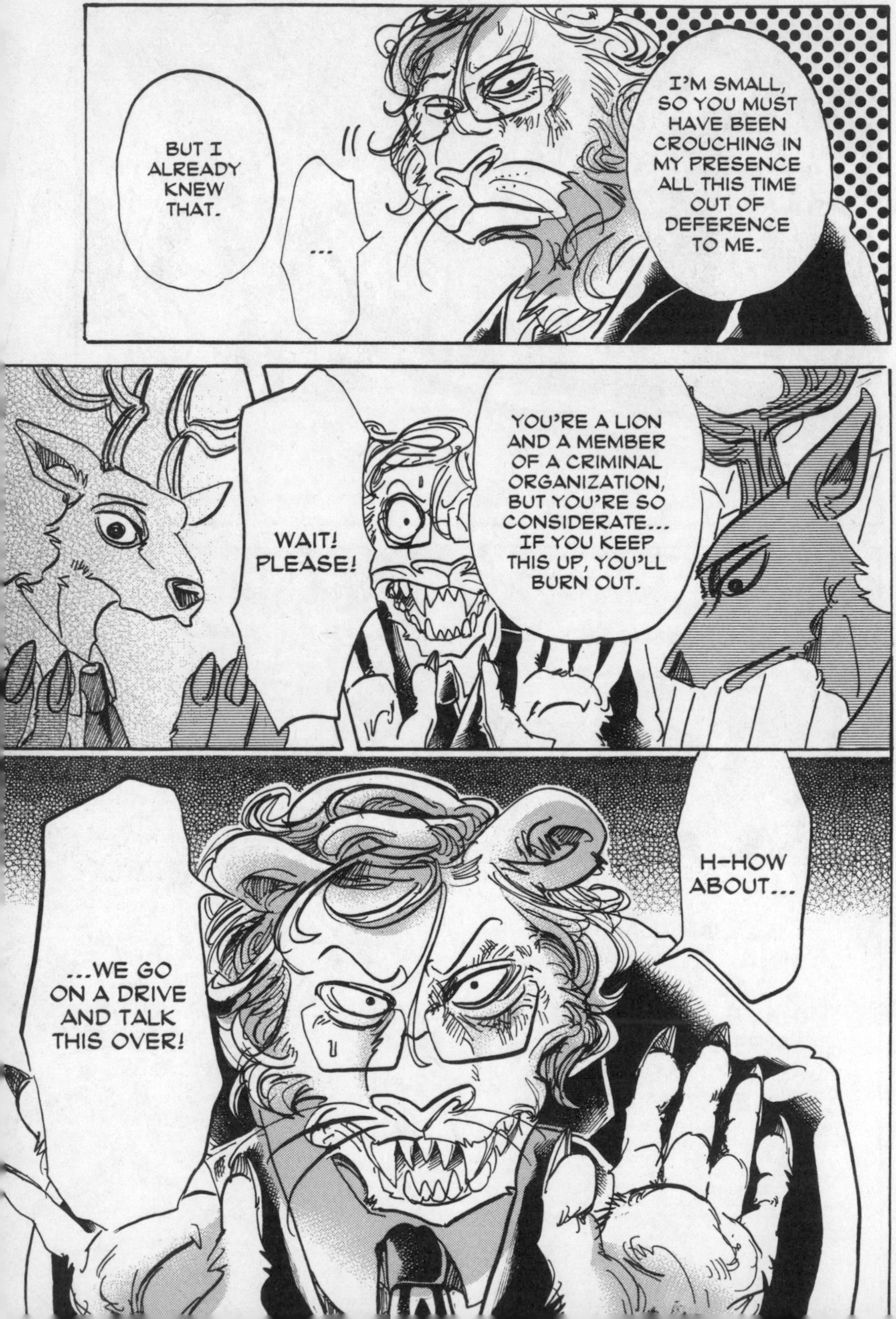
I'M SMALL, SO YOU MUST HAVE BEEN CROUCHING IN MY PRESENCE ALL THIS TIME OUT OF DEFERENCE TO ME.
...
BUT I ALREADY KNEW THAT.
YOU'RE A LION AND A MEMBER OF A CRIMINAL ORGANIZATION, BUT YOU'RE SO CONSIDERATE... IF YOU KEEP THIS UP, YOU'LL BURN OUT.
WAIT! PLEASE!
H-HOW ABOUT...
...WE GO ON A DRIVE AND TALK THIS OVER!

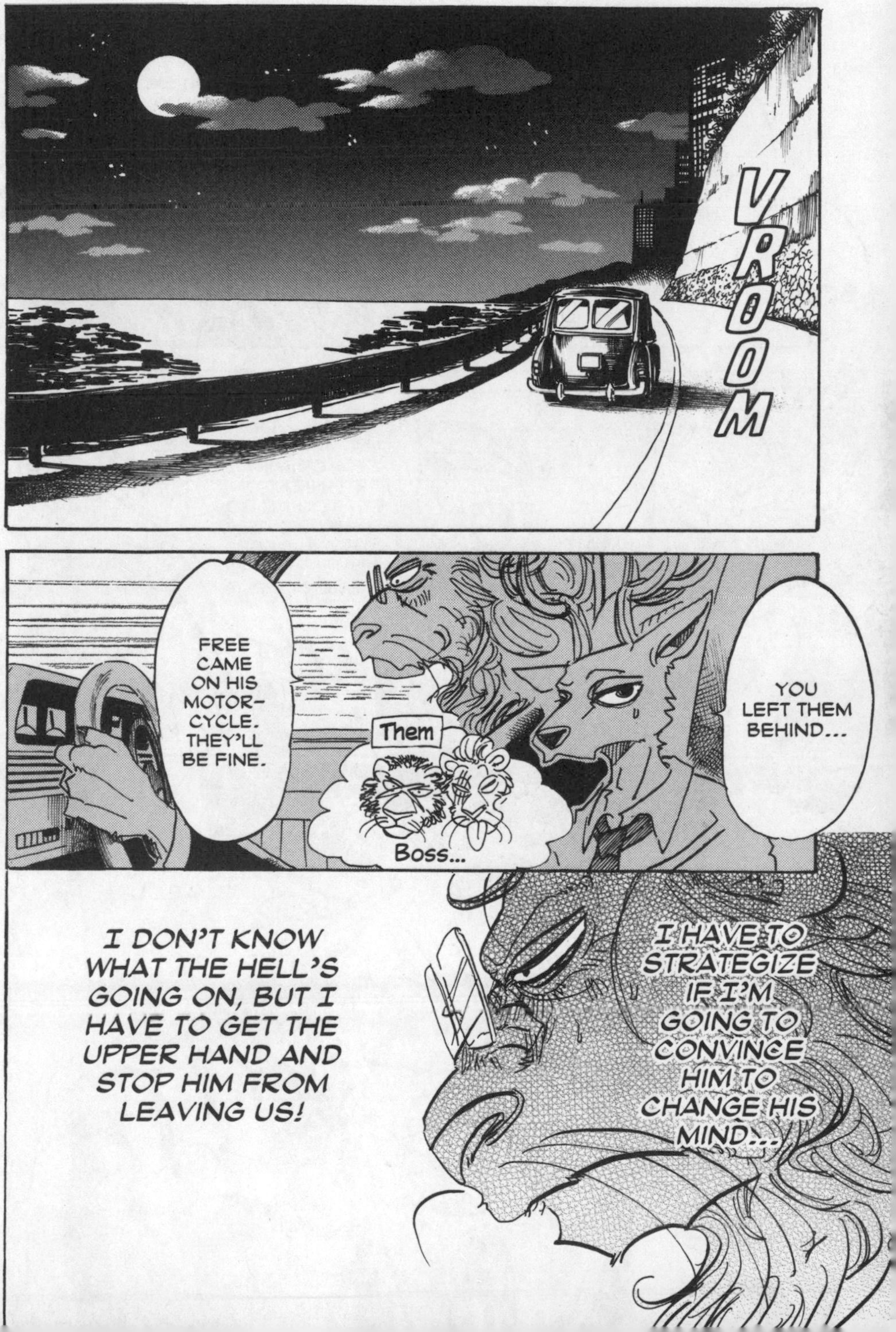
VROOM
YOU LEFT THEM BEHIND...
Them
Boss...
FREE CAME ON HIS MOTORCYCLE. THEY'LL BE FINE.
I HAVE TO STRATEGIZE IF I'M GOING TO CONVINCE HIM TO CHANGE HIS MIND...
I DON'T KNOW WHAT THE HELL'S GOING ON, BUT I HAVE TO GET THE UPPER HAND AND STOP HIM FROM LEAVING US!

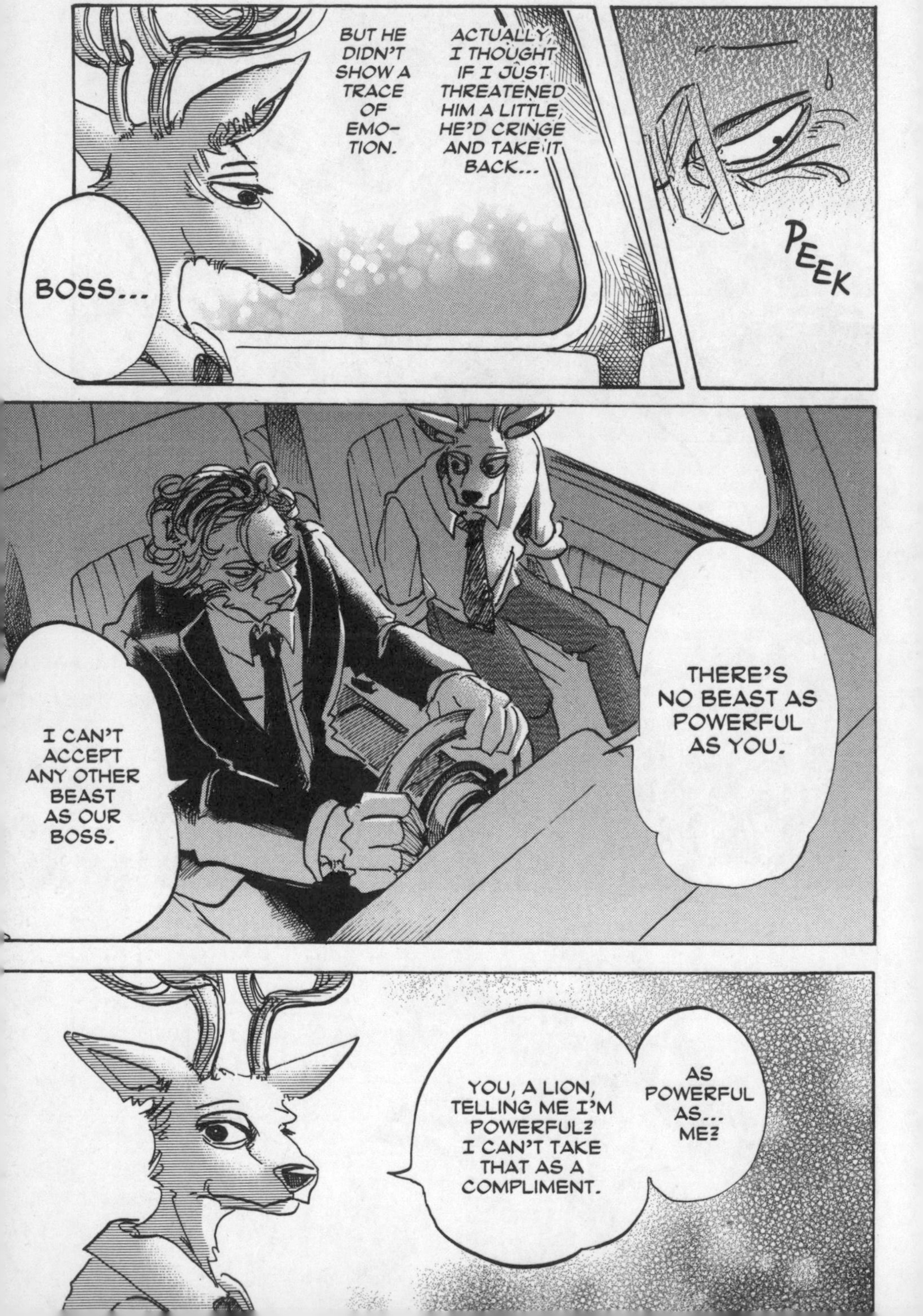
PEEK
ACTUALLY, I THOUGHT IF I JUST THREATENED HIM A LITTLE, HE'D CRINGE AND TAKE IT BACK...
BUT HE DIDN'T SHOW A TRACE OF EMO-TION.
BOSS...
THERE'S NO BEAST AS POWERFUL AS YOU.
I CAN'T ACCEPT ANY OTHER BEAST AS OUR BOSS.
AS POWERFUL AS... ME?
YOU, A LION, TELLING ME I'M POWERFUL? I CAN'T TAKE THAT AS A COMPLIMENT.

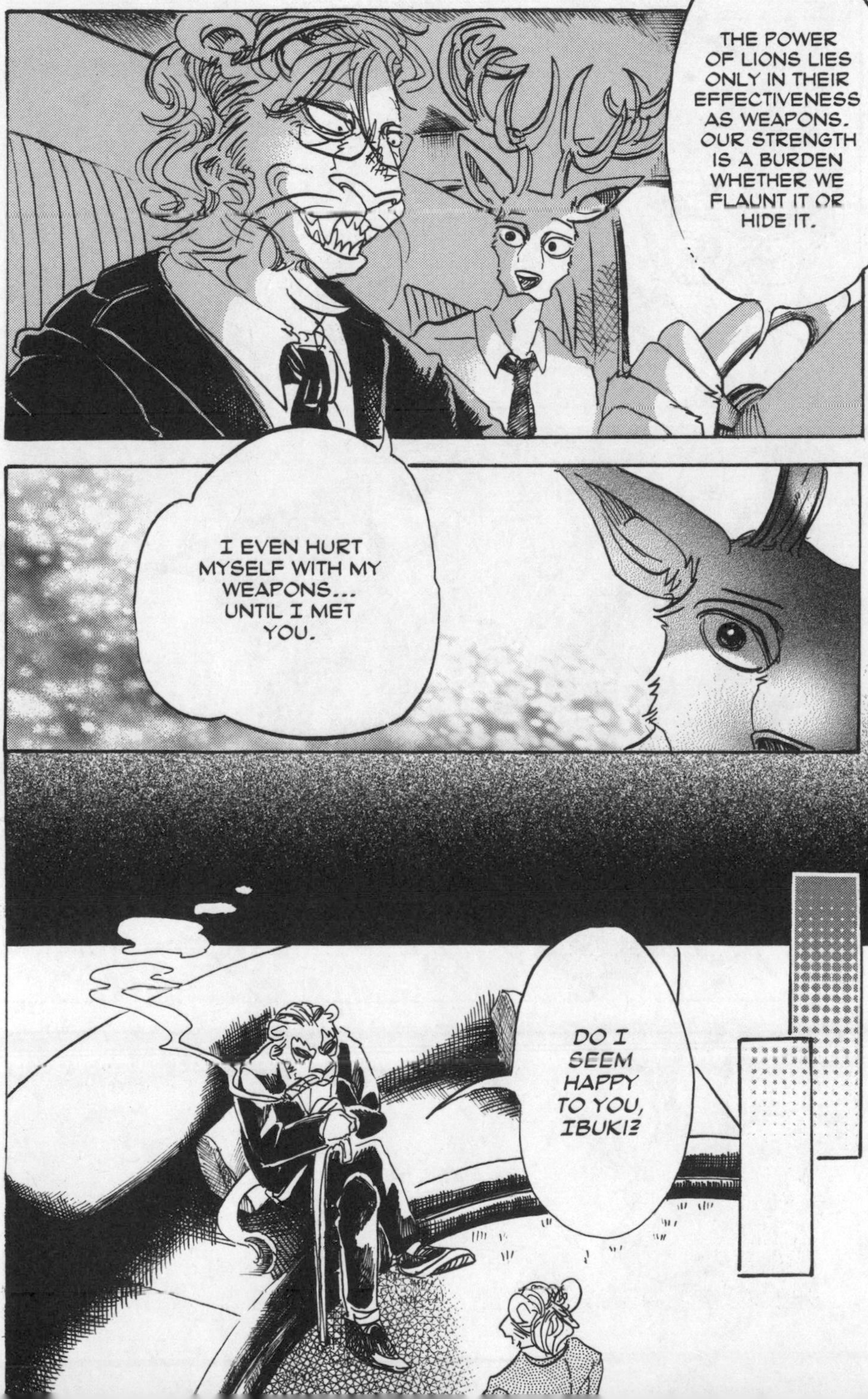
THE POWER OF LIONS LIES ONLY IN THEIR EFFECTIVENESS AS WEAPONS. OUR STRENGTH IS A BURDEN WHETHER WE FLAUNT IT OR HIDE IT.
I EVEN HURT MYSELF WITH MY WEAPONS... UNTIL I MET YOU.
DO I SEEM HAPPY TO YOU, IBUKI?

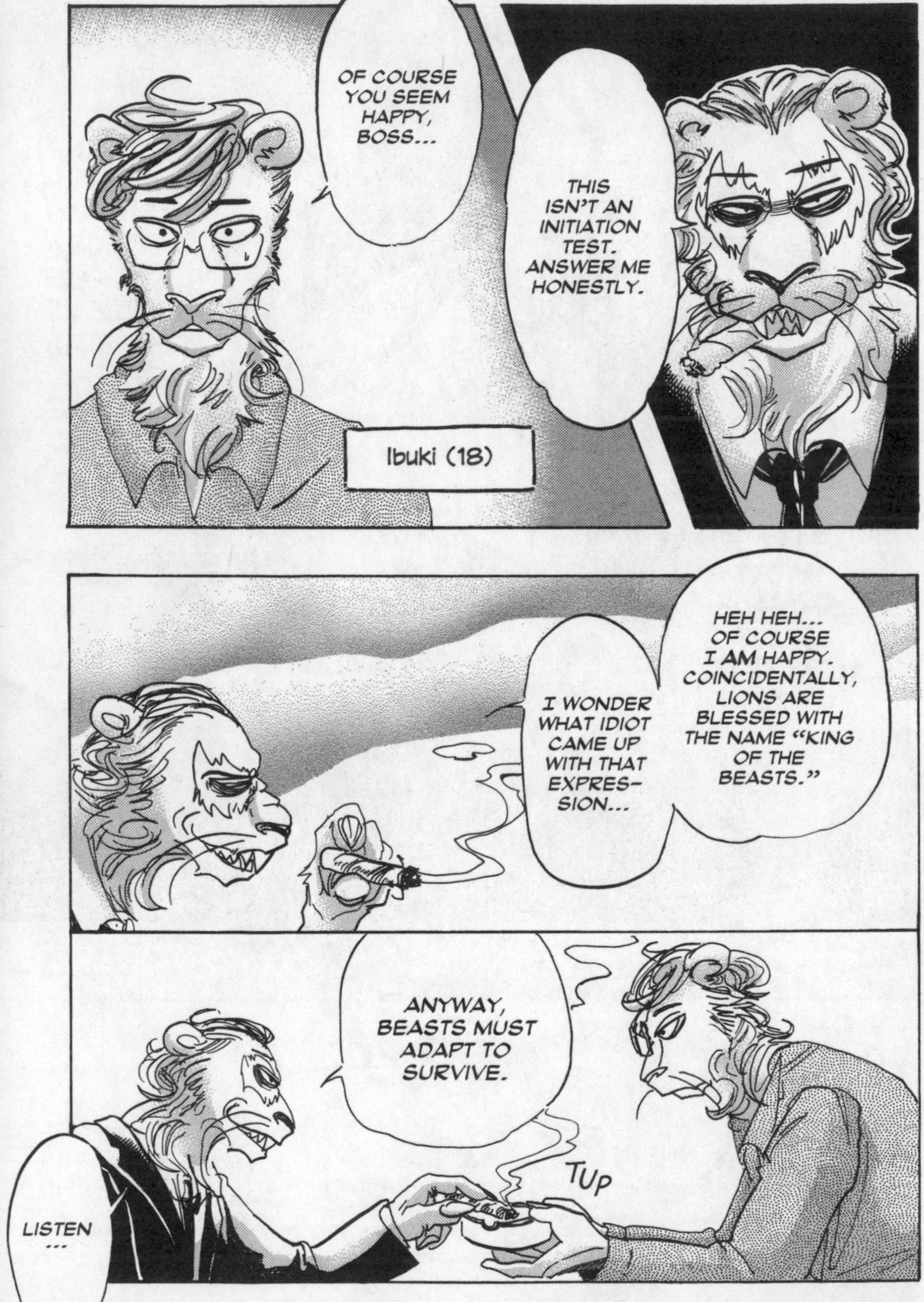
THIS ISN'T AN INITIATION TEST. ANSWER ME HONESTLY.
OF COURSE YOU SEEM HAPPY, BOSS...
Ibuki (18)
HEH HEH... OF COURSE I AM HAPPY. COINCIDENTALLY, LIONS ARE BLESSED WITH THE NAME "KING OF THE BEASTS."
I WONDER WHAT IDIOT CAME UP WITH THAT EXPRES-SION...
ANYWAY, BEASTS MUST ADAPT TO SURVIVE.
TUP
LISTEN...

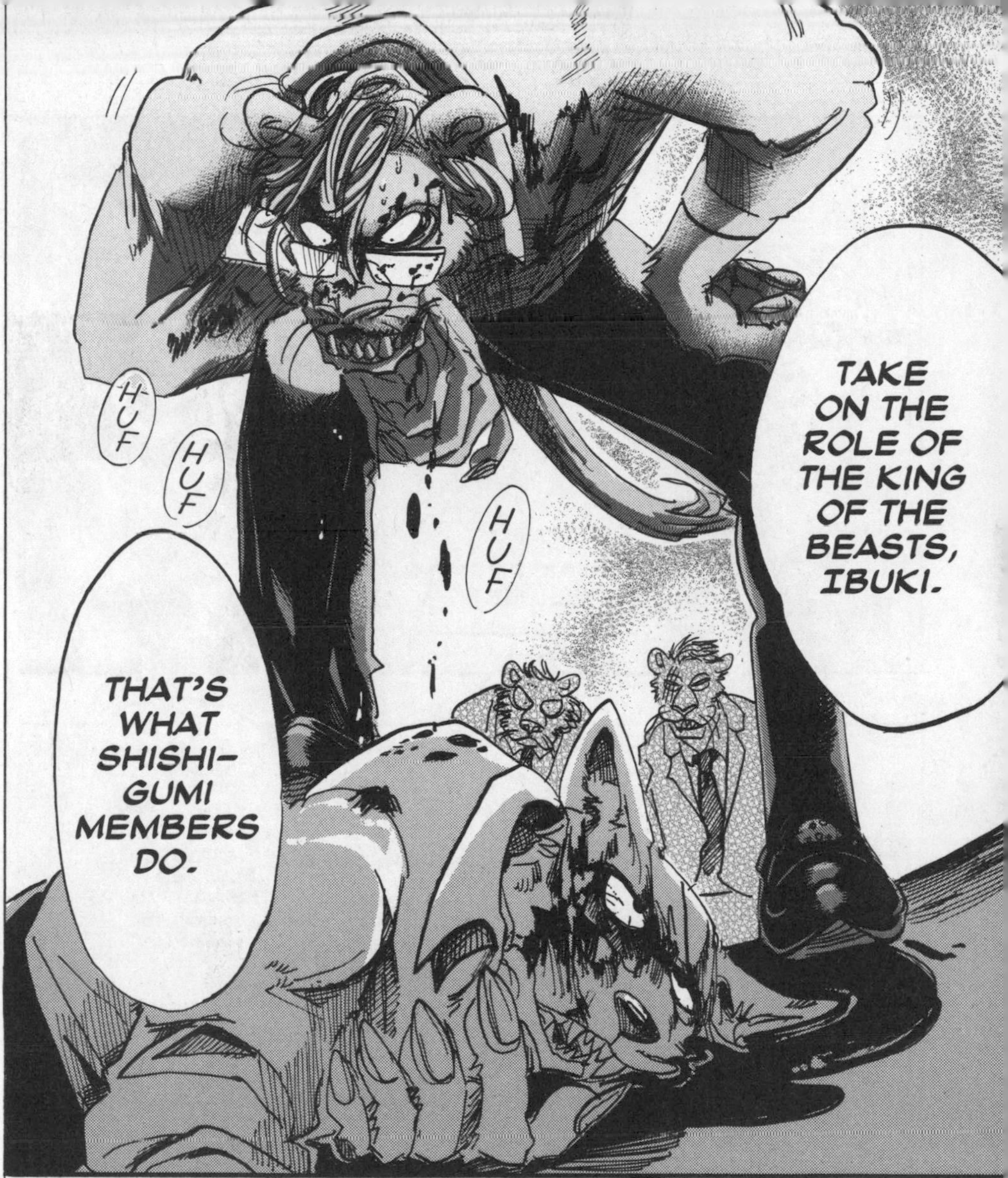
TAKE ON THE ROLE OF THE KING OF THE BEASTS, IBUKI.
HUF
HUF
HUF
THAT'S WHAT SHISHI-GUMI MEMBERS DO.
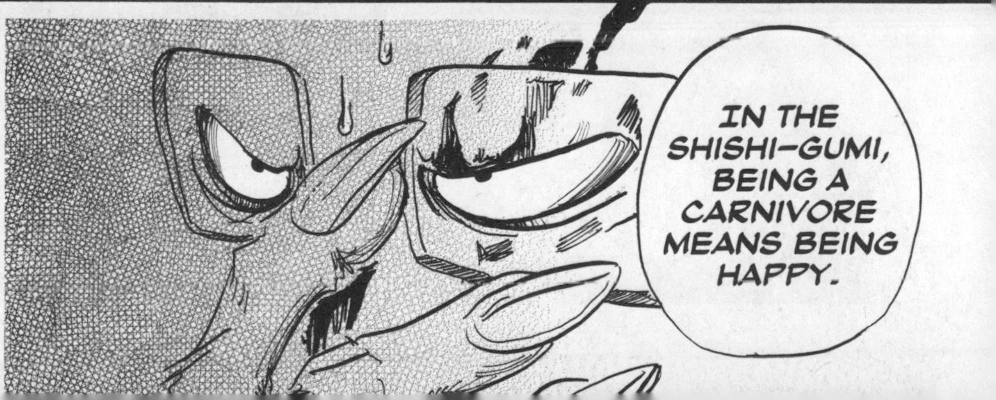
IN THE SHISHI-GUMI, BEING A CARNIVORE MEANS BEING HAPPY.

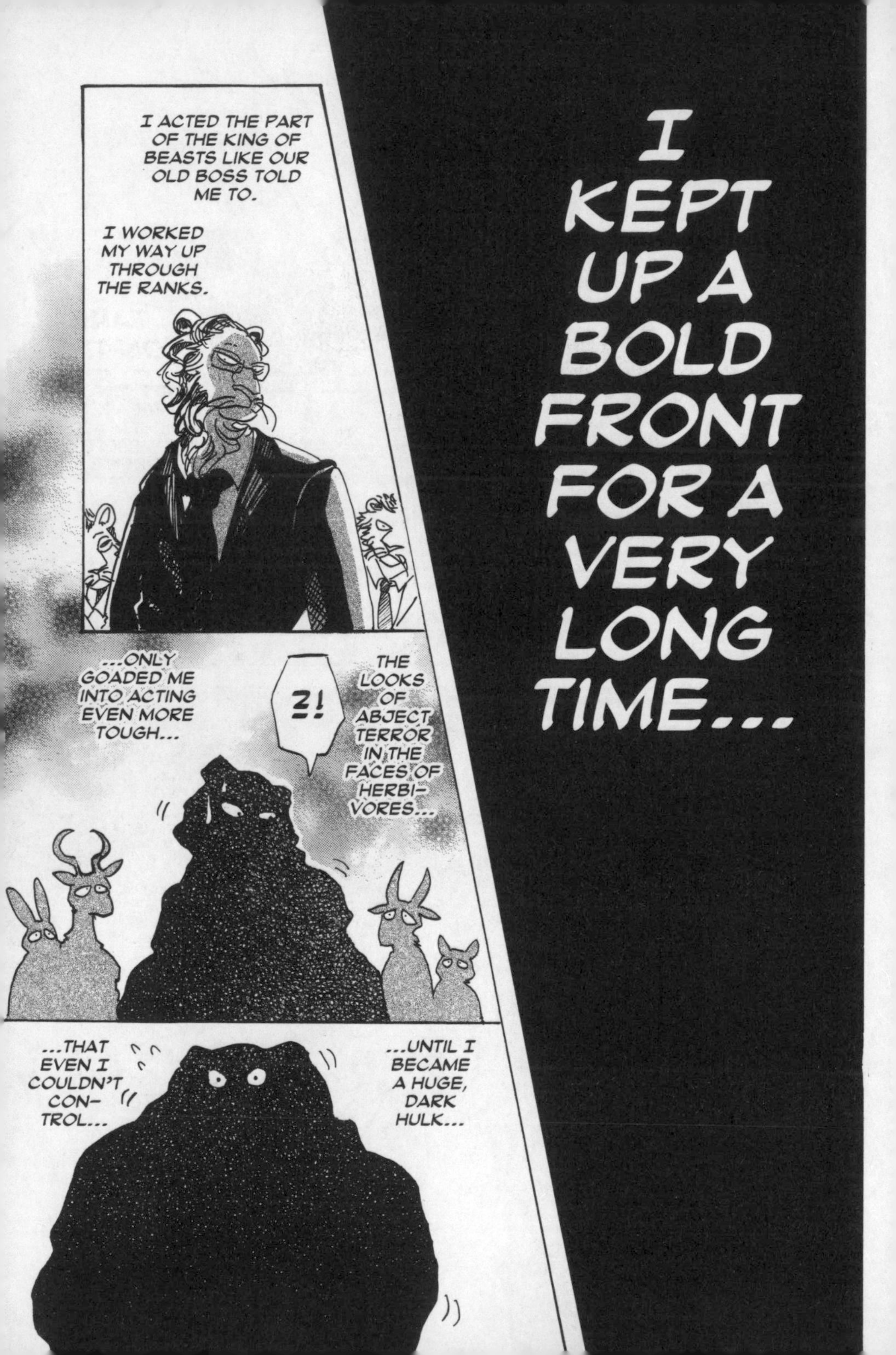
I KEPT UP A BOLD FRONT FOR A VERY LONG TIME...
I ACTED THE PART OF THE KING OF BEASTS LIKE OUR OLD BOSS TOLD ME TO.
I WORKED MY WAY UP THROUGH THE RANKS.
THE LOOKS OF ABJECT TERROR IN THE FACES OF HERBI-VORES...
?!
...ONLY GOADED ME INTO ACTING EVEN MORE TOUGH...
...UNTIL I BECAME A HUGE, DARK HULK...
...THAT EVEN I COULDN'T CON-TROL...

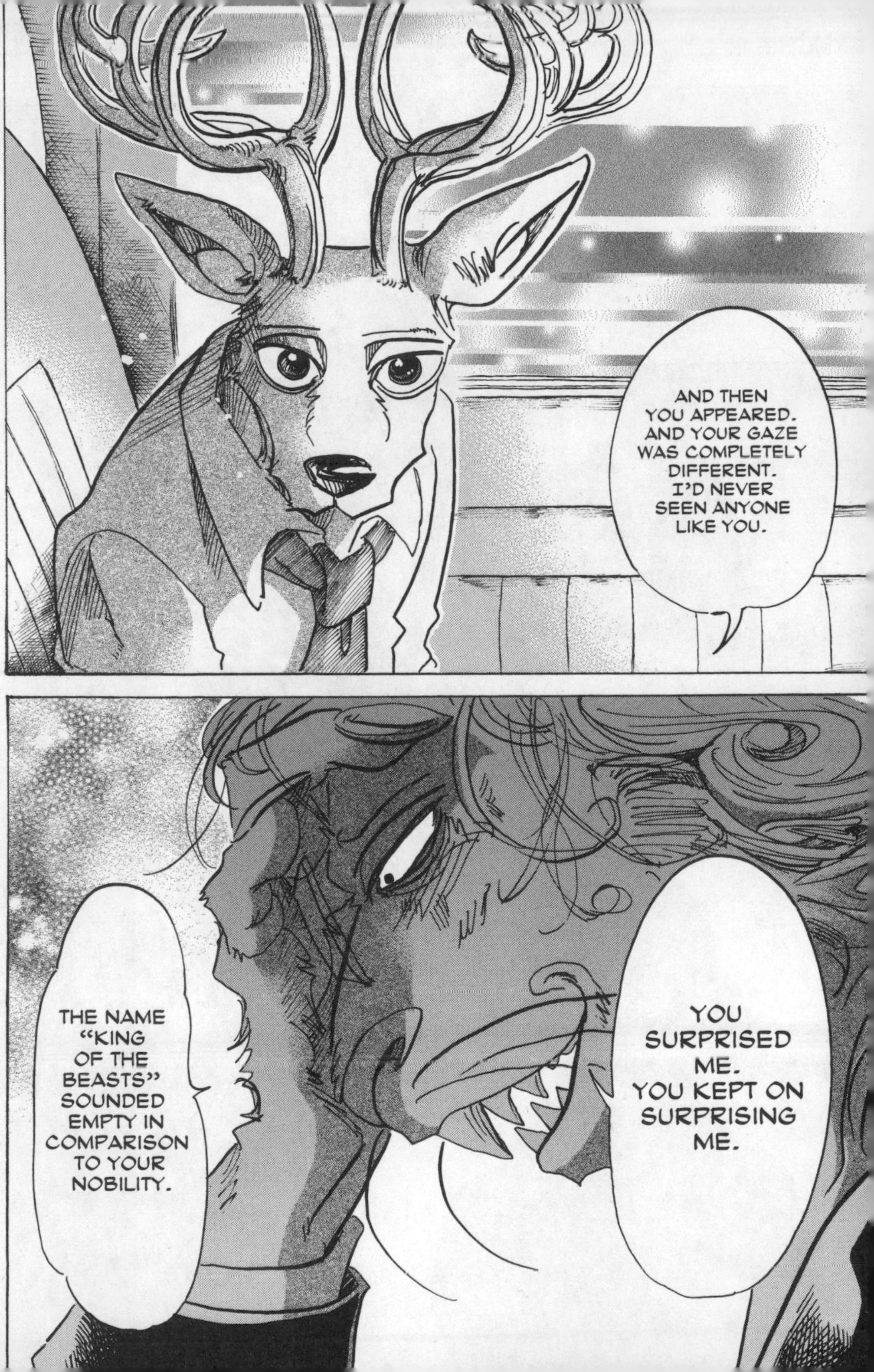
AND THEN YOU APPEARED. AND YOUR GAZE WAS COMPLETELY DIFFERENT. I'D NEVER SEEN ANYONE LIKE YOU.
YOU SURPRISED ME. YOU KEPT ON SURPRISING ME.
THE NAME "KING OF THE BEASTS" SOUNDED EMPTY IN COMPARISON TO YOUR NOBILITY.

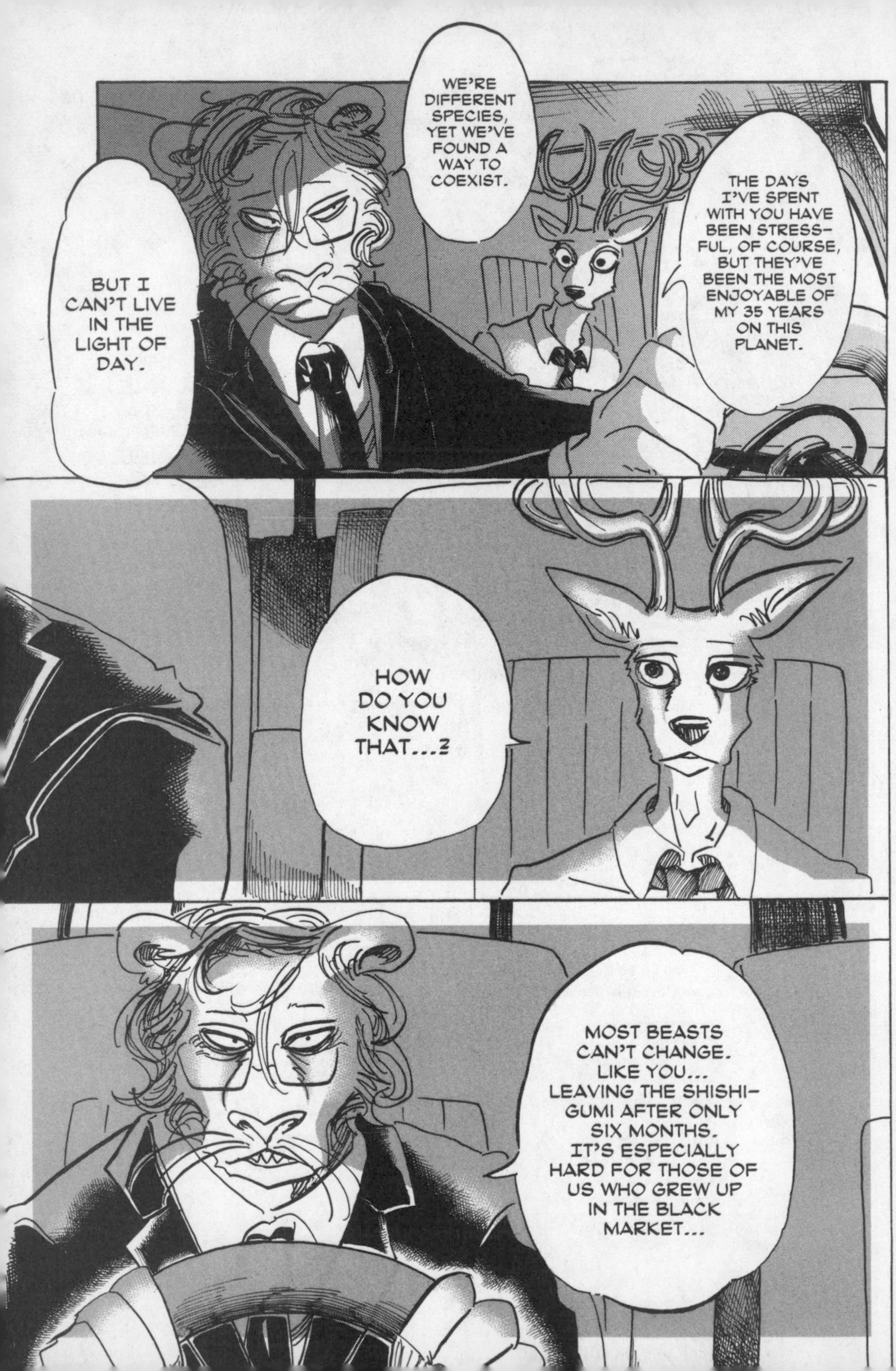
THE DAYS I'VE SPENT WITH YOU HAVE BEEN STRESS-FUL, OF COURSE, BUT THEY'VE BEEN THE MOST ENJOYABLE OF MY 35 YEARS ON THIS PLANET.
WE'RE DIFFERENT SPECIES, YET WE'VE FOUND A WAY TO COEXIST.
BUT I CAN'T LIVE IN THE LIGHT OF DAY.
HOW DO YOU KNOW THAT...?
MOST BEASTS CAN'T CHANGE. LIKE YOU... LEAVING THE SHISHI-GUMI AFTER ONLY SIX MONTHS. IT'S ESPECIALLY HARD FOR THOSE OF US WHO GREW UP IN THE BLACK MARKET...

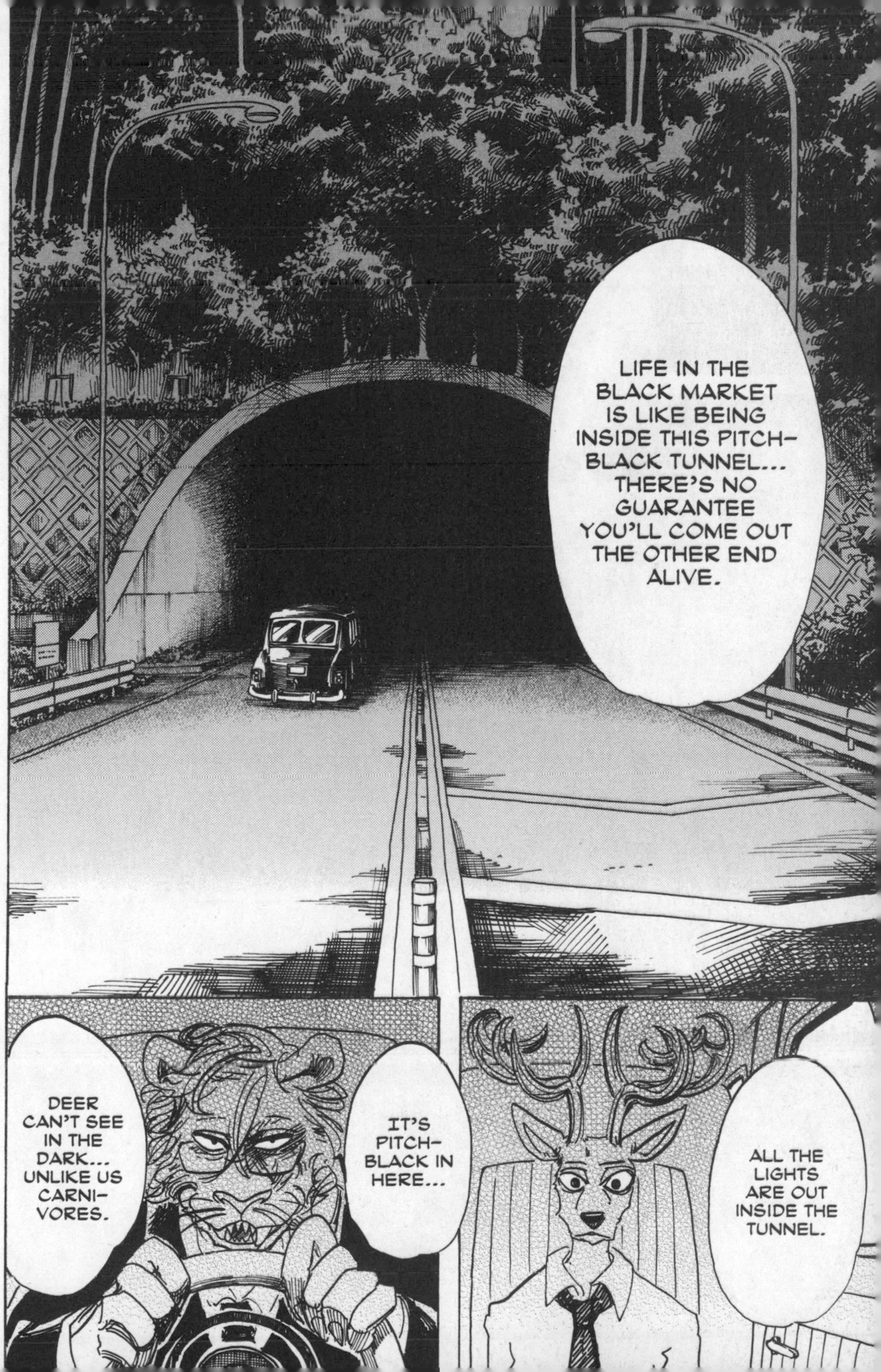
LIFE IN THE BLACK MARKET IS LIKE BEING INSIDE THIS PITCH-BLACK TUNNEL... THERE'S NO GUARANTEE YOU'LL COME OUT THE OTHER END ALIVE.
ALL THE LIGHTS ARE OUT INSIDE THE TUNNEL.
IT'S PITCH-BLACK IN HERE...
DEER CAN'T SEE IN THE DARK... UNLIKE US CARNI-VORES.

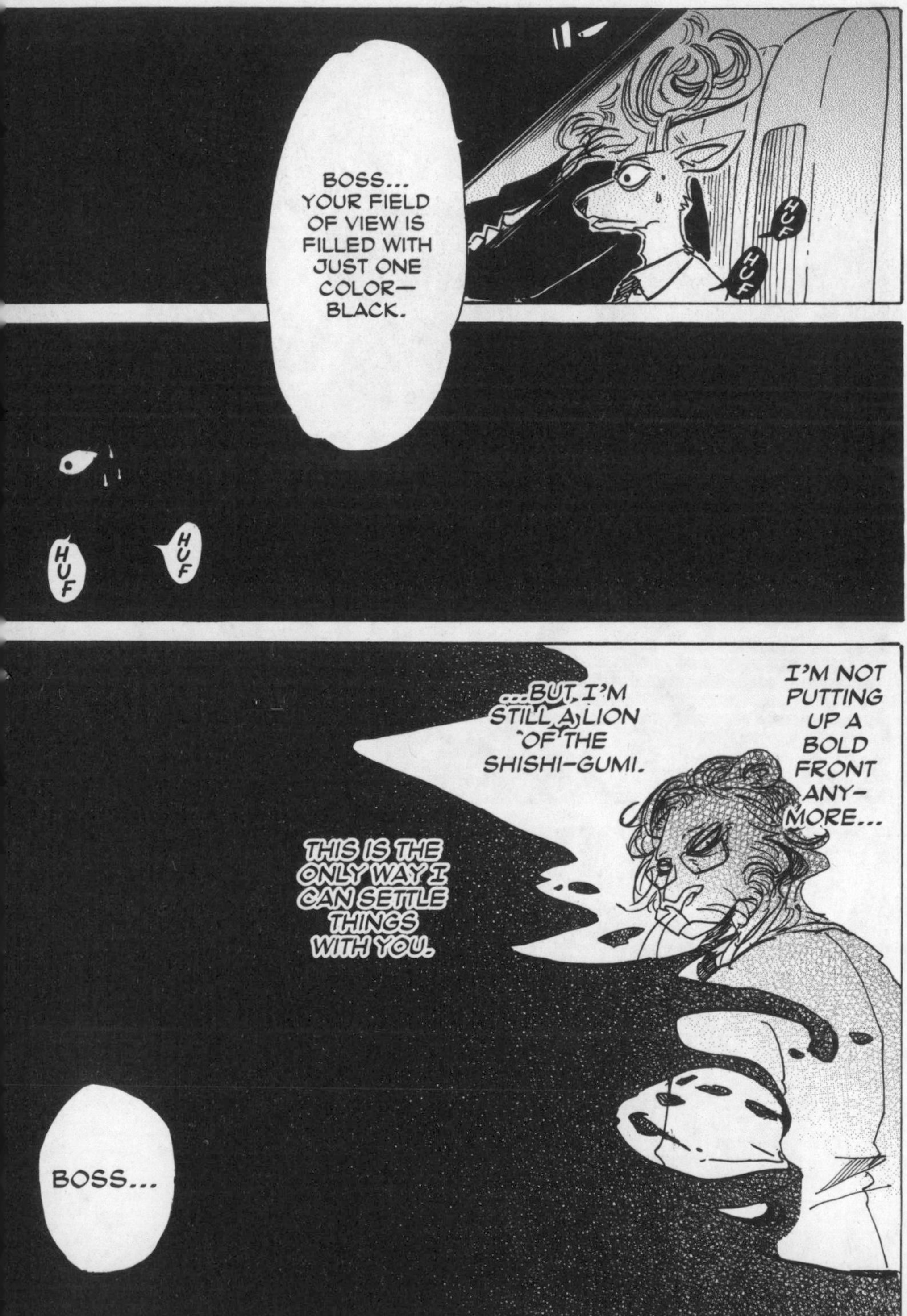
HUF
HUF
BOSS... YOUR FIELD OF VIEW IS FILLED WITH JUST ONE COLOR—BLACK.
HUF
HUF
I'M NOT PUTTING UP A BOLD FRONT ANYMORE...
...BUT, I'M STILL A LION OF THE SHISHI-GUMI.
THIS IS THE ONLY WAY I CAN SETTLE THINGS WITH YOU.
BOSS...

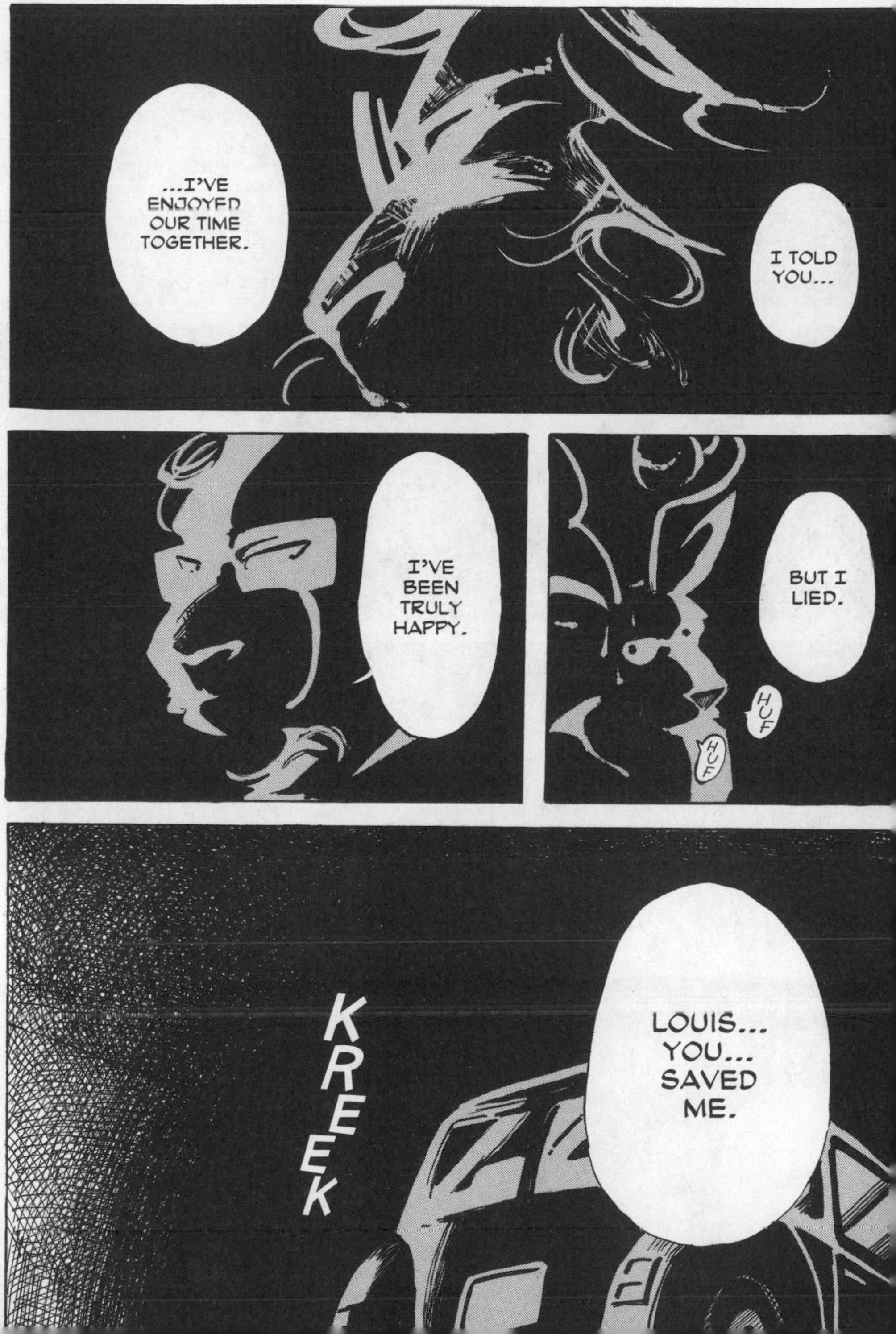
I TOLD YOU...
...I'VE ENJOYED OUR TIME TOGETHER.
BUT I LIED.
HUF
HUF
I'VE BEEN TRULY HAPPY.
LOUIS... YOU... SAVED ME.
KREEK

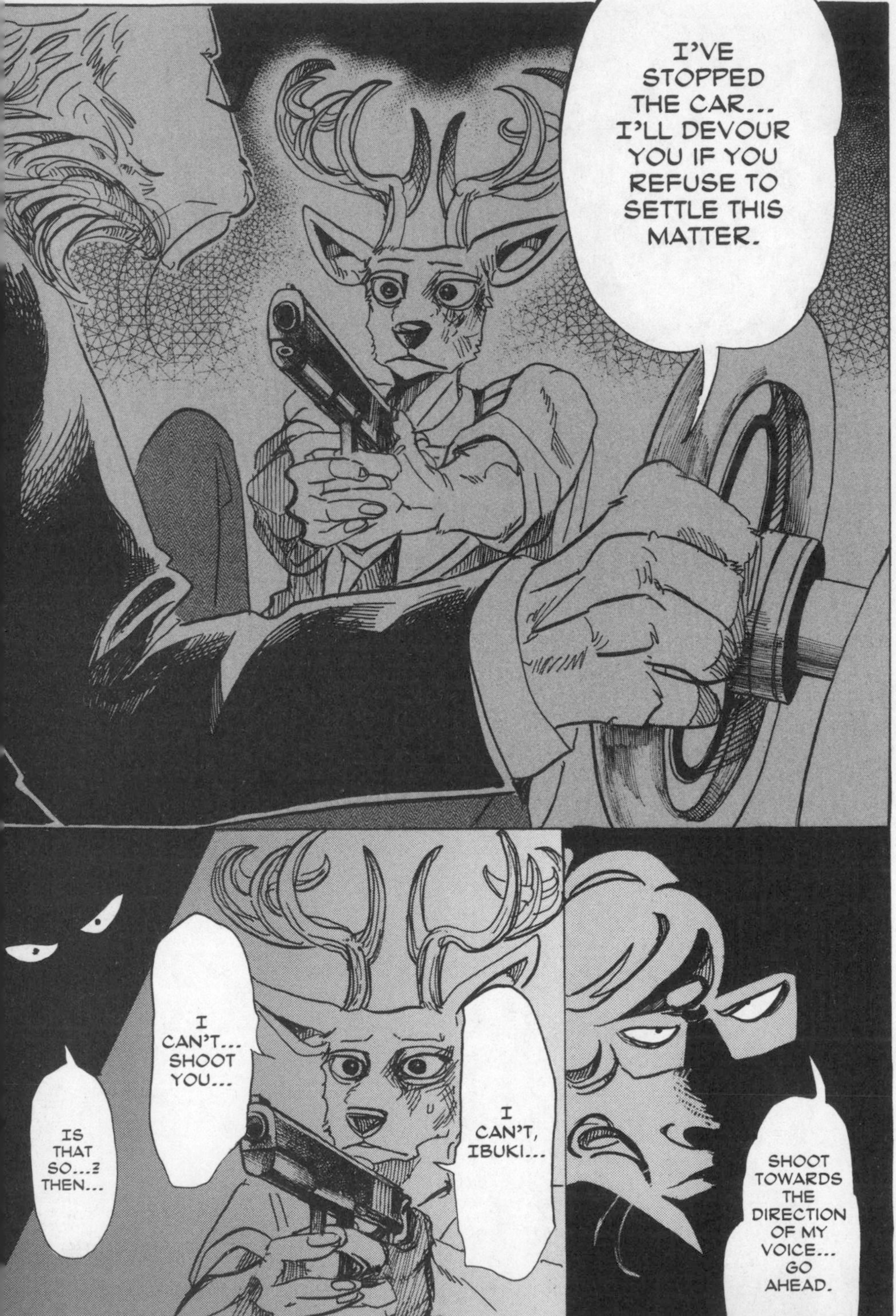
I'VE STOPPED THE CAR... I'LL DEVOUR YOU IF YOU REFUSE TO SETTLE THIS MATTER.
SHOOT TOWARDS THE DIRECTION OF MY VOICE... GO AHEAD.
I CAN'T... SHOOT YOU...
I CAN'T, IBUKI...
IS THAT SO...? THEN...

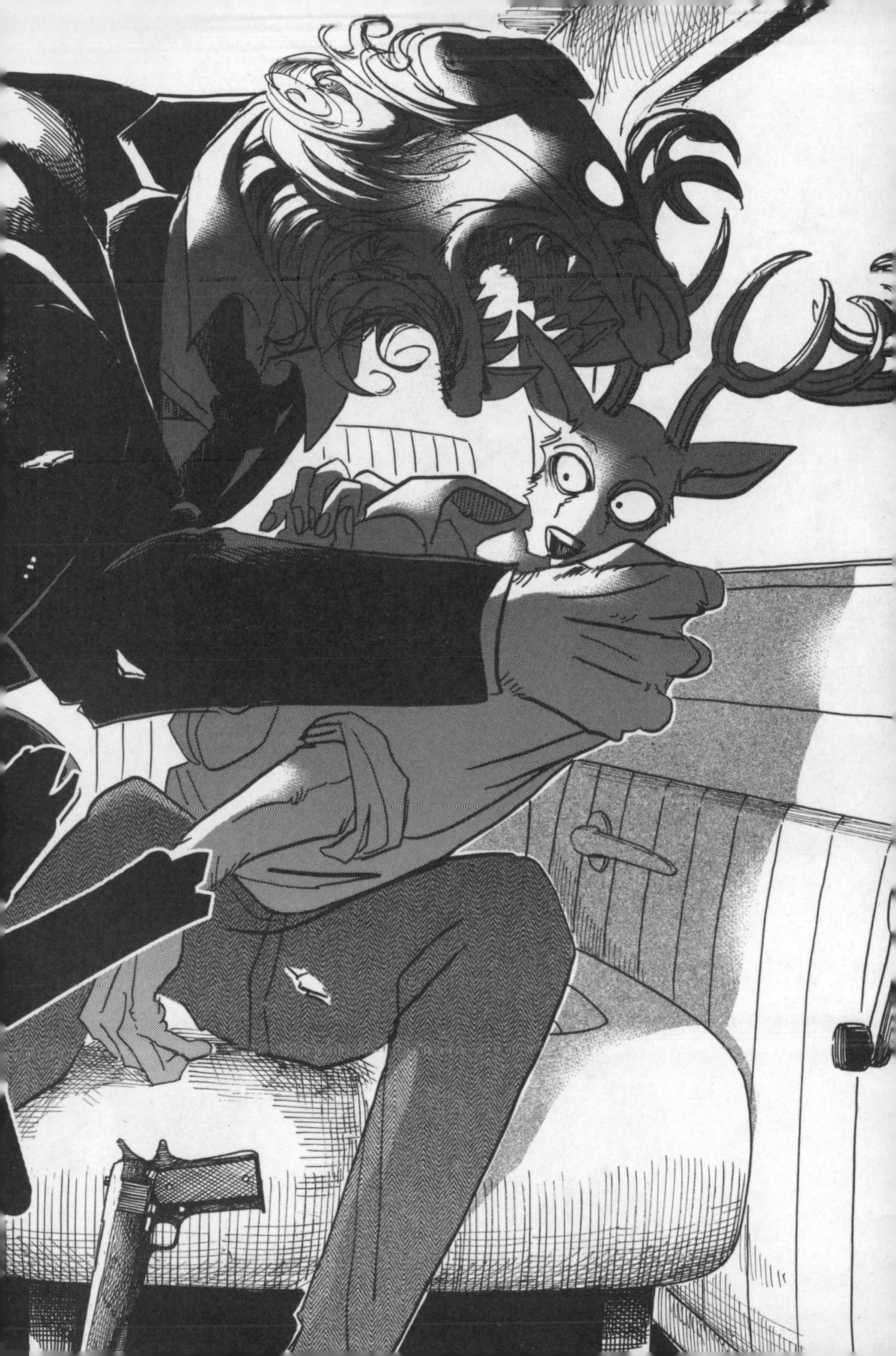

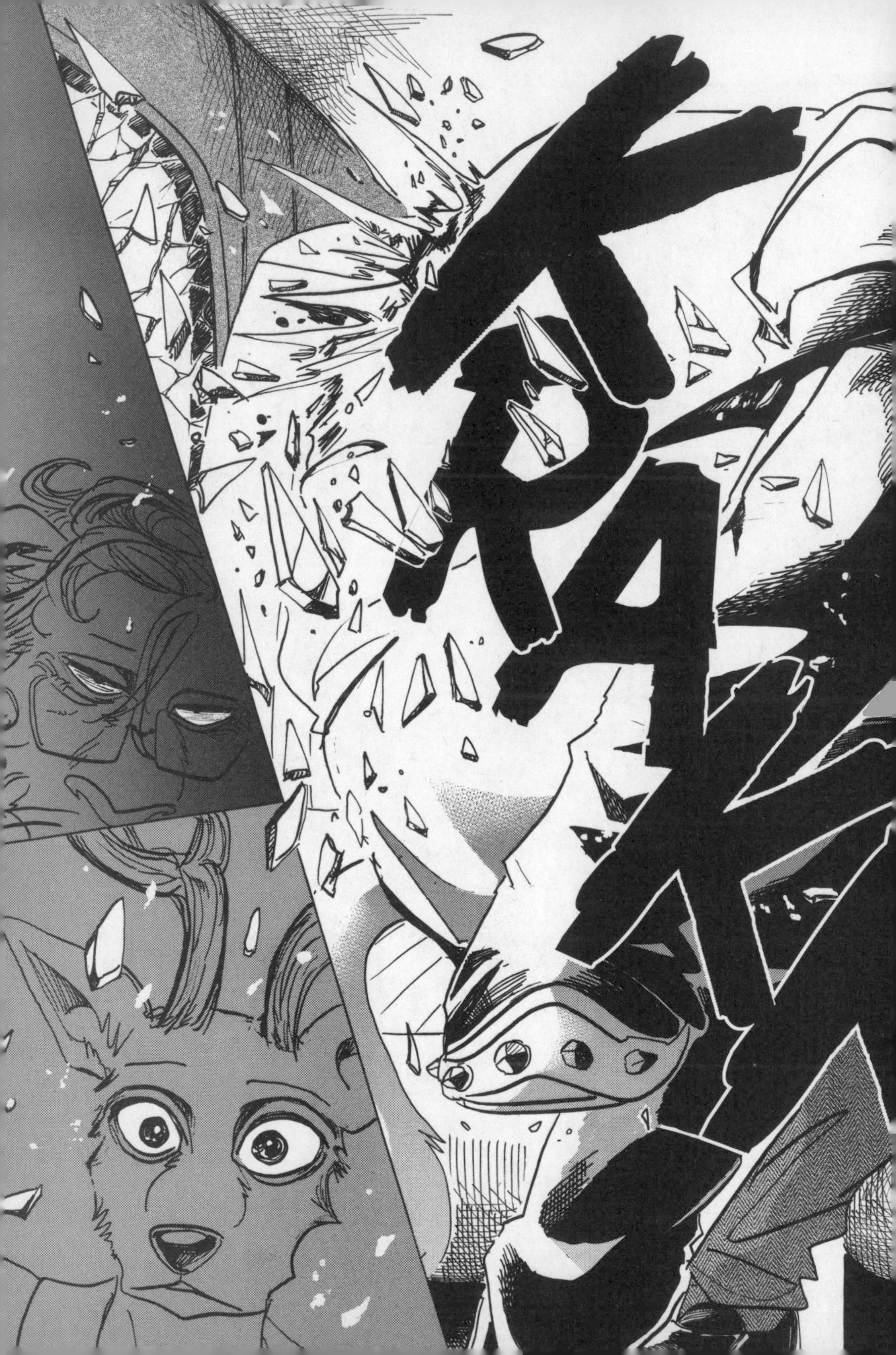

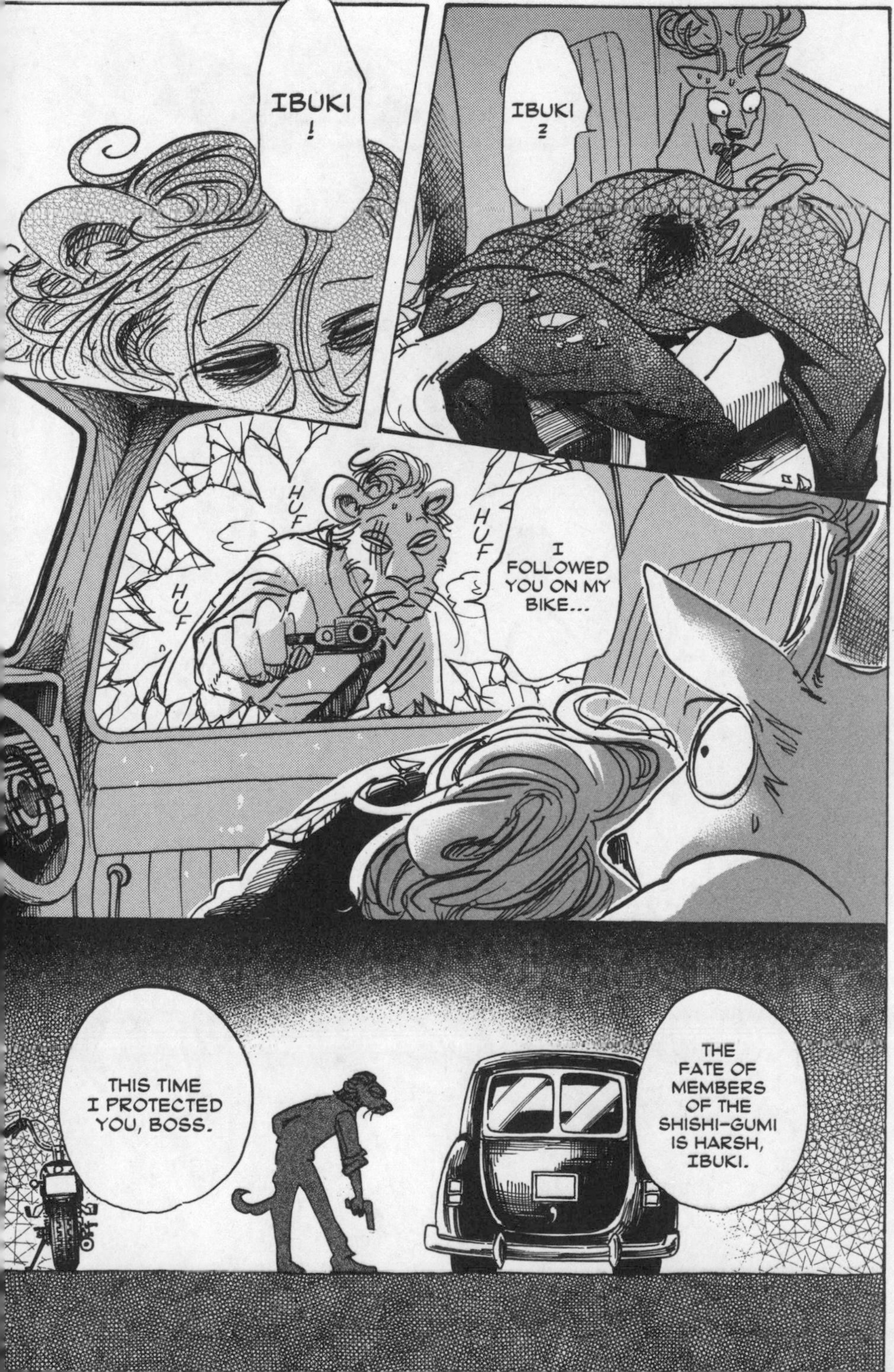
IBUKI?
IBUKI!
HUF
HUF
HUF
I FOLLOWED YOU ON MY BIKE...
THE FATE OF MEMBERS OF THE SHISHI-GUMI IS HARSH, IBUKI.
THIS TIME I PROTECTED YOU, BOSS.

Chapter 93: Pluck the Golden Hairs from the Shirt and Place Them into Your Pocket

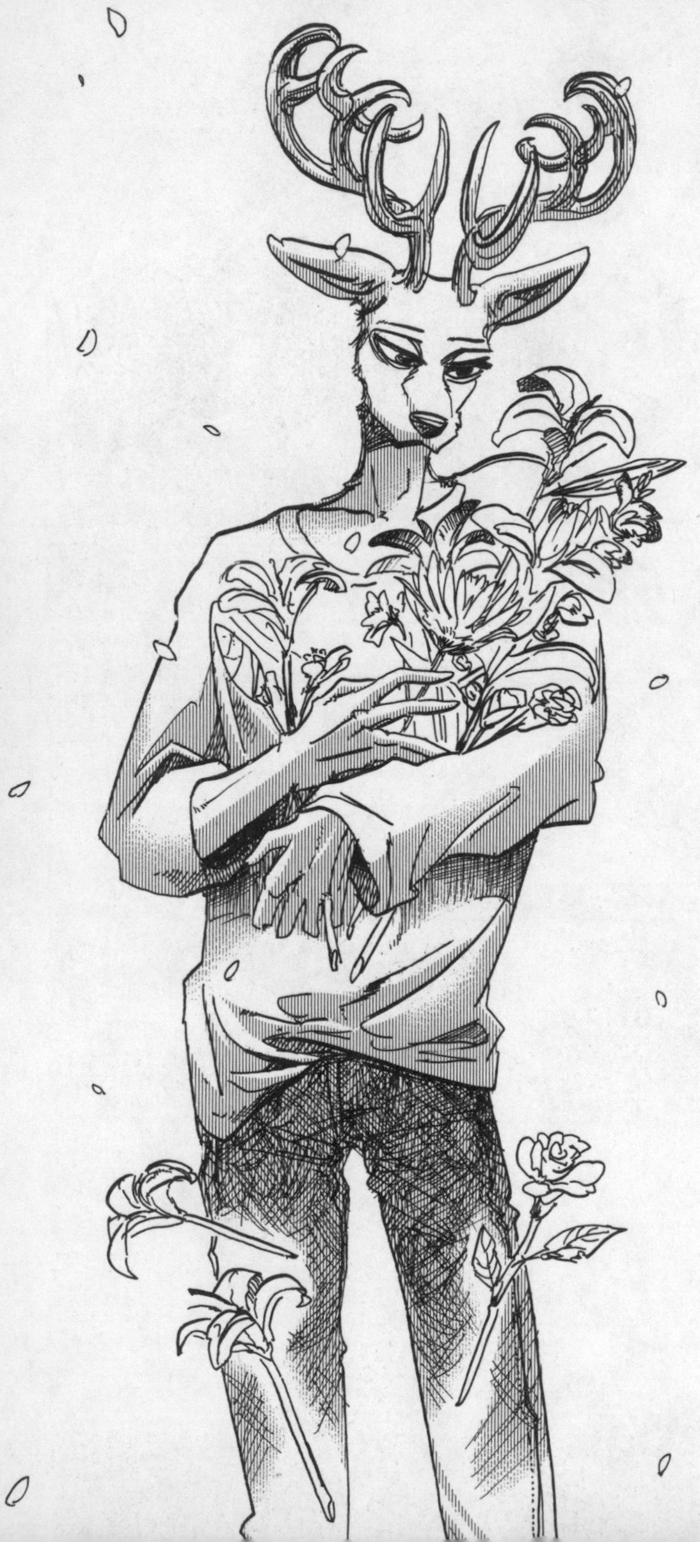

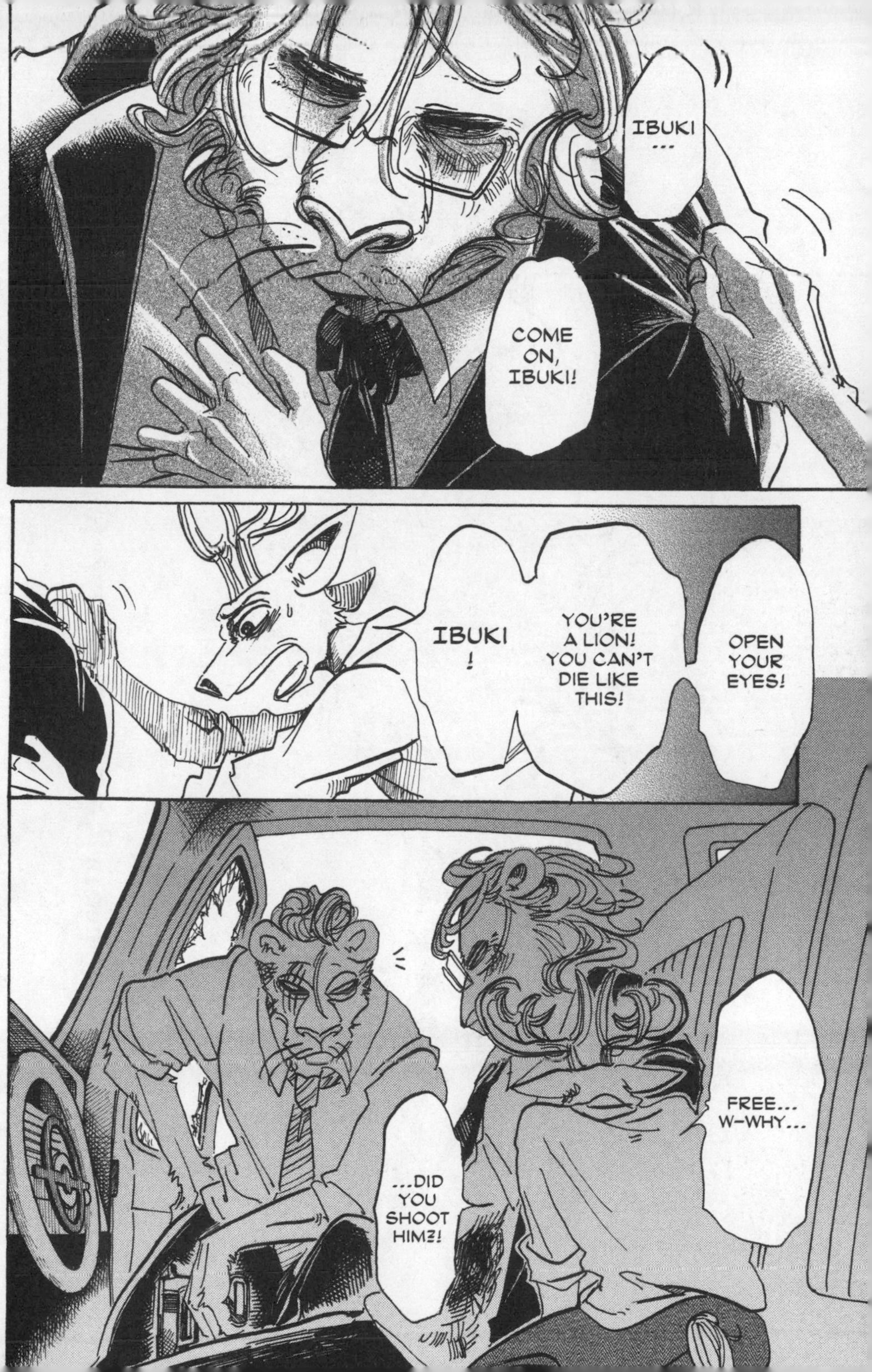
IBUKI ...
COME ON, IBUKI!
OPEN YOUR EYES!
YOU'RE A LION! YOU CAN'T DIE LIKE THIS!
IBUKI!
FREE... W-WHY...
...DID YOU SHOOT HIM?!

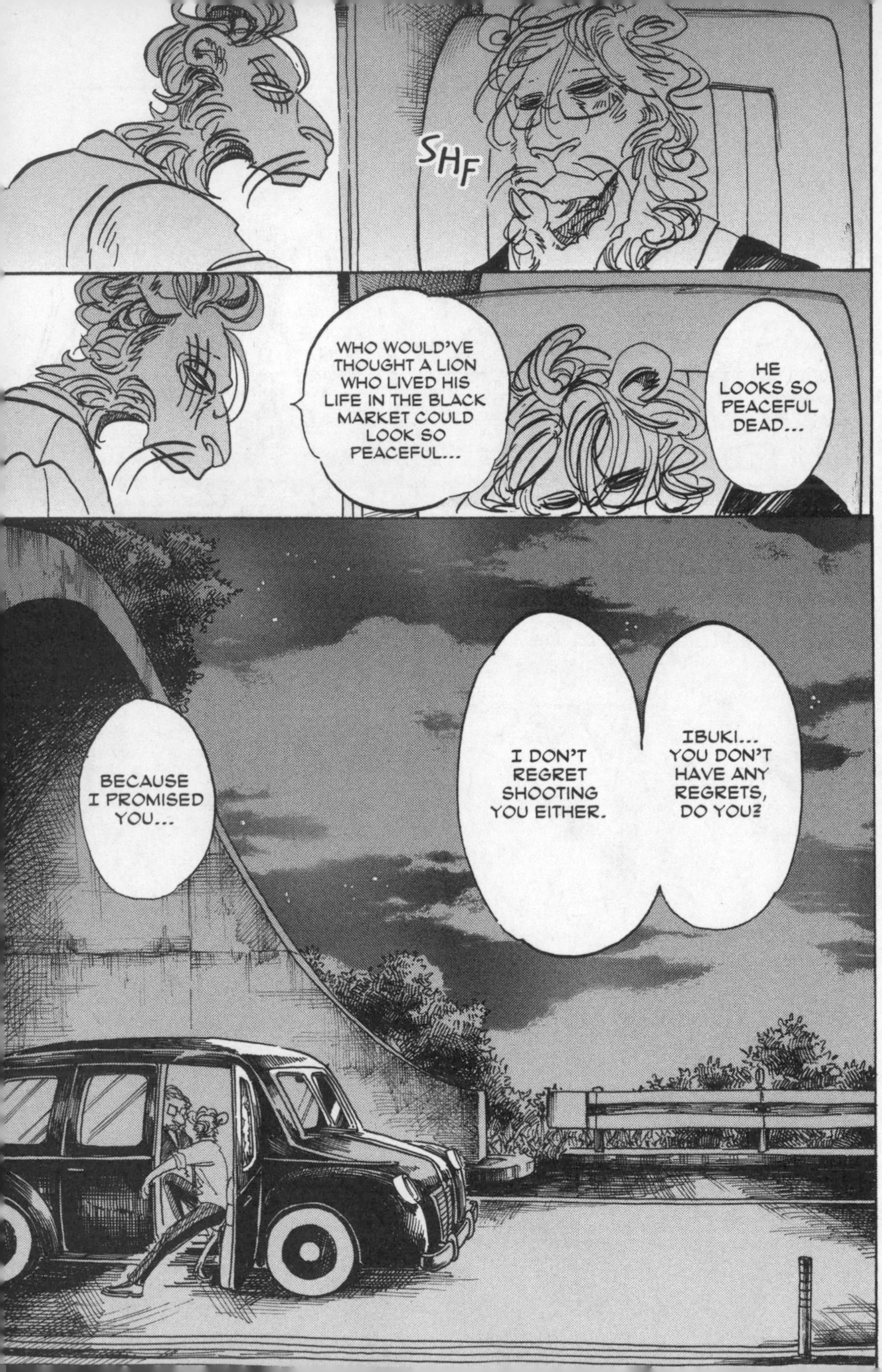
SHF
HE LOOKS SO PEACEFUL DEAD...
WHO WOULD'VE THOUGHT A LION WHO LIVED HIS LIFE IN THE BLACK MARKET COULD LOOK SO PEACEFUL...
IBUKI... YOU DON'T HAVE ANY REGRETS, DO YOU?
I DON'T REGRET SHOOTING YOU EITHER.
BECAUSE I PROMISED YOU...

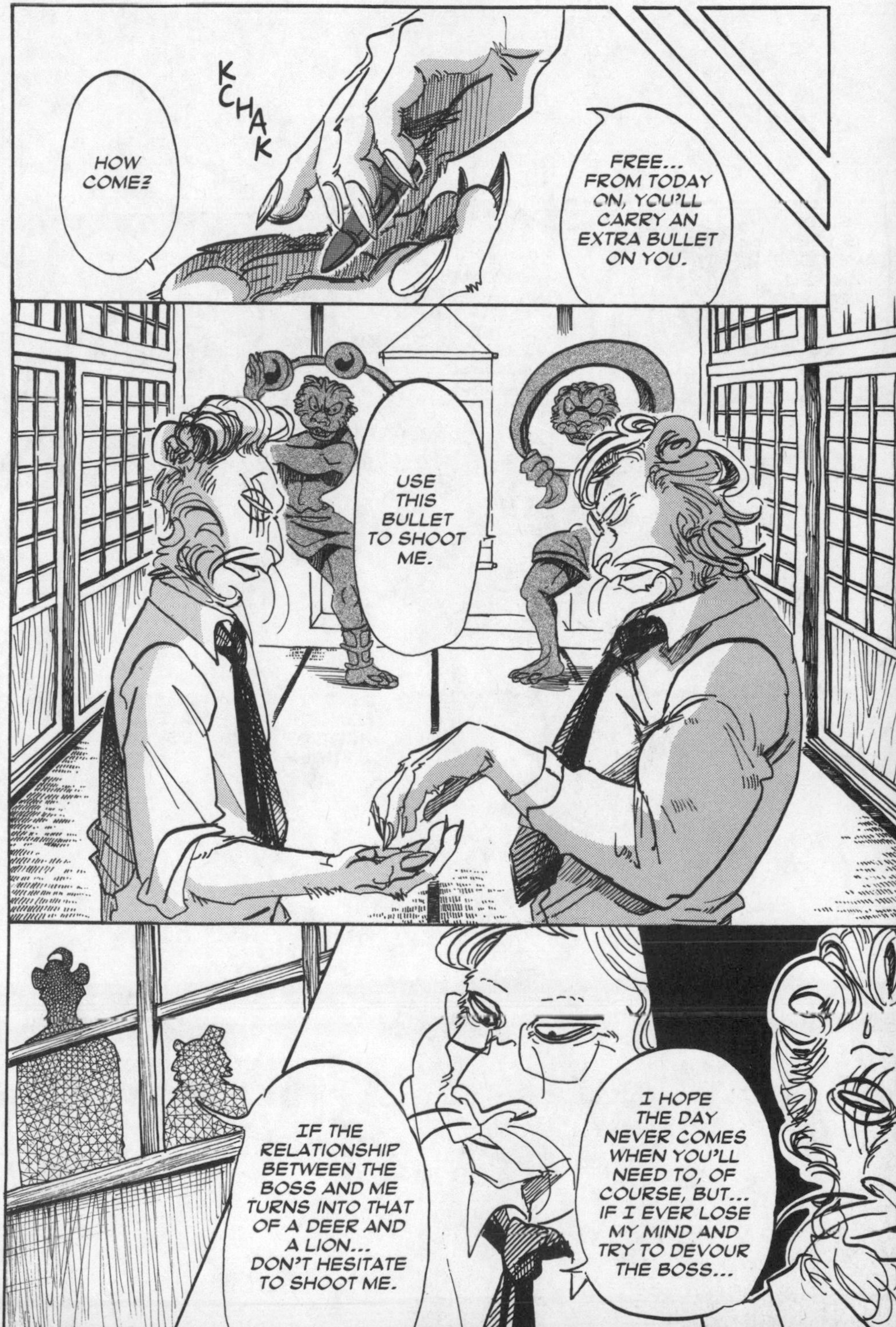
FREE... FROM TODAY ON, YOU'LL CARRY AN EXTRA BULLET ON YOU.
KCHAK
HOW COME?
USE THIS BULLET TO SHOOT ME.
I HOPE THE DAY NEVER COMES WHEN YOU'LL NEED TO, OF COURSE, BUT... IF I EVER LOSE MY MIND AND TRY TO DEVOUR THE BOSS...
IF THE RELATIONSHIP BETWEEN THE BOSS AND ME TURNS INTO THAT OF A DEER AND A LION... DON'T HESITATE TO SHOOT ME.

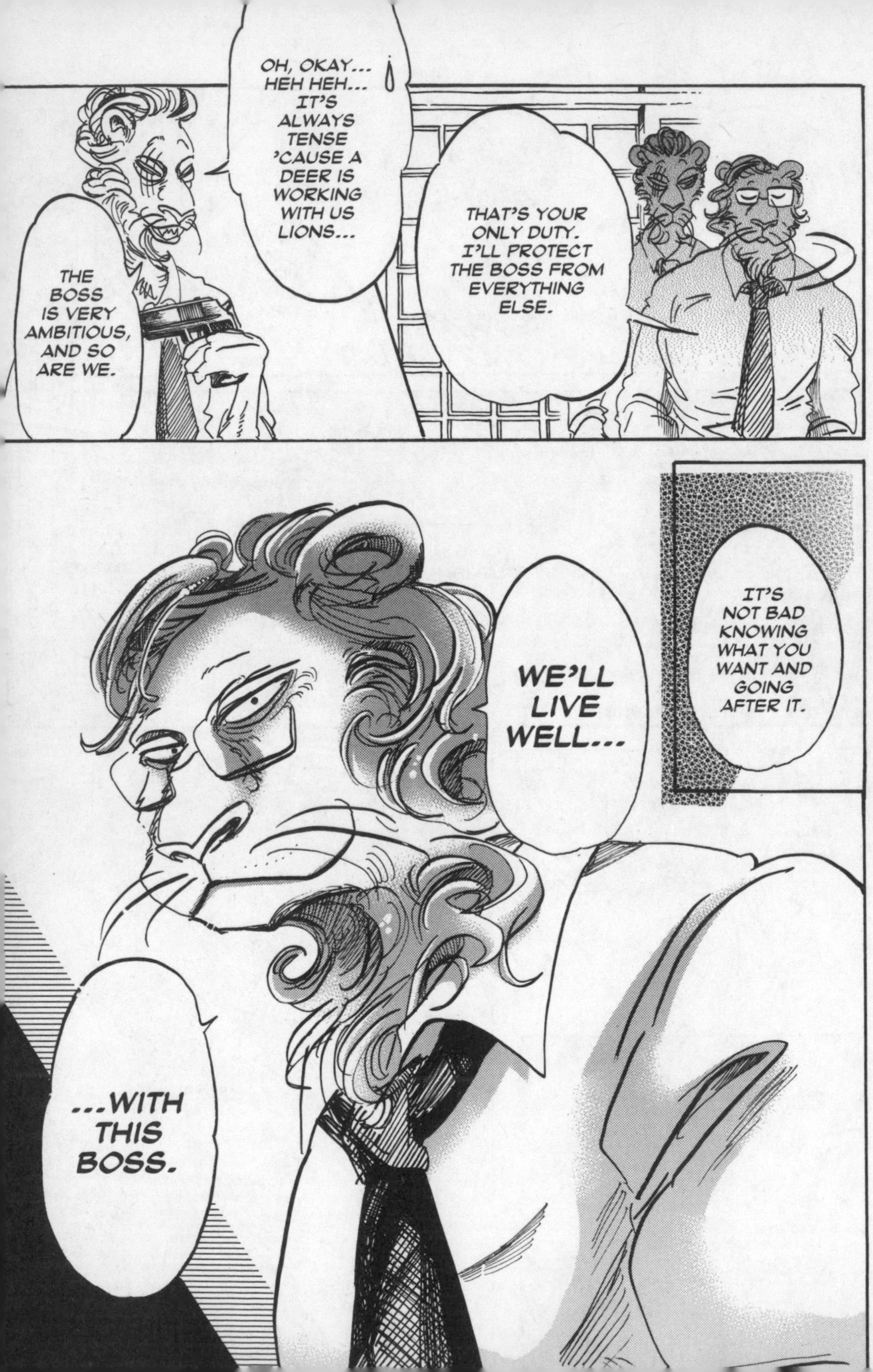
THAT'S YOUR ONLY DUTY. I'LL PROTECT THE BOSS FROM EVERYTHING ELSE.
OH, OKAY... HEH HEH... IT'S ALWAYS TENSE 'CAUSE A DEER IS WORKING WITH US LIONS...
THE BOSS IS VERY AMBITIOUS, AND SO ARE WE.
IT'S NOT BAD KNOWING WHAT YOU WANT AND GOING AFTER IT.
WE'LL LIVE WELL...
...WITH THIS BOSS.

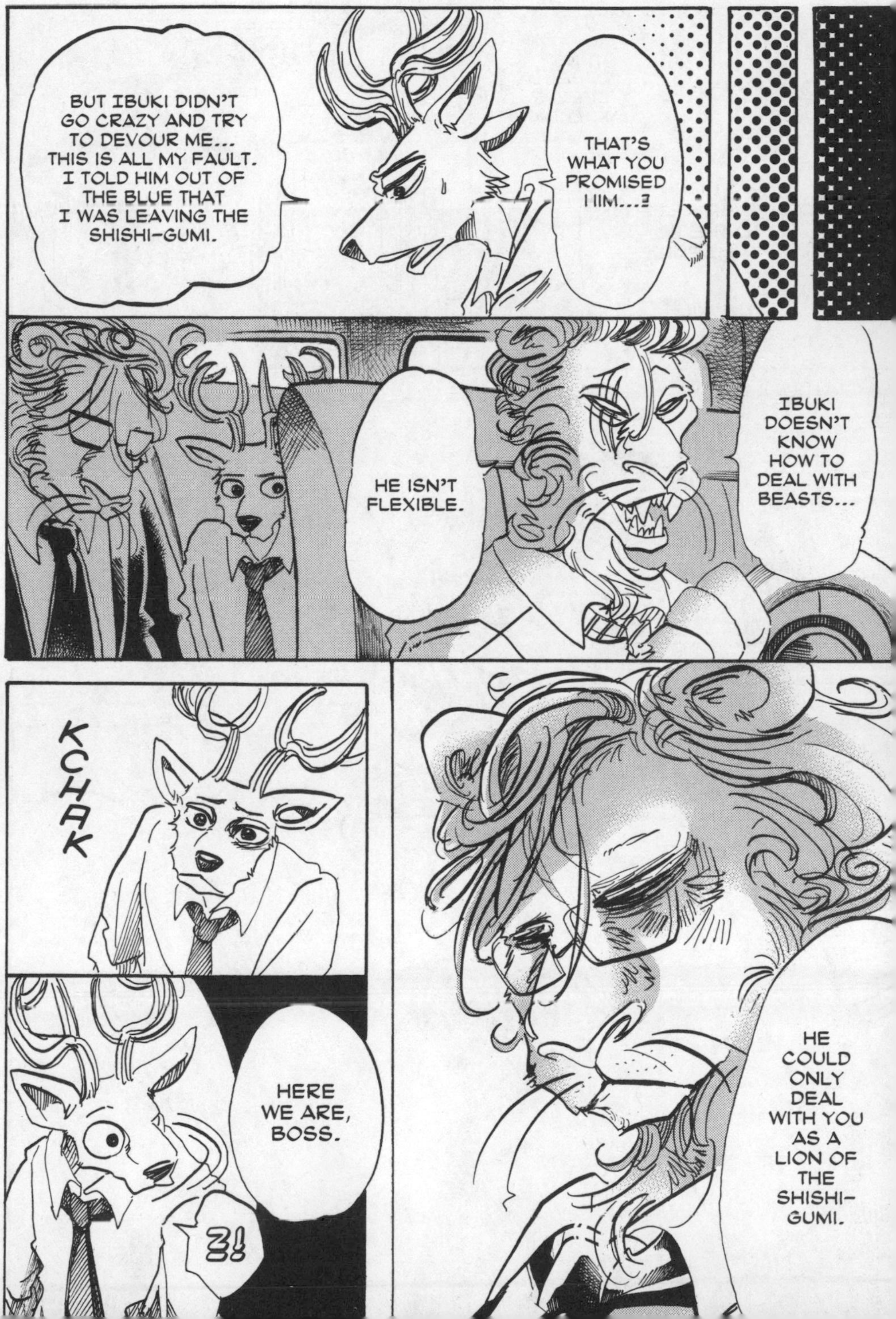
THAT'S WHAT YOU PROMISED HIM...?
BUT IBUKI DIDN'T GO CRAZY AND TRY TO DEVOUR ME... THIS IS ALL MY FAULT. I TOLD HIM OUT OF THE BLUE THAT I WAS LEAVING THE SHISHI-GUMI.
IBUKI DOESN'T KNOW HOW TO DEAL WITH BEASTS...
HE ISN'T FLEXIBLE.
HE COULD ONLY DEAL WITH YOU AS A LION OF THE SHISHI-GUMI.
KCHAK
HERE WE ARE, BOSS.
!?

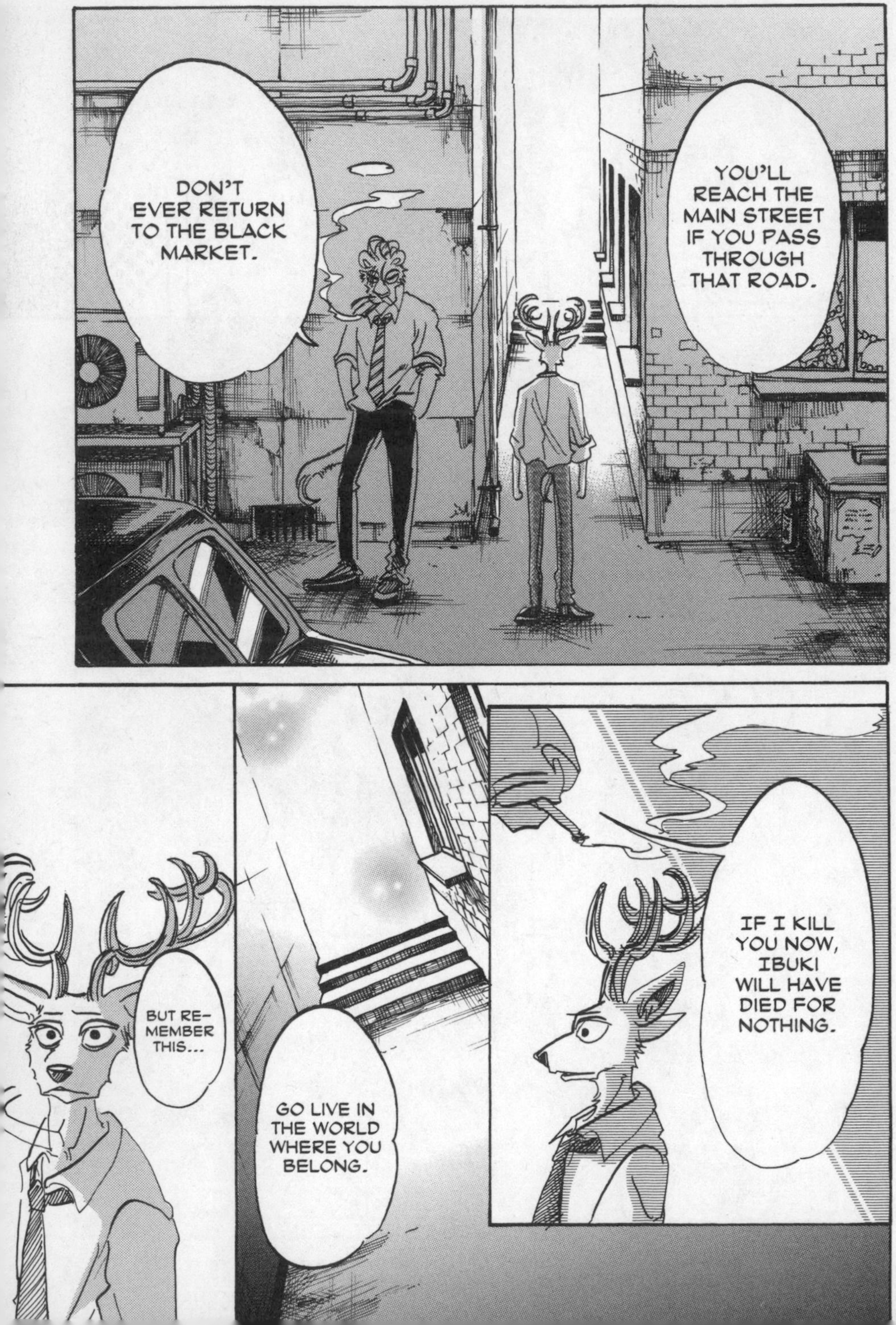
YOU'LL REACH THE MAIN STREET IF YOU PASS THROUGH THAT ROAD.
DON'T EVER RETURN TO THE BLACK MARKET.
IF I KILL YOU NOW, IBUKI WILL HAVE DIED FOR NOTHING.
GO LIVE IN THE WORLD WHERE YOU BELONG.
BUT RE-MEMBER THIS...

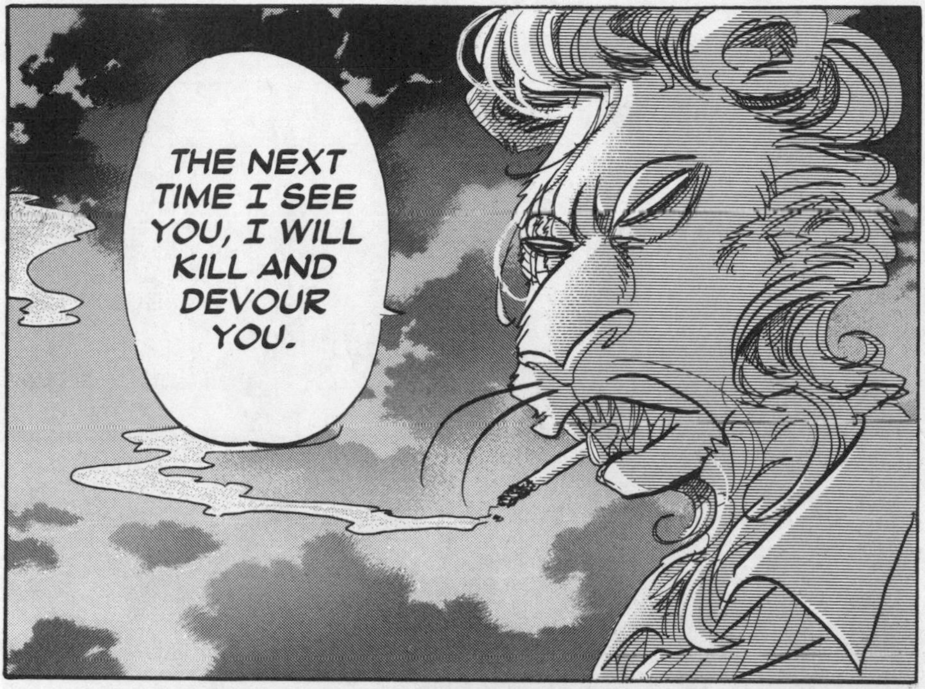
THE NEXT TIME I SEE YOU, I WILL KILL AND DEVOUR YOU.
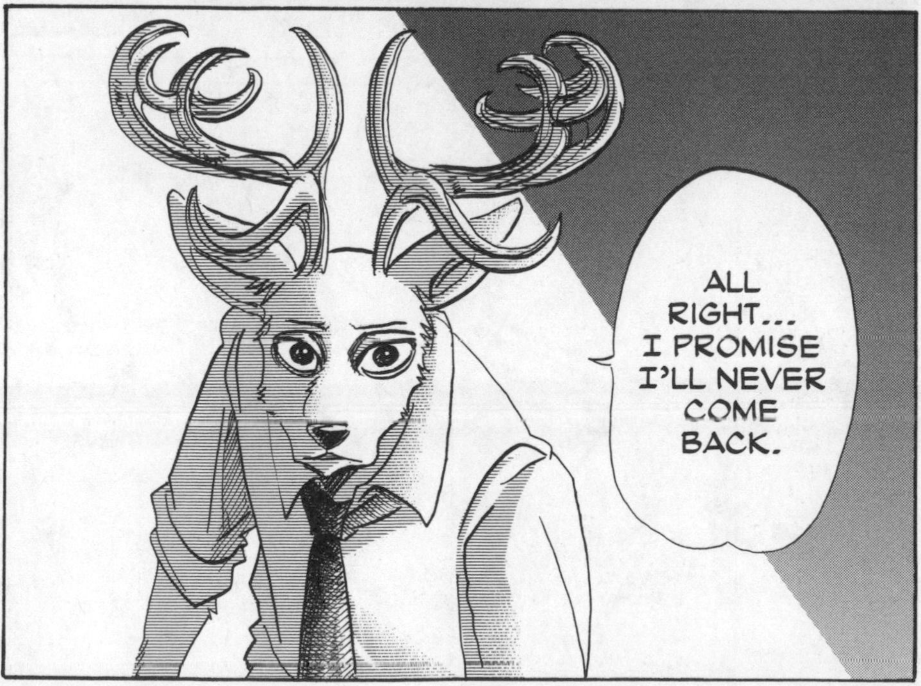
ALL RIGHT... I PROMISE I'LL NEVER COME BACK.

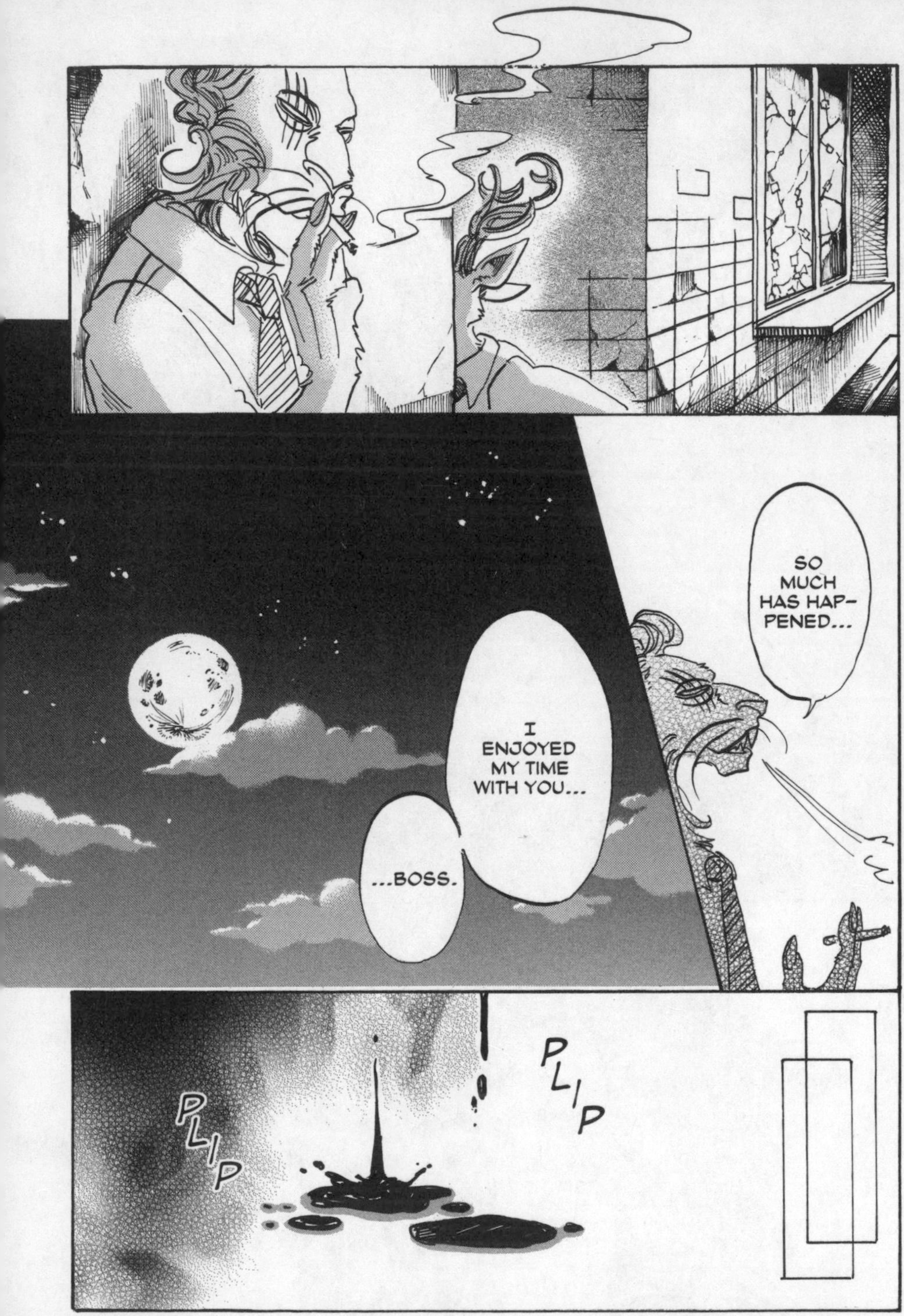

SO MUCH HAS HAP- PENED...
I ENJOYED MY TIME WITH YOU...
...BOSS.
PLIP
PLIP

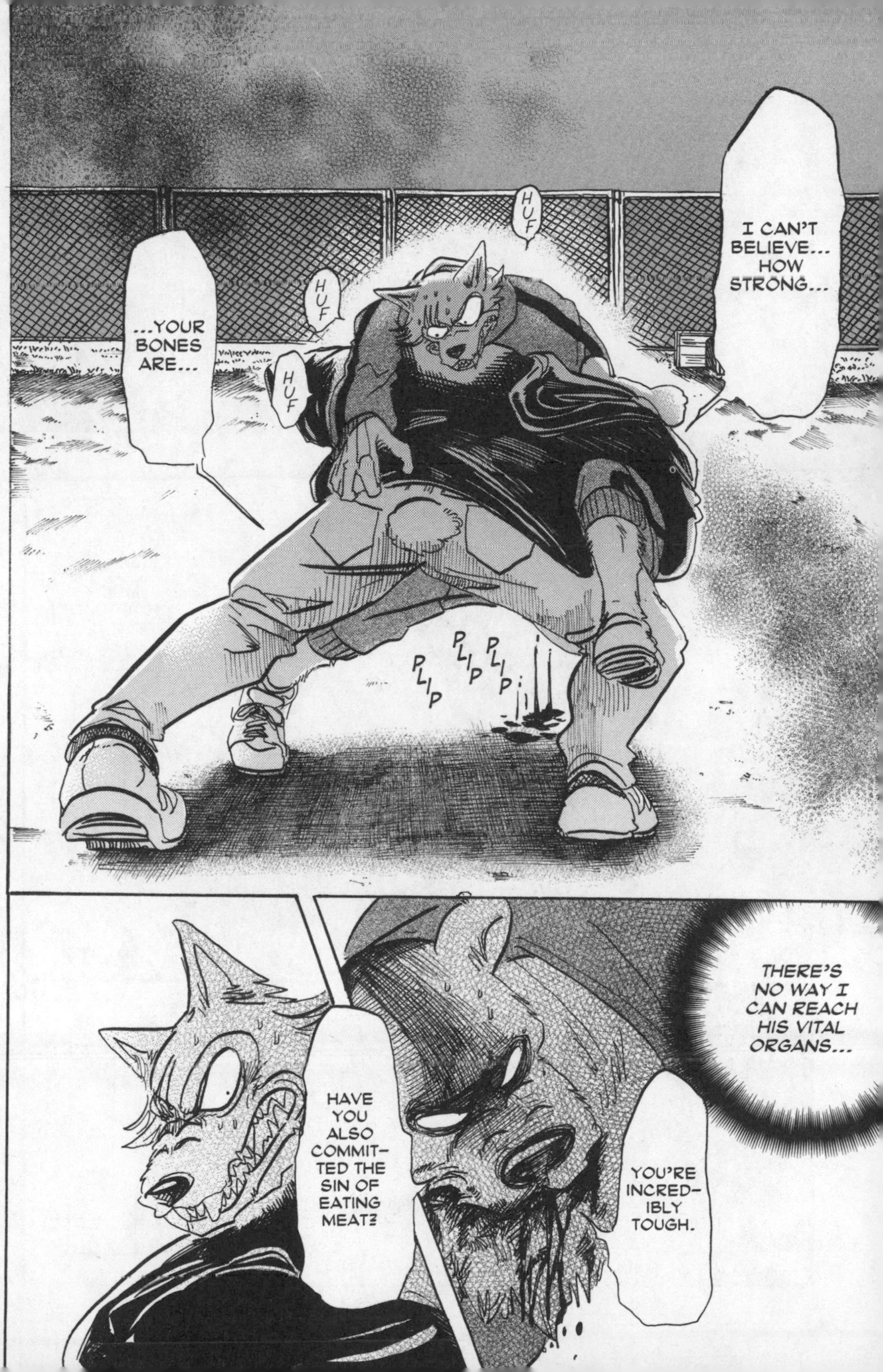
I CAN'T BELIEVE... HOW STRONG...
HUF
HUF
HUF
...YOUR BONES ARE...
PLIP
PLIP
PLIP
THERE'S NO WAY I CAN REACH HIS VITAL ORGANS...
YOU'RE INCREDIBLY TOUGH.
HAVE YOU ALSO COMMITTED THE SIN OF EATING MEAT?

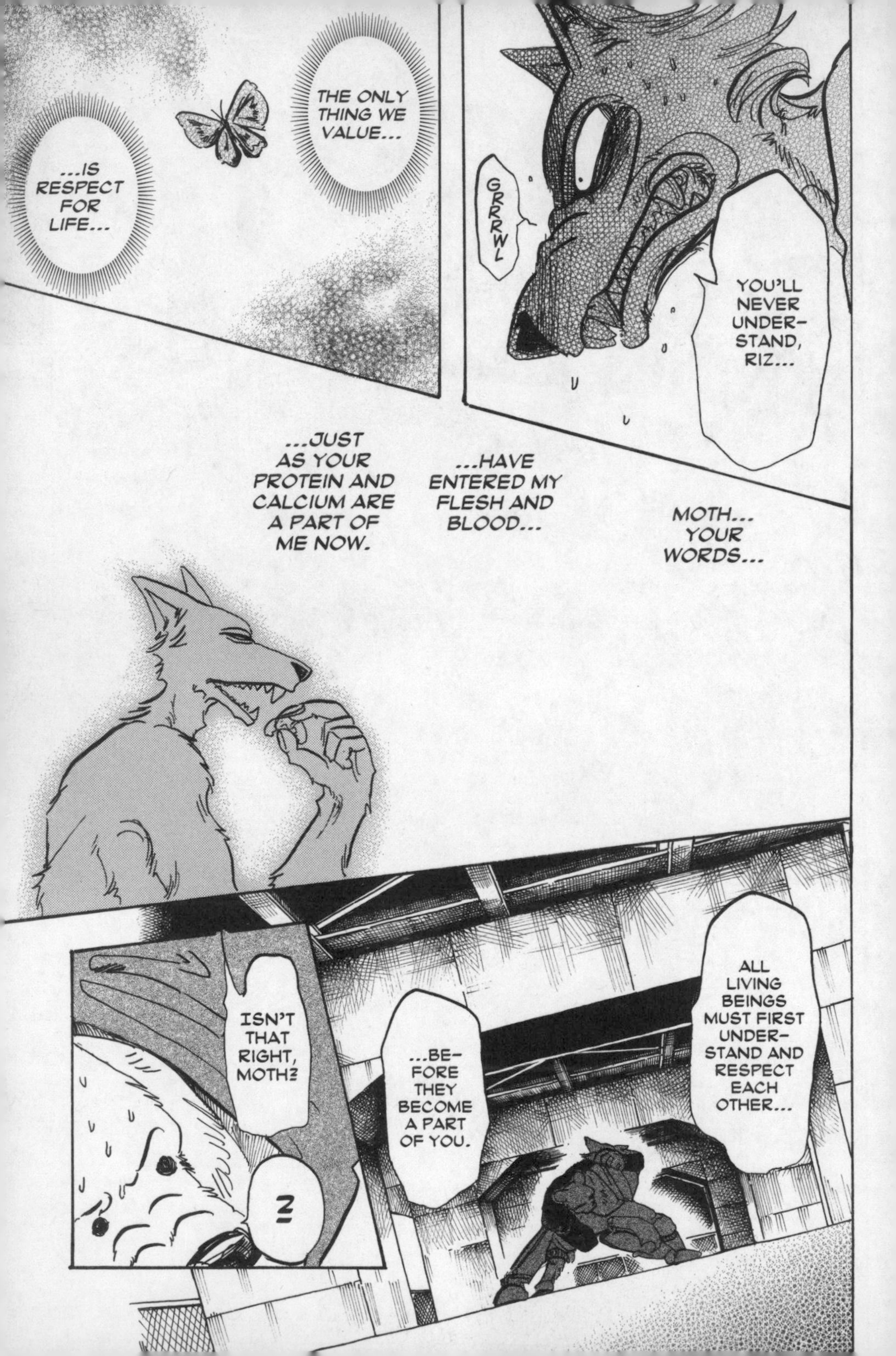
YOU'LL NEVER UNDER-STAND, RIZ...
GRRRWL
THE ONLY THING WE VALUE...
...IS RESPECT FOR LIFE...
MOTH... YOUR WORDS...
...HAVE ENTERED MY FLESH AND BLOOD...
...JUST AS YOUR PROTEIN AND CALCIUM ARE A PART OF ME NOW.
ALL LIVING BEINGS MUST FIRST UNDER-STAND AND RESPECT EACH OTHER...
...BE-FORE THEY BECOME A PART OF YOU.
ISN'T THAT RIGHT, MOTH?
?!

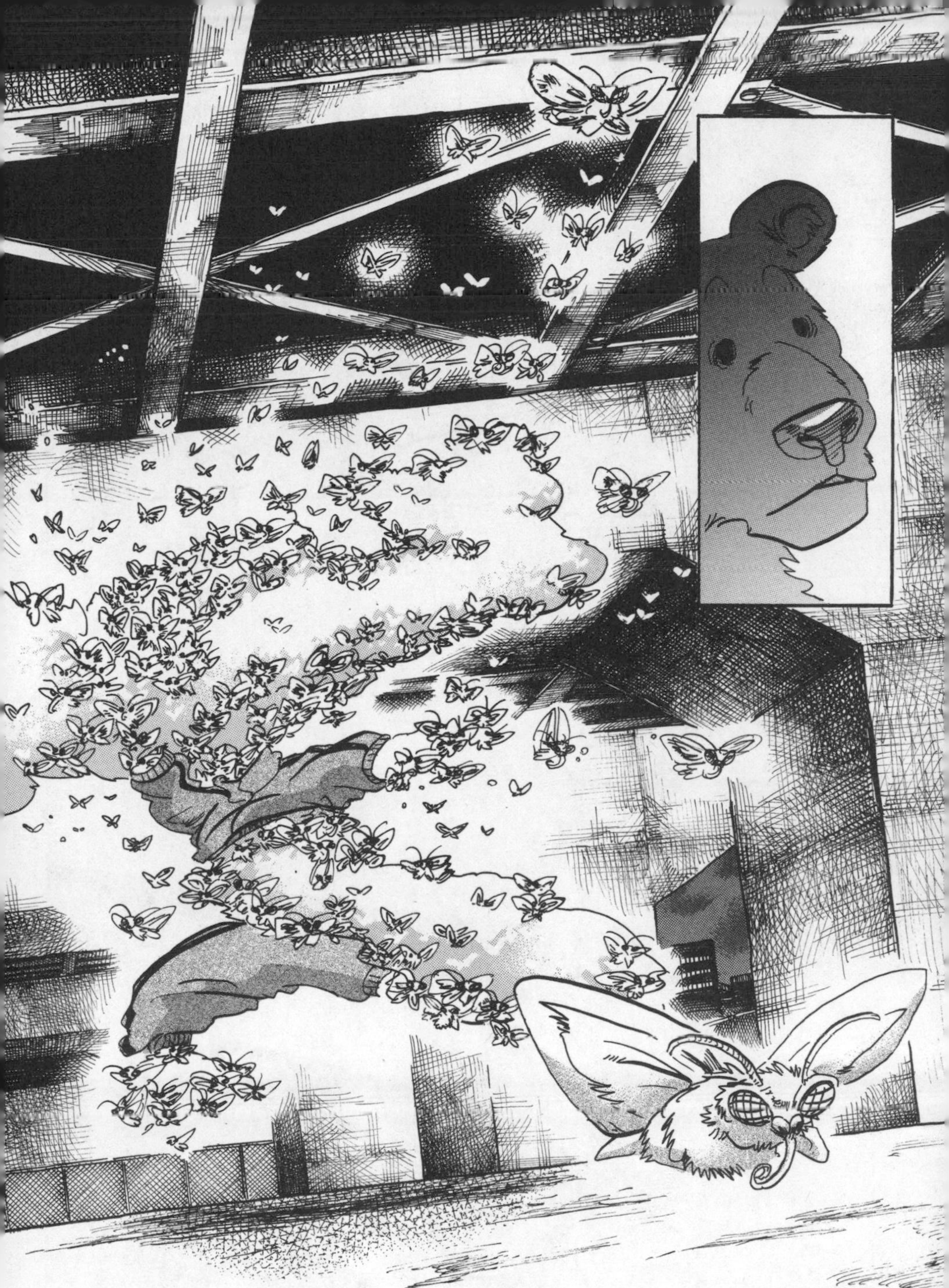

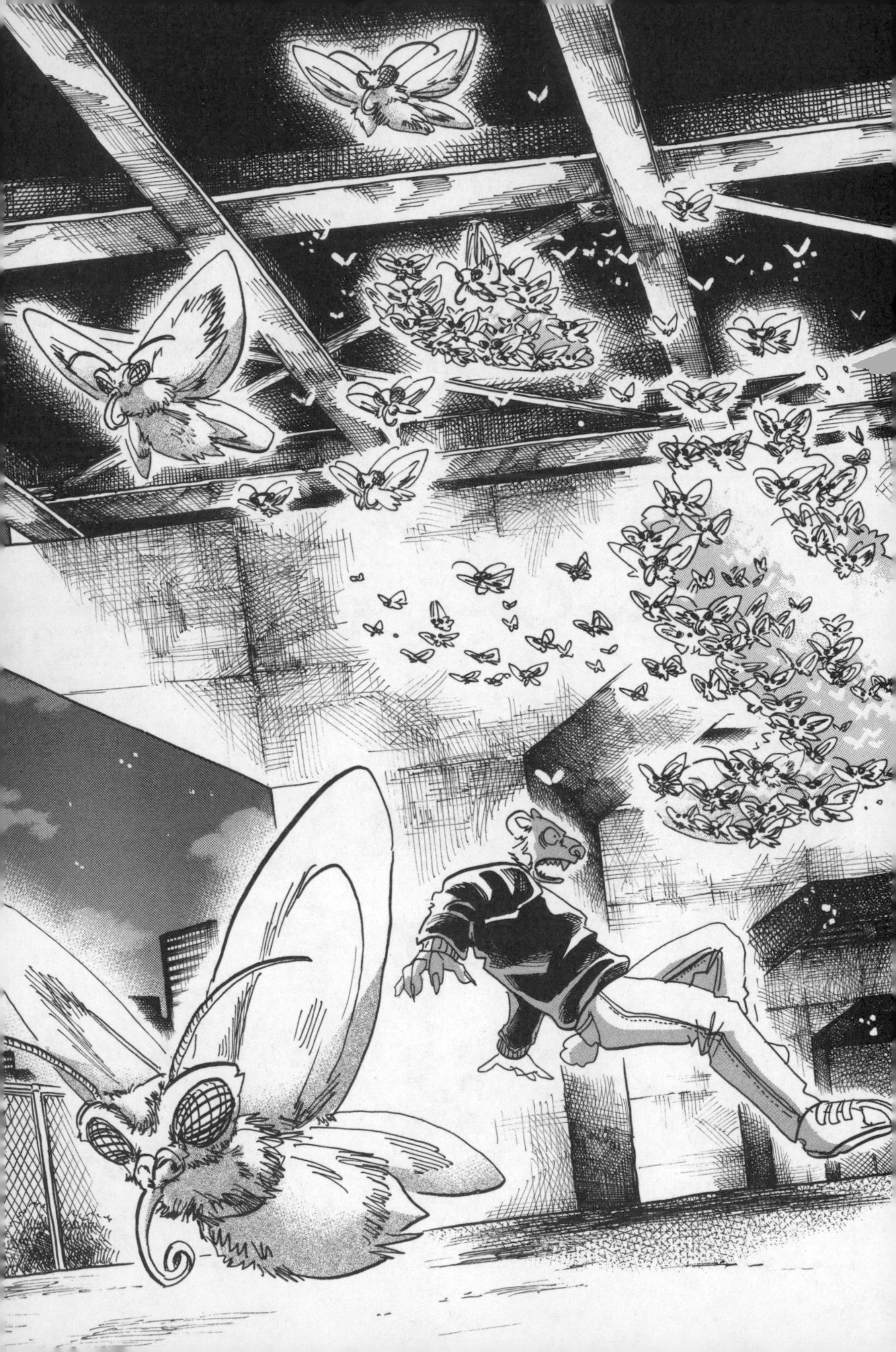

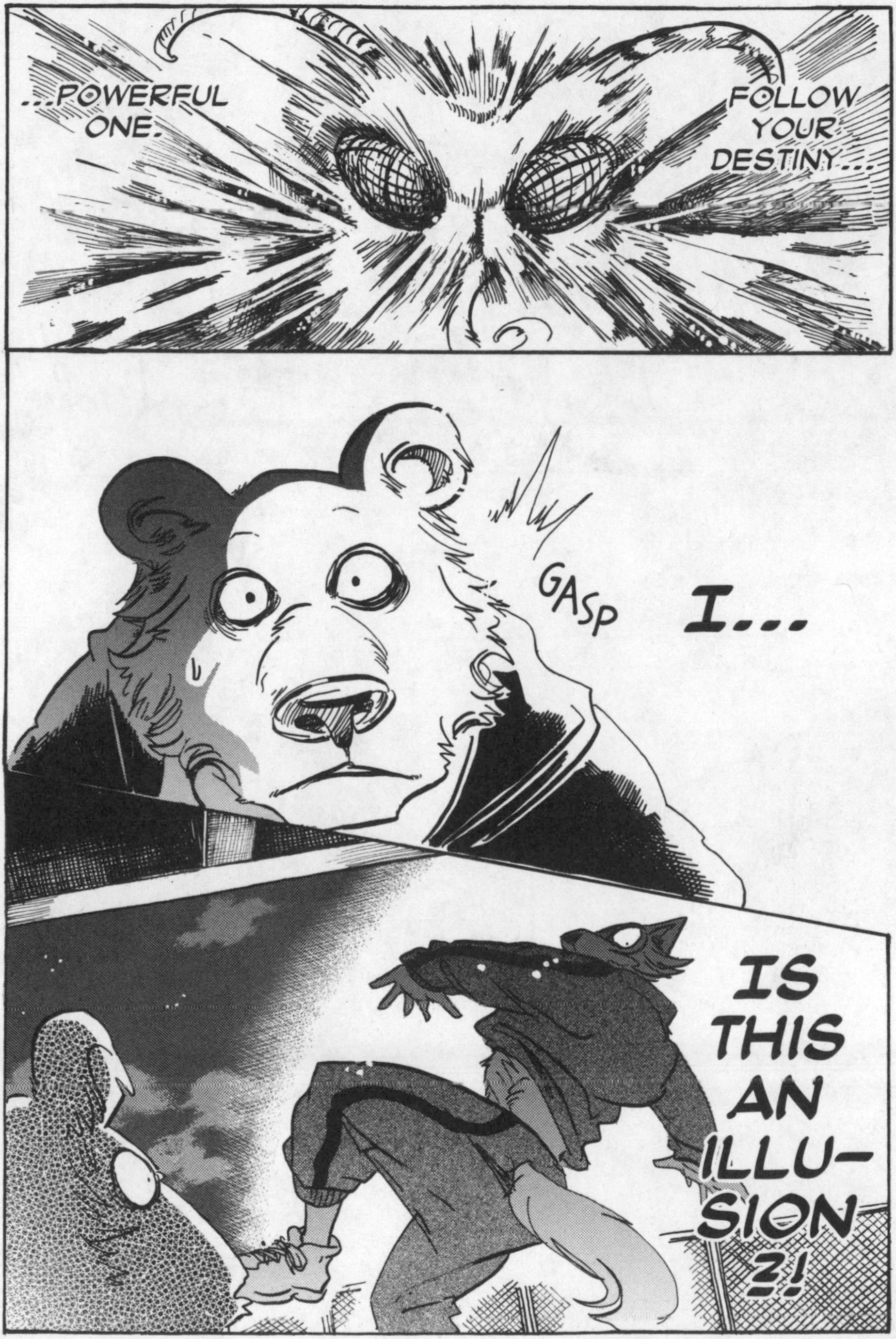
FOLLOW YOUR DESTINY...
...POWERFUL ONE.
GASP
I...
IS THIS AN ILLU-SION?!

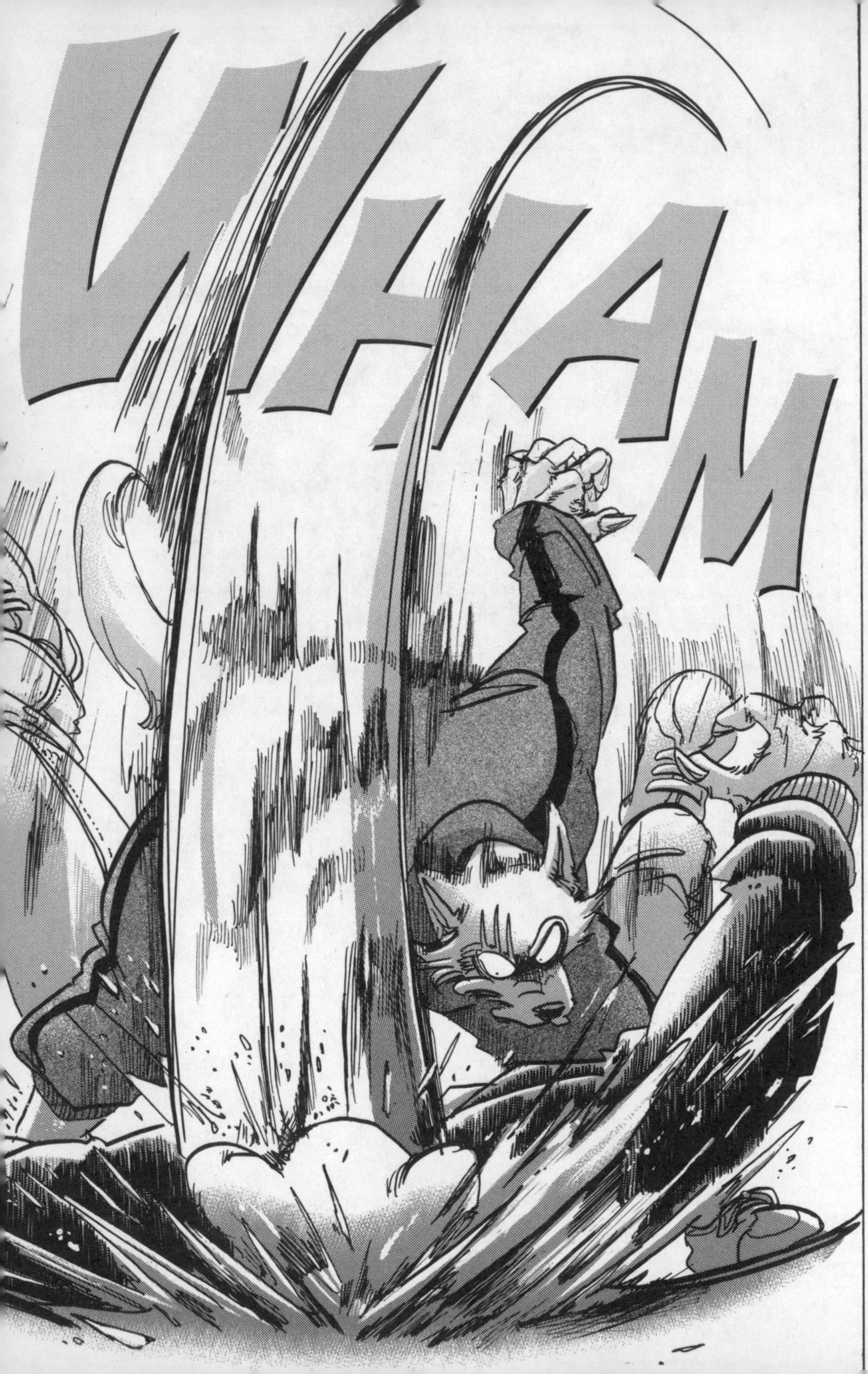
WHAM

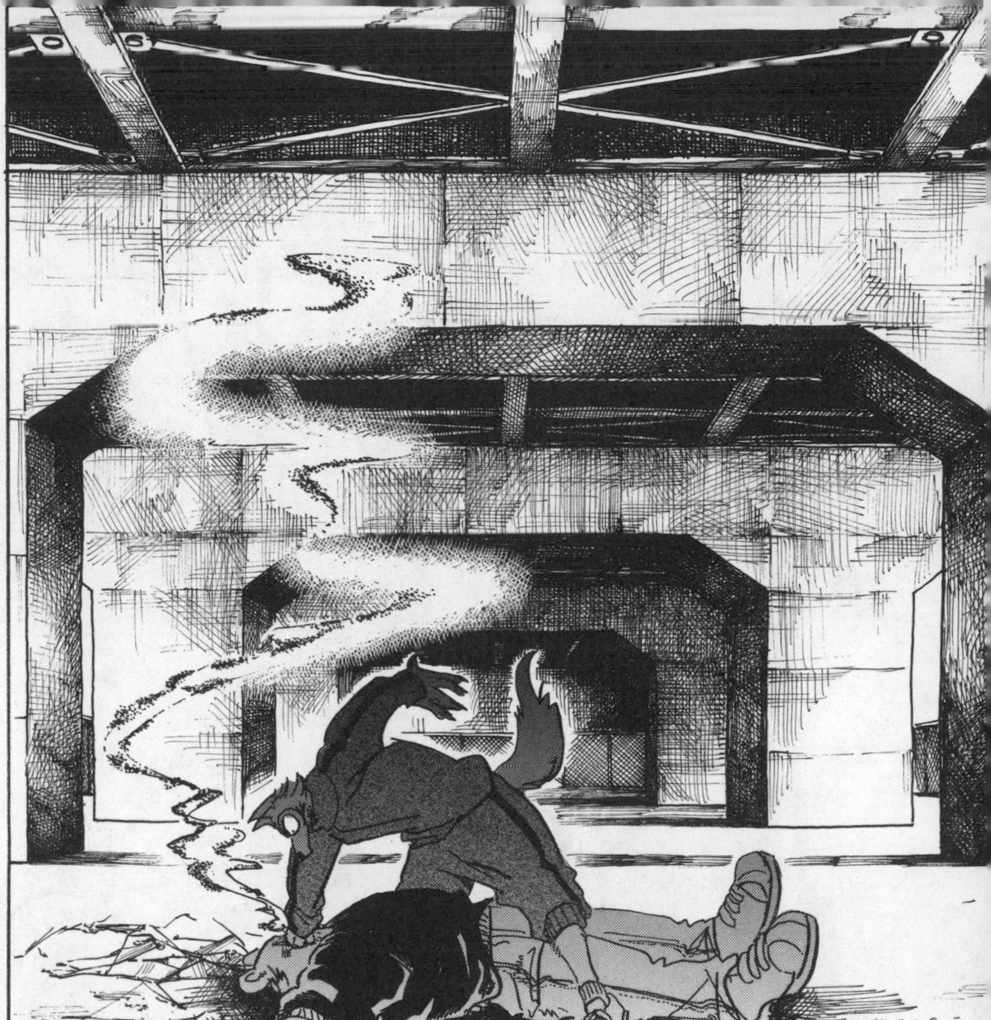
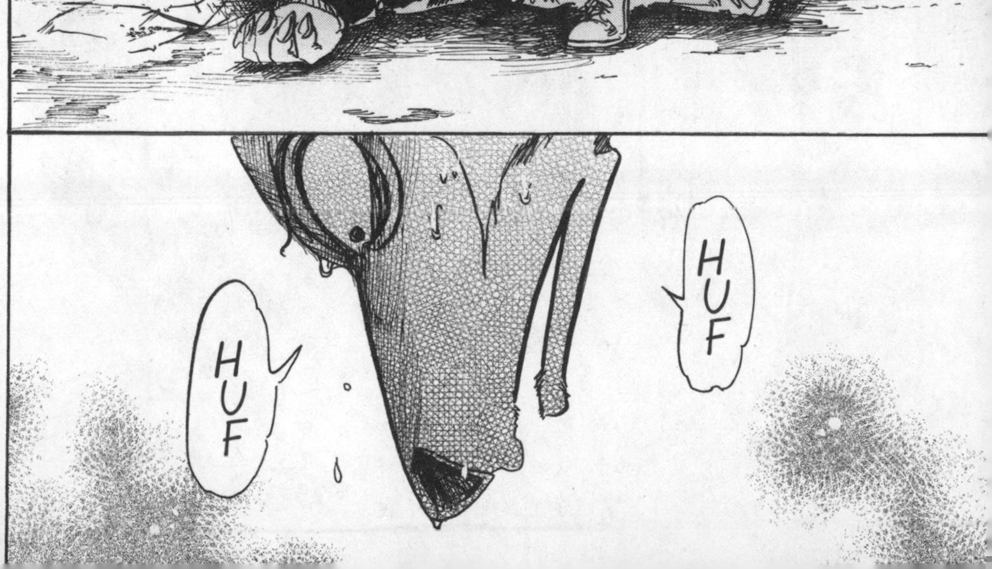
HUF
HUF

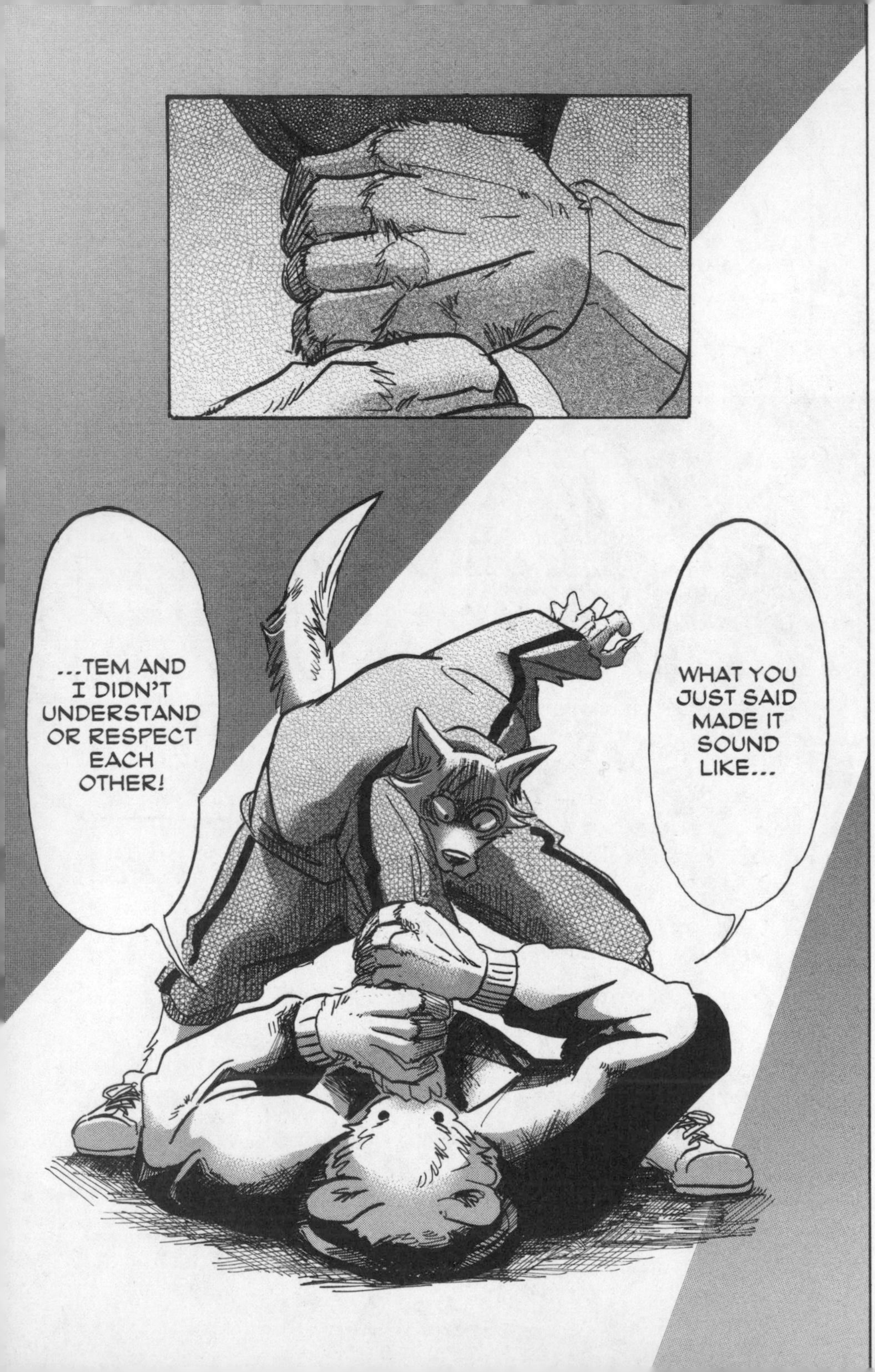
WHAT YOU JUST SAID MADE IT SOUND LIKE...
...TEM AND I DIDN'T UNDERSTAND OR RESPECT EACH OTHER!

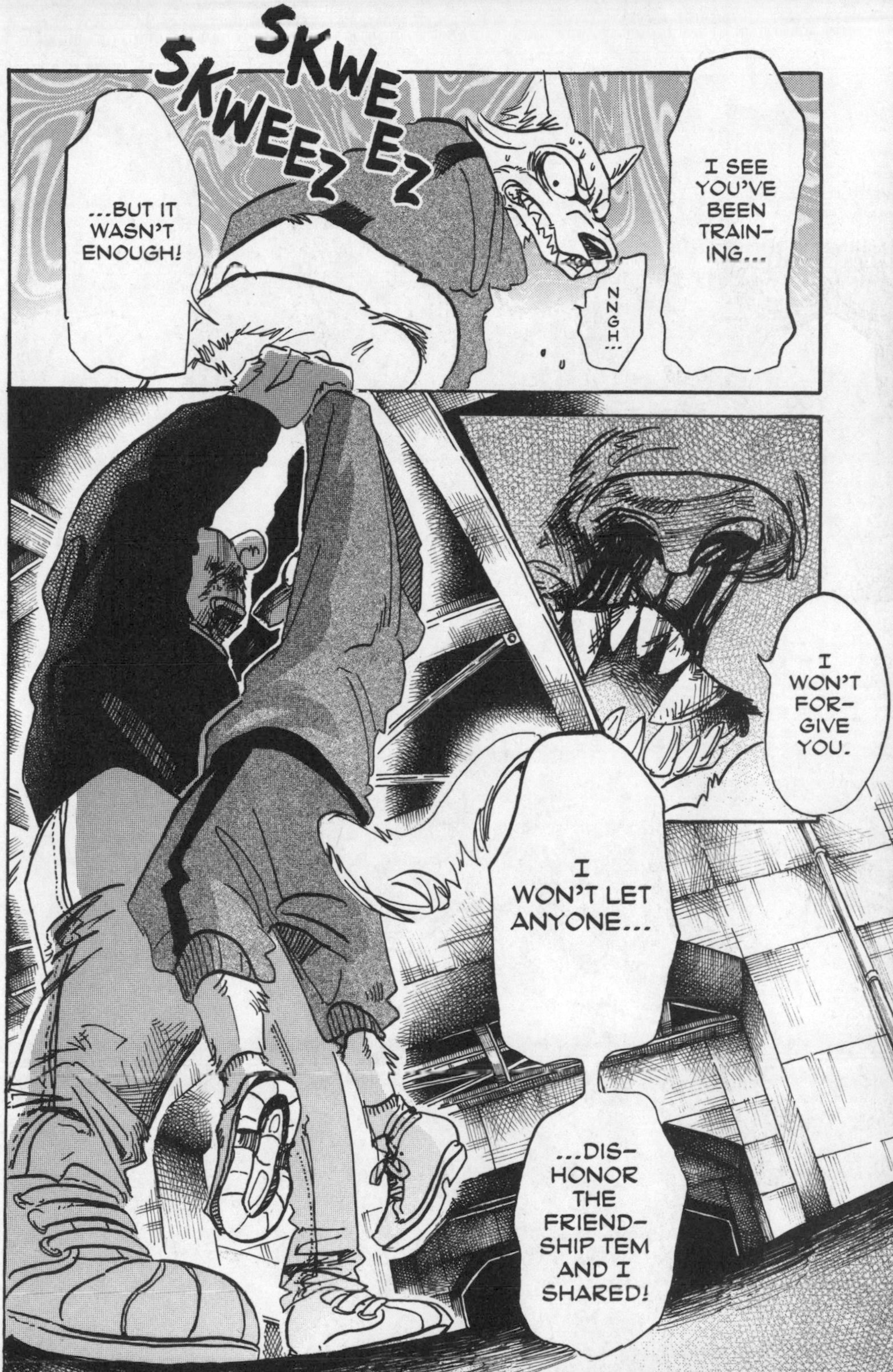
I SEE YOU'VE BEEN TRAIN-ING...
NNGH...
SKWEEZ
SKWEEZ
...BUT IT WASN'T ENOUGH!
I WON'T FOR-GIVE YOU.
I WON'T LET ANYONE...
...DIS-HONOR THE FRIEND-SHIP TEM AND I SHARED!

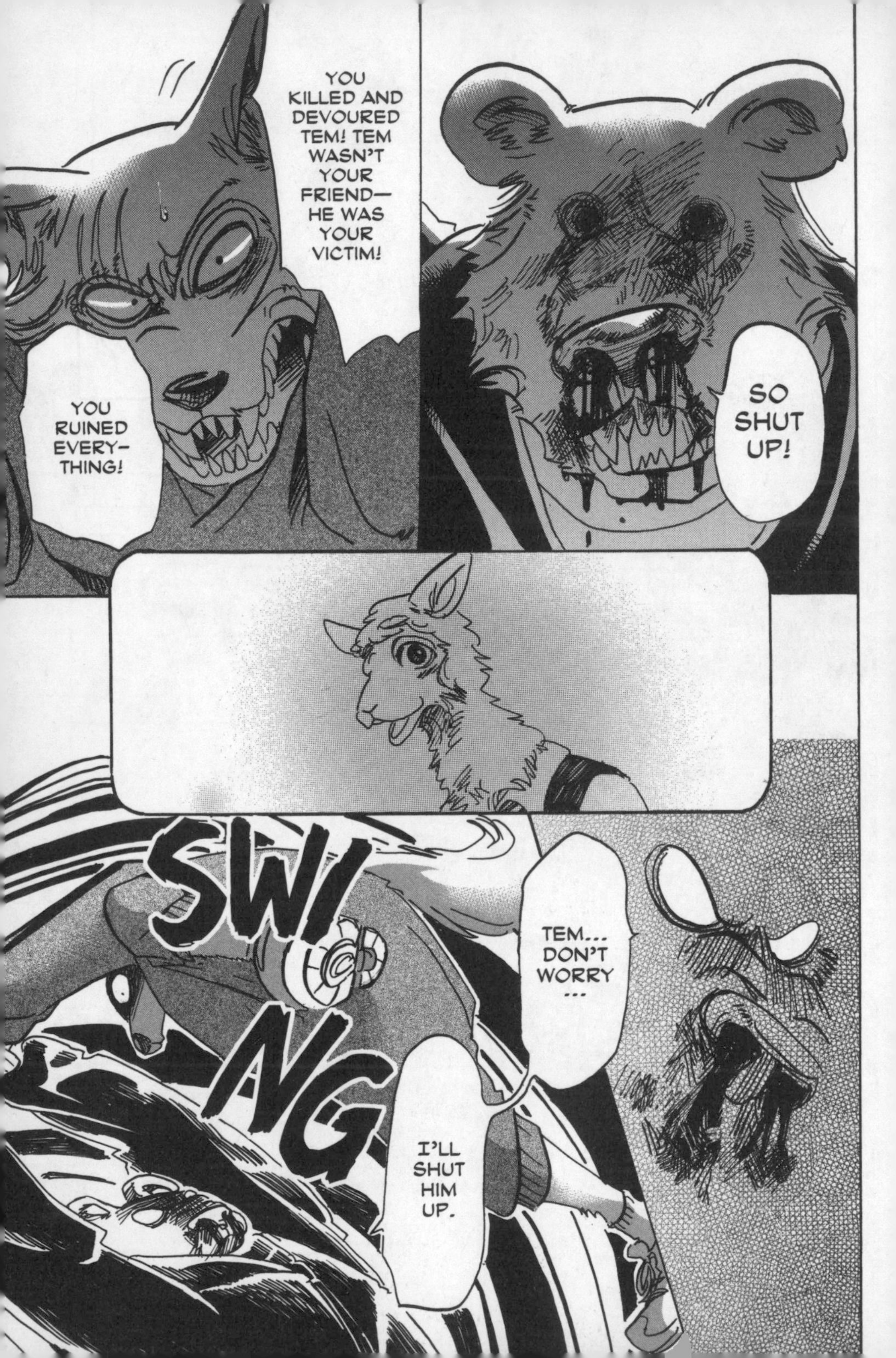
SO SHUT UP!
YOU KILLED AND DEVOURED TEM! TEM WASN'T YOUR FRIEND—HE WAS YOUR VICTIM!
YOU RUINED EVERY-THING!
TEM... DON'T WORRY...
SWING
I'LL SHUT HIM UP.

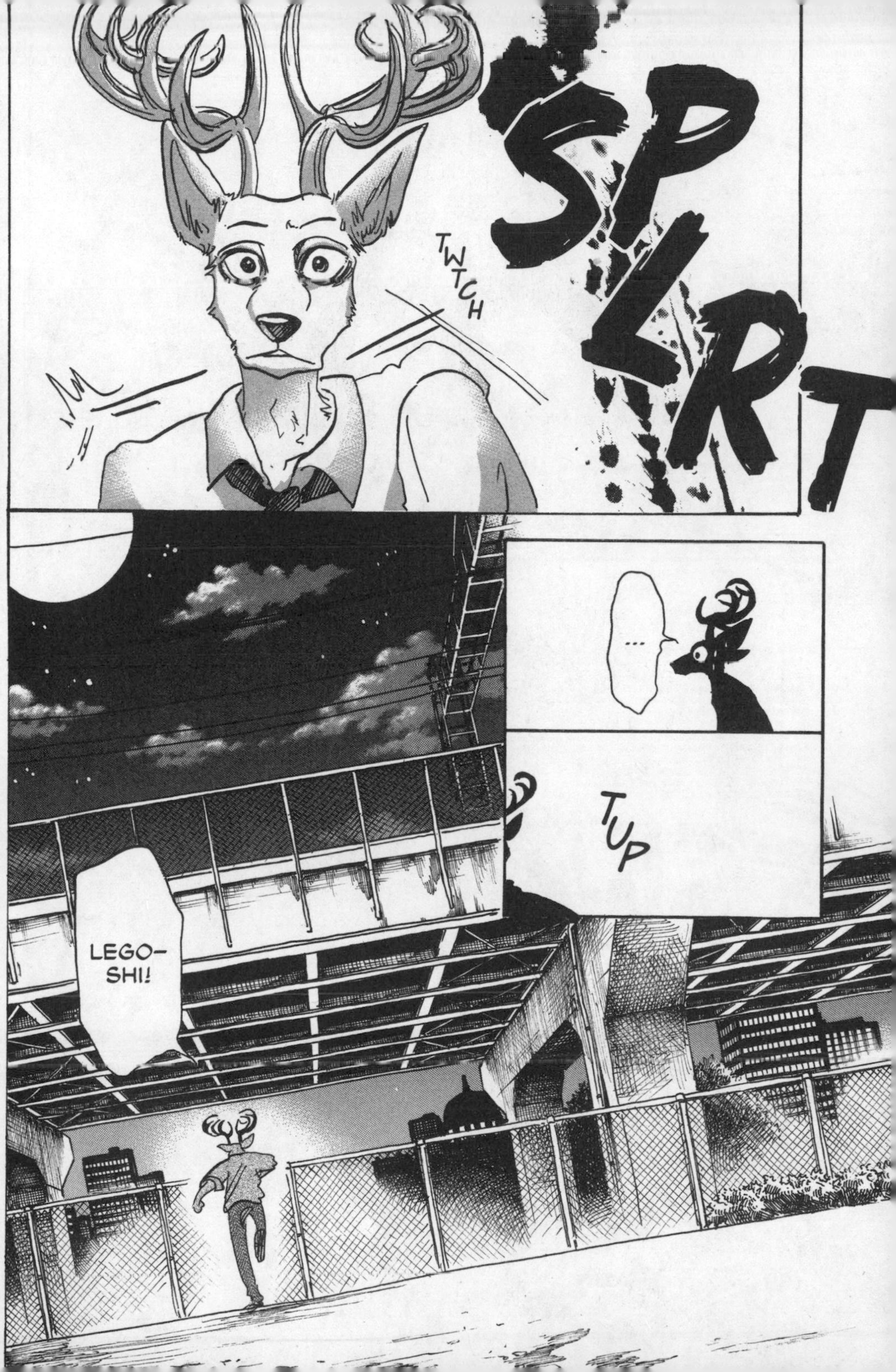
SPLRT
TWTCH
...
TUP
LEGO-SHI!

Chapter 94: Beasts' School ☆ Wars

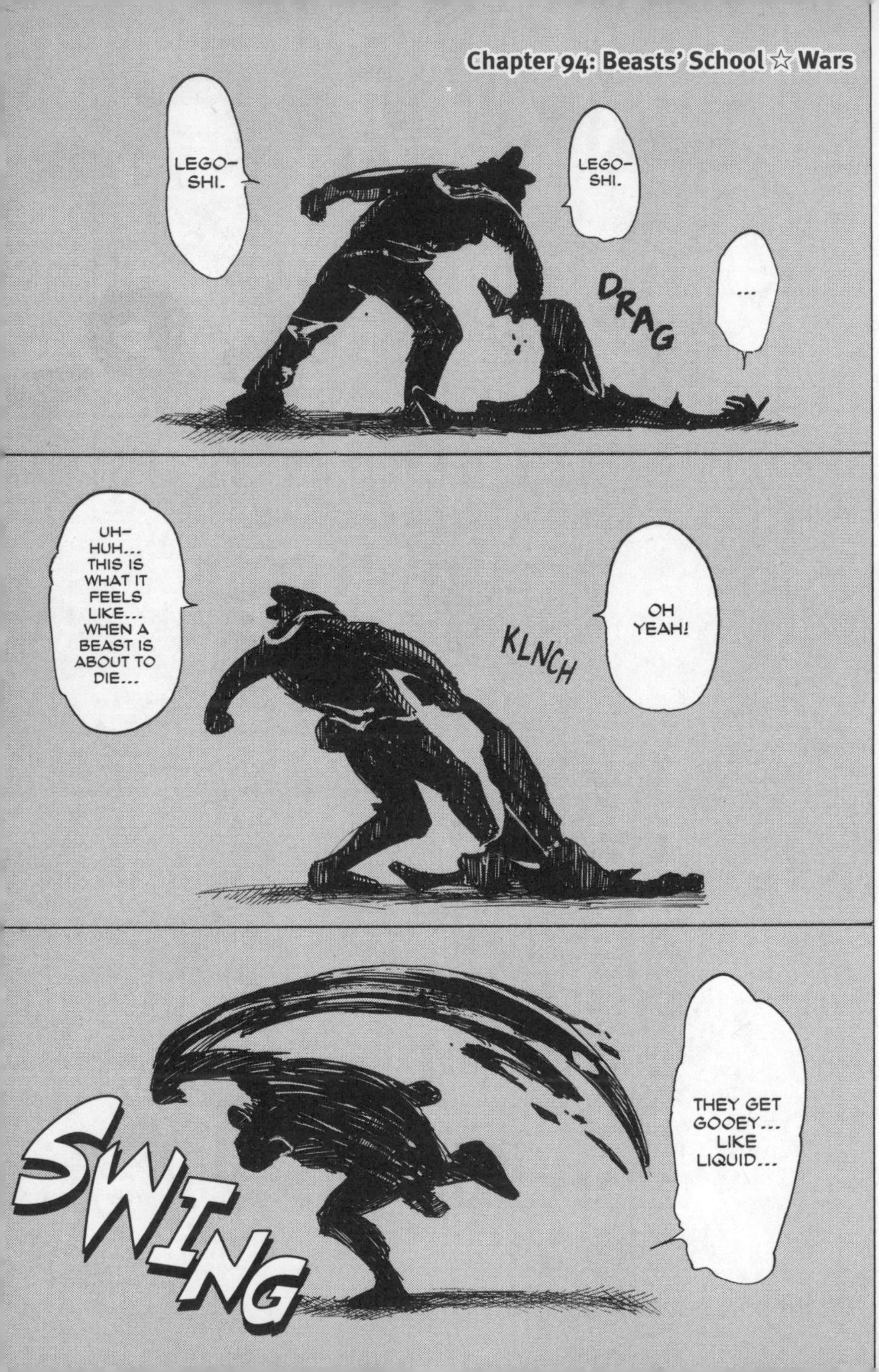
...
DRAG
LEGO-SHI.
LEGO-SHI.
OH YEAH!
KLNCH
UH-HUH... THIS IS WHAT IT FEELS LIKE... WHEN A BEAST IS ABOUT TO DIE...
THEY GET GOOEY... LIKE LIQUID...
SWING

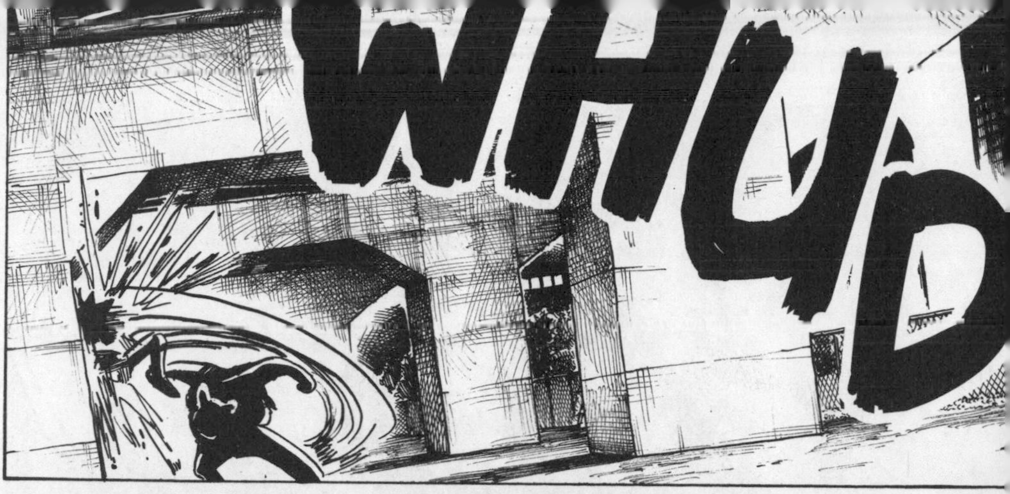
WHUD

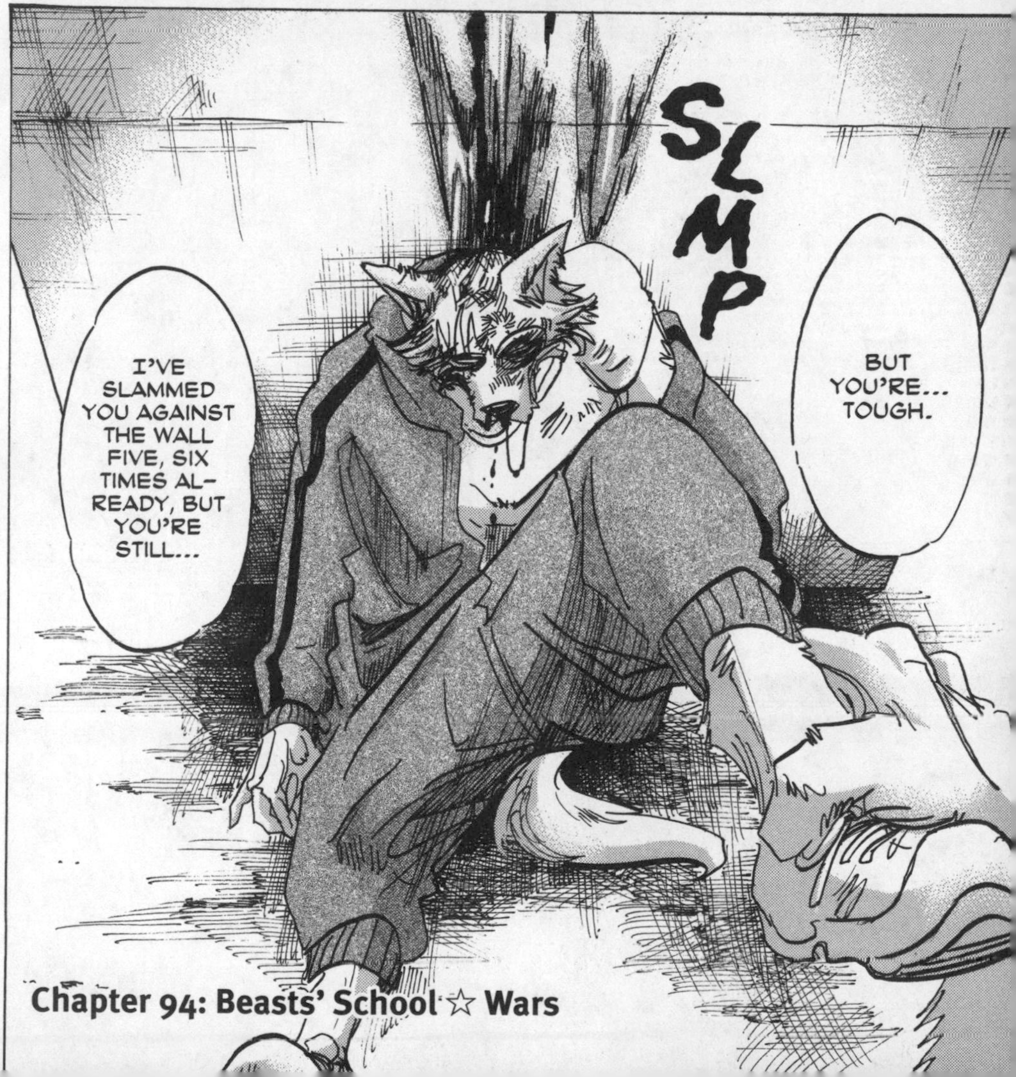
SLMP
I'VE SLAMMED YOU AGAINST THE WALL FIVE, SIX TIMES AL-READY, BUT YOU'RE STILL...
BUT YOU'RE... TOUGH.

Chapter 94: Beasts' School ☆ Wars

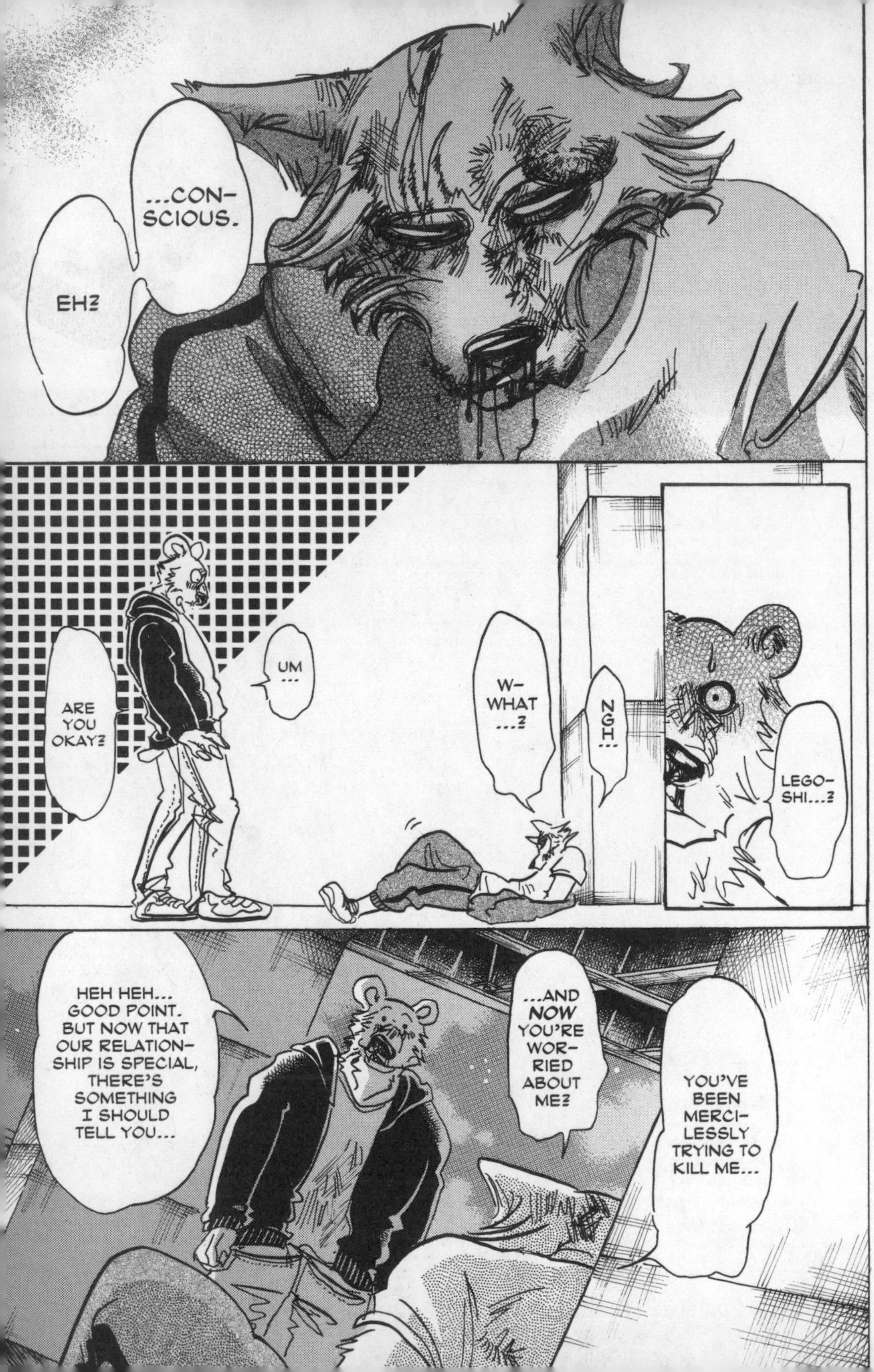
...CON-SCIOUS.
EH?
LEGO-SHI...?
NGH...
W-WHAT...?
UM...
ARE YOU OKAY?
YOU'VE BEEN MERCI-LESSLY TRYING TO KILL ME...
...AND NOW YOU'RE WOR-RIED ABOUT ME?
HEH HEH... GOOD POINT. BUT NOW THAT OUR RELATION-SHIP IS SPECIAL, THERE'S SOMETHING I SHOULD TELL YOU...

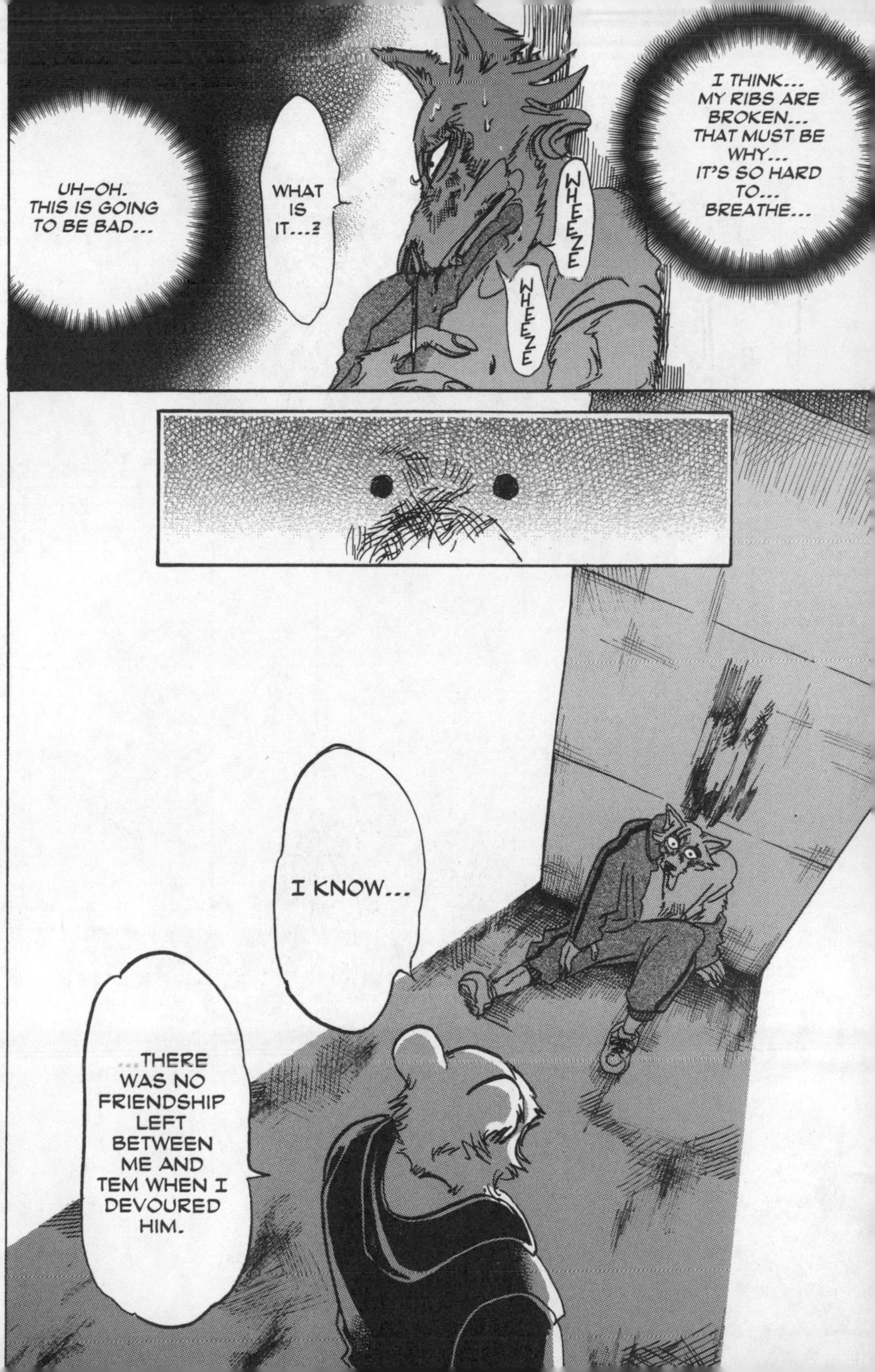
I THINK... MY RIBS ARE BROKEN... THAT MUST BE WHY... IT'S SO HARD TO... BREATHE...
WHEEZE
WHEEZE
WHAT IS IT...?
UH-OH. THIS IS GOING TO BE BAD...
I KNOW...
...THERE WAS NO FRIENDSHIP LEFT BETWEEN ME AND TEM WHEN I DEVOURED HIM.

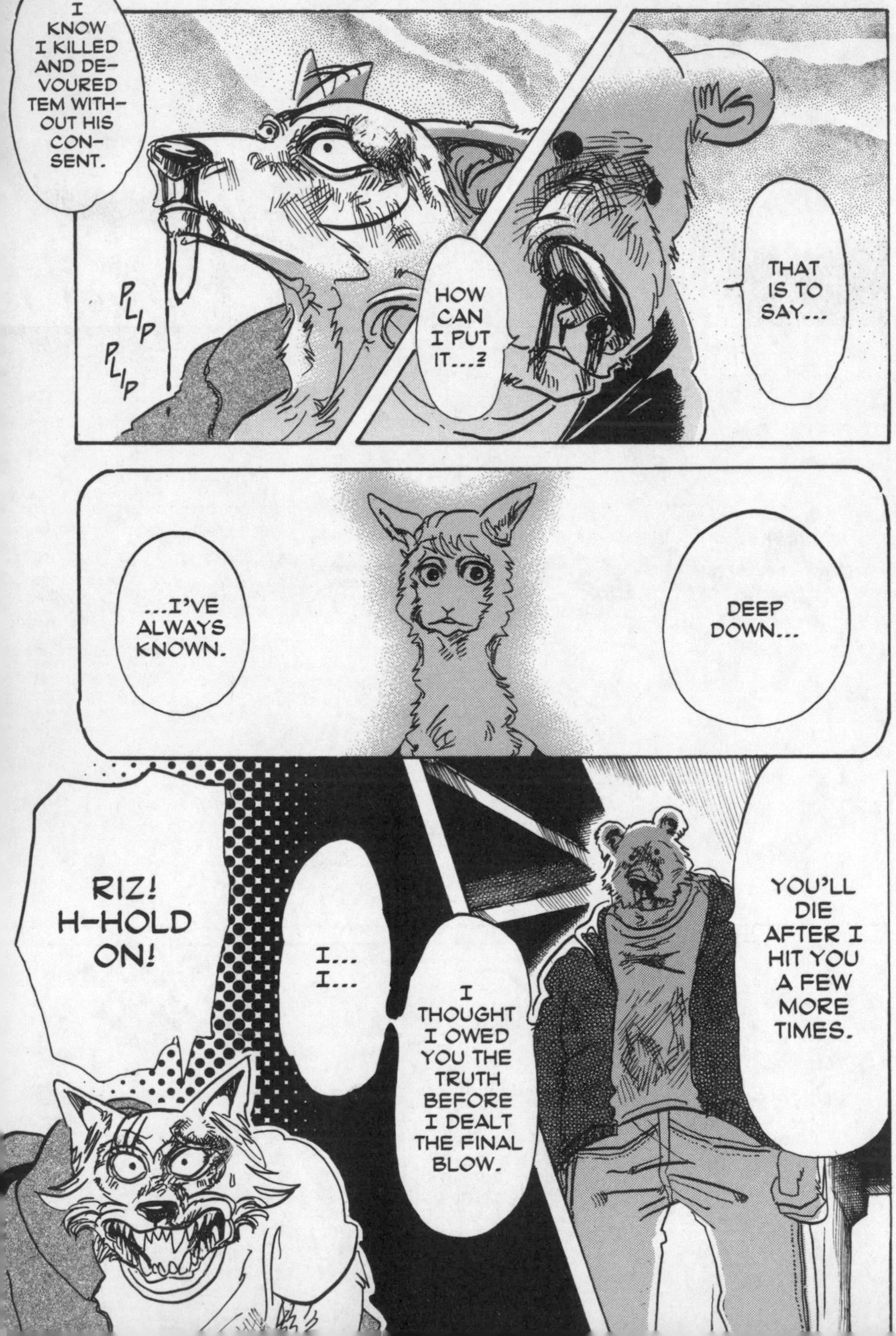
THAT IS TO SAY...
HOW CAN I PUT IT...?
I KNOW I KILLED AND DE-VOURED TEM WITH-OUT HIS CON-SENT.
PLIP PLIP
DEEP DOWN...
...I'VE ALWAYS KNOWN.
YOU'LL DIE AFTER I HIT YOU A FEW MORE TIMES.
I THOUGHT I OWED YOU THE TRUTH BEFORE I DEALT THE FINAL BLOW.
I... I...
RIZ! H-HOLD ON!

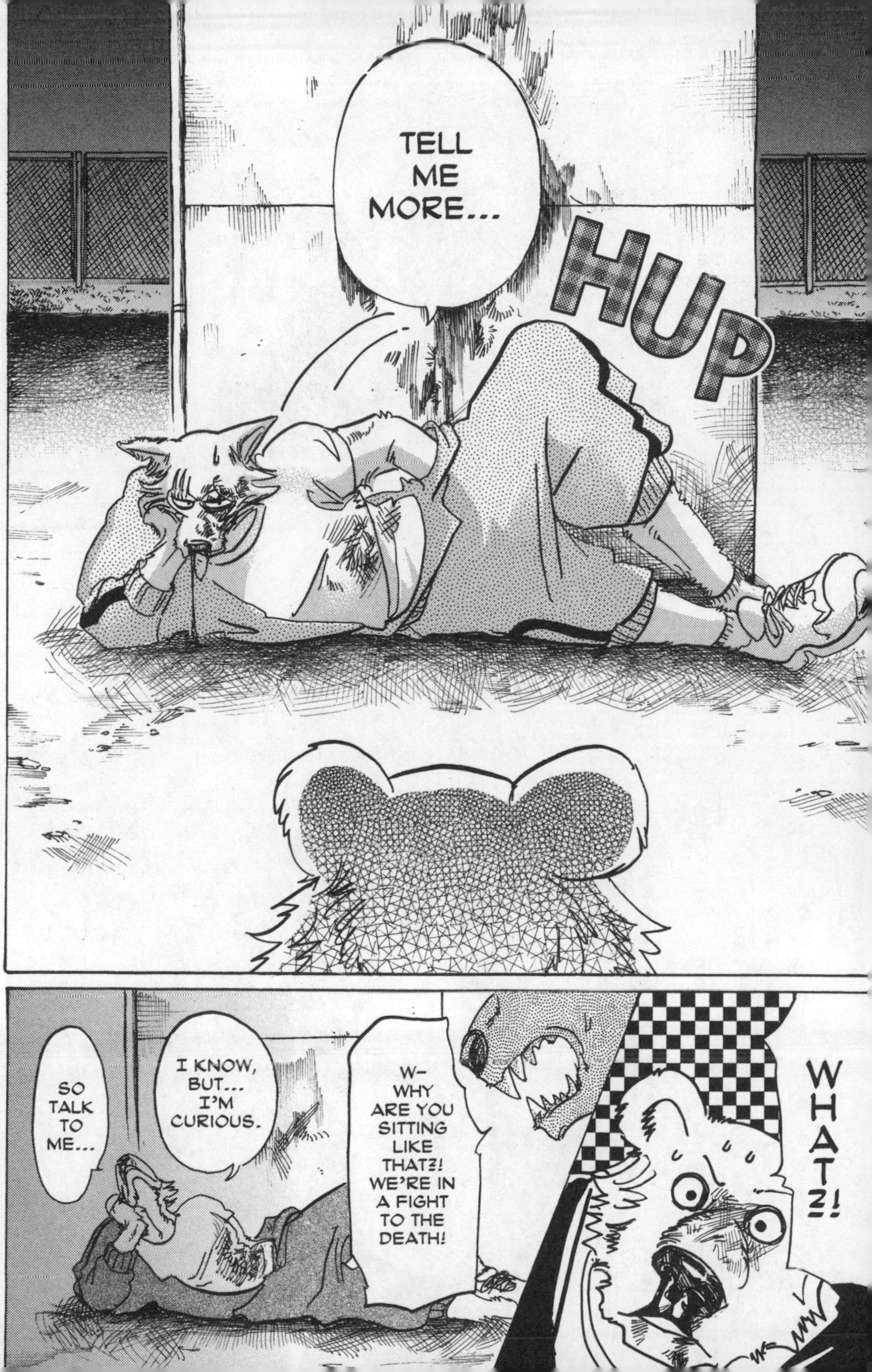
TELL ME MORE...
HUP
WHAT?!
W-WHY ARE YOU SITTING LIKE THAT?! WE'RE IN A FIGHT TO THE DEATH!
I KNOW, BUT... I'M CURIOUS.
SO TALK TO ME...

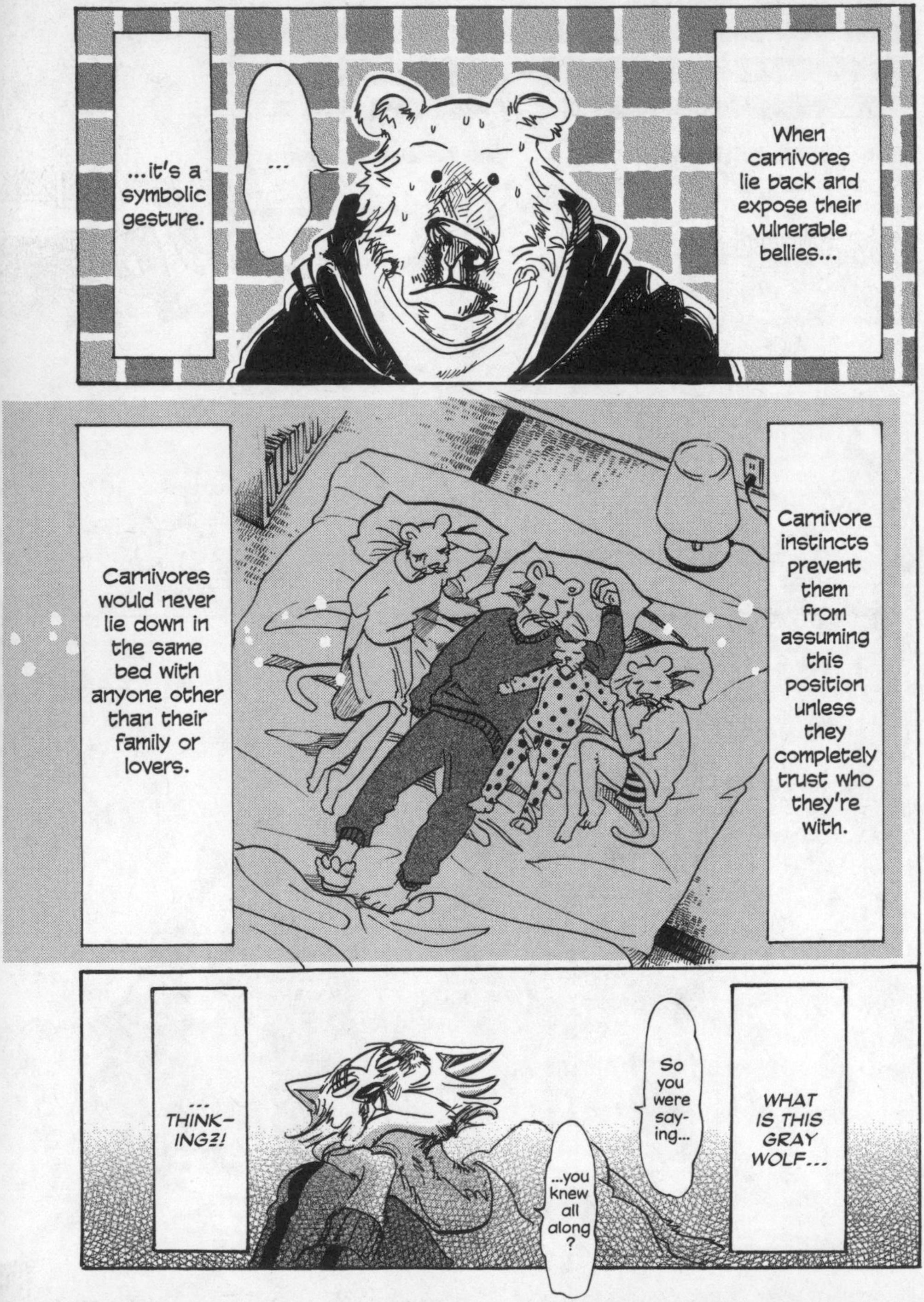
When carnivores lie back and expose their vulnerable bellies...
...
...it's a symbolic gesture.
Carnivore instincts prevent them from assuming this position unless they completely trust who they're with.
Carnivores would never lie down in the same bed with anyone other than their family or lovers.
WHAT IS THIS GRAY WOLF...
So you were saying...
...you knew all along?
...THINKING?!

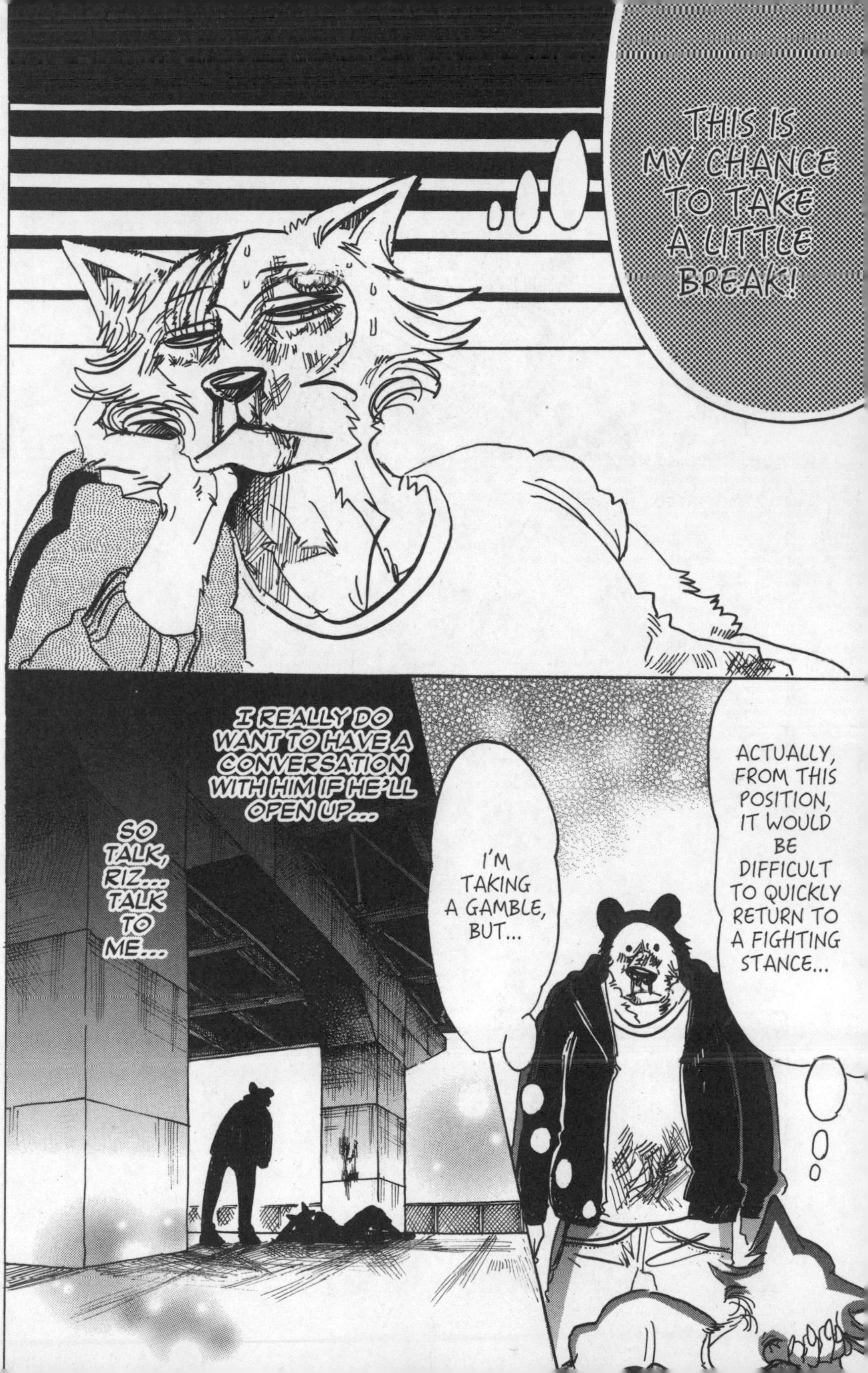
THIS IS MY CHANCE TO TAKE A LITTLE BREAK!
ACTUALLY, FROM THIS POSITION, IT WOULD BE DIFFICULT TO QUICKLY RETURN TO A FIGHTING STANCE...
I'M TAKING A GAMBLE, BUT...
I REALLY DO WANT TO HAVE A CONVERSATION WITH HIM IF HE'LL OPEN UP...
SO TALK, RIZ... TALK TO ME...

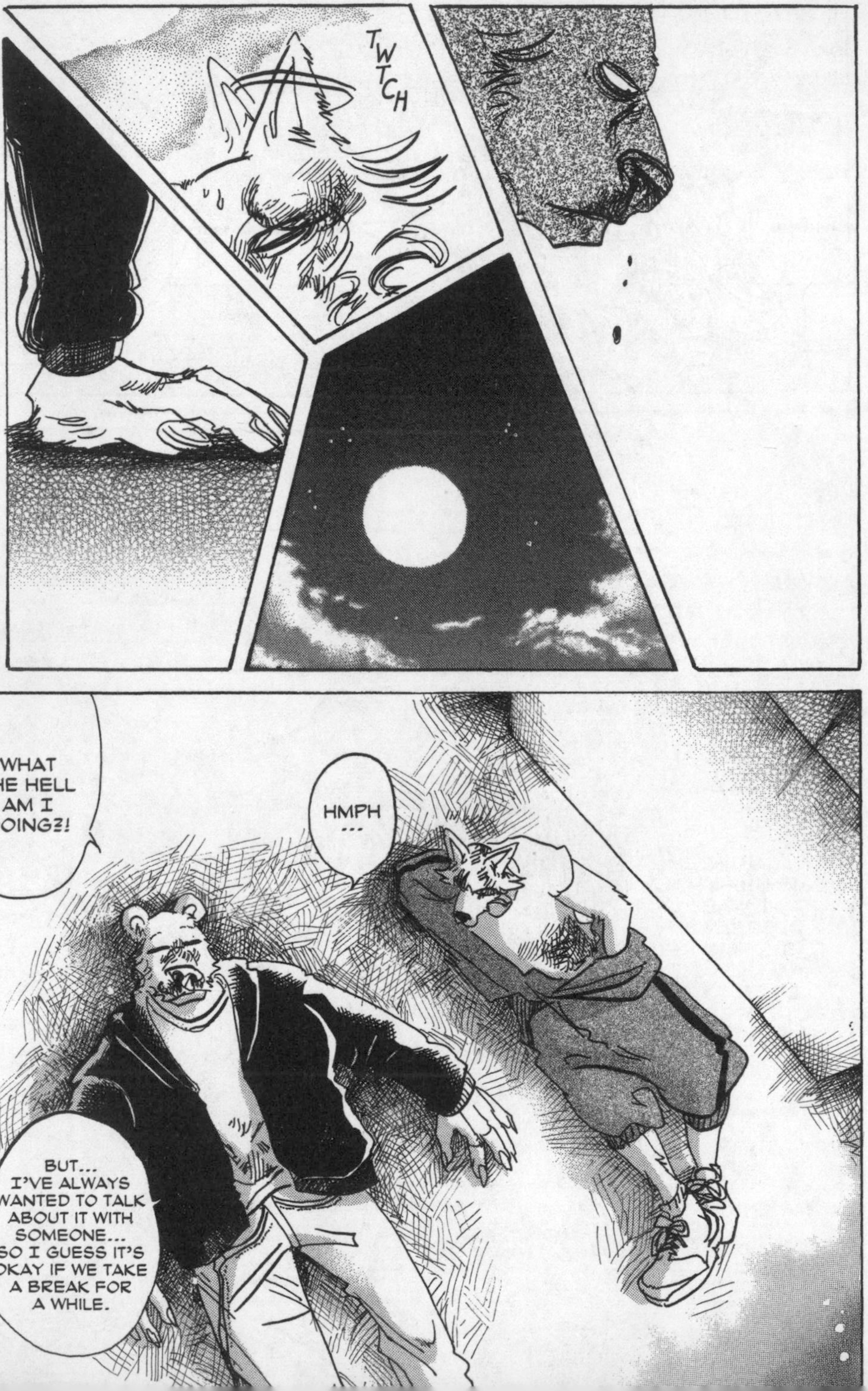
TWTCH
HMPH...
WHAT THE HELL AM I DOING?!
BUT... I'VE ALWAYS WANTED TO TALK ABOUT IT WITH SOMEONE... SO I GUESS IT'S OKAY IF WE TAKE A BREAK FOR A WHILE.

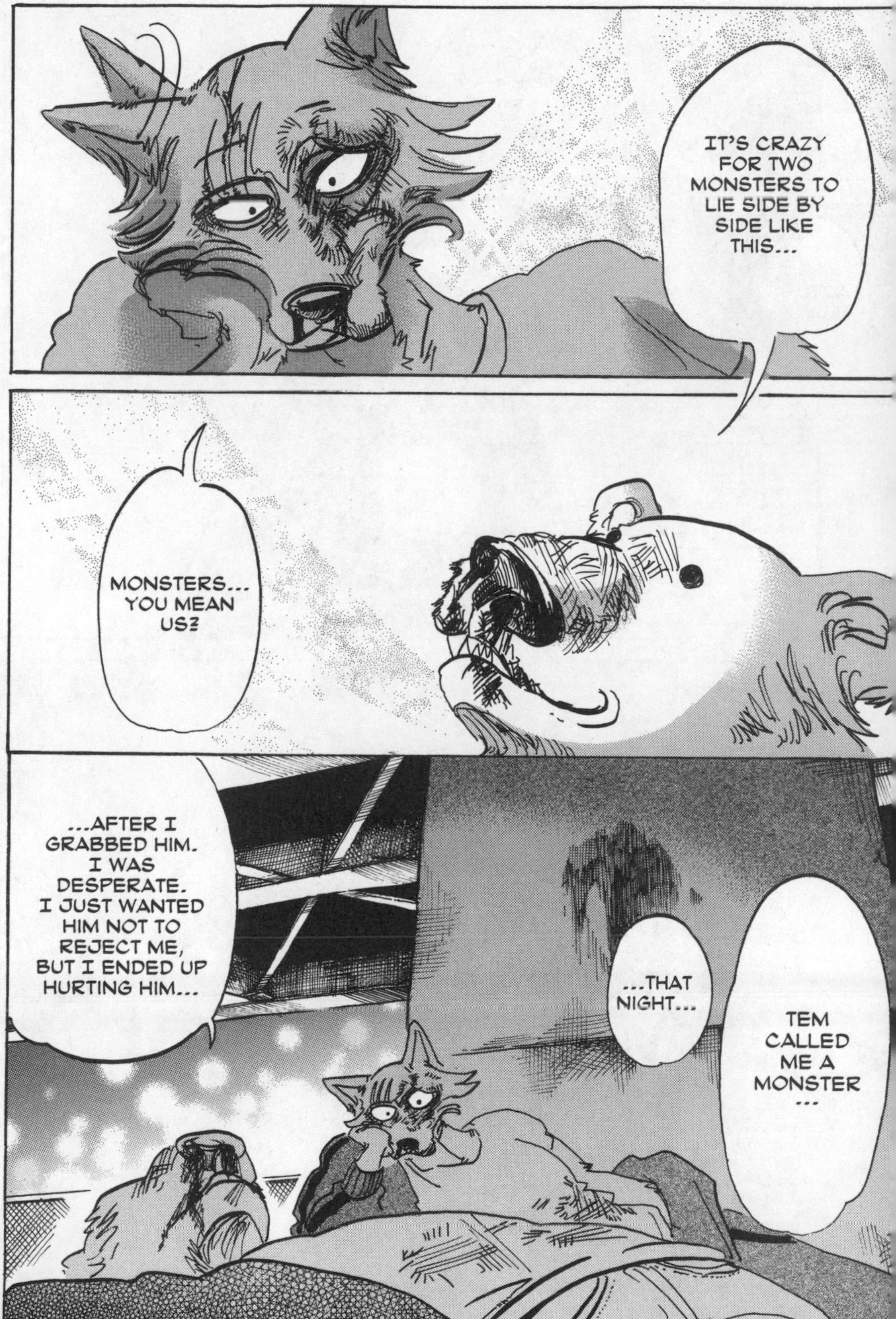
IT'S CRAZY FOR TWO MONSTERS TO LIE SIDE BY SIDE LIKE THIS...
MONSTERS... YOU MEAN US?
TEM CALLED ME A MONSTER ...
...THAT NIGHT...
...AFTER I GRABBED HIM. I WAS DESPERATE. I JUST WANTED HIM NOT TO REJECT ME, BUT I ENDED UP HURTING HIM...

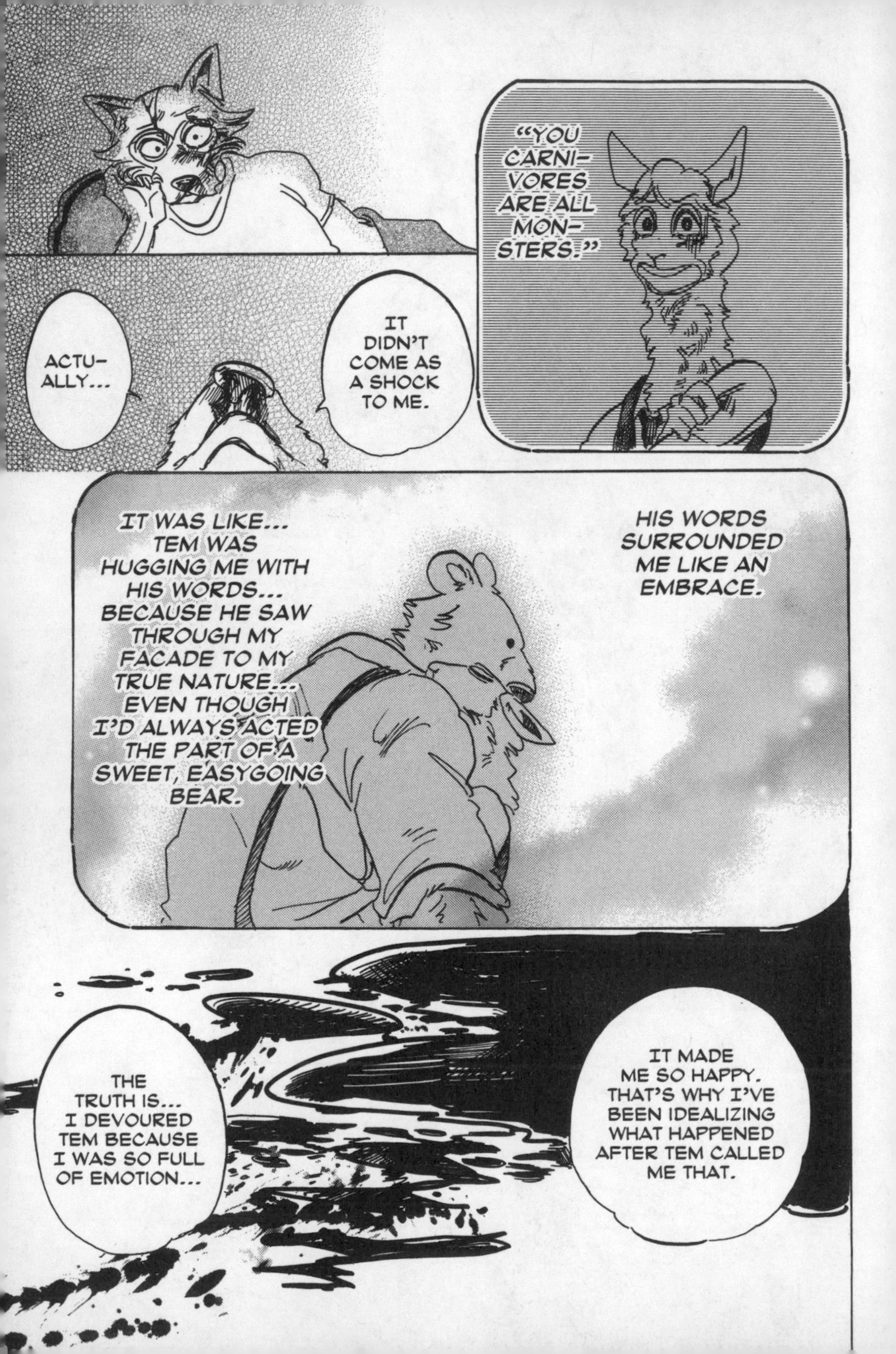
"YOU CARNIVORES ARE ALL MONSTERS."
IT DIDN'T COME AS A SHOCK TO ME.
ACTUALLY...
HIS WORDS SURROUNDED ME LIKE AN EMBRACE.
IT WAS LIKE... TEM WAS HUGGING ME WITH HIS WORDS... BECAUSE HE SAW THROUGH MY FACADE TO MY TRUE NATURE... EVEN THOUGH I'D ALWAYS ACTED THE PART OF A SWEET, EASYGOING BEAR.
IT MADE ME SO HAPPY. THAT'S WHY I'VE BEEN IDEALIZING WHAT HAPPENED AFTER TEM CALLED ME THAT.
THE TRUTH IS... I DEVOURED TEM BECAUSE I WAS SO FULL OF EMOTION...

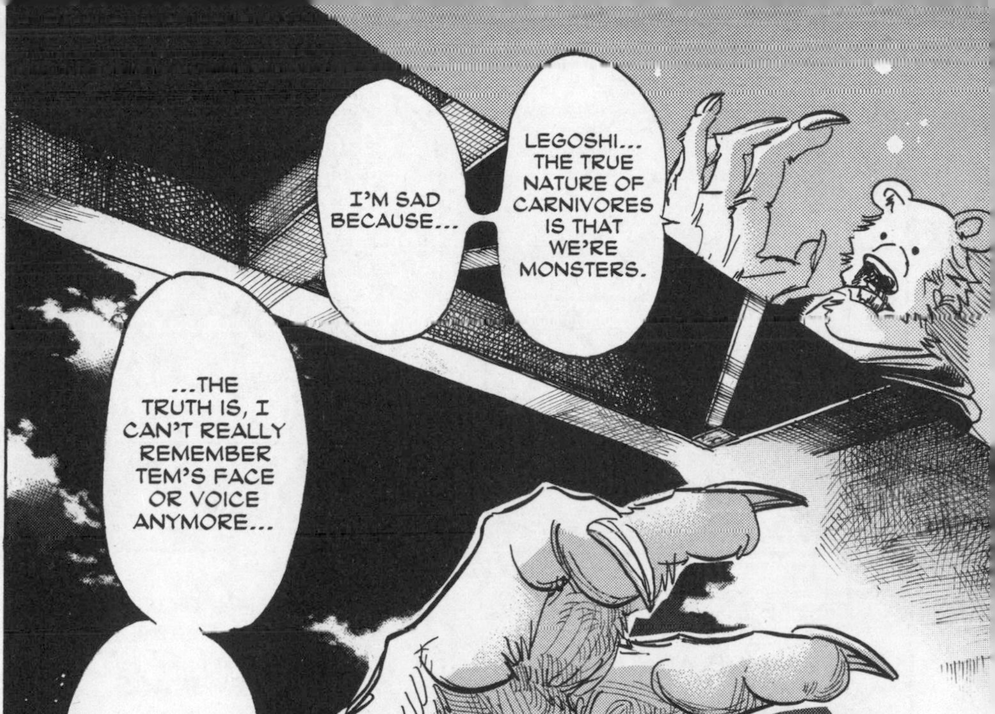
LEGOSHI... THE TRUE NATURE OF CARNIVORES IS THAT WE'RE MONSTERS.
I'M SAD BECAUSE...
...THE TRUTH IS, I CAN'T REALLY REMEMBER TEM'S FACE OR VOICE ANYMORE...
...BUT I CAN STILL VIVIDLY RECALL HIS TASTE AND SMELL.
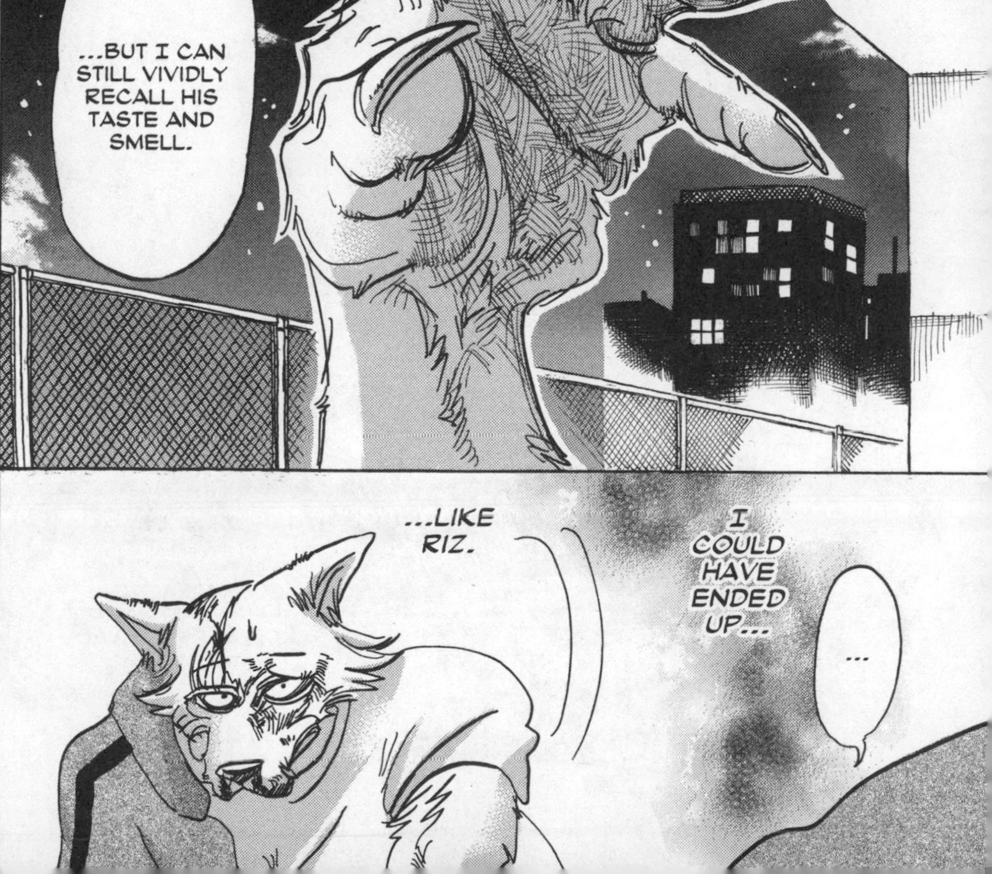
...
I COULD HAVE ENDED UP...
...LIKE RIZ.

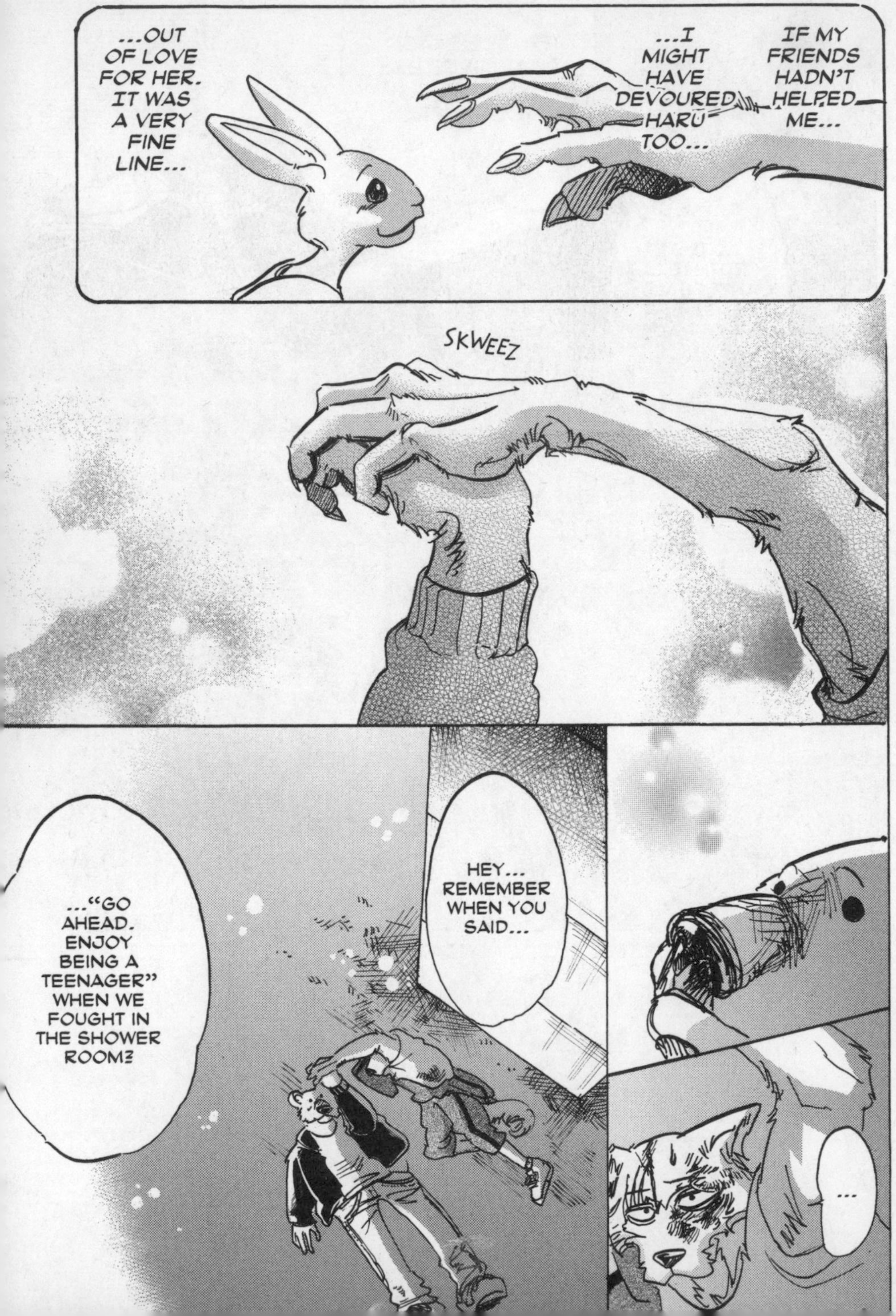
IF MY FRIENDS HADN'T HELPED ME...
...I MIGHT HAVE DEVOURED HARU TOO...
...OUT OF LOVE FOR HER. IT WAS A VERY FINE LINE...
SKWEEZ
...
HEY... REMEMBER WHEN YOU SAID...
..."GO AHEAD. ENJOY BEING A TEENAGER" WHEN WE FOUGHT IN THE SHOWER ROOM?

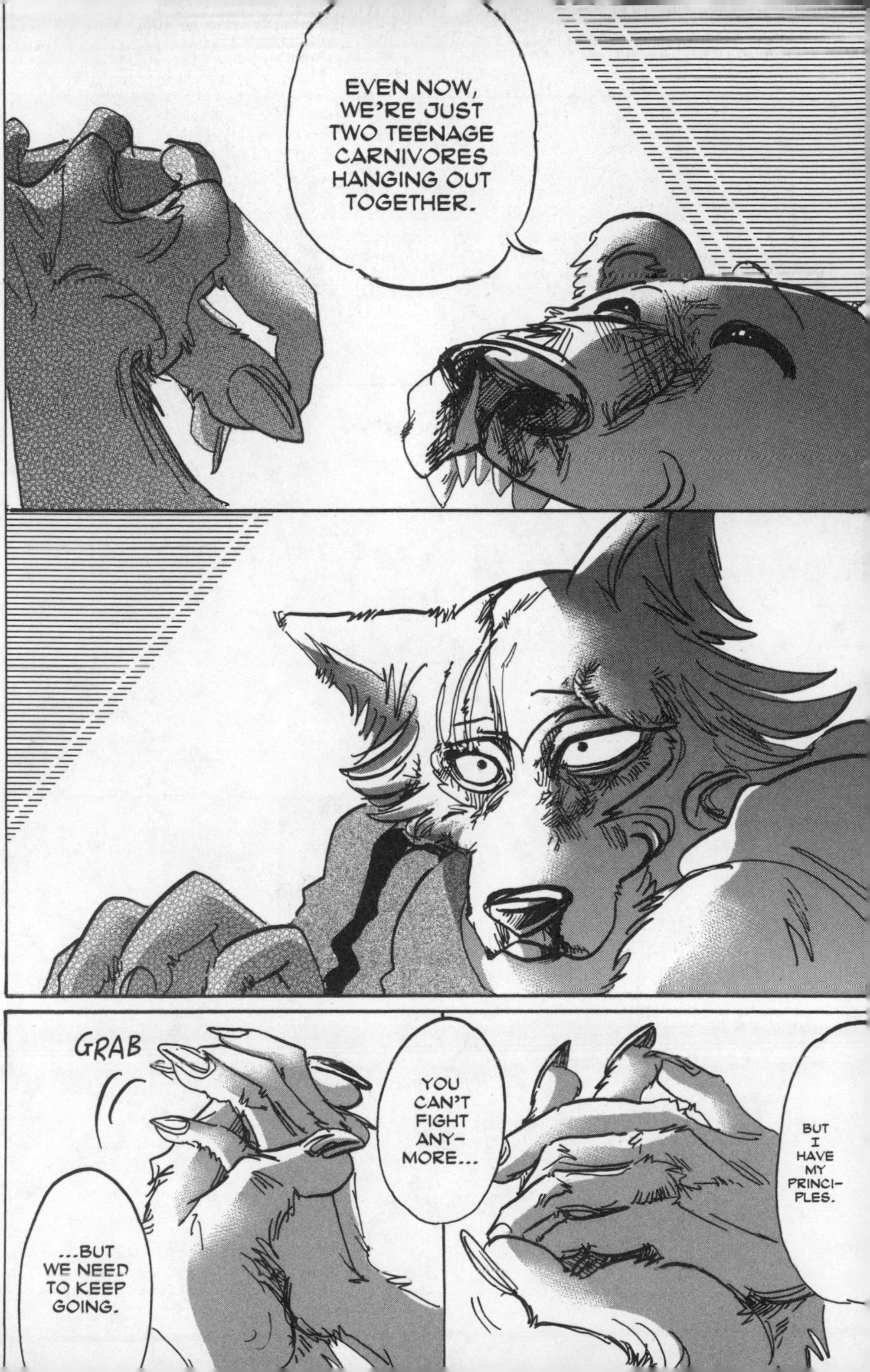
EVEN NOW, WE'RE JUST TWO TEENAGE CARNIVORES HANGING OUT TOGETHER.
BUT I HAVE MY PRINCI-PLES.
YOU CAN'T FIGHT ANY-MORE...
GRAB
...BUT WE NEED TO KEEP GOING.

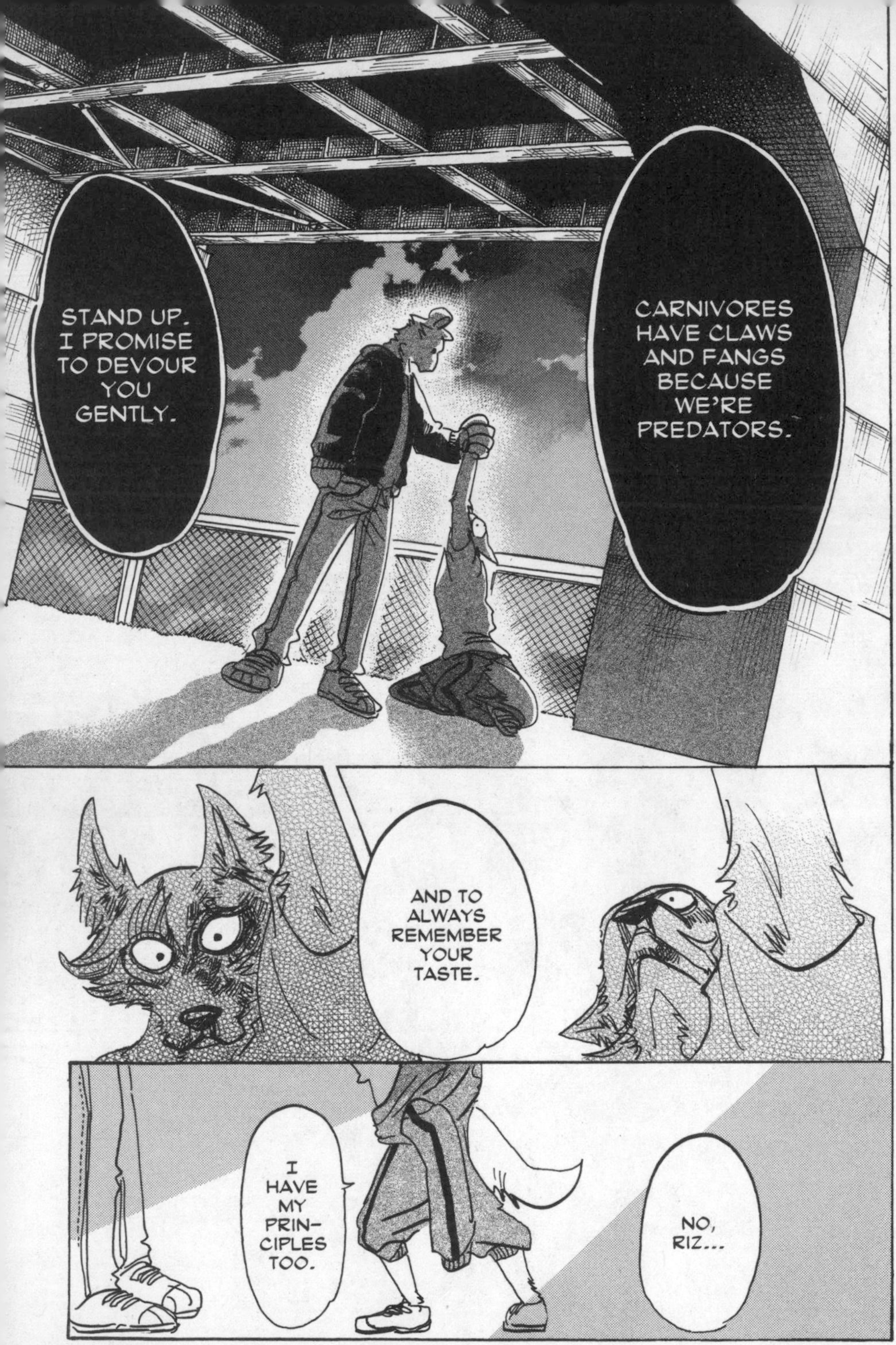
CARNIVORES HAVE CLAWS AND FANGS BECAUSE WE'RE PREDATORS.
STAND UP. I PROMISE TO DEVOUR YOU GENTLY.
AND TO ALWAYS REMEMBER YOUR TASTE.
NO, RIZ...
I HAVE MY PRIN-CIPLES TOO.

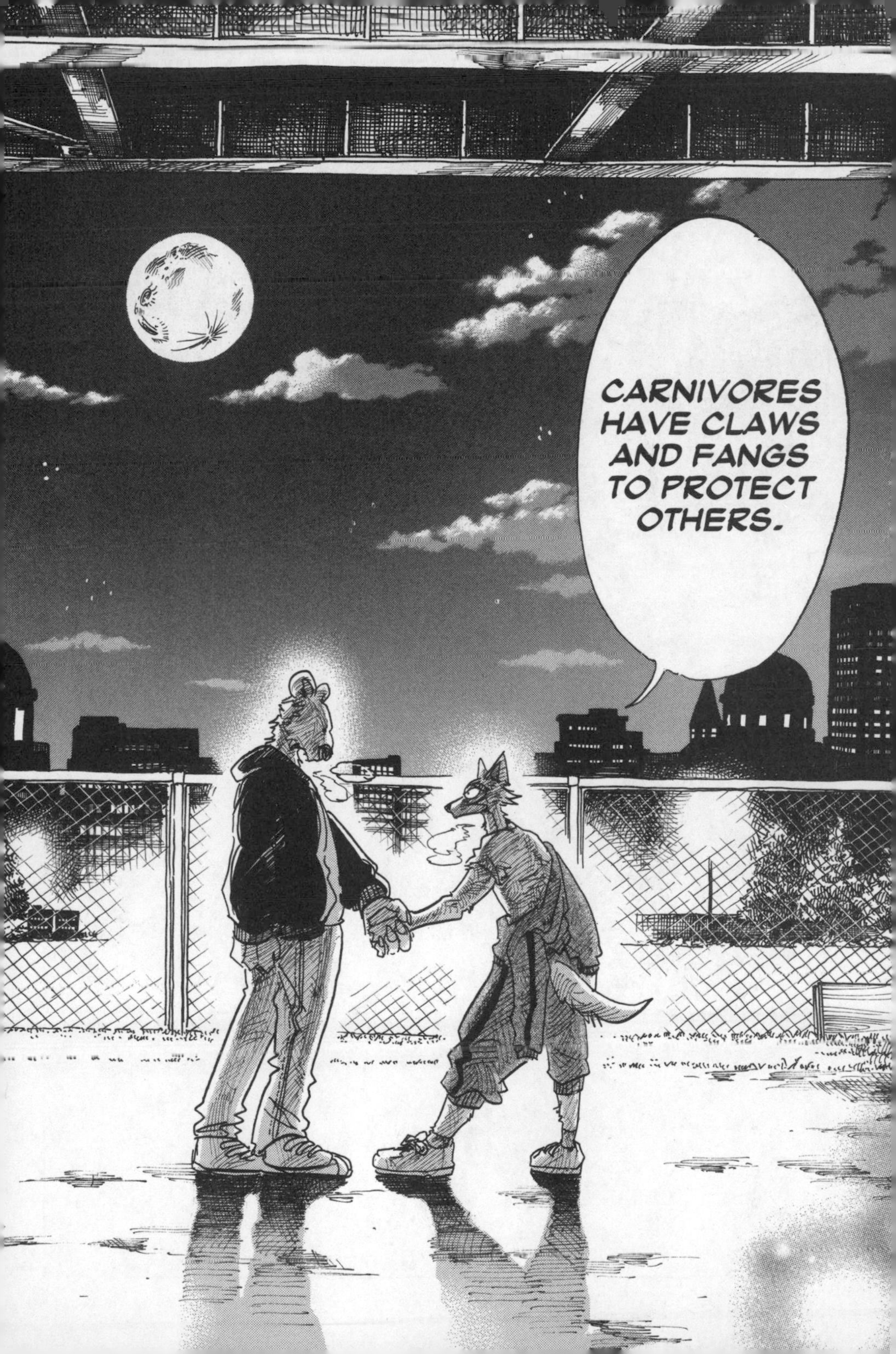
CARNIVORES HAVE CLAWS AND FANGS TO PROTECT OTHERS.

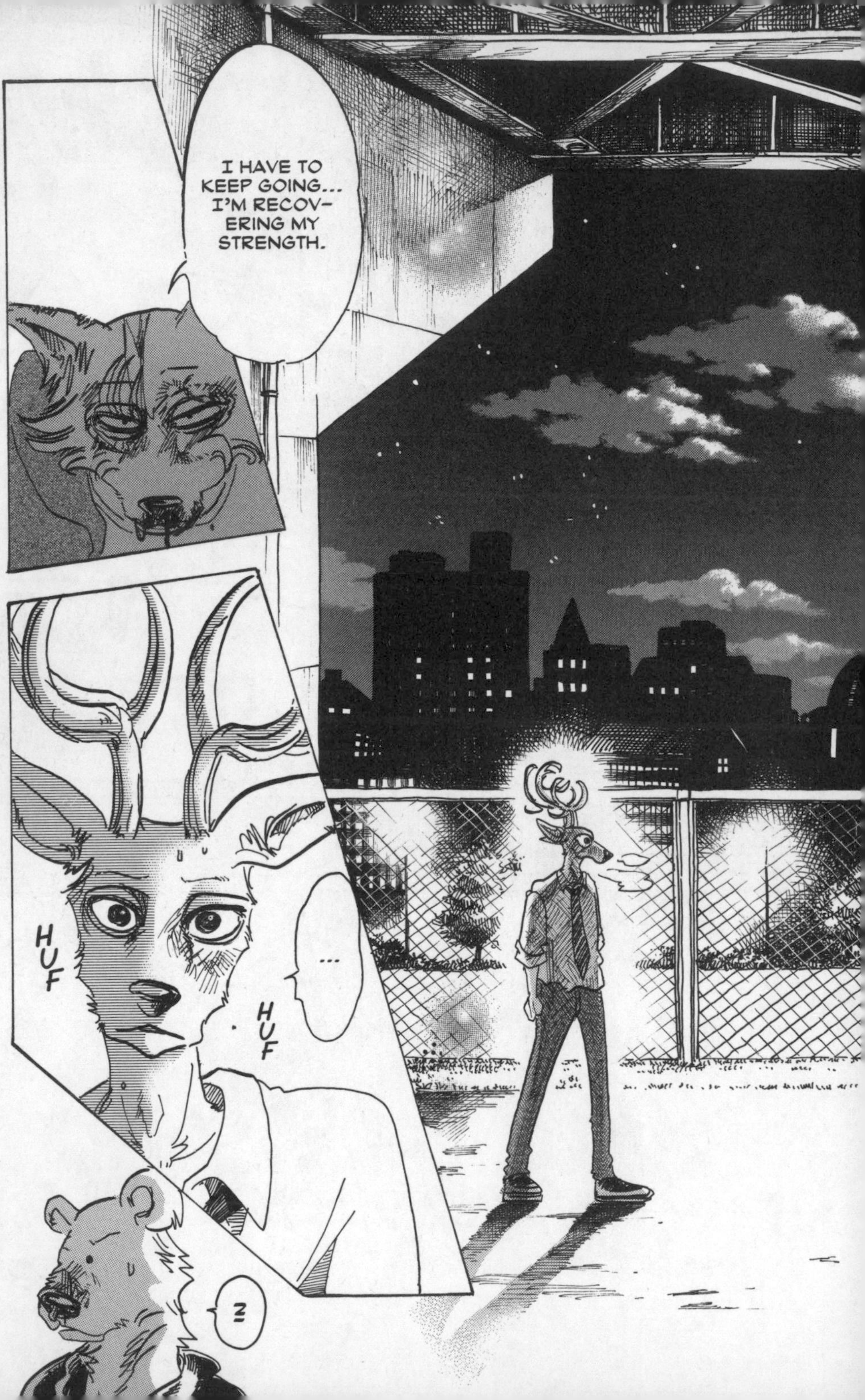
I HAVE TO KEEP GOING... I'M RECOVERING MY STRENGTH.
HUF HUF
...

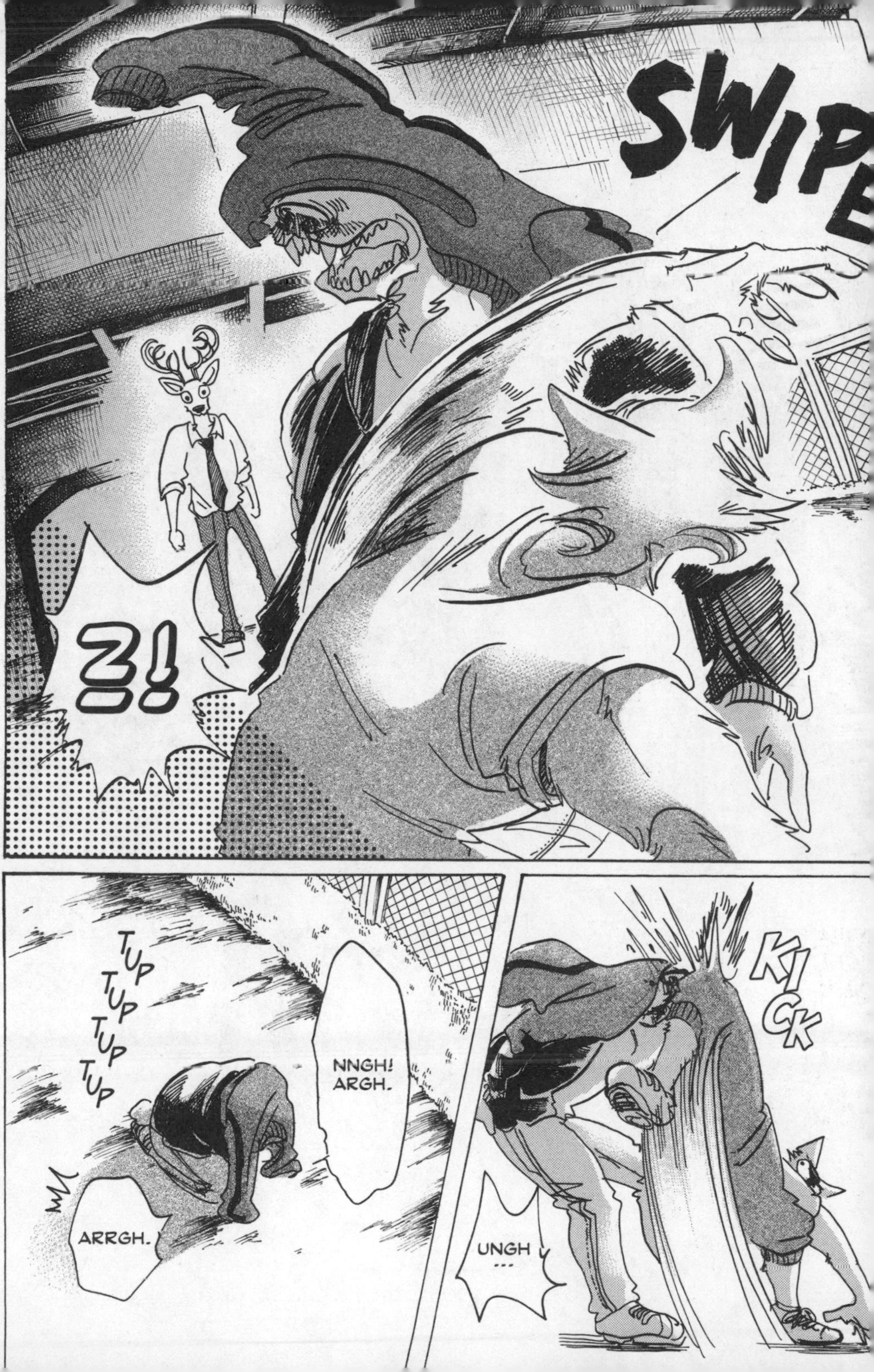
SWIPE
Z!
KICK
UNGH ...
NNGH! ARGH.
TUP TUP TUP TUP TUP
ARRGH.

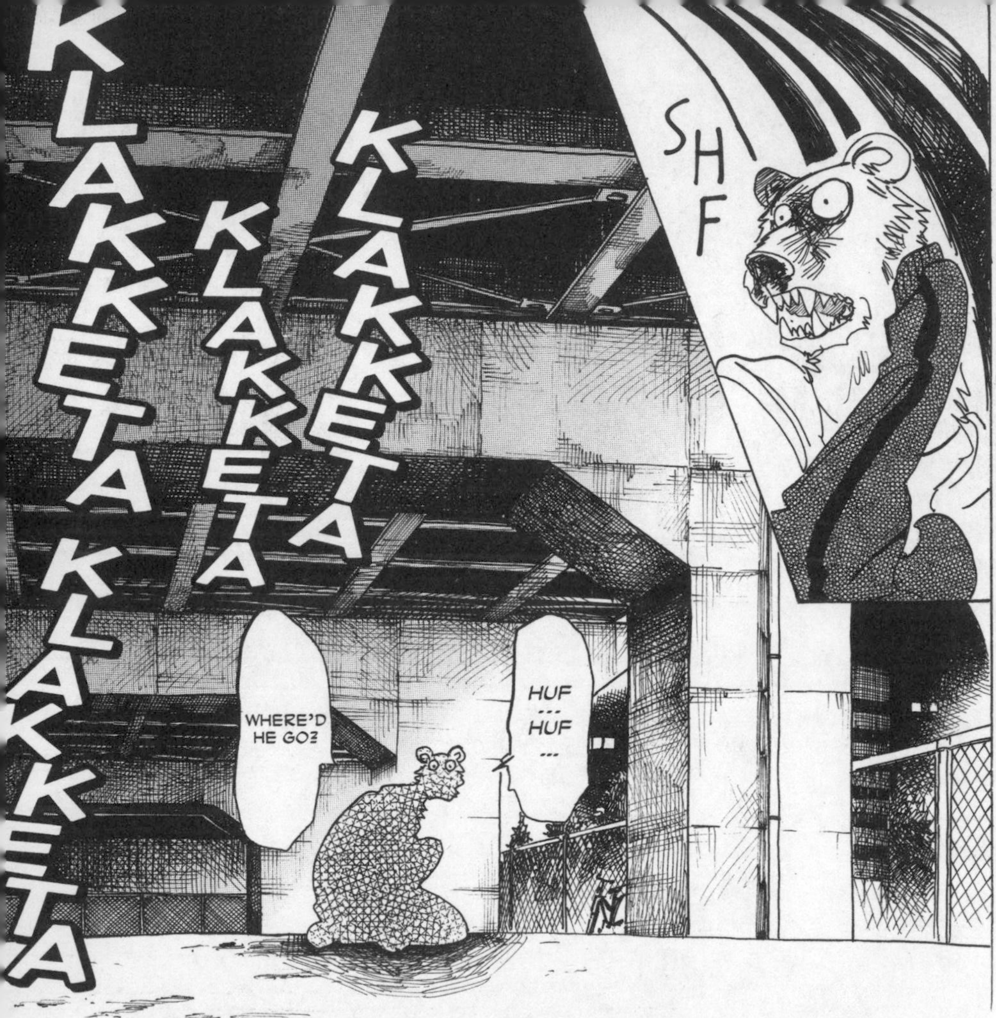
SHF
HUF ... HUF ...
WHERE'D HE GO?
KLAKKETA KLAKKETA
KLAKKETA
KLAKKETA KLAKKETA
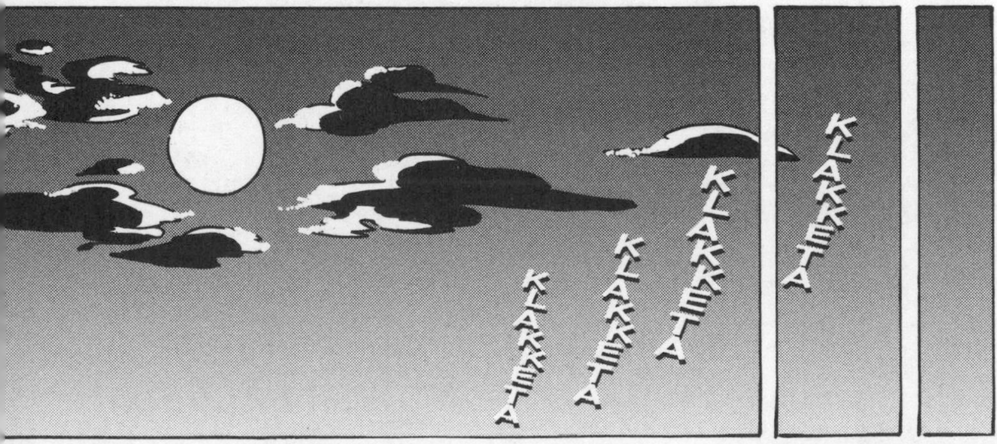
KLAKKETA
KLAKKETA
KLAKKETA
KLAKKETA

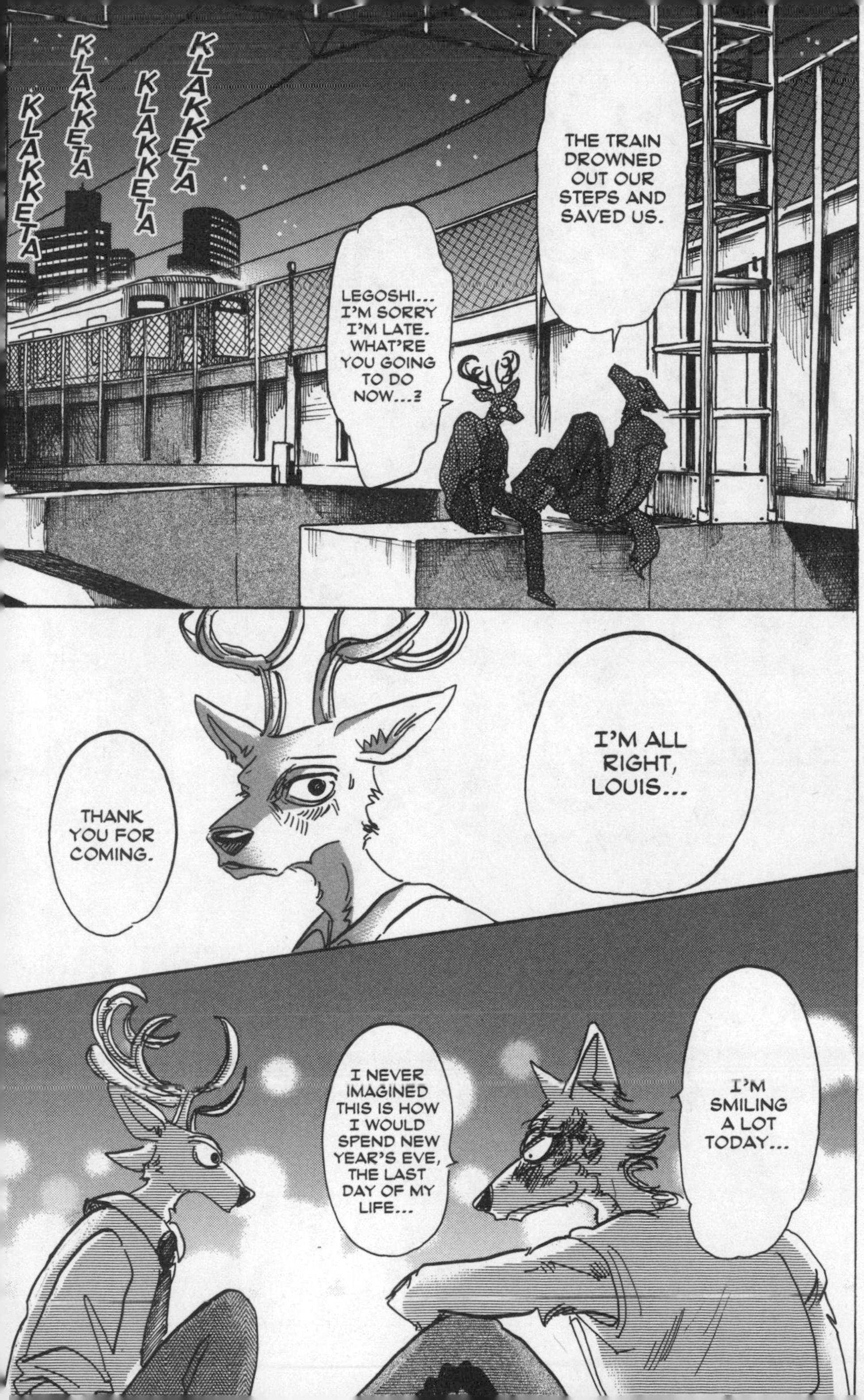
THE TRAIN DROWNED OUT OUR STEPS AND SAVED US.
LEGOSHI... I'M SORRY I'M LATE. WHAT'RE YOU GOING TO DO NOW...?
KLAKKETA
KLAKKETA
KLAKKETA
I'M ALL RIGHT, LOUIS...
THANK YOU FOR COMING.
I'M SMILING A LOT TODAY...
I NEVER IMAGINED THIS IS HOW I WOULD SPEND NEW YEAR'S EVE, THE LAST DAY OF MY LIFE...

Chapter 95: Eighteenfold Concentrated Drop

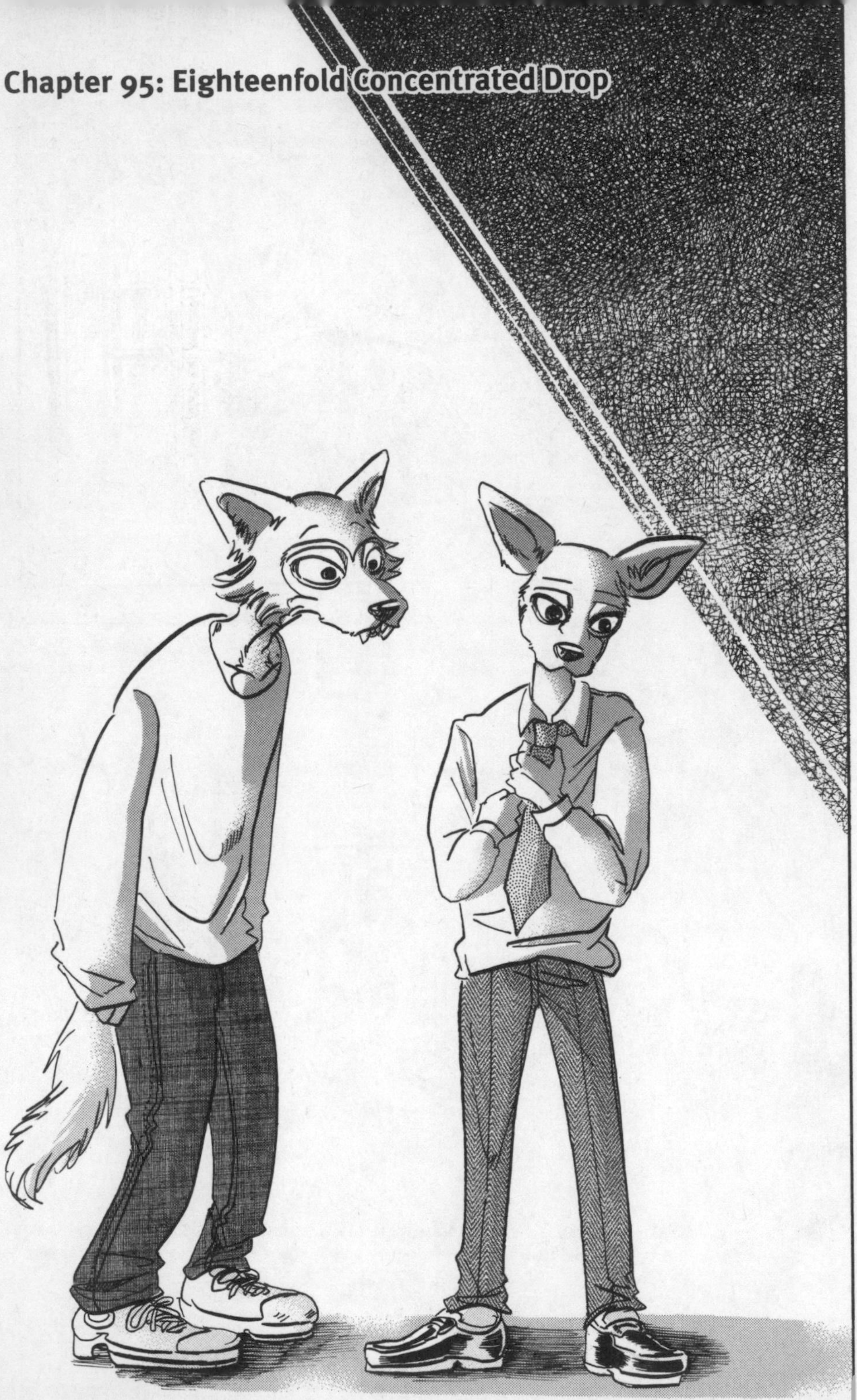

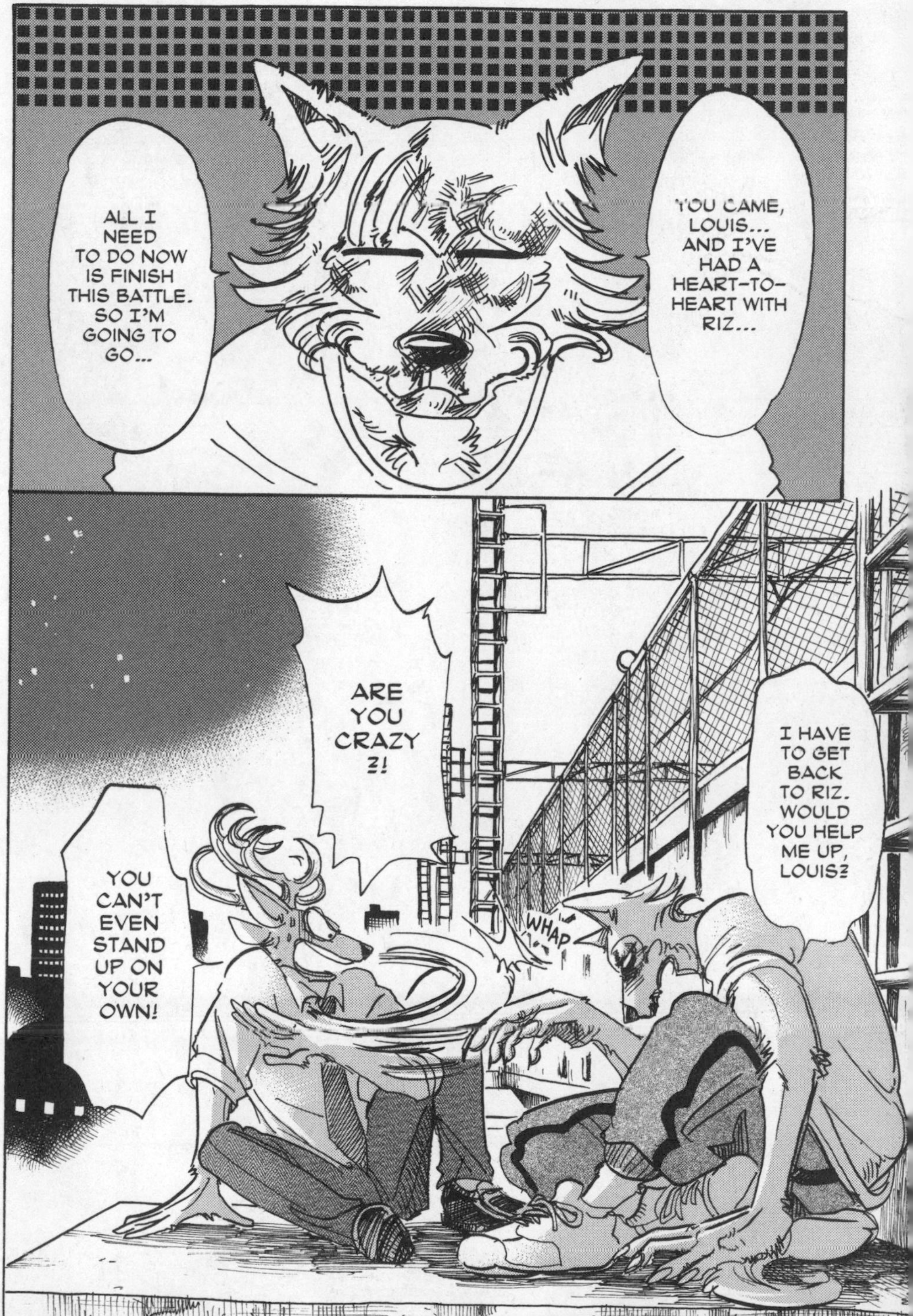
YOU CAME, LOUIS... AND I'VE HAD A HEART-TO-HEART WITH RIZ...
ALL I NEED TO DO NOW IS FINISH THIS BATTLE. SO I'M GOING TO GO...
I HAVE TO GET BACK TO RIZ. WOULD YOU HELP ME UP, LOUIS?
WHAP
ARE YOU CRAZY?!
YOU CAN'T EVEN STAND UP ON YOUR OWN!

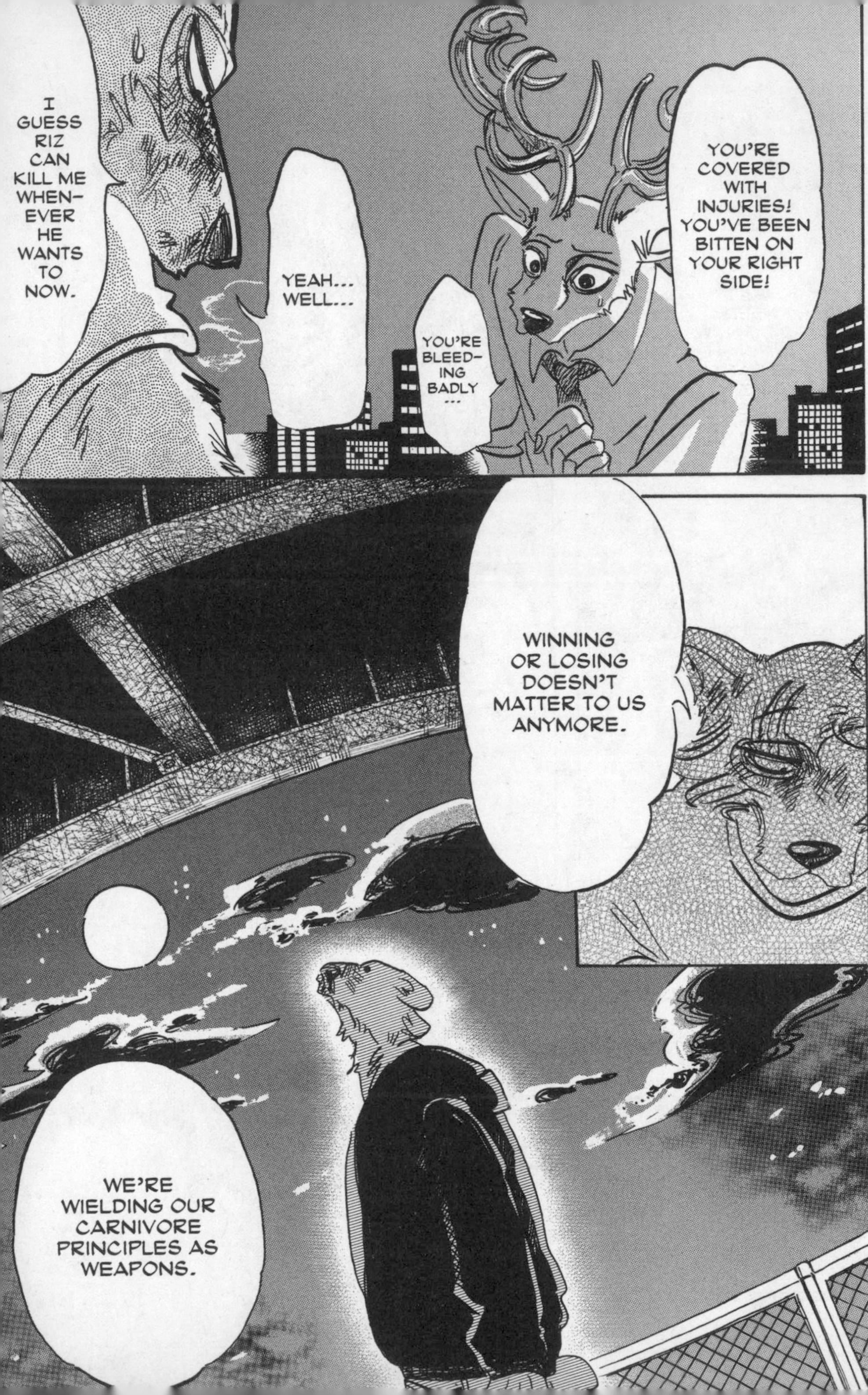
YOU'RE COVERED WITH INJURIES! YOU'VE BEEN BITTEN ON YOUR RIGHT SIDE!
YOU'RE BLEEDING BADLY...
YEAH... WELL...
I GUESS RIZ CAN KILL ME WHENEVER HE WANTS TO NOW.
WINNING OR LOSING DOESN'T MATTER TO US ANYMORE.
WE'RE WIELDING OUR CARNIVORE PRINCIPLES AS WEAPONS.

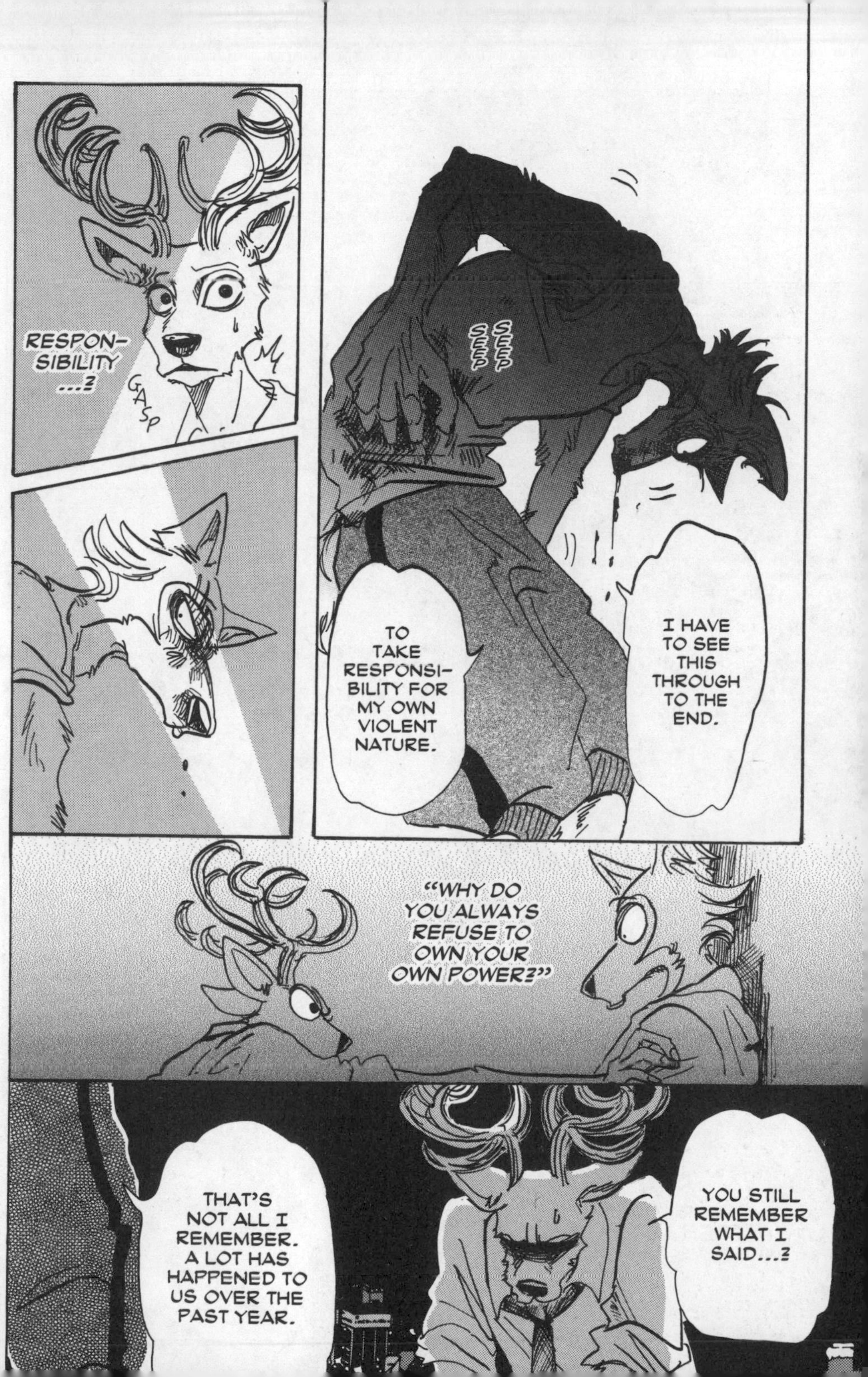
SEEP SEEP
I HAVE TO SEE THIS THROUGH TO THE END.
TO TAKE RESPONSIBILITY FOR MY OWN VIOLENT NATURE.
RESPONSIBILITY ...?
GASP
"WHY DO YOU ALWAYS REFUSE TO OWN YOUR OWN POWER?"
YOU STILL REMEMBER WHAT I SAID...?
THAT'S NOT ALL I REMEMBER. A LOT HAS HAPPENED TO US OVER THE PAST YEAR.

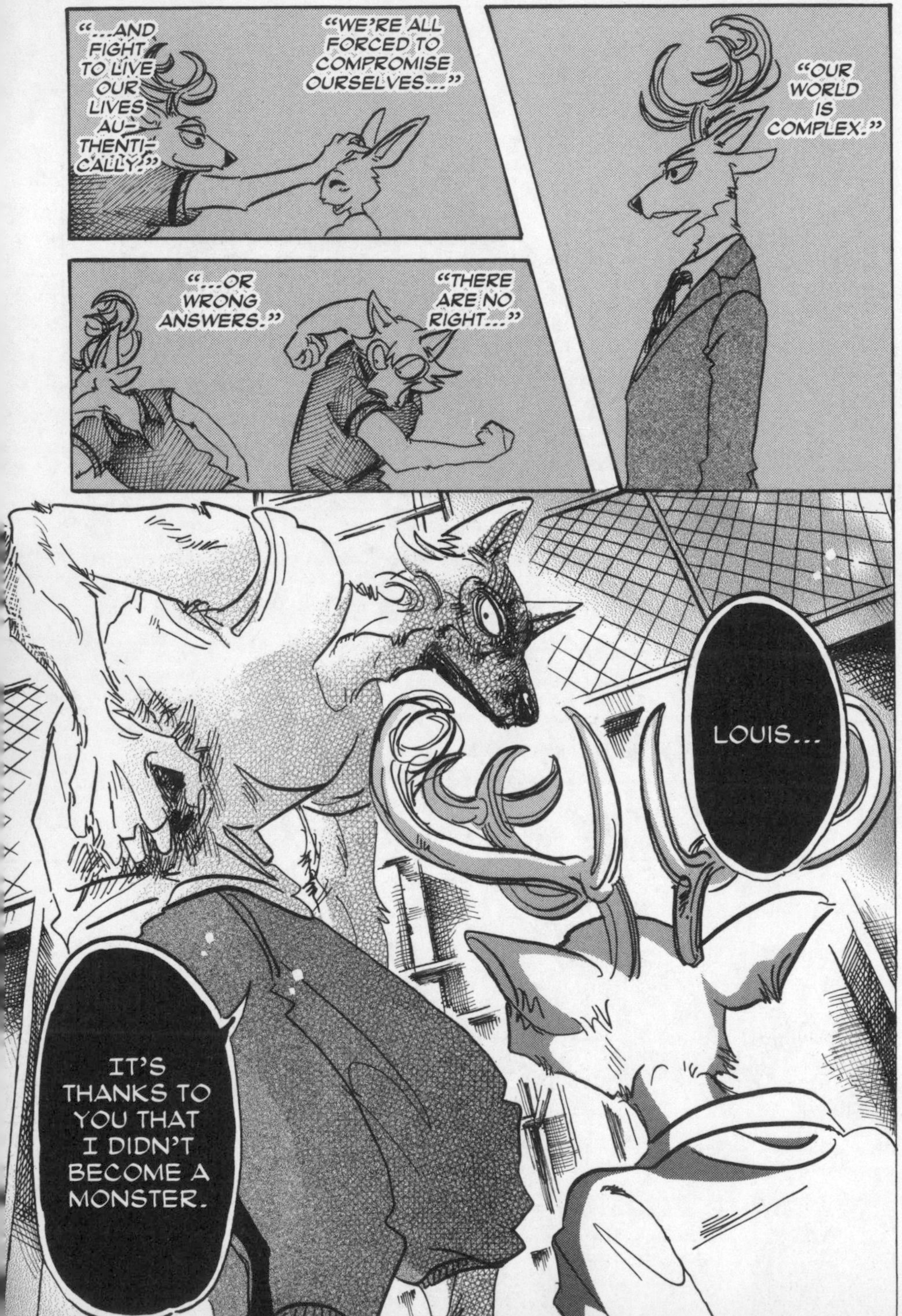
"OUR WORLD IS COMPLEX."
"WE'RE ALL FORCED TO COMPROMISE OURSELVES..."
"...AND FIGHT TO LIVE OUR LIVES AUTHENTICALLY."
"THERE ARE NO RIGHT..."
"...OR WRONG ANSWERS."
LOUIS...
IT'S THANKS TO YOU THAT I DIDN'T BECOME A MONSTER.

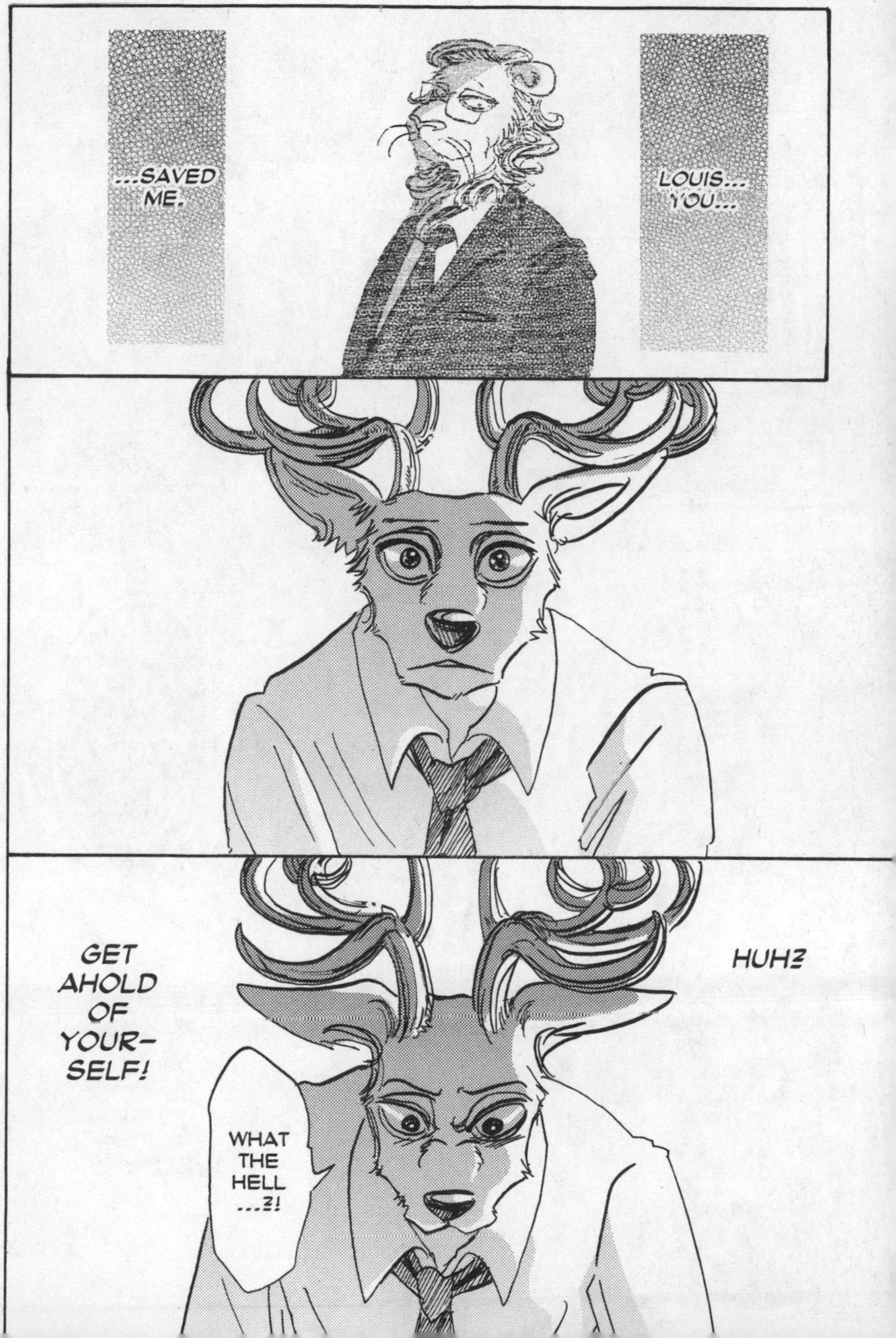
LOUIS... YOU...
...SAVED ME.
HUH?
GET AHOLD OF YOUR-SELF!
WHAT THE HELL ...?!

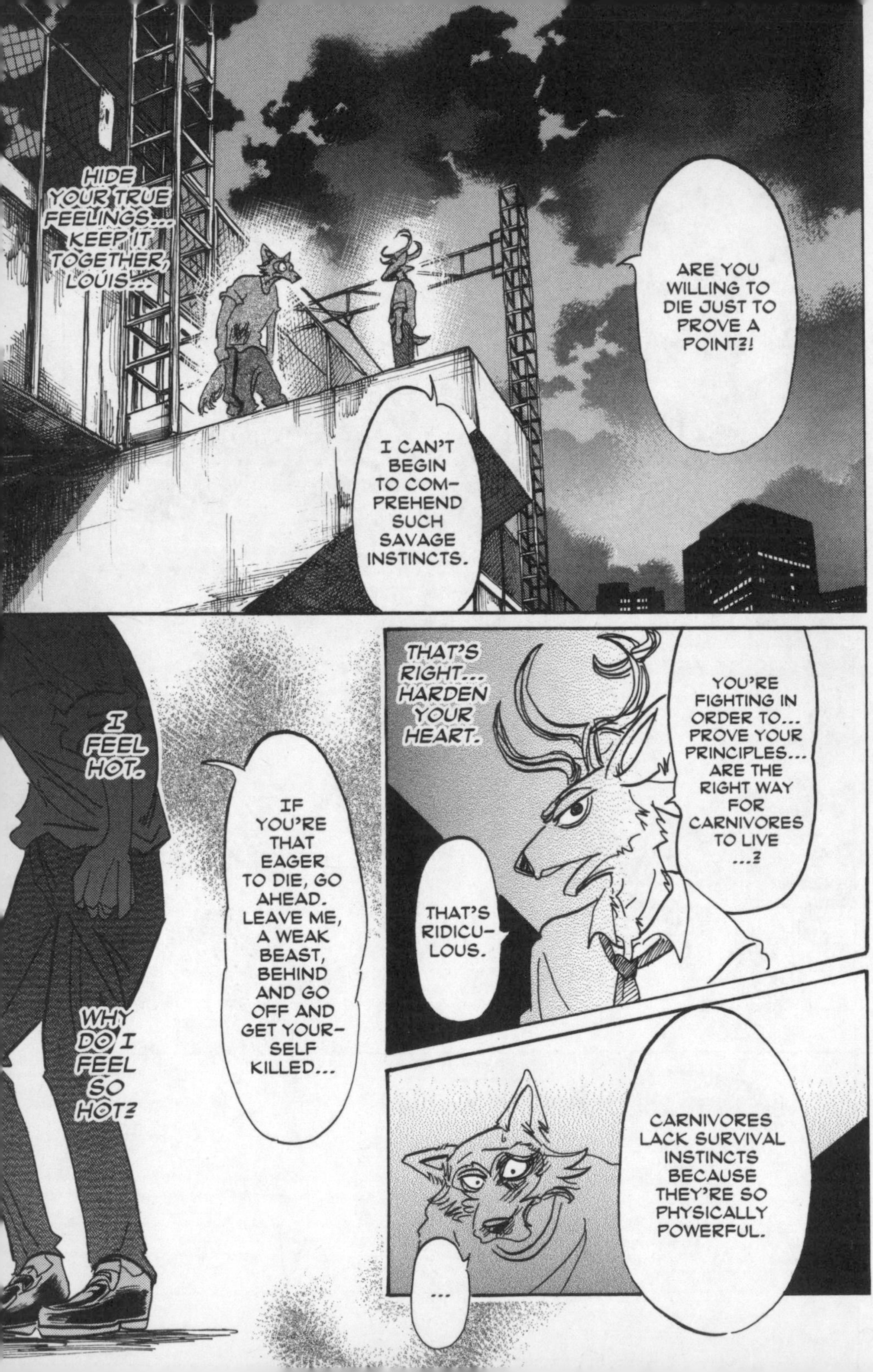
ARE YOU WILLING TO DIE JUST TO PROVE A POINT?!
I CAN'T BEGIN TO COMPREHEND SUCH SAVAGE INSTINCTS.
HIDE YOUR TRUE FEELINGS... KEEP IT TOGETHER, LOUIS...
YOU'RE FIGHTING IN ORDER TO... PROVE YOUR PRINCIPLES... ARE THE RIGHT WAY FOR CARNIVORES TO LIVE...?
THAT'S RIGHT... HARDEN YOUR HEART.
THAT'S RIDICULOUS.
CARNIVORES LACK SURVIVAL INSTINCTS BECAUSE THEY'RE SO PHYSICALLY POWERFUL.
...
IF YOU'RE THAT EAGER TO DIE, GO AHEAD. LEAVE ME, A WEAK BEAST, BEHIND AND GO OFF AND GET YOURSELF KILLED...
I FEEL HOT.
WHY DO I FEEL SO HOT?

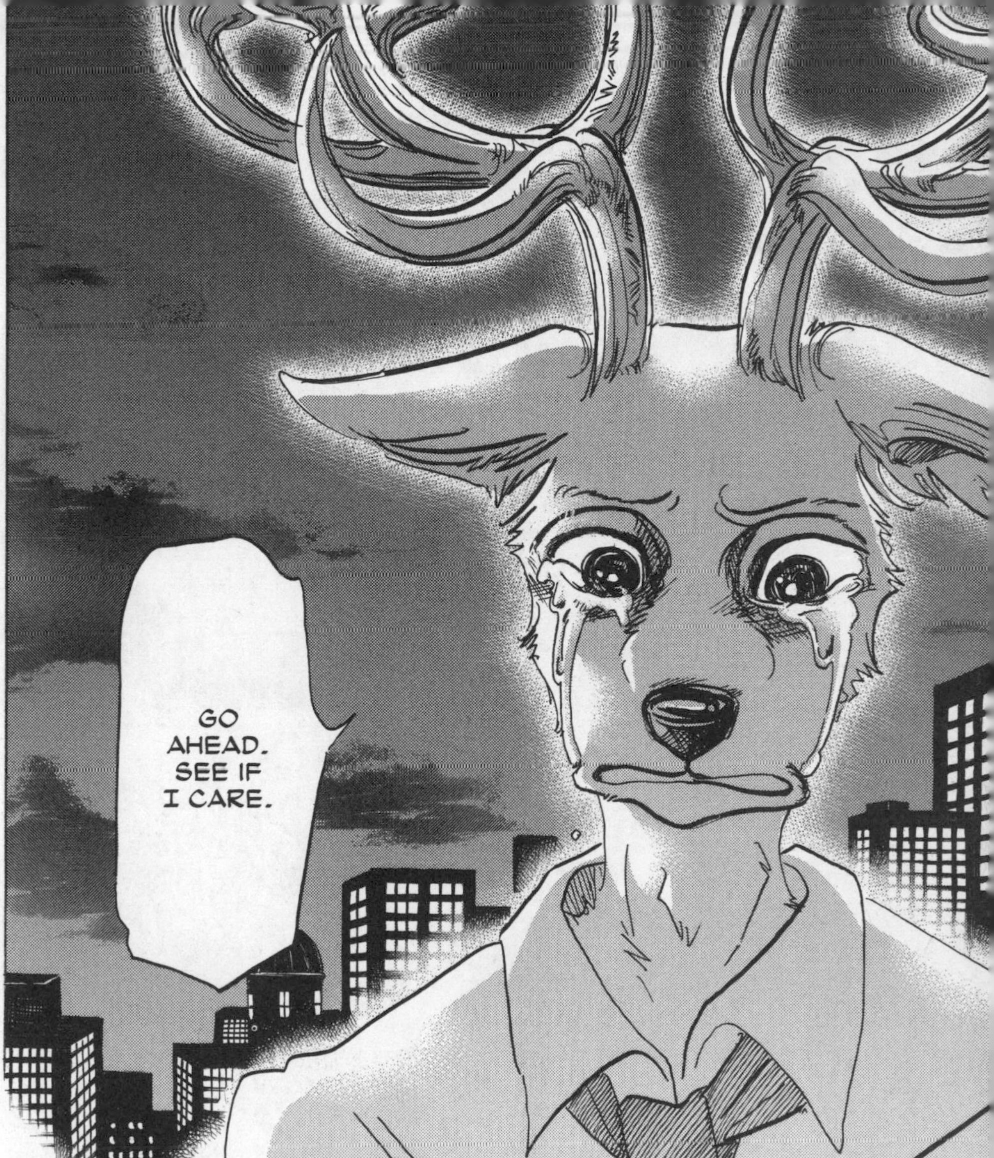
GO AHEAD. SEE IF I CARE.
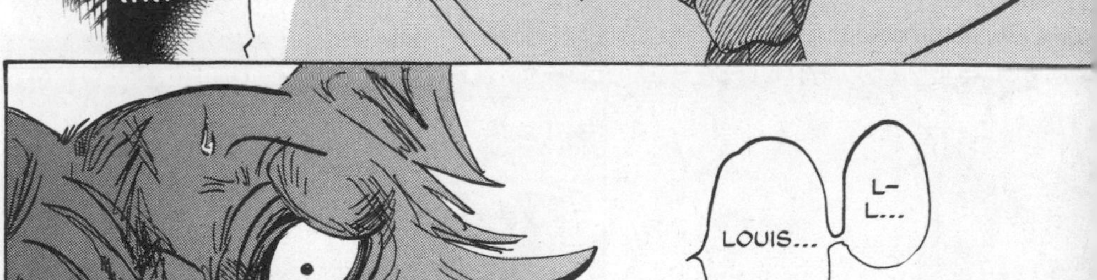
L- L...
LOUIS...

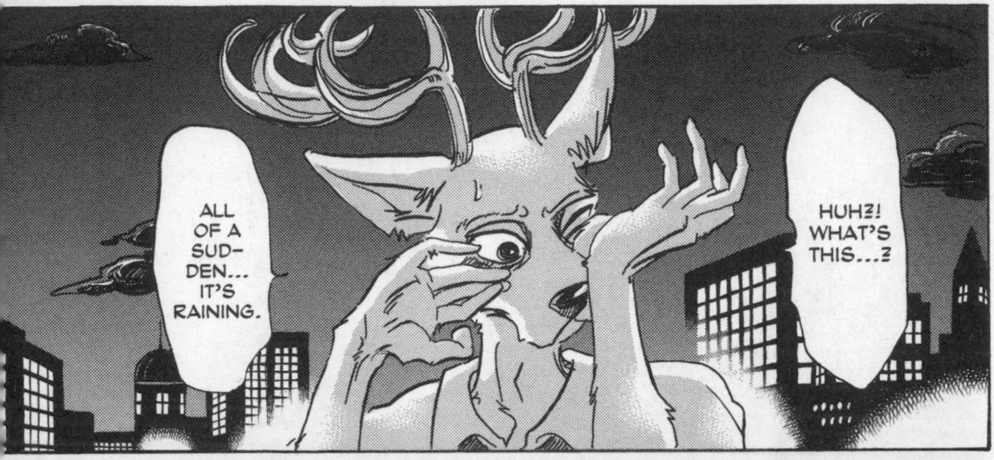
HUH?! WHAT'S THIS...?
ALL OF A SUDDEN... IT'S RAINING.
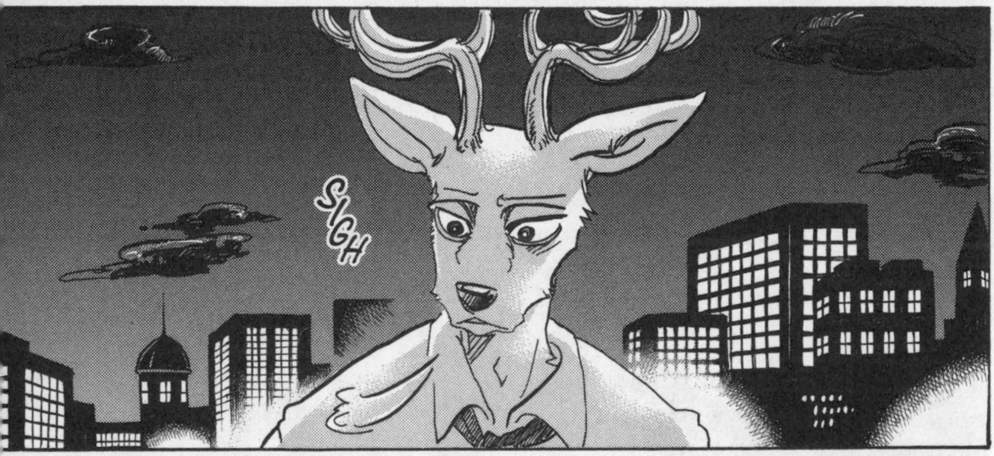
SIGH
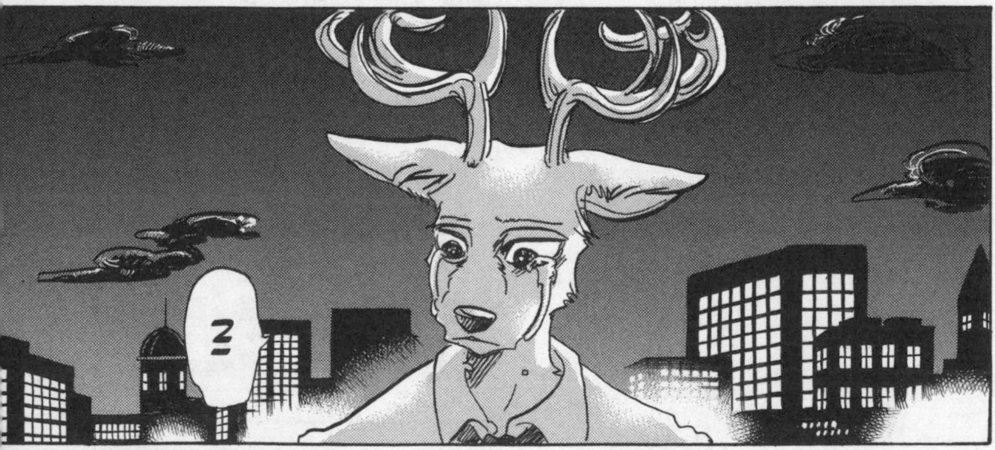
?

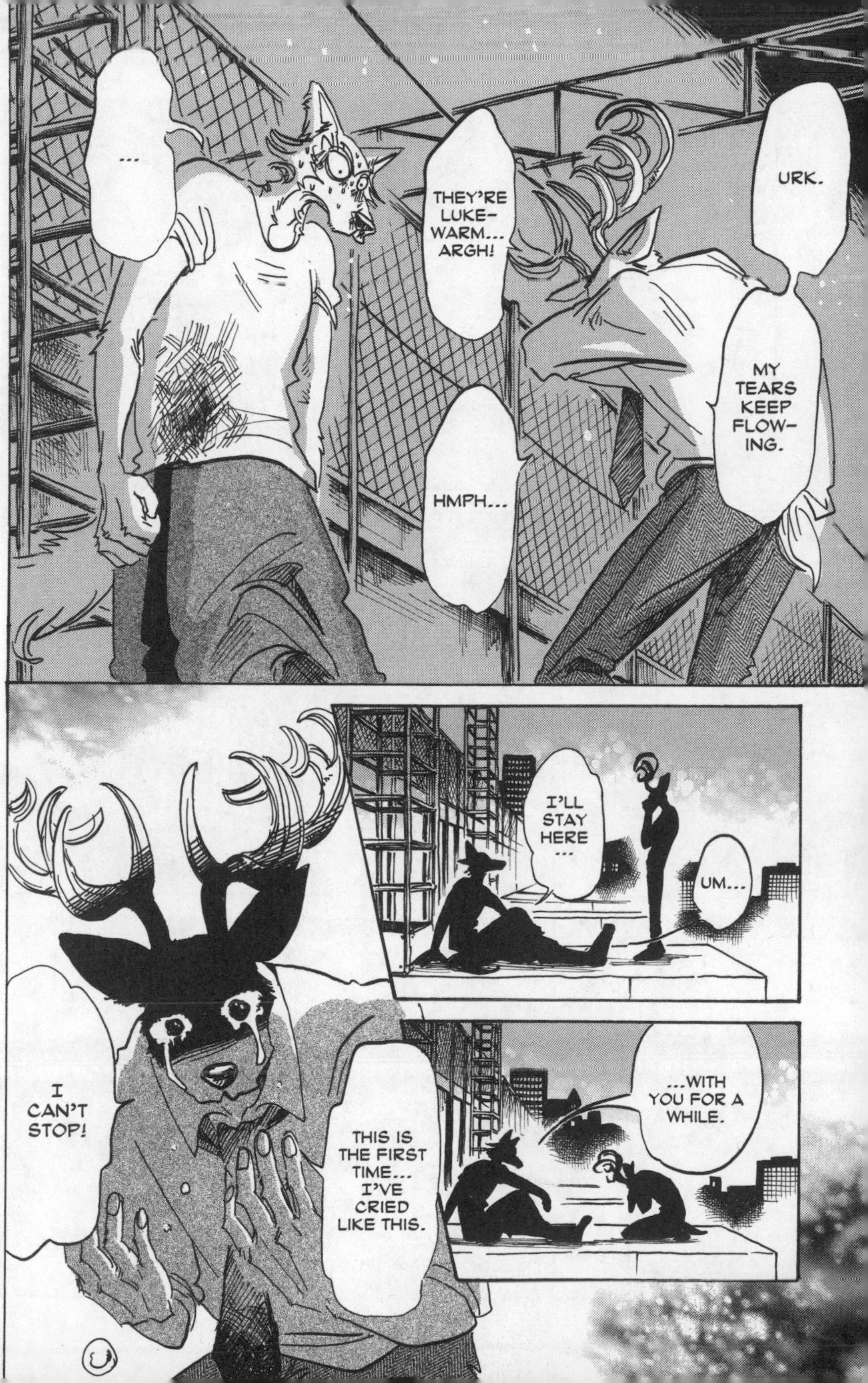
URK.
THEY'RE LUKEWARM... ARGH!
...
MY TEARS KEEP FLOWING.
HMPH...
UM...
I'LL STAY HERE ...
...WITH YOU FOR A WHILE.
THIS IS THE FIRST TIME... I'VE CRIED LIKE THIS.
I CAN'T STOP!

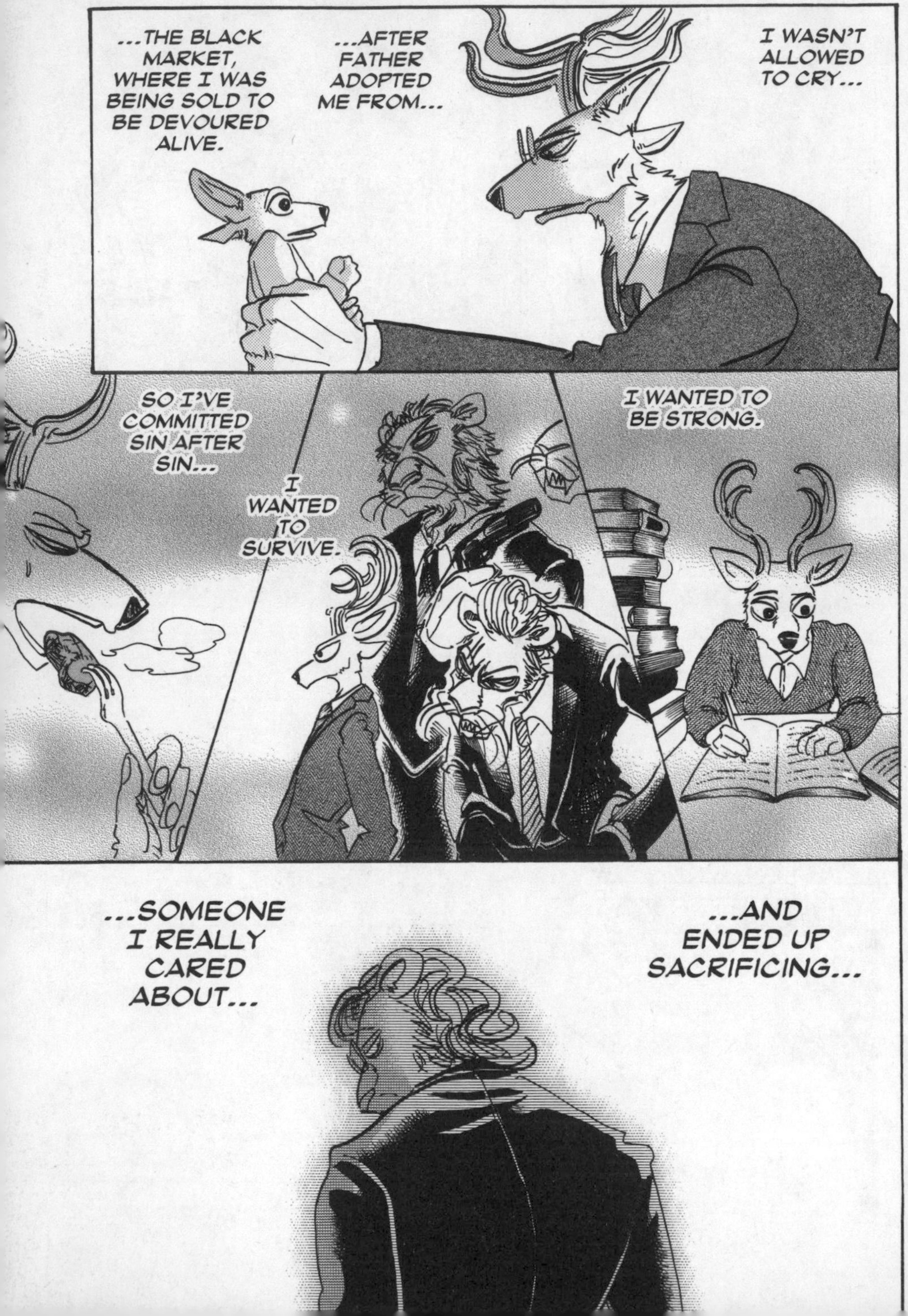
I WASN'T ALLOWED TO CRY...
...AFTER FATHER ADOPTED ME FROM...
...THE BLACK MARKET, WHERE I WAS BEING SOLD TO BE DEVOURED ALIVE.
I WANTED TO BE STRONG.
I WANTED TO SURVIVE.
SO I'VE COMMITTED SIN AFTER SIN...
...AND ENDED UP SACRIFICING...
...SOMEONE I REALLY CARED ABOUT...

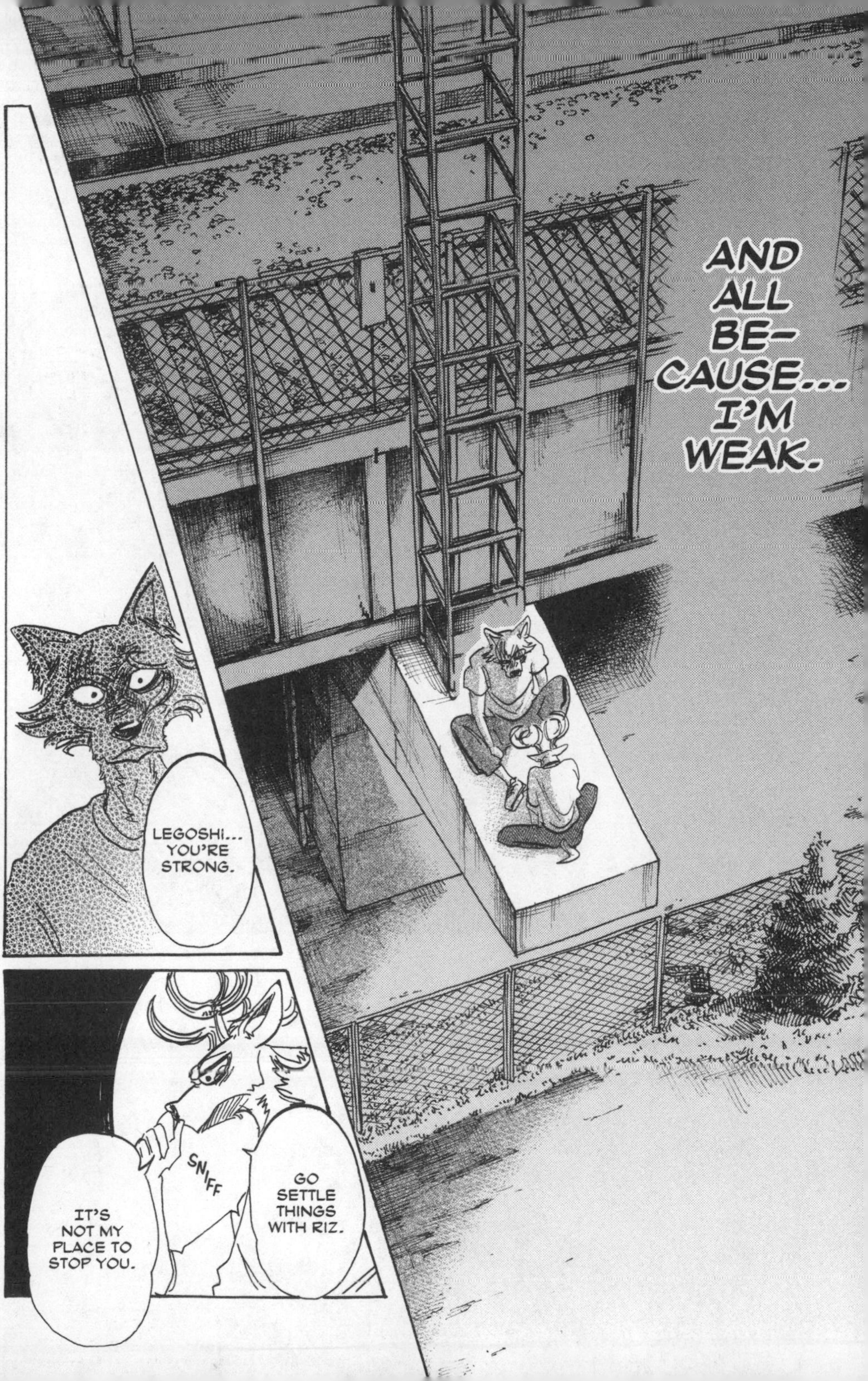
AND ALL BE-CAUSE... I'M WEAK.
LEGOSHI... YOU'RE STRONG.
GO SETTLE THINGS WITH RIZ.
SNIFF
IT'S NOT MY PLACE TO STOP YOU.

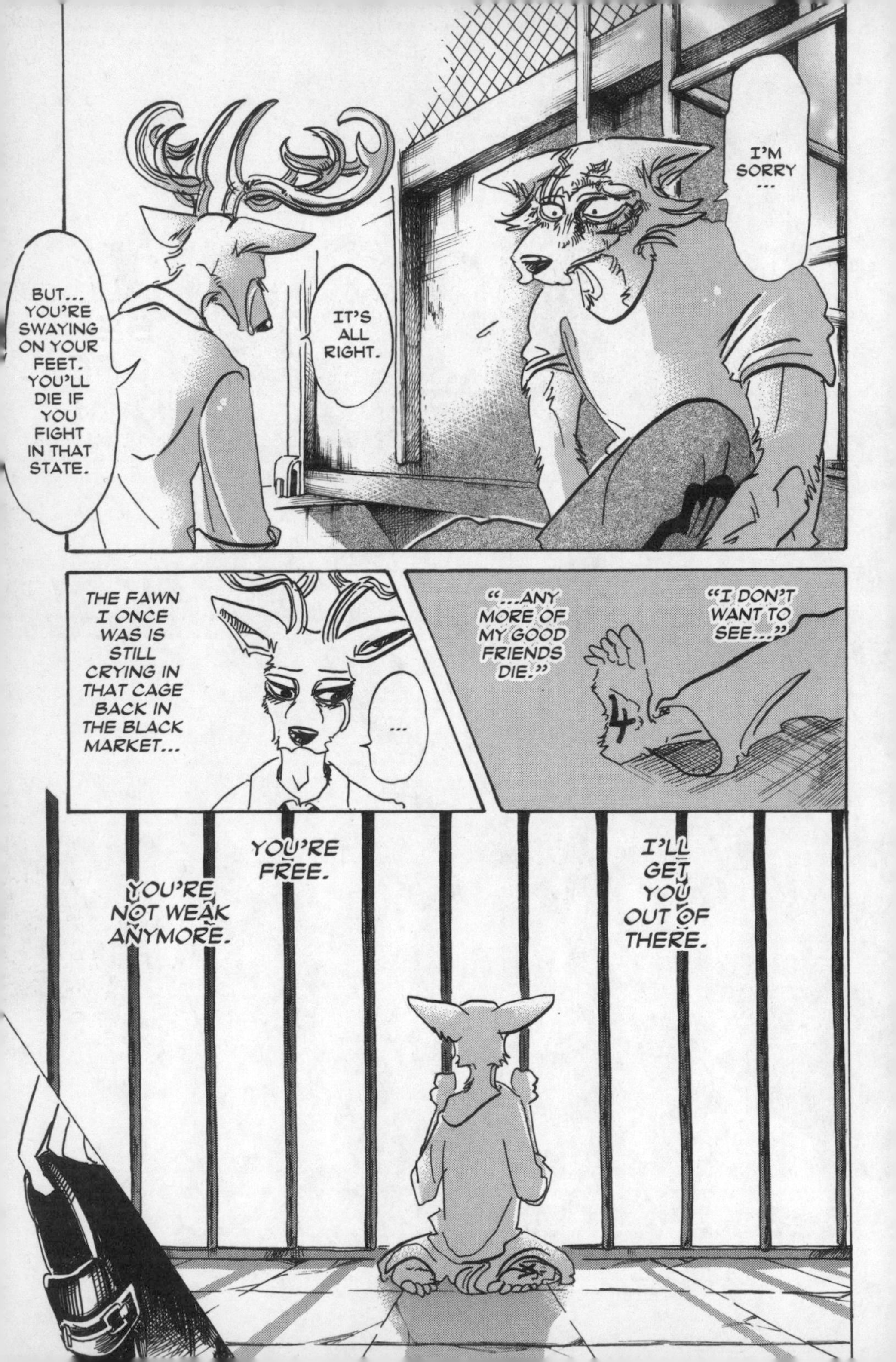
I'M SORRY ...
IT'S ALL RIGHT.
BUT... YOU'RE SWAYING ON YOUR FEET. YOU'LL DIE IF YOU FIGHT IN THAT STATE.
"I DON'T WANT TO SEE..."
"...ANY MORE OF MY GOOD FRIENDS DIE."
THE FAWN I ONCE WAS IS STILL CRYING IN THAT CAGE BACK IN THE BLACK MARKET...
...
I'LL GET YOU OUT OF THERE.
YOU'RE FREE.
YOU'RE NOT WEAK ANYMORE.

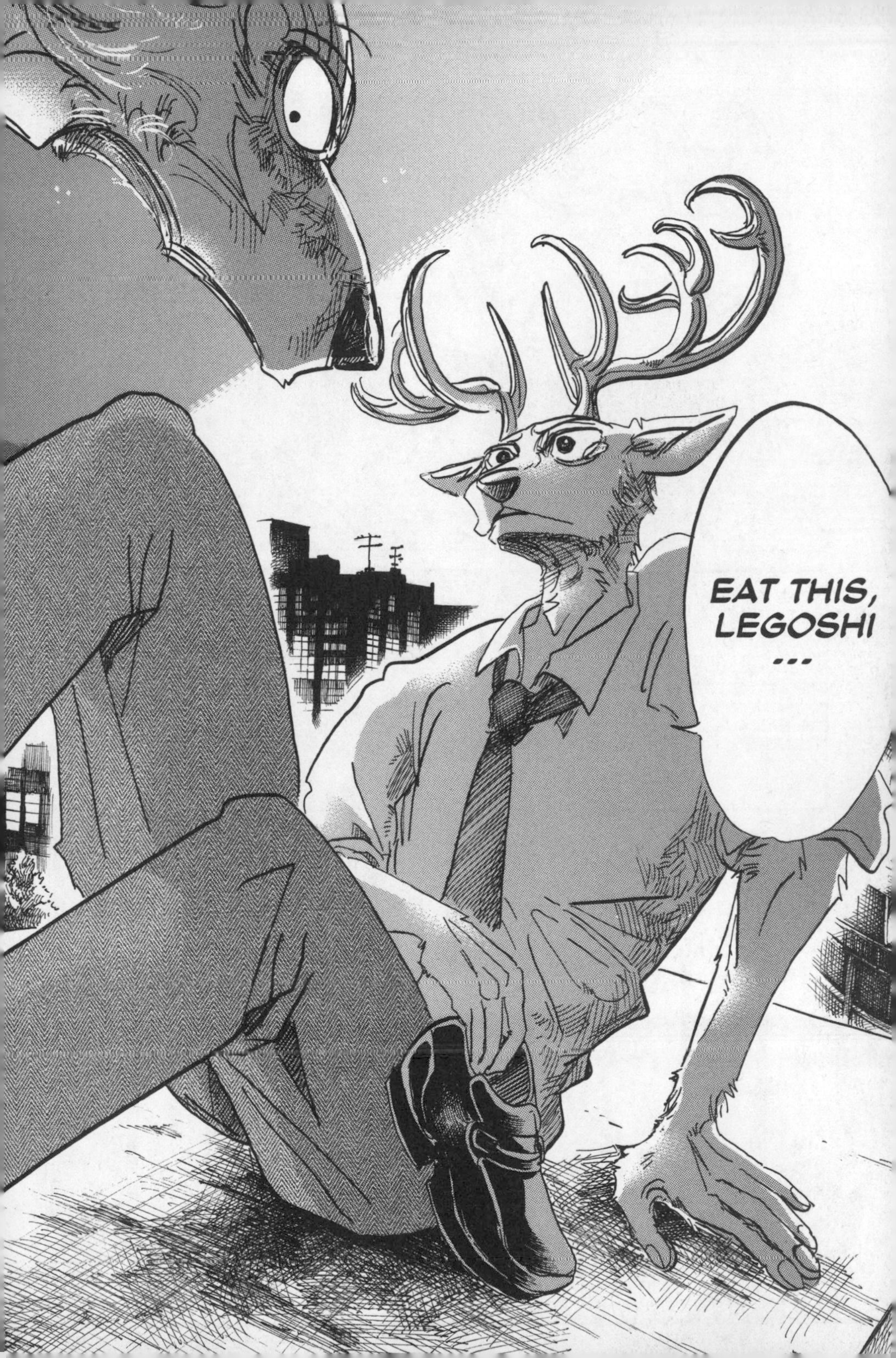
EAT THIS, LEGOSHI ...

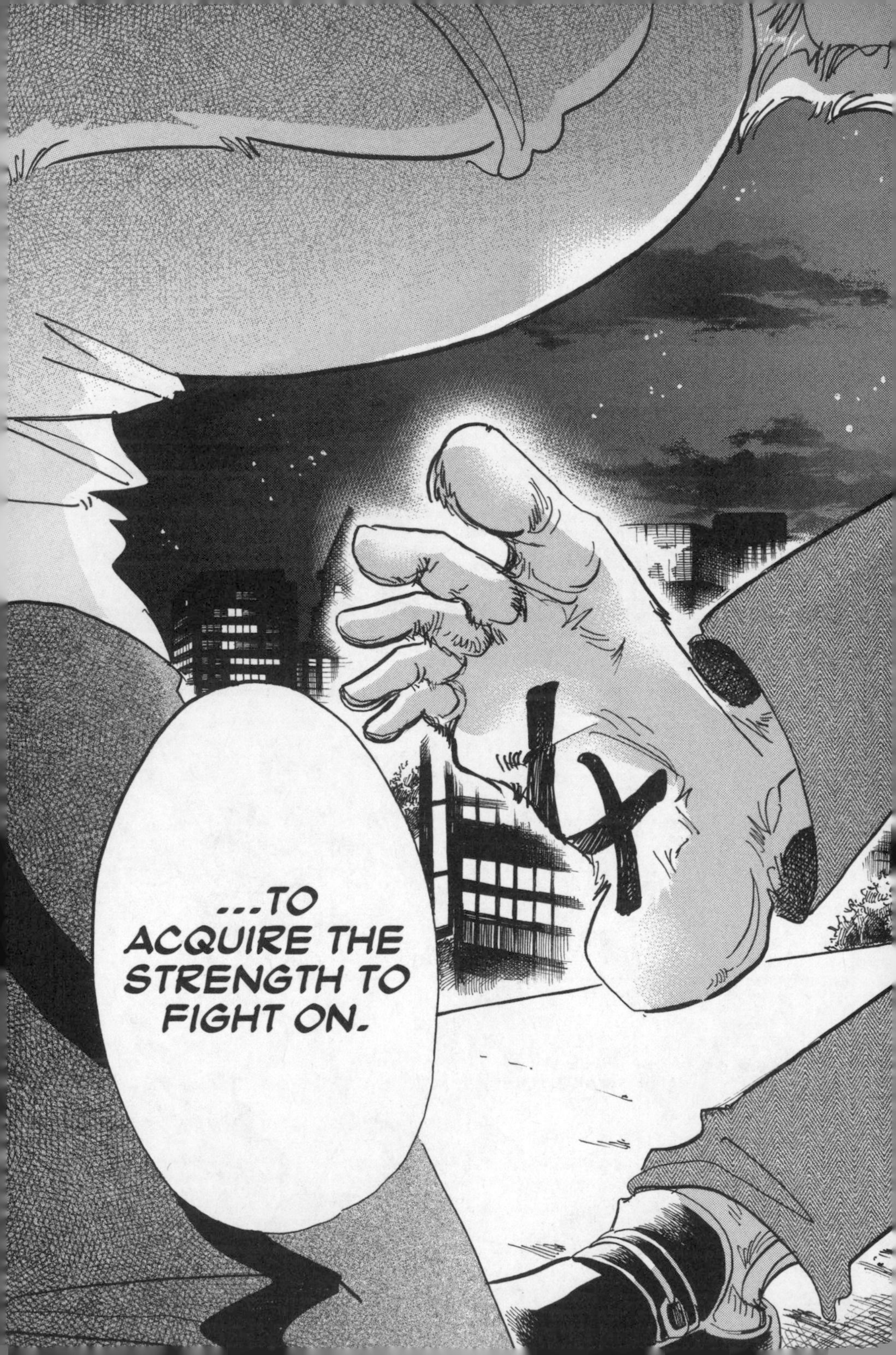
...TO ACQUIRE THE STRENGTH TO FIGHT ON.

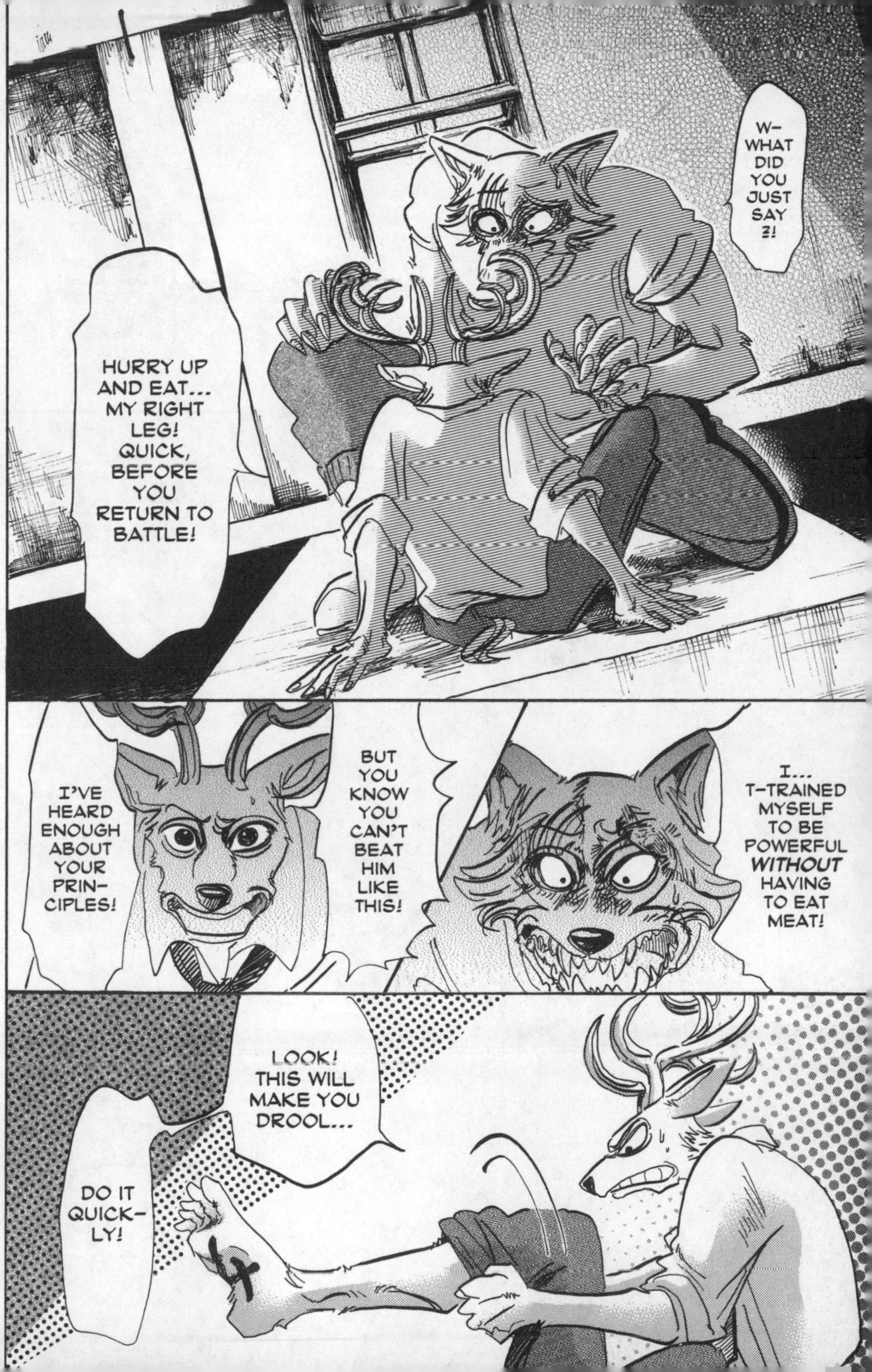
W-WHAT DID YOU JUST SAY?!
HURRY UP AND EAT... MY RIGHT LEG! QUICK, BEFORE YOU RETURN TO BATTLE!
I... T-TRAINED MYSELF TO BE POWERFUL *WITHOUT* HAVING TO EAT MEAT!
BUT YOU KNOW YOU CAN'T BEAT HIM LIKE THIS!
I'VE HEARD ENOUGH ABOUT YOUR PRIN-CIPLES!
LOOK! THIS WILL MAKE YOU DROOL...
DO IT QUICK-LY!

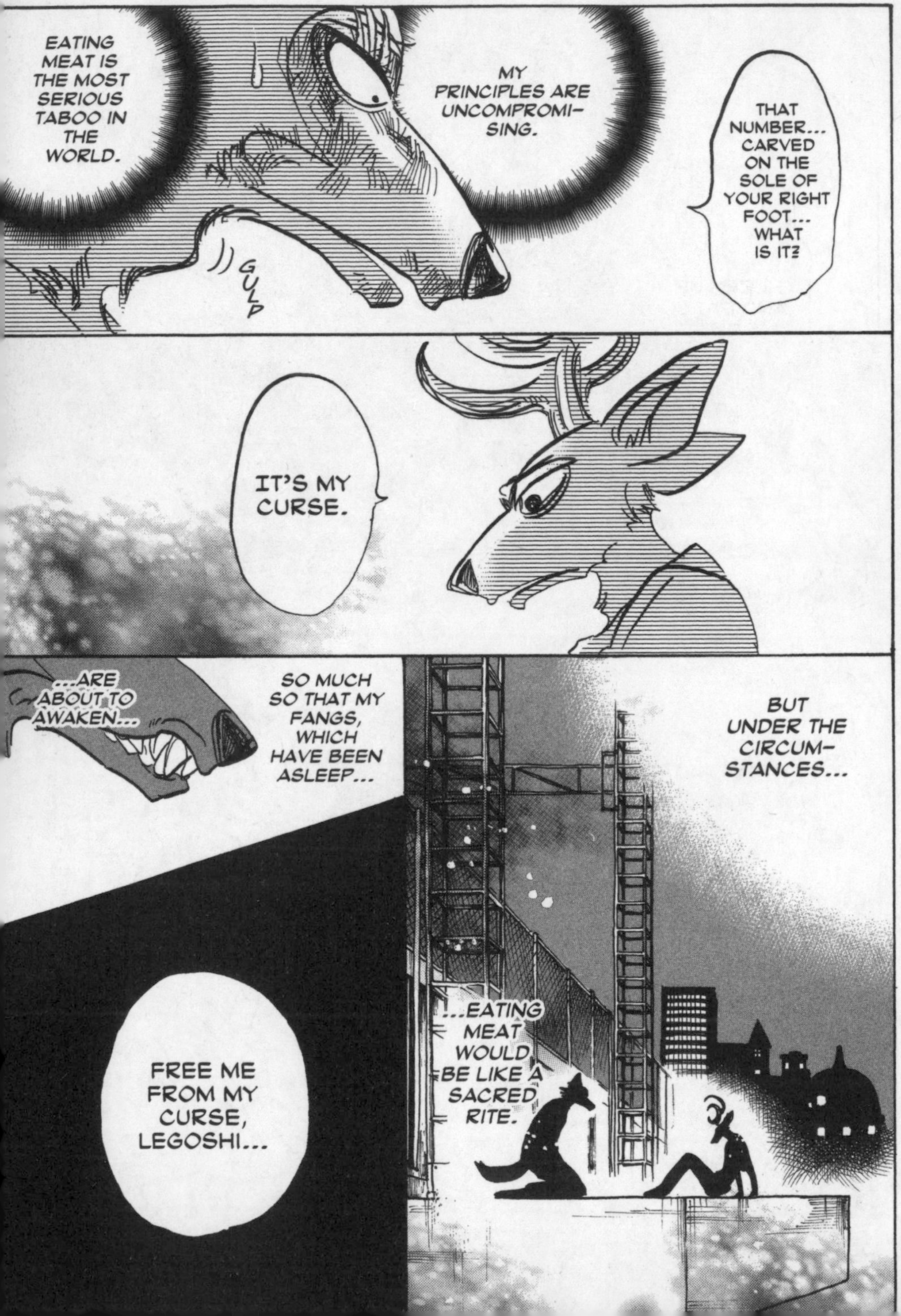
THAT NUMBER... CARVED ON THE SOLE OF YOUR RIGHT FOOT... WHAT IS IT?
MY PRINCIPLES ARE UNCOMPROMISING.
GULP
EATING MEAT IS THE MOST SERIOUS TABOO IN THE WORLD.
IT'S MY CURSE.
BUT UNDER THE CIRCUMSTANCES...
...EATING MEAT WOULD BE LIKE A SACRED RITE.
SO MUCH SO THAT MY FANGS, WHICH HAVE BEEN ASLEEP...
...ARE ABOUT TO AWAKEN...
FREE ME FROM MY CURSE, LEGOSHI...

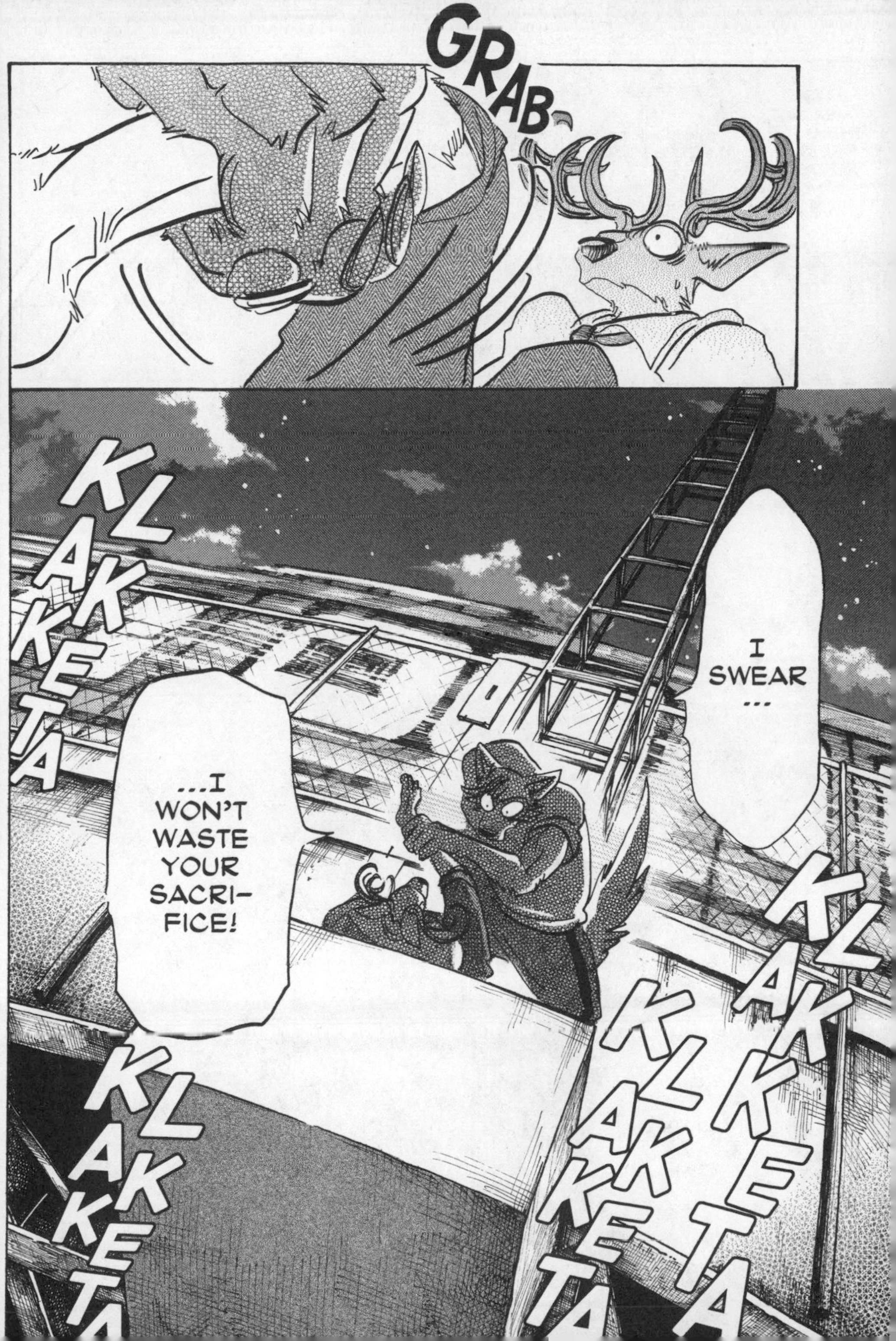
GRAB-
I SWEAR ...
...I WON'T WASTE YOUR SACRI-FICE!
KLAKKETA
KLAKKETA
KLAKKETA
KLAKKETA

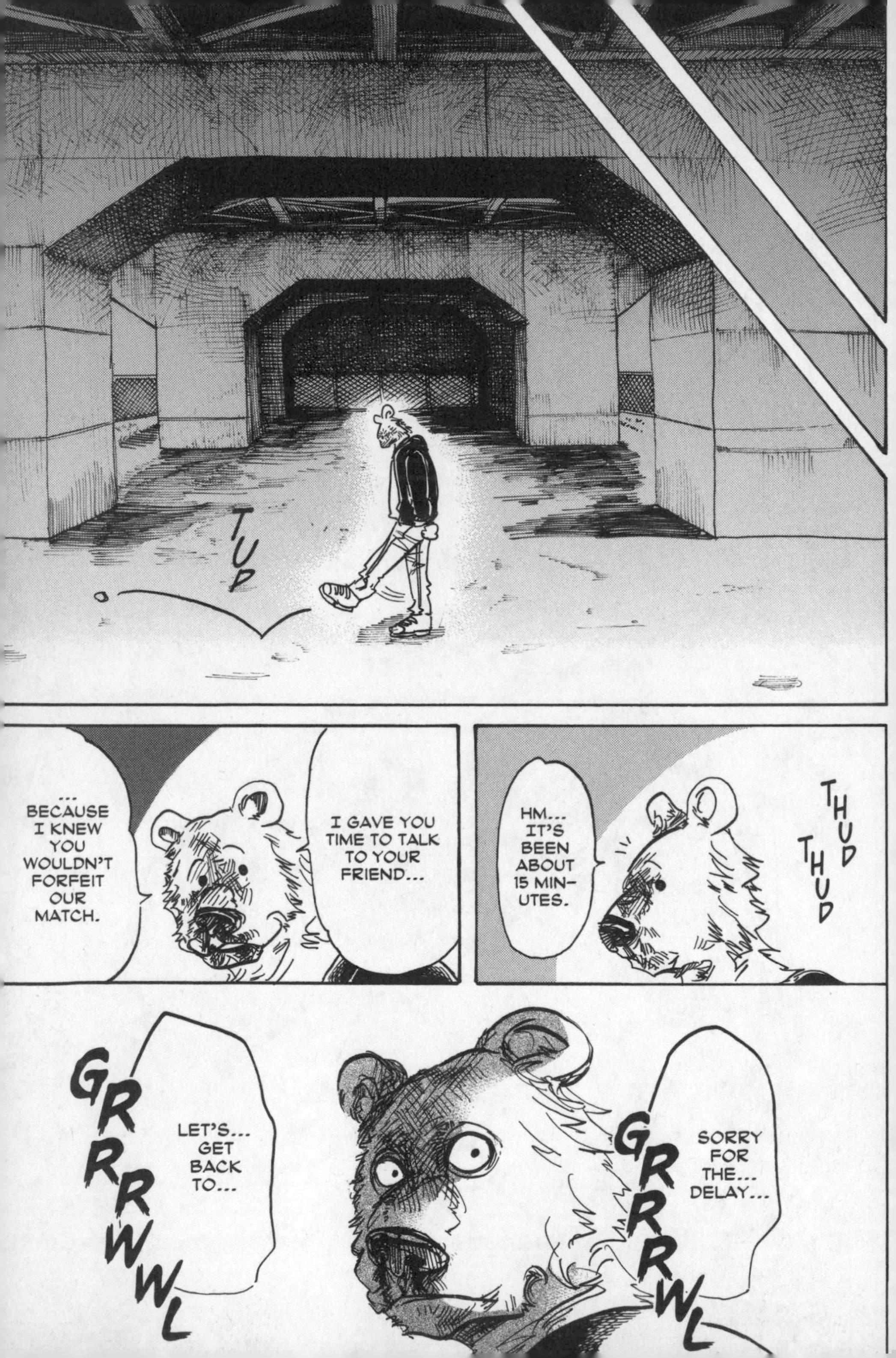
TUD
THUD THUD
HM... IT'S BEEN ABOUT 15 MIN-UTES.
I GAVE YOU TIME TO TALK TO YOUR FRIEND...
...BECAUSE I KNEW YOU WOULDN'T FORFEIT OUR MATCH.
SORRY FOR THE... DELAY...
GRRRWL
LET'S... GET BACK TO...
GRRRWWL

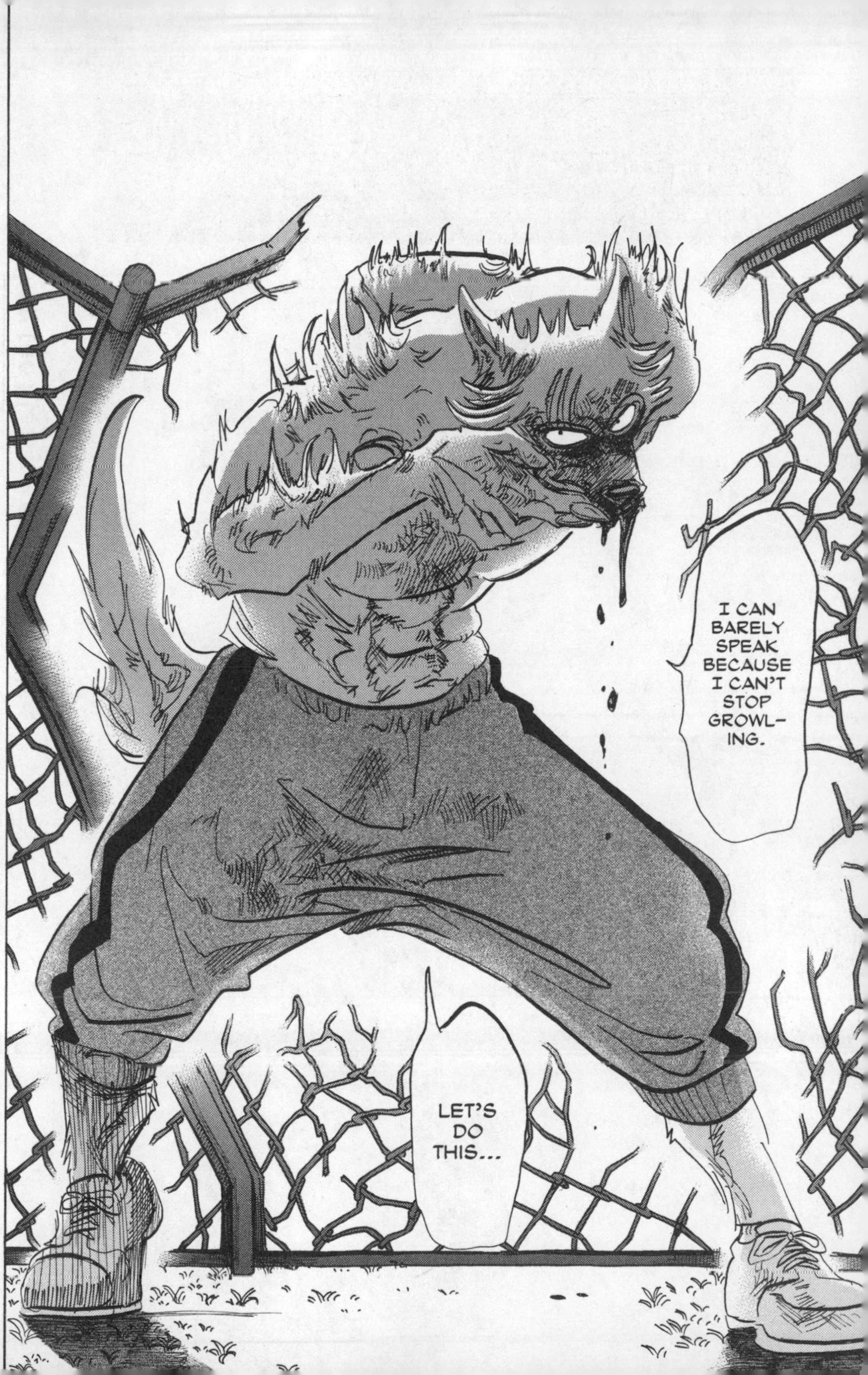
I CAN BARELY SPEAK BECAUSE I CAN'T STOP GROWL-ING.
LET'S DO THIS...

Chapter 96: Sealing the Pledge with Vermilion Ink

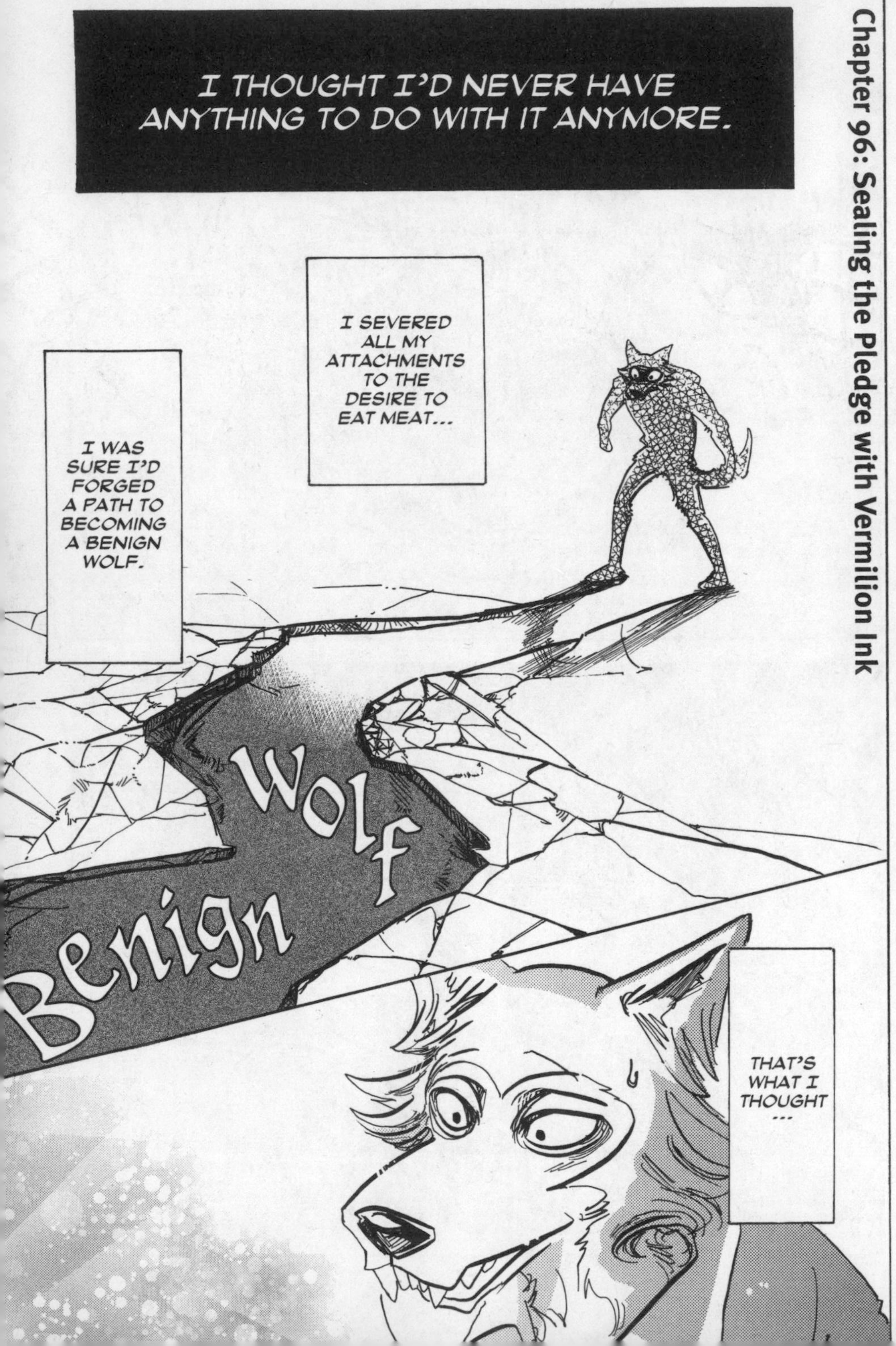

I THOUGHT I'D NEVER HAVE ANYTHING TO DO WITH IT ANYMORE.
I SEVERED ALL MY ATTACHMENTS TO THE DESIRE TO EAT MEAT...
I WAS SURE I'D FORGED A PATH TO BECOMING A BENIGN WOLF.
Benign Wolf
THAT'S WHAT I THOUGHT...

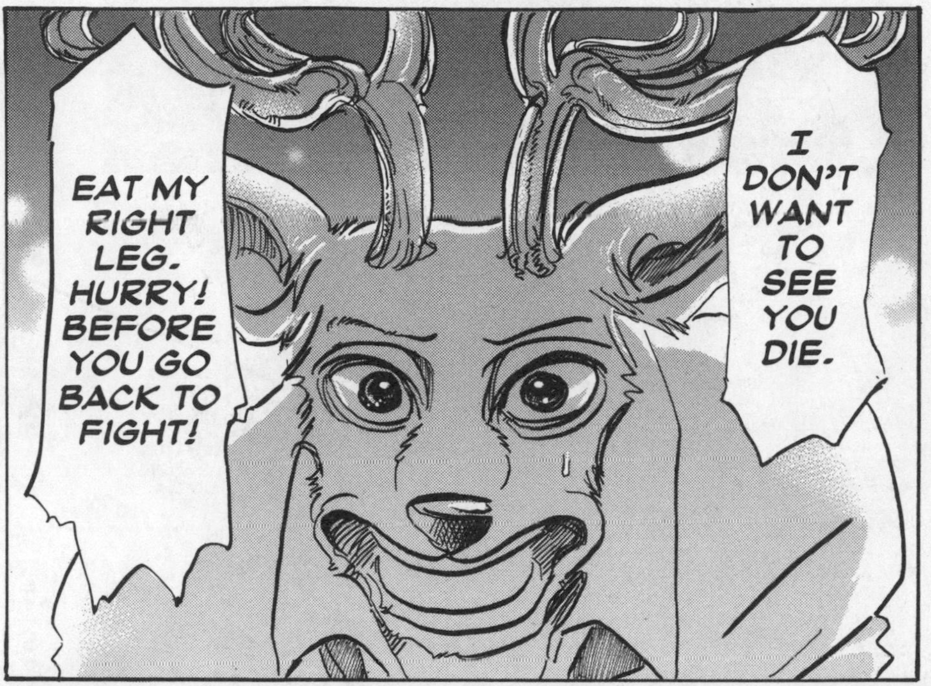
I DON'T WANT TO SEE YOU DIE.
EAT MY RIGHT LEG. HURRY! BEFORE YOU GO BACK TO FIGHT!

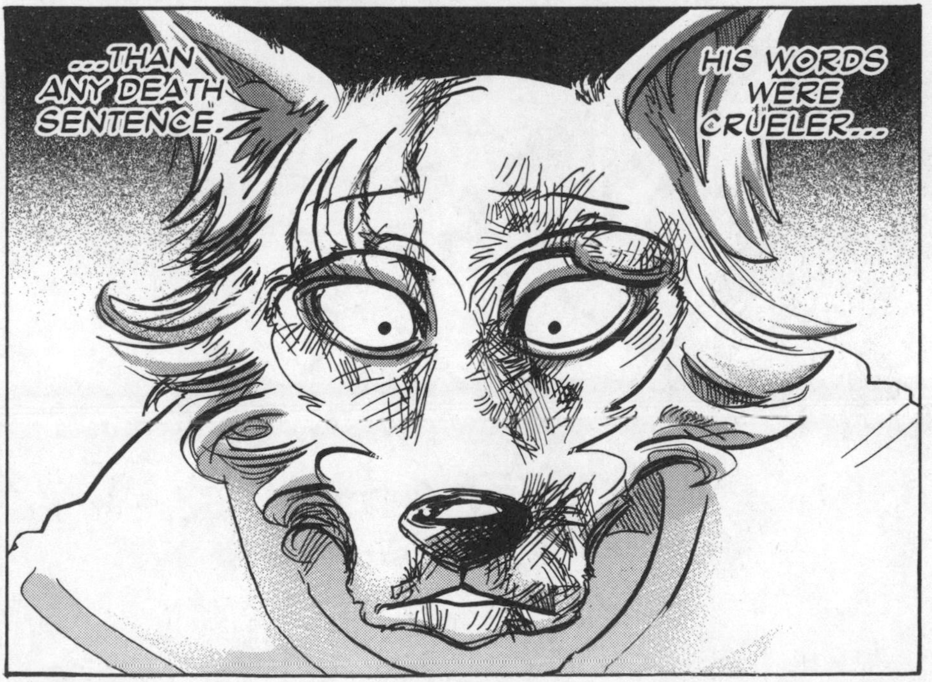
HIS WORDS WERE CRUELER...
...THAN ANY DEATH SENTENCE.

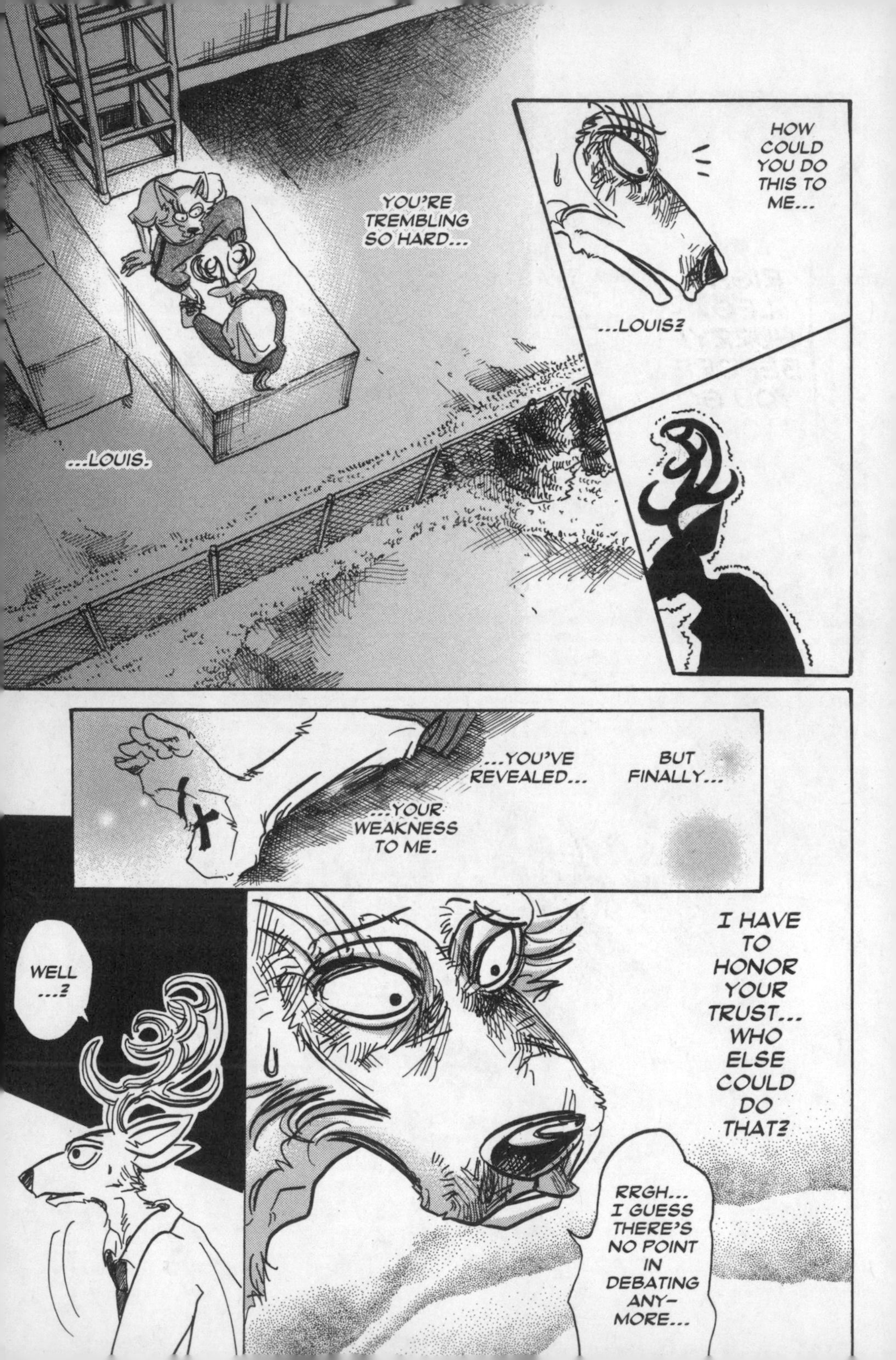
HOW COULD YOU DO THIS TO ME...
...LOUIS?
YOU'RE TREMBLING SO HARD...
...LOUIS.
BUT FINALLY...
...YOU'VE REVEALED...
...YOUR WEAKNESS TO ME.
I HAVE TO HONOR YOUR TRUST... WHO ELSE COULD DO THAT?
RRGH... I GUESS THERE'S NO POINT IN DEBATING ANY-MORE...
WELL...?

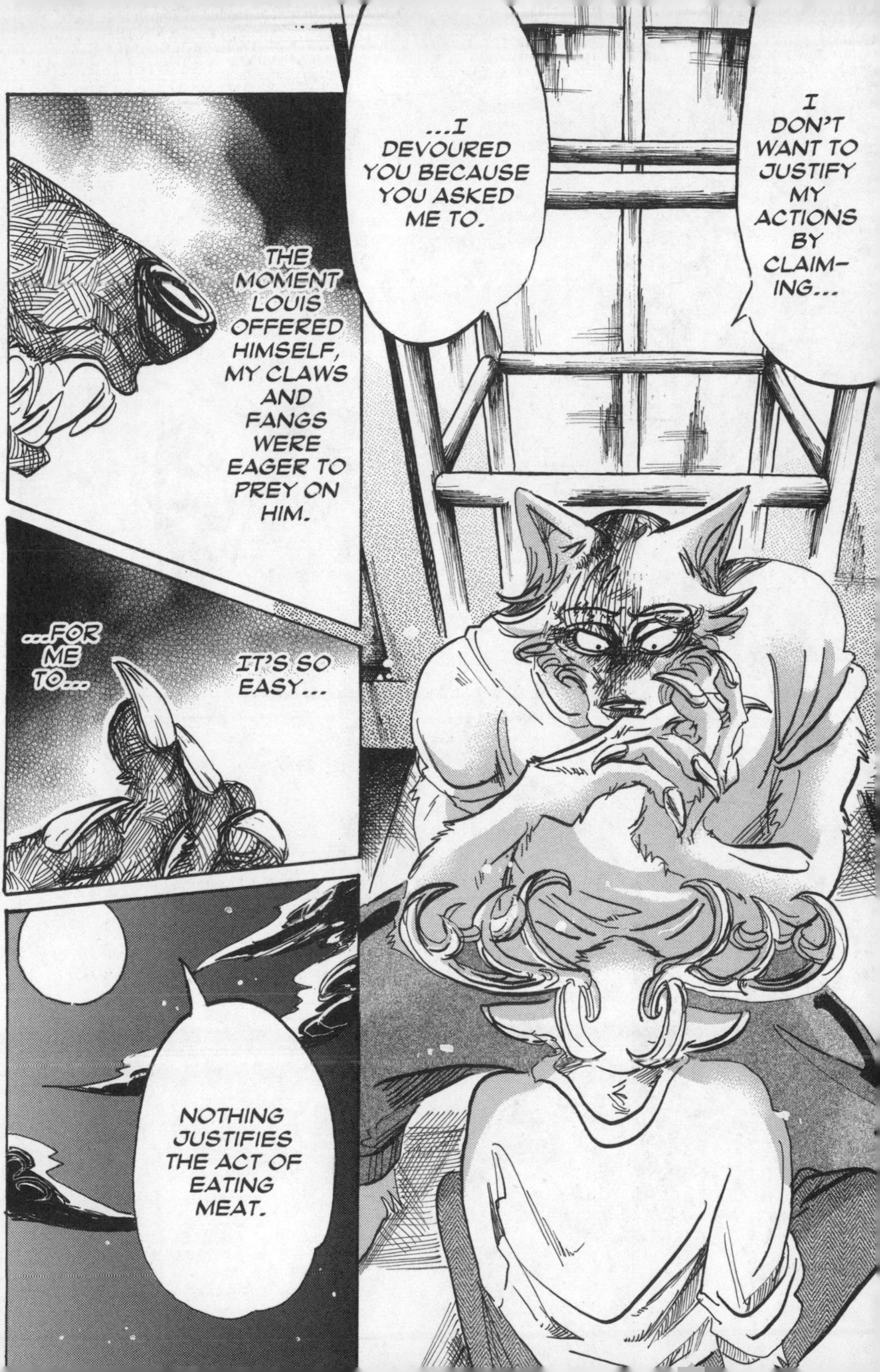
I DON'T WANT TO JUSTIFY MY ACTIONS BY CLAIMING...
...I DEVOURED YOU BECAUSE YOU ASKED ME TO.
THE MOMENT LOUIS OFFERED HIMSELF, MY CLAWS AND FANGS WERE EAGER TO PREY ON HIM.
IT'S SO EASY...
...FOR ME TO...
NOTHING JUSTIFIES THE ACT OF EATING MEAT.

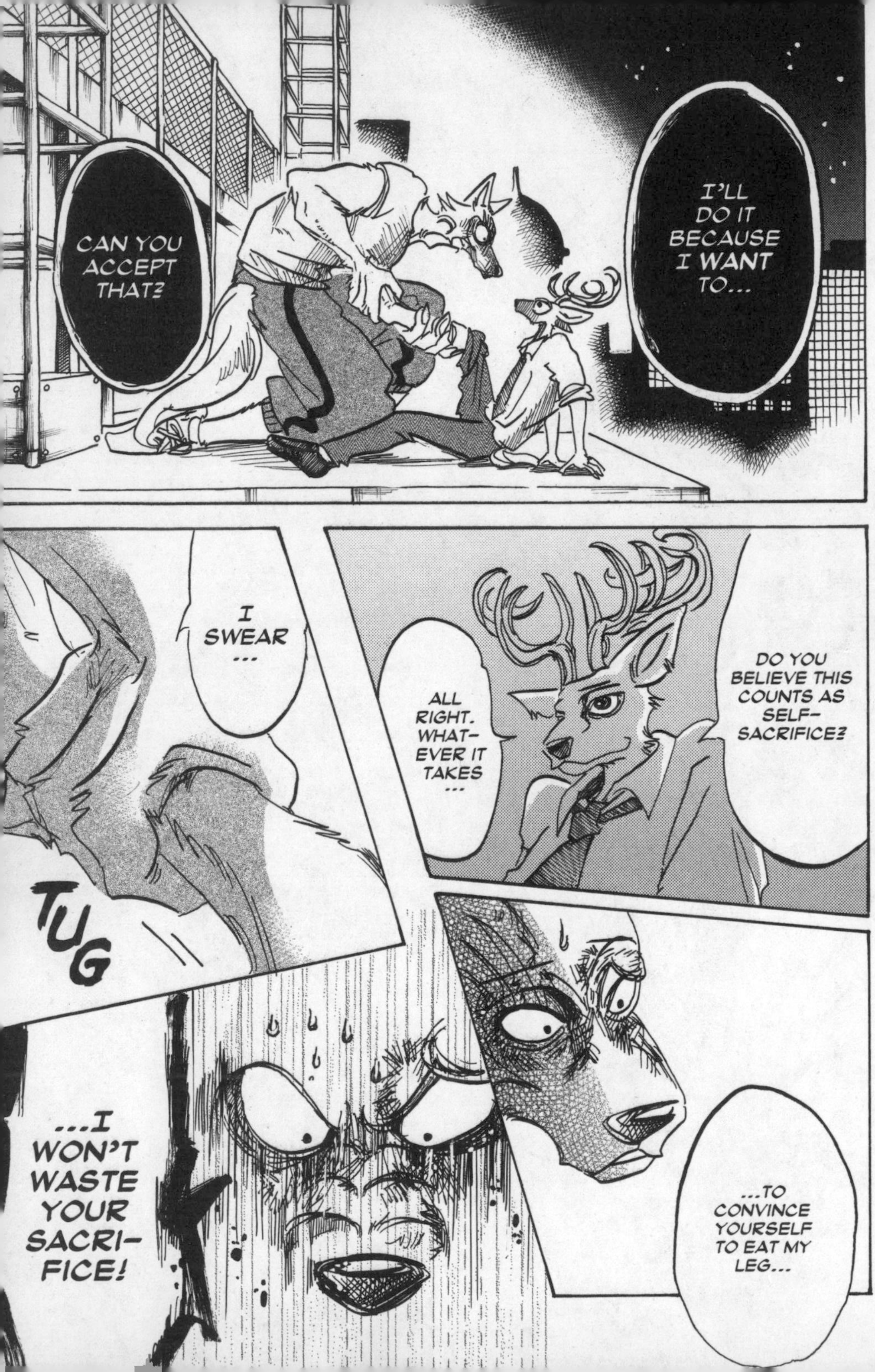
I'LL DO IT BECAUSE I WANT TO...
CAN YOU ACCEPT THAT?
DO YOU BELIEVE THIS COUNTS AS SELF-SACRIFICE?
ALL RIGHT. WHAT-EVER IT TAKES...
I SWEAR...
TUG
...TO CONVINCE YOURSELF TO EAT MY LEG...
...I WON'T WASTE YOUR SACRIFICE!

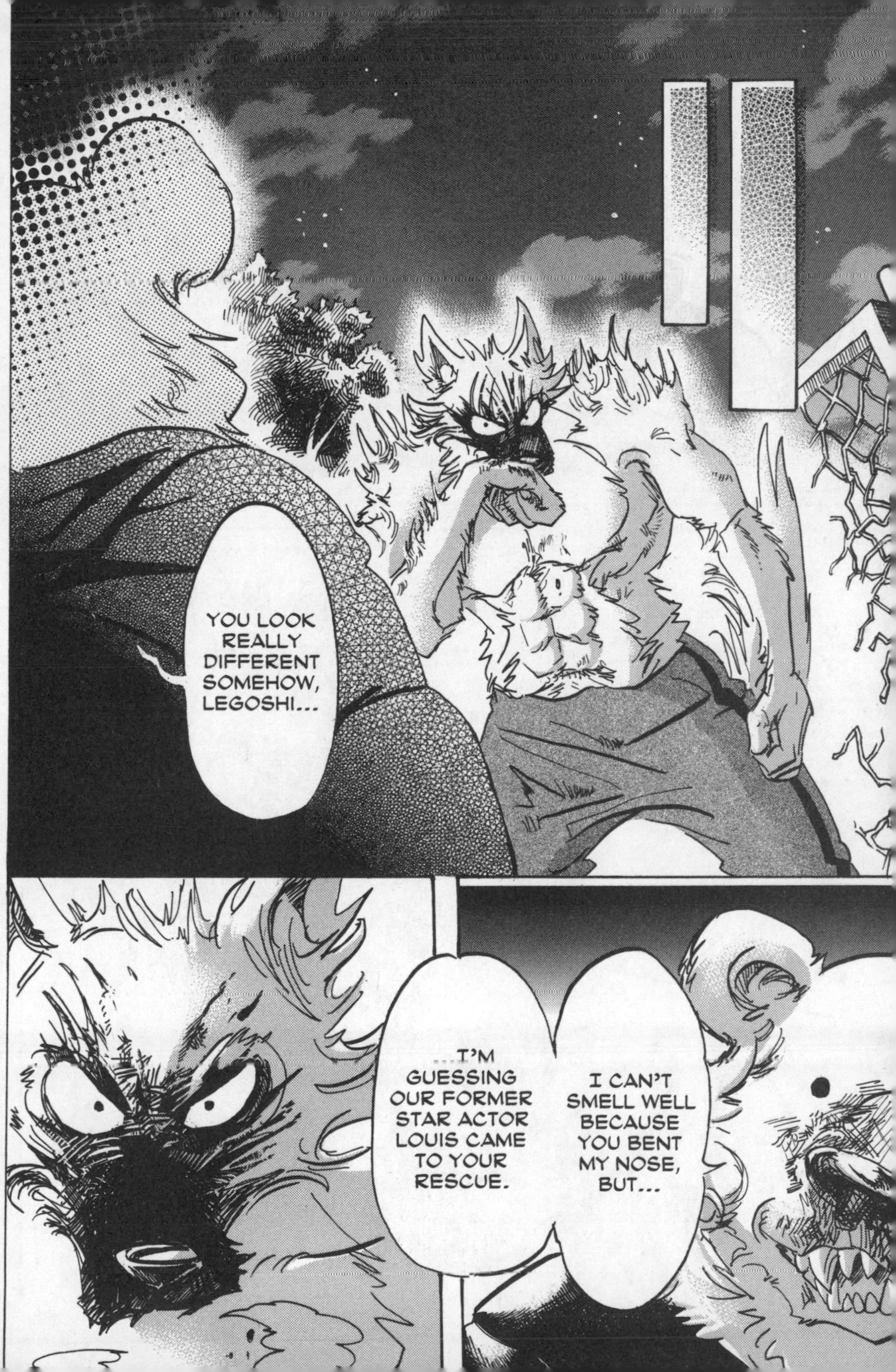
YOU LOOK REALLY DIFFERENT SOMEHOW, LEGOSHI...
I CAN'T SMELL WELL BECAUSE YOU BENT MY NOSE, BUT...
...I'M GUESSING OUR FORMER STAR ACTOR LOUIS CAME TO YOUR RESCUE.

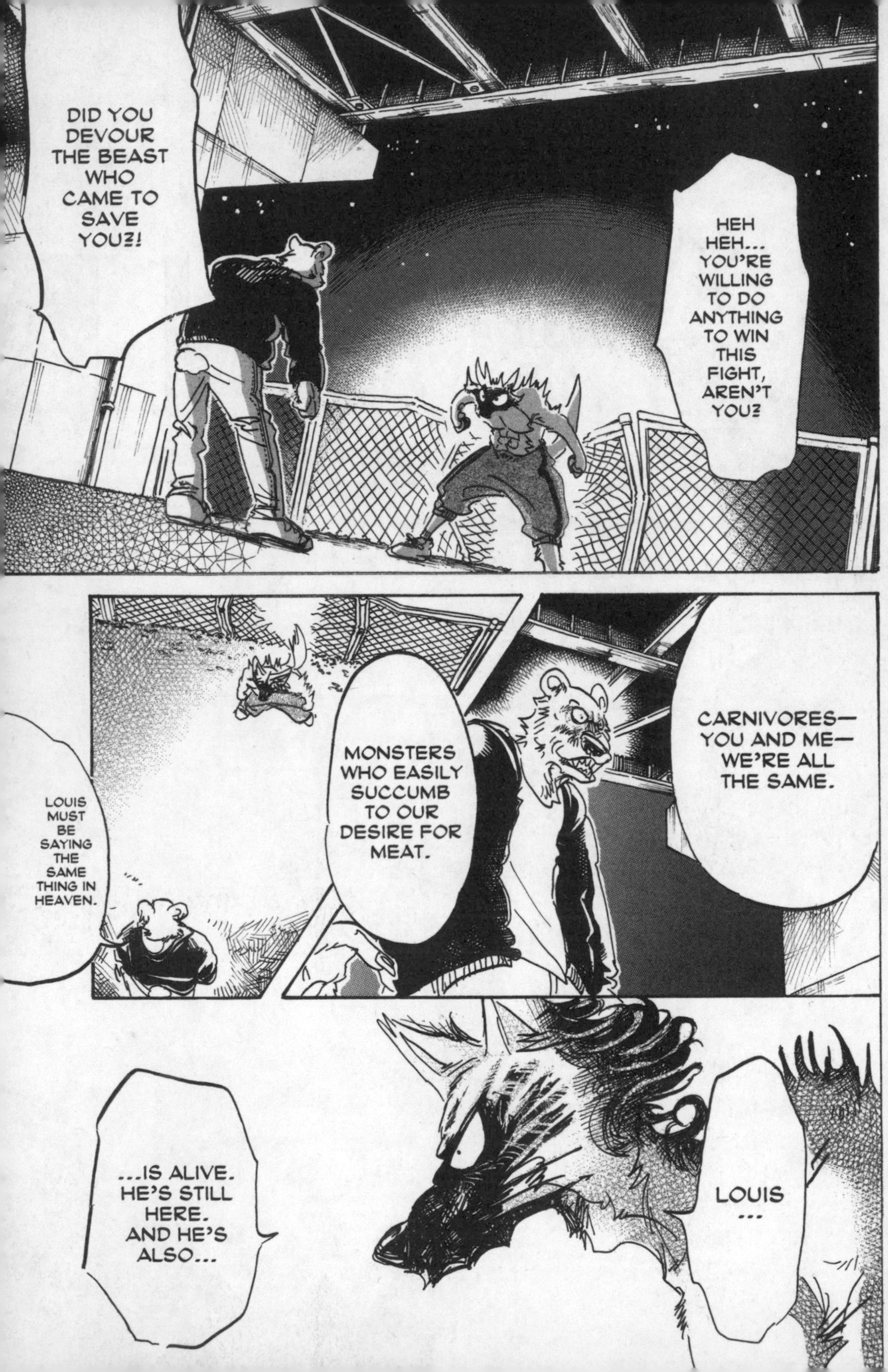
DID YOU DEVOUR THE BEAST WHO CAME TO SAVE YOU?!
HEH HEH... YOU'RE WILLING TO DO ANYTHING TO WIN THIS FIGHT, AREN'T YOU?
CARNIVORES— YOU AND ME— WE'RE ALL THE SAME.
MONSTERS WHO EASILY SUCCUMB TO OUR DESIRE FOR MEAT.
LOUIS MUST BE SAYING THE SAME THING IN HEAVEN.
LOUIS ...
...IS ALIVE. HE'S STILL HERE. AND HE'S ALSO...

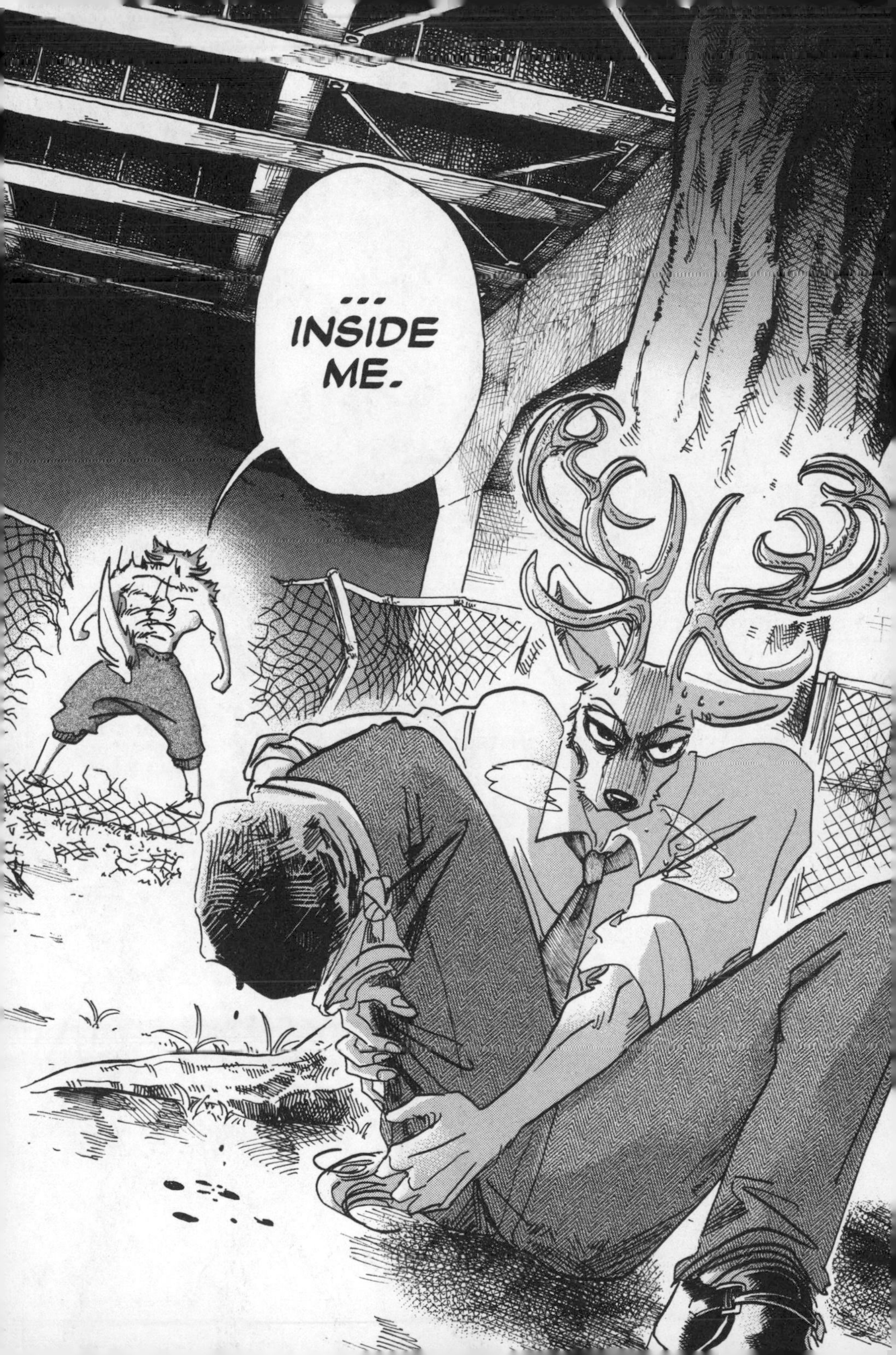
...
INSIDE
ME.

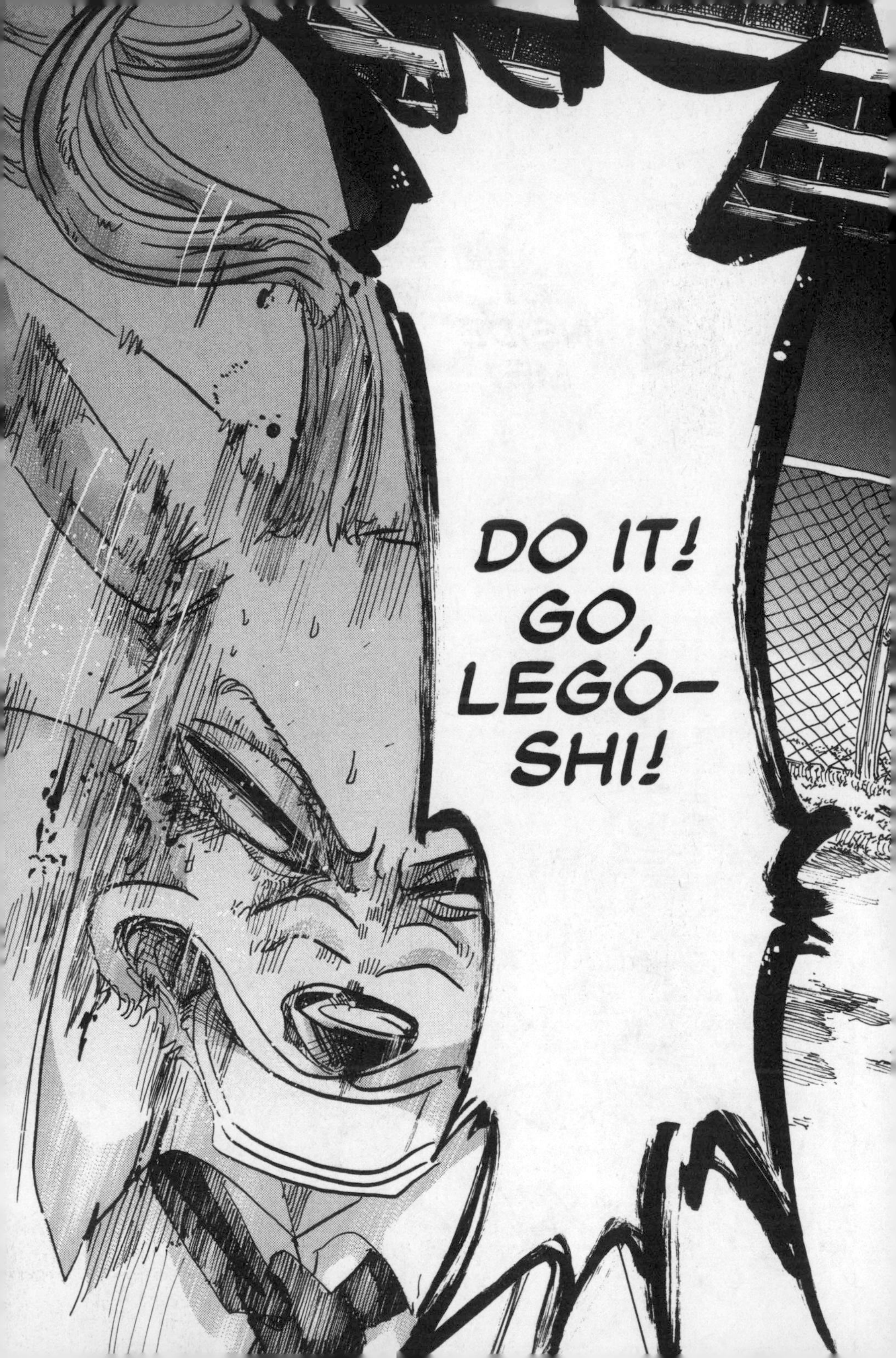
DO IT! GO, LEGO-SHI!

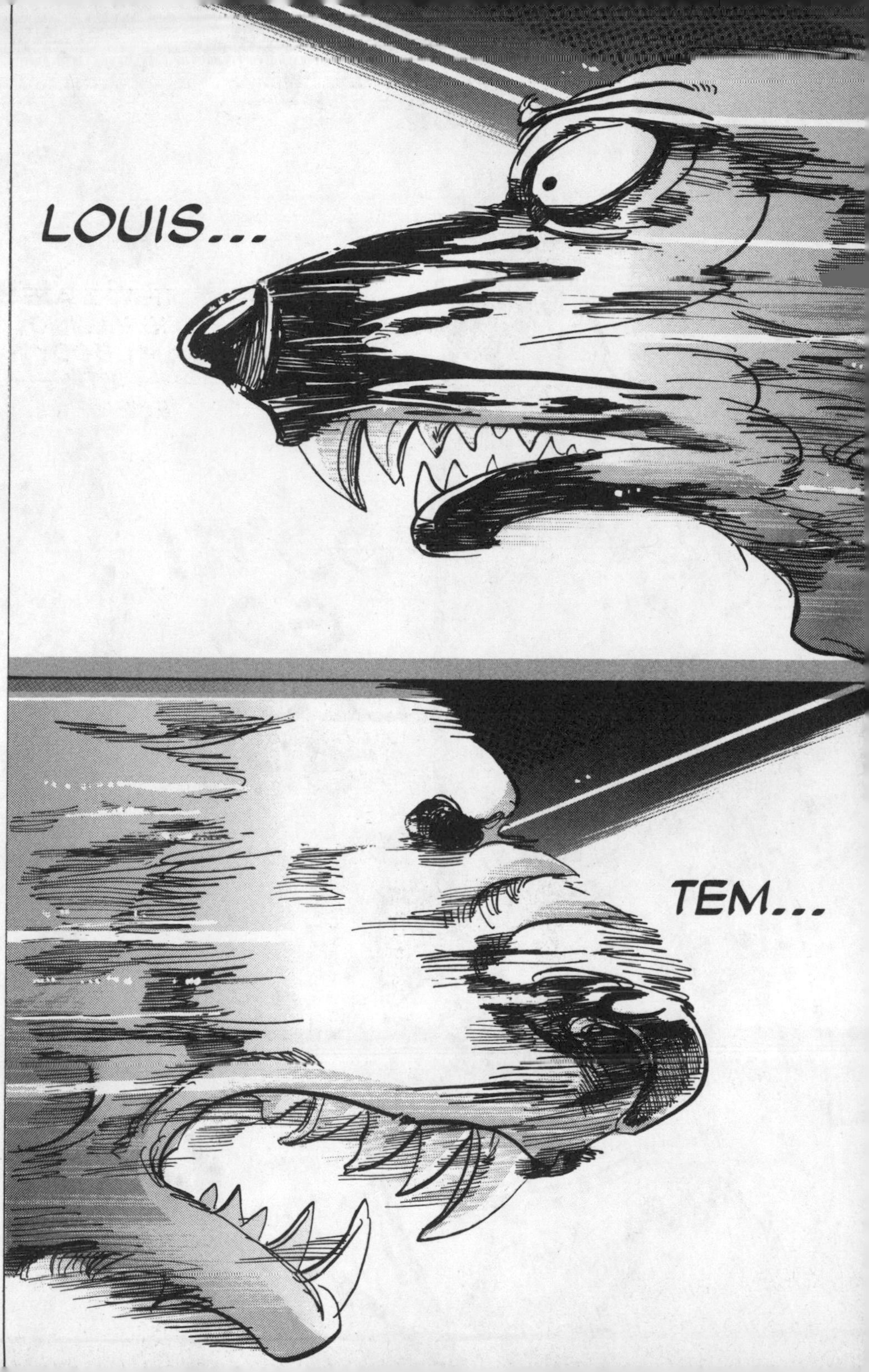
LOUIS...
TEM...

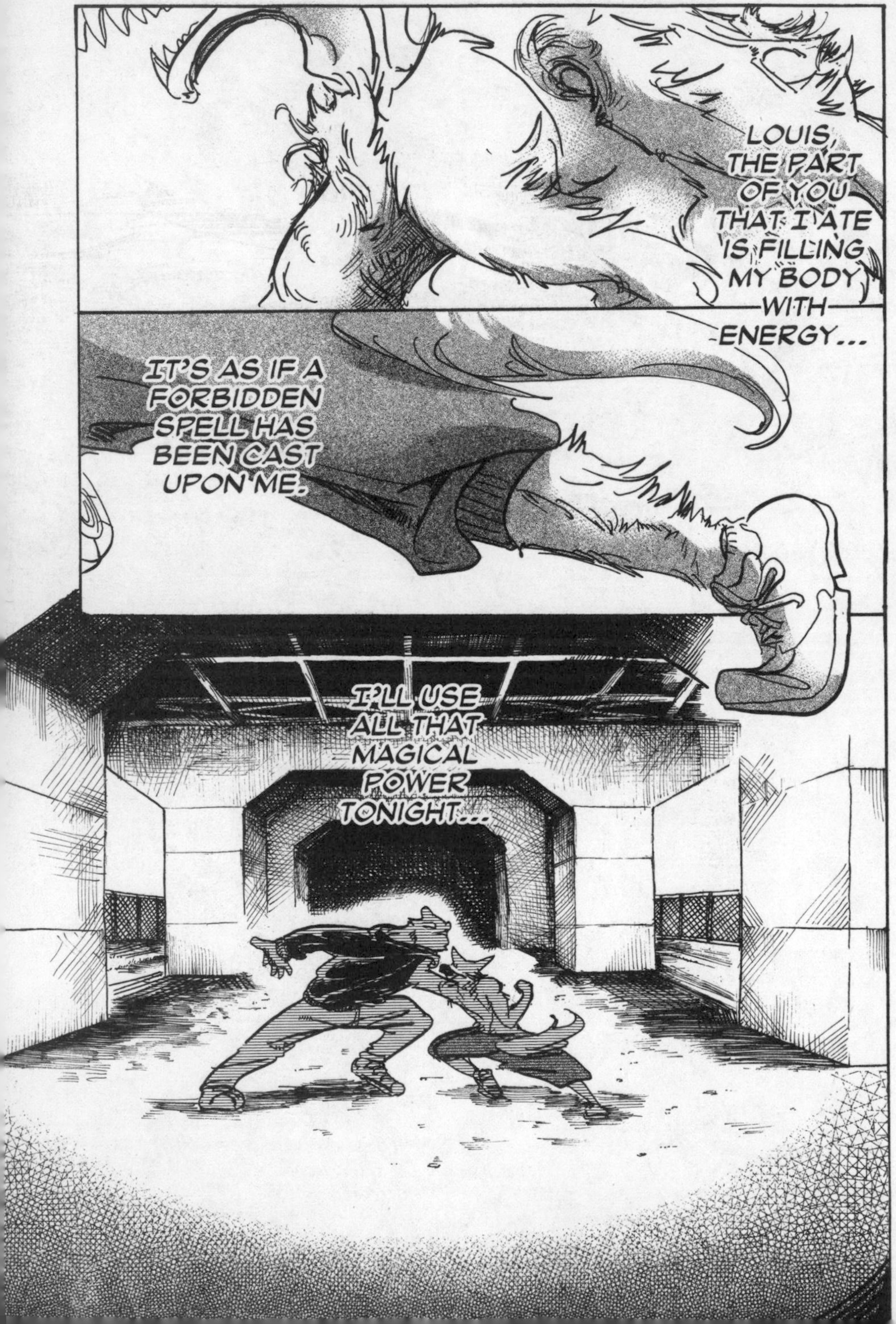
LOUIS, THE PART OF YOU THAT I ATE IS FILLING MY BODY WITH ENERGY...
IT'S AS IF A FORBIDDEN SPELL HAS BEEN CAST UPON ME.
I'LL USE ALL THAT MAGICAL POWER TONIGHT...

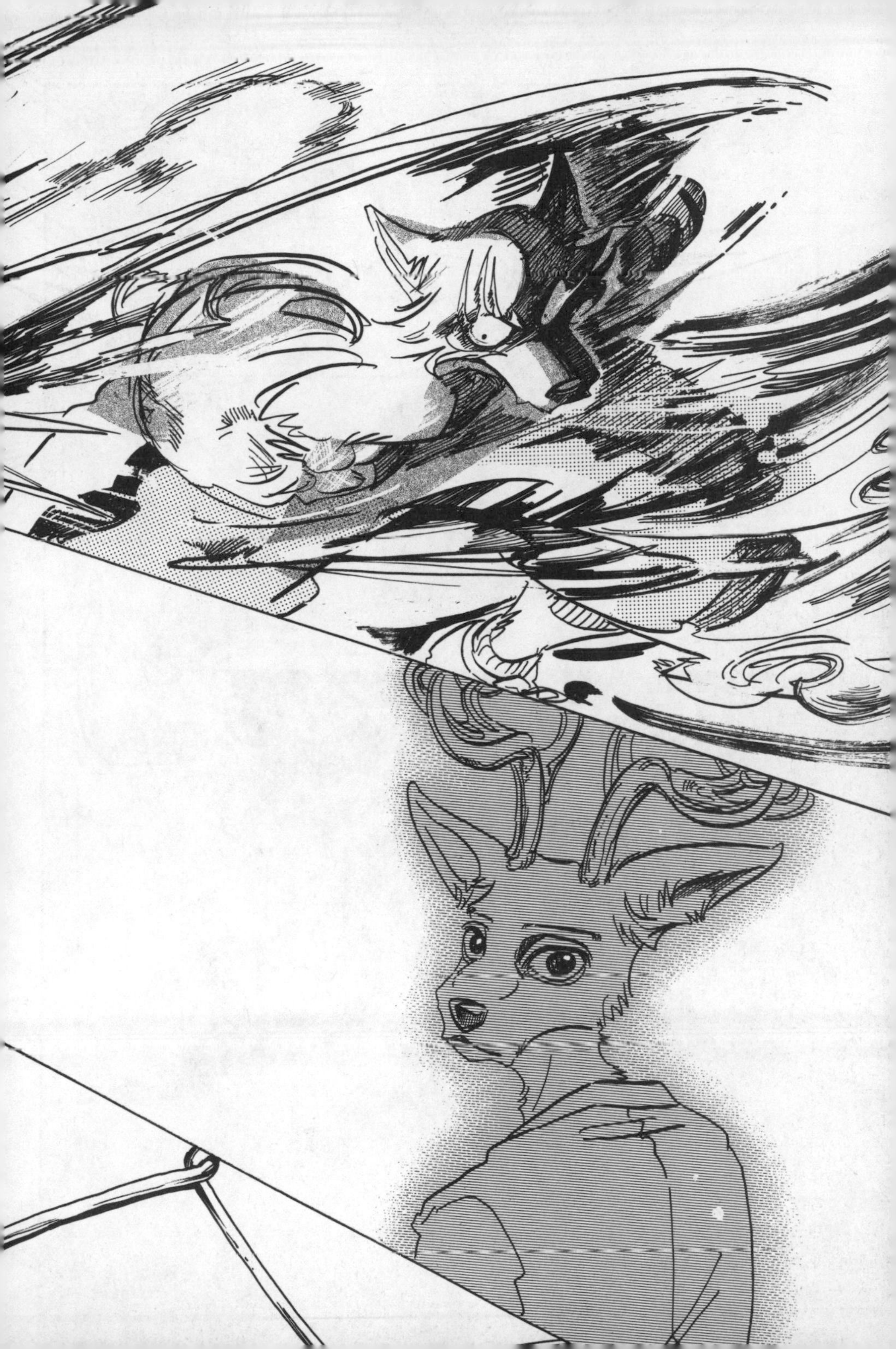

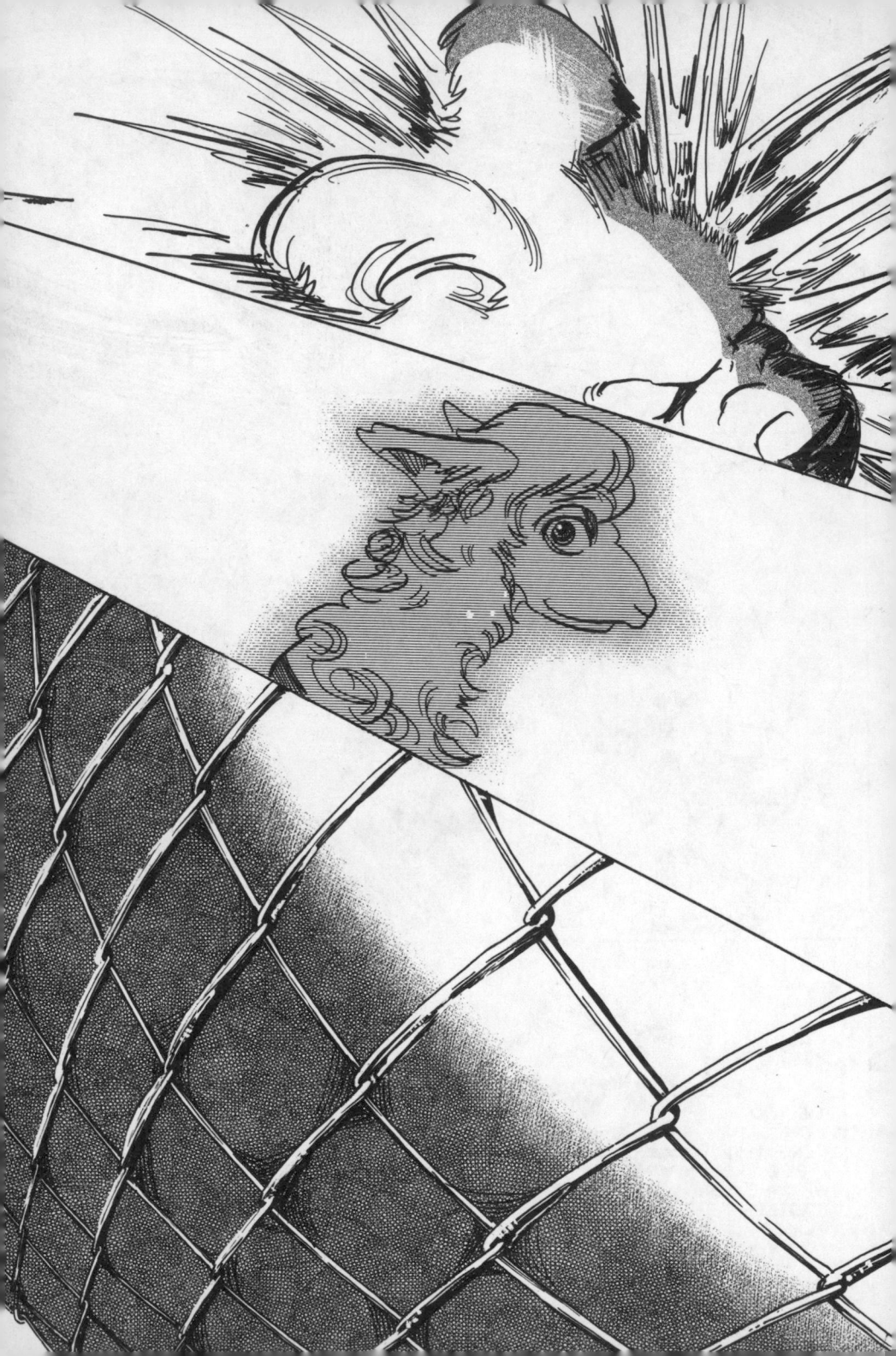

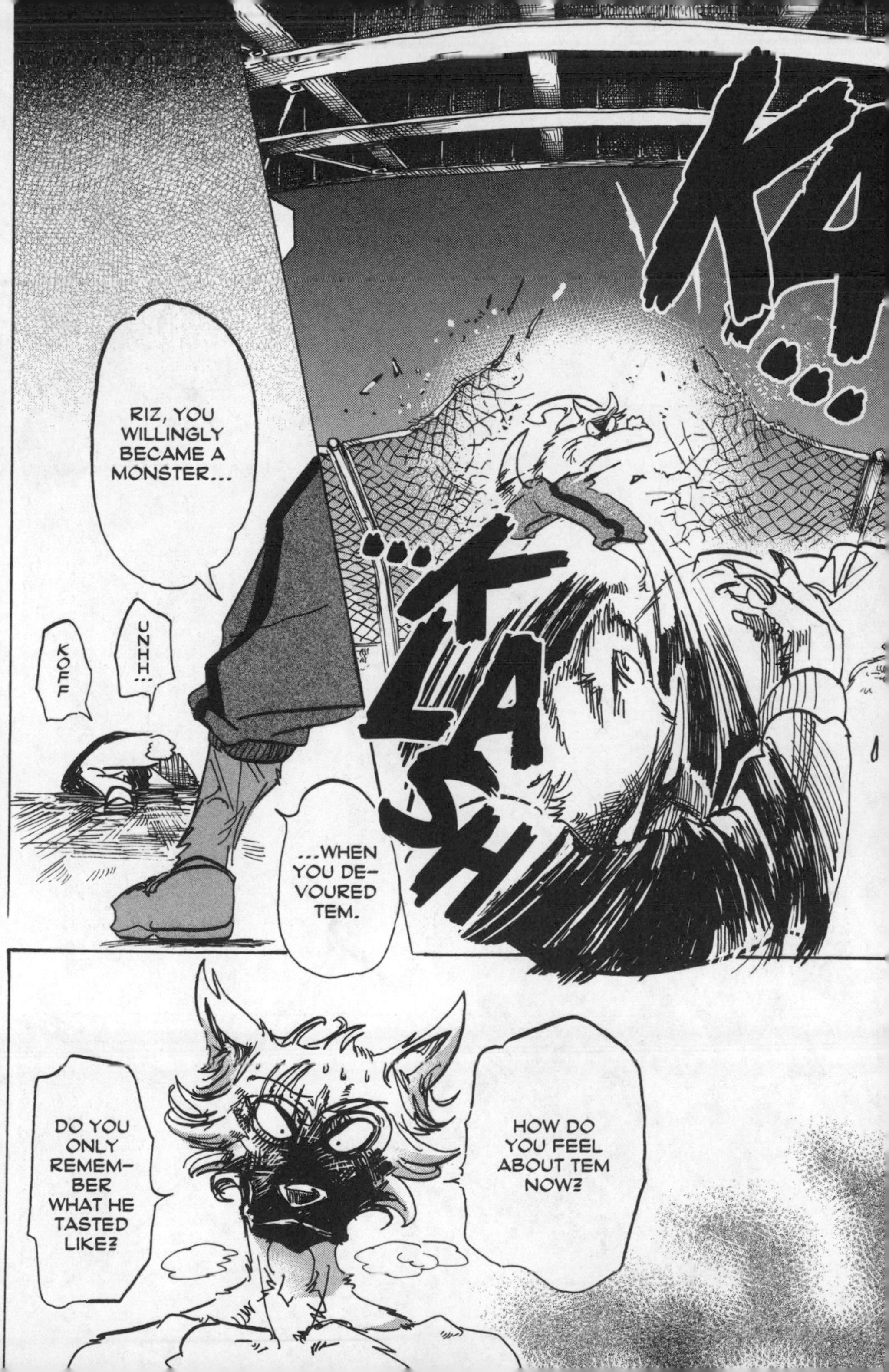
KA...
...KLASH
RIZ, YOU WILLINGLY BECAME A MONSTER...
...WHEN YOU DE-VOURED TEM.
UNHH...
KOFF
HOW DO YOU FEEL ABOUT TEM NOW?
DO YOU ONLY REMEM-BER WHAT HE TASTED LIKE?

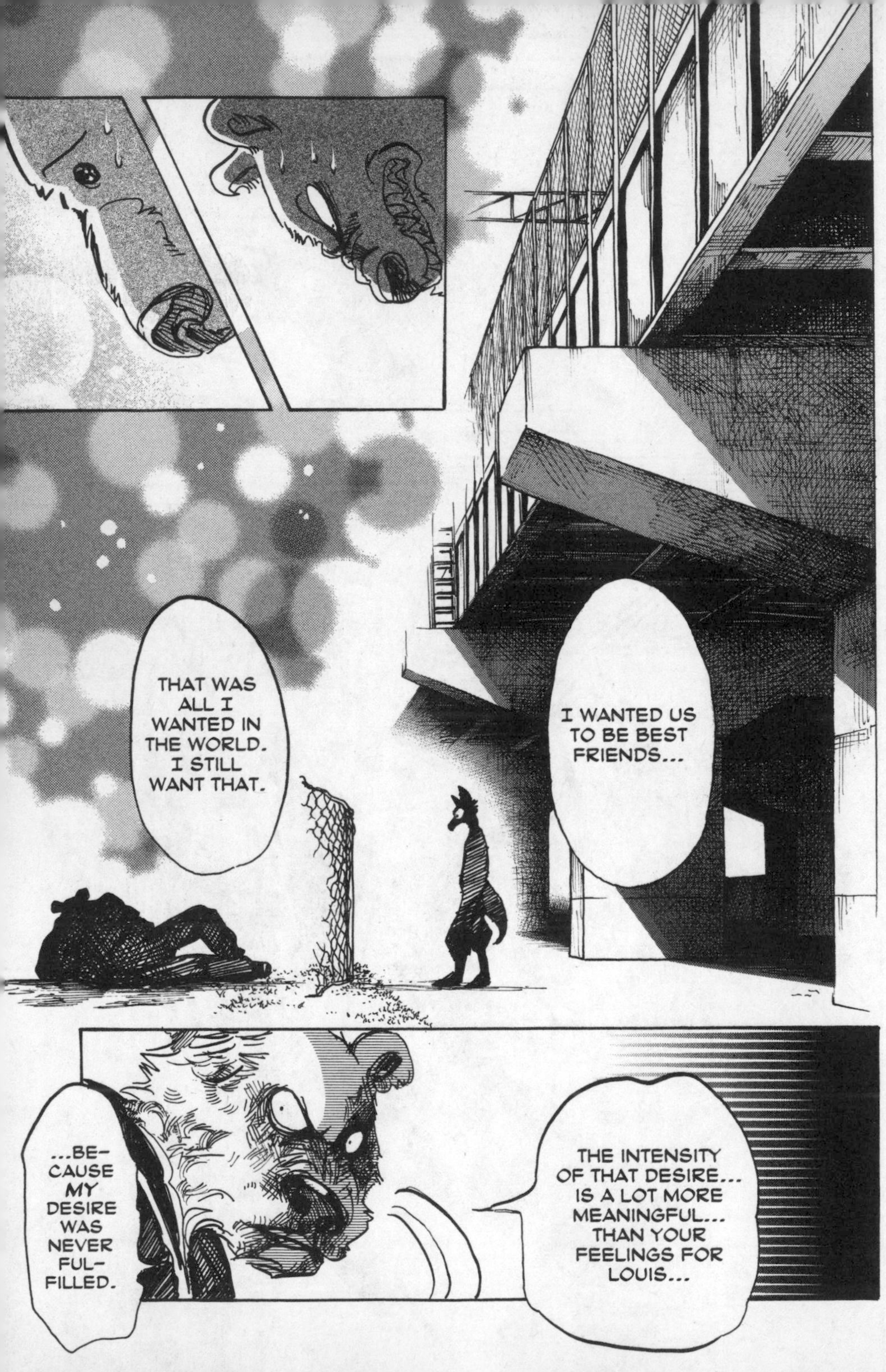
I WANTED US TO BE BEST FRIENDS...
THAT WAS ALL I WANTED IN THE WORLD. I STILL WANT THAT.
THE INTENSITY OF THAT DESIRE... IS A LOT MORE MEANINGFUL... THAN YOUR FEELINGS FOR LOUIS...
...BE-CAUSE MY DESIRE WAS NEVER FUL-FILLED.

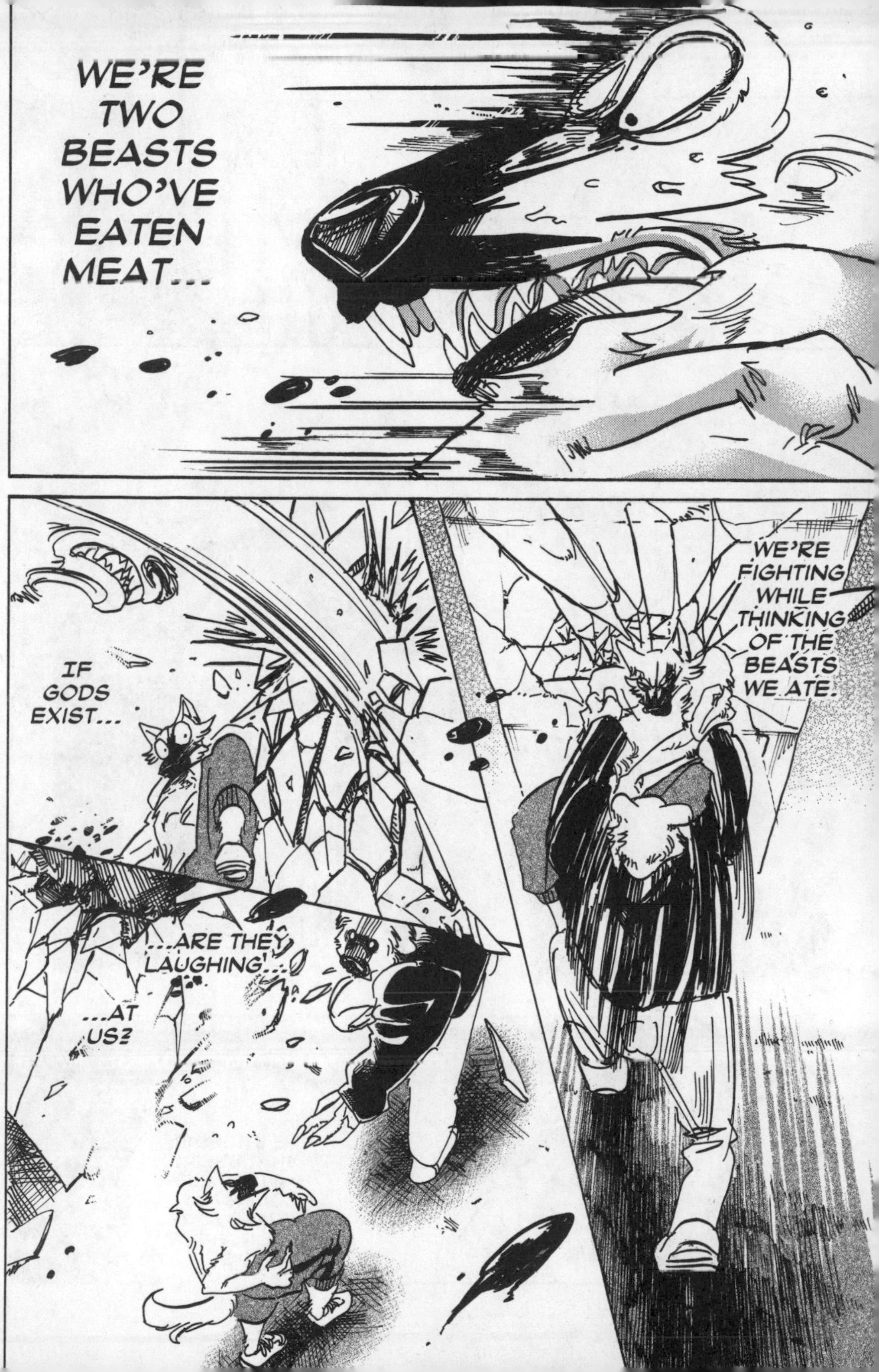
WE'RE TWO BEASTS WHO'VE EATEN MEAT...
WE'RE FIGHTING WHILE THINKING OF THE BEASTS WE ATE.
IF GODS EXIST...
...ARE THEY LAUGHING...
...AT US?

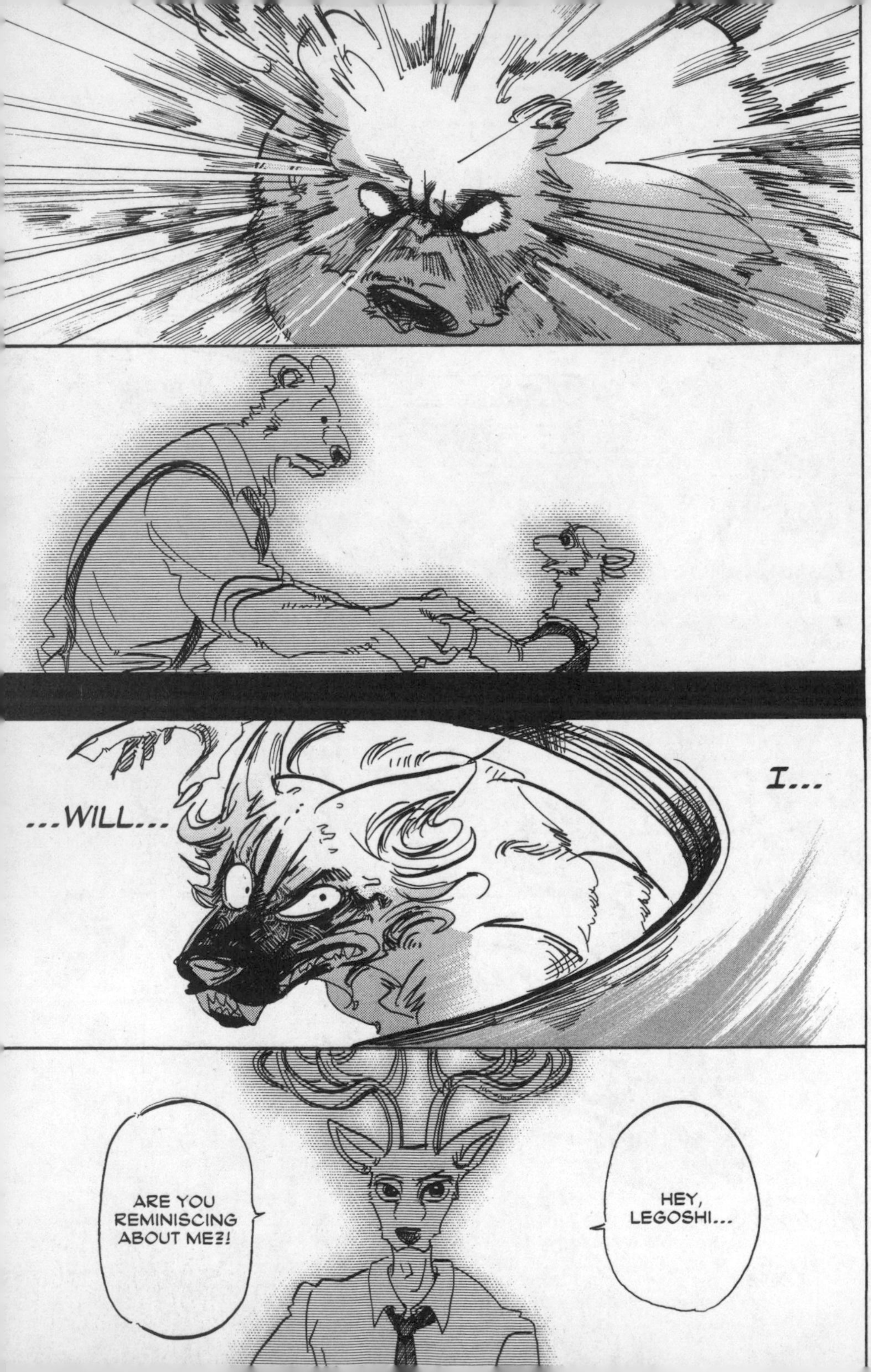
I...
...WILL...
HEY, LEGOSHI...
ARE YOU REMINISCING ABOUT ME?!

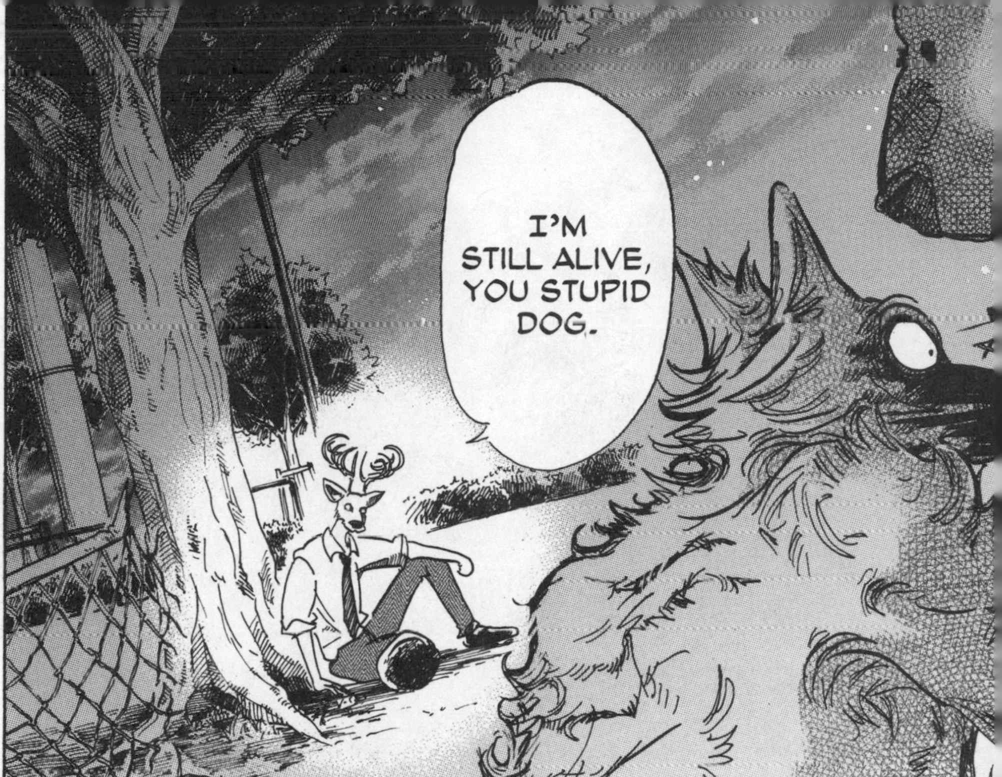
I'M STILL ALIVE, YOU STUPID DOG.
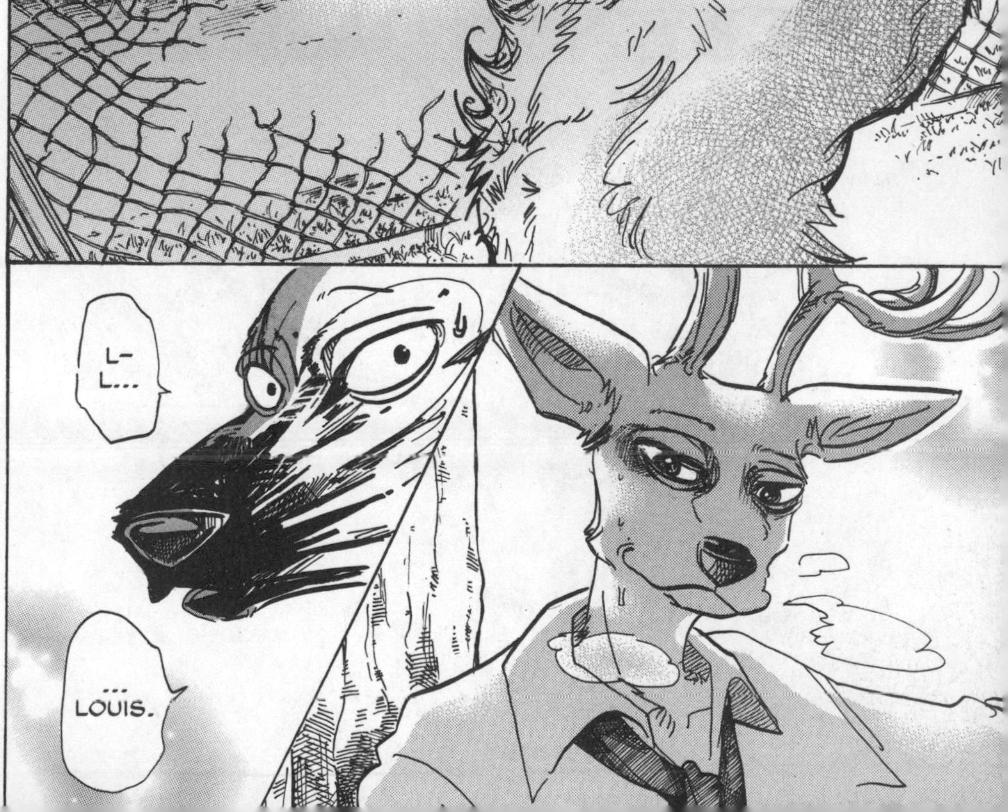
L- L...
... LOUIS.

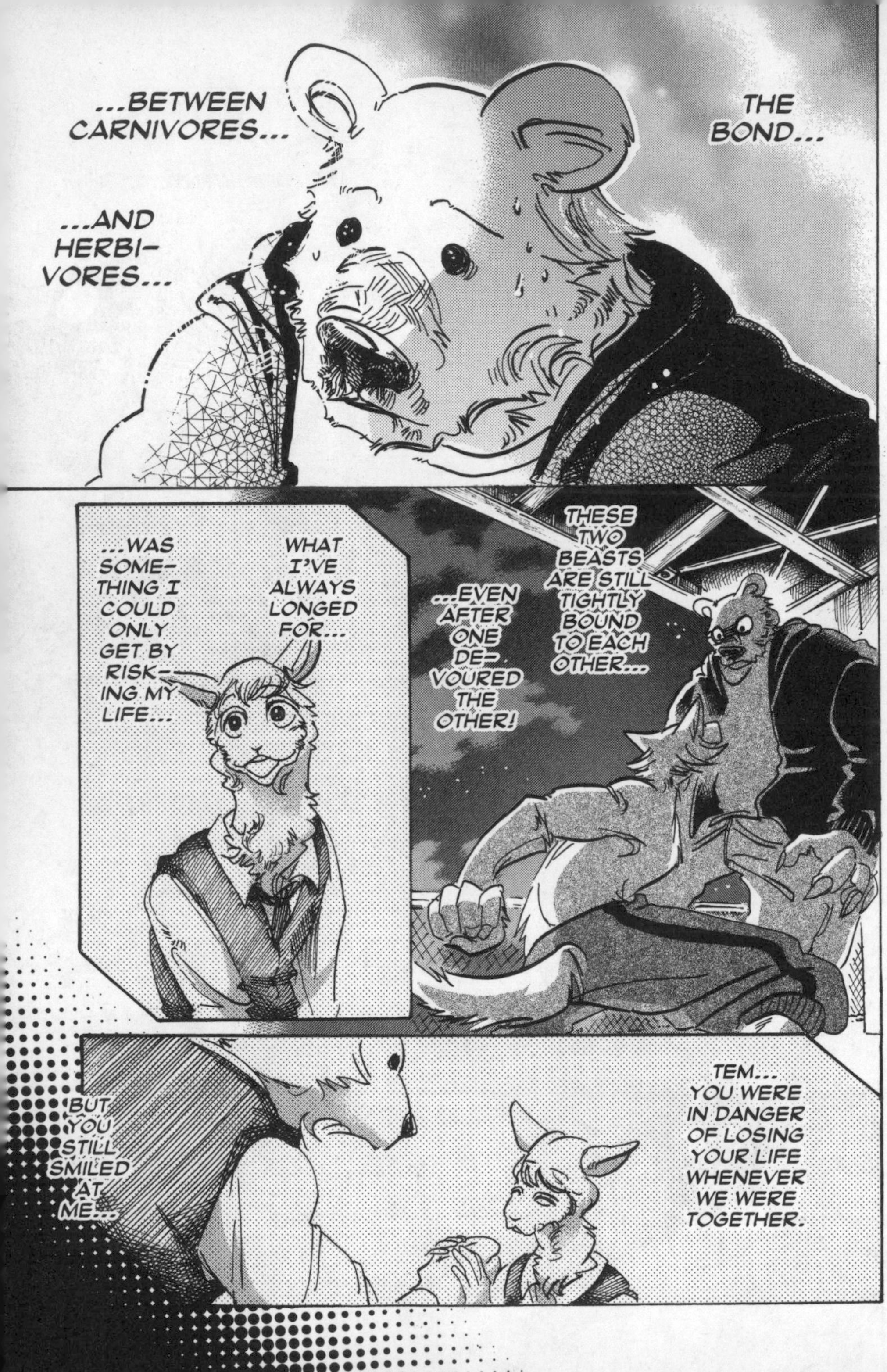
THE BOND...
...BETWEEN CARNIVORES...
...AND HERBI-VORES...
THESE TWO BEASTS ARE STILL TIGHTLY BOUND TO EACH OTHER...
...EVEN AFTER ONE DE-VOURED THE OTHER!
WHAT I'VE ALWAYS LONGED FOR...
...WAS SOME-THING I COULD ONLY GET BY RISK-ING MY LIFE...
TEM... YOU WERE IN DANGER OF LOSING YOUR LIFE WHENEVER WE WERE TOGETHER.
BUT YOU STILL SMILED AT ME...

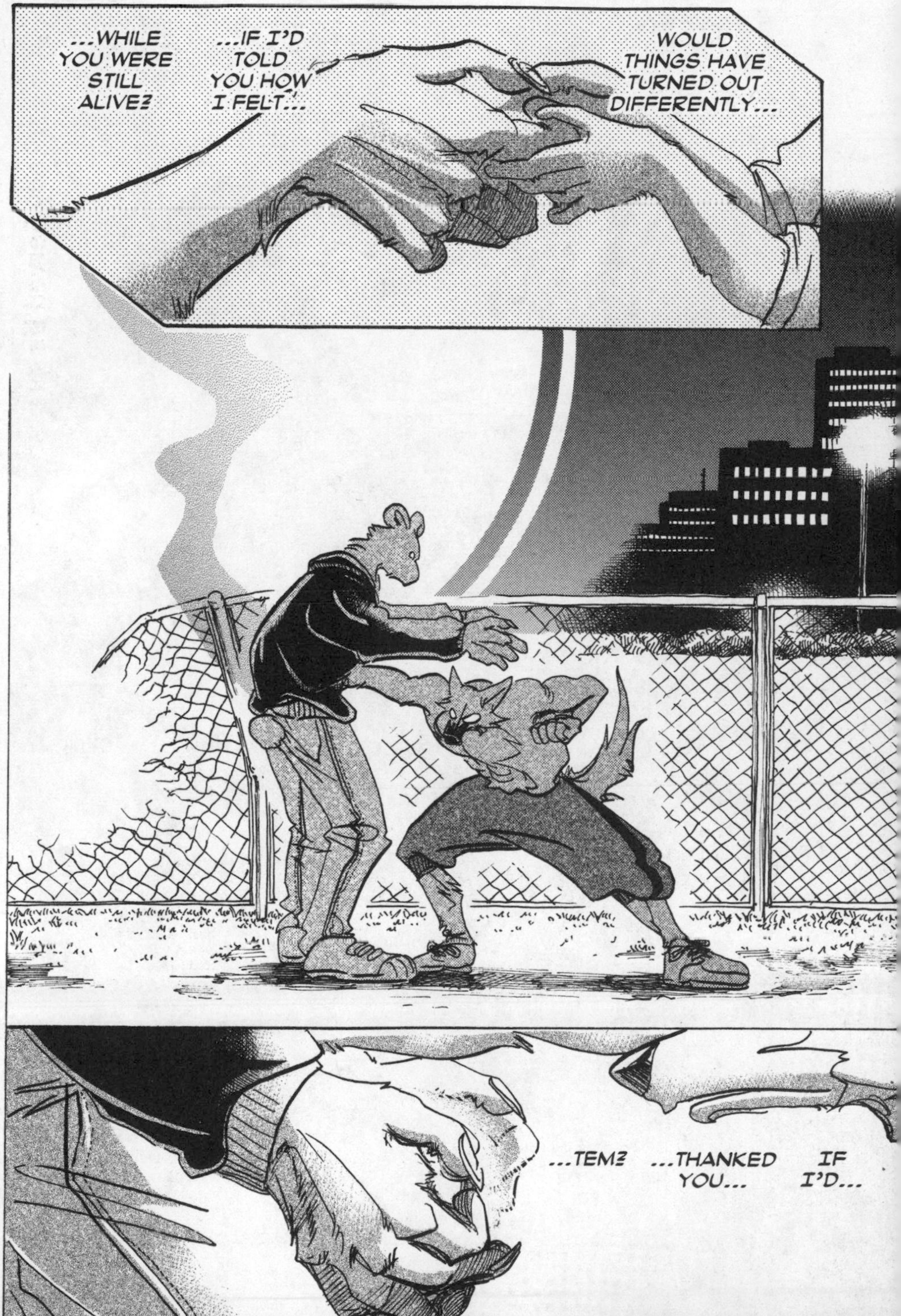
WOULD THINGS HAVE TURNED OUT DIFFERENTLY...
...IF I'D TOLD YOU HOW I FELT...
...WHILE YOU WERE STILL ALIVE?
IF I'D...
...THANKED YOU...
...TEM?

Chapter 97: They Served Us a Feast

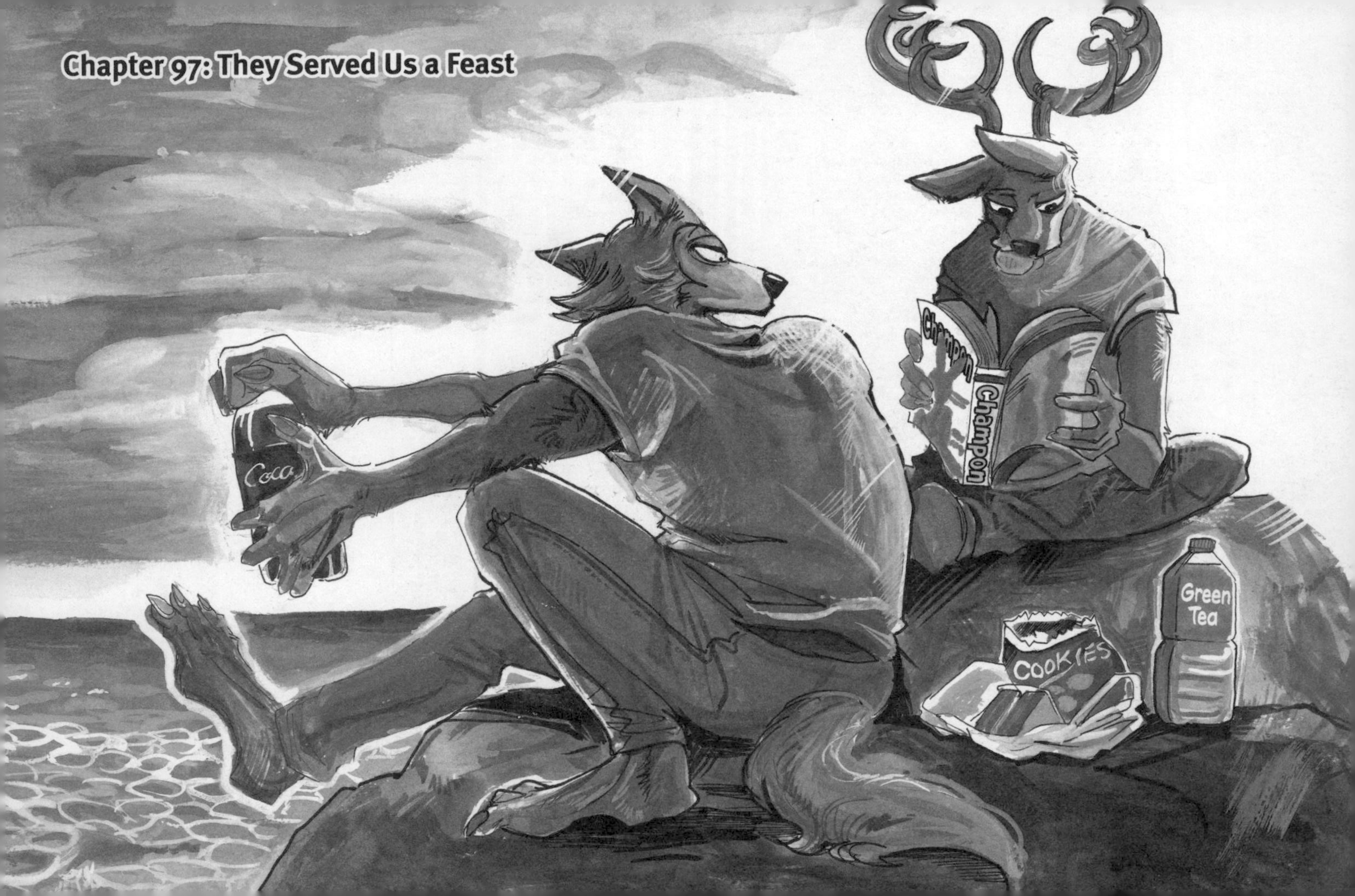
Coca
Champon
Champon
COOKIES
Green Tea

BEASTARS
Vol. 11

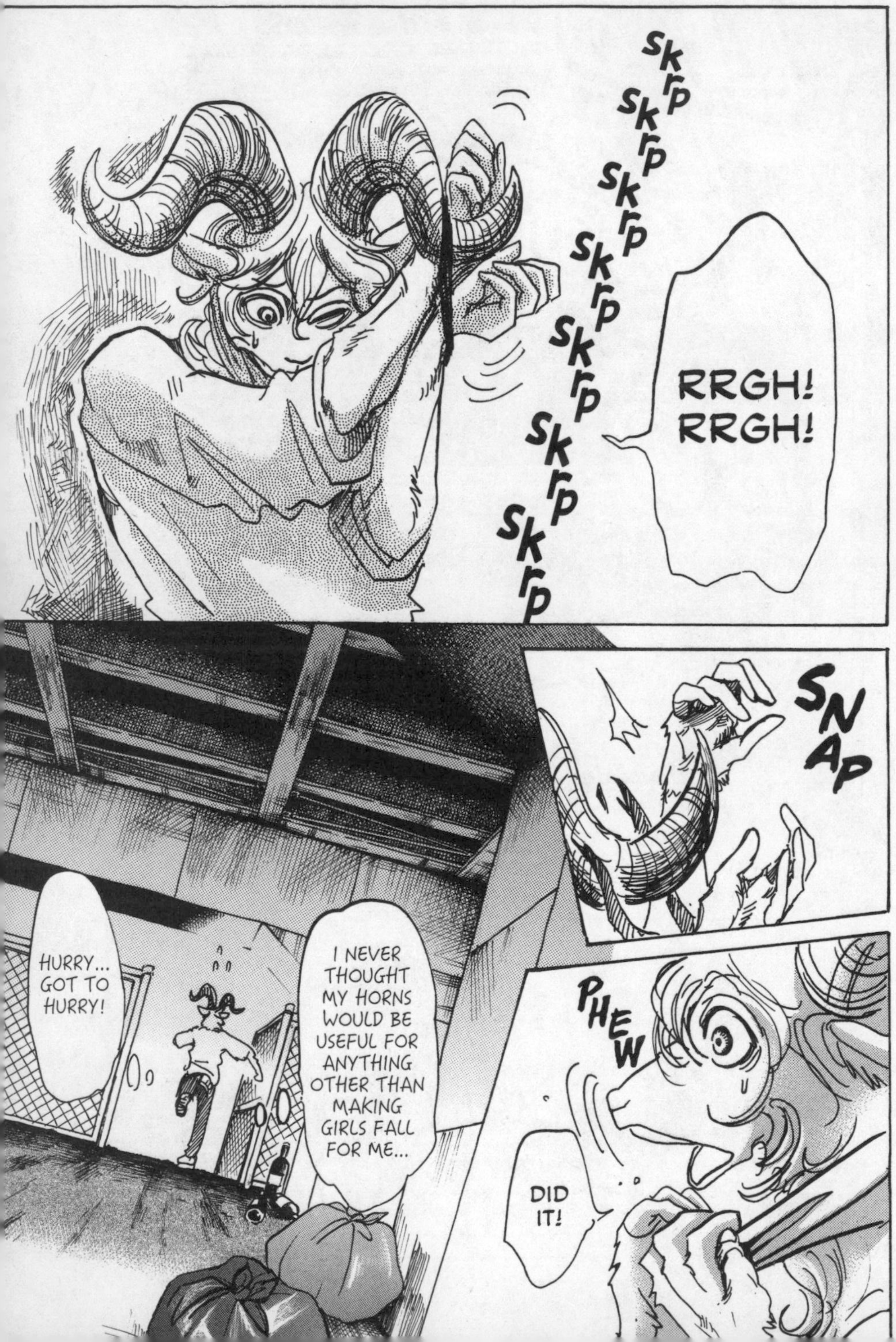
RRGH! RRGH!
SKRP SKRP SKRP SKRP SKRP SKRP SKRP SKRP
SNAP
PHEW
DID IT!
I NEVER THOUGHT MY HORNS WOULD BE USEFUL FOR ANYTHING OTHER THAN MAKING GIRLS FALL FOR ME...
HURRY... GOT TO HURRY!

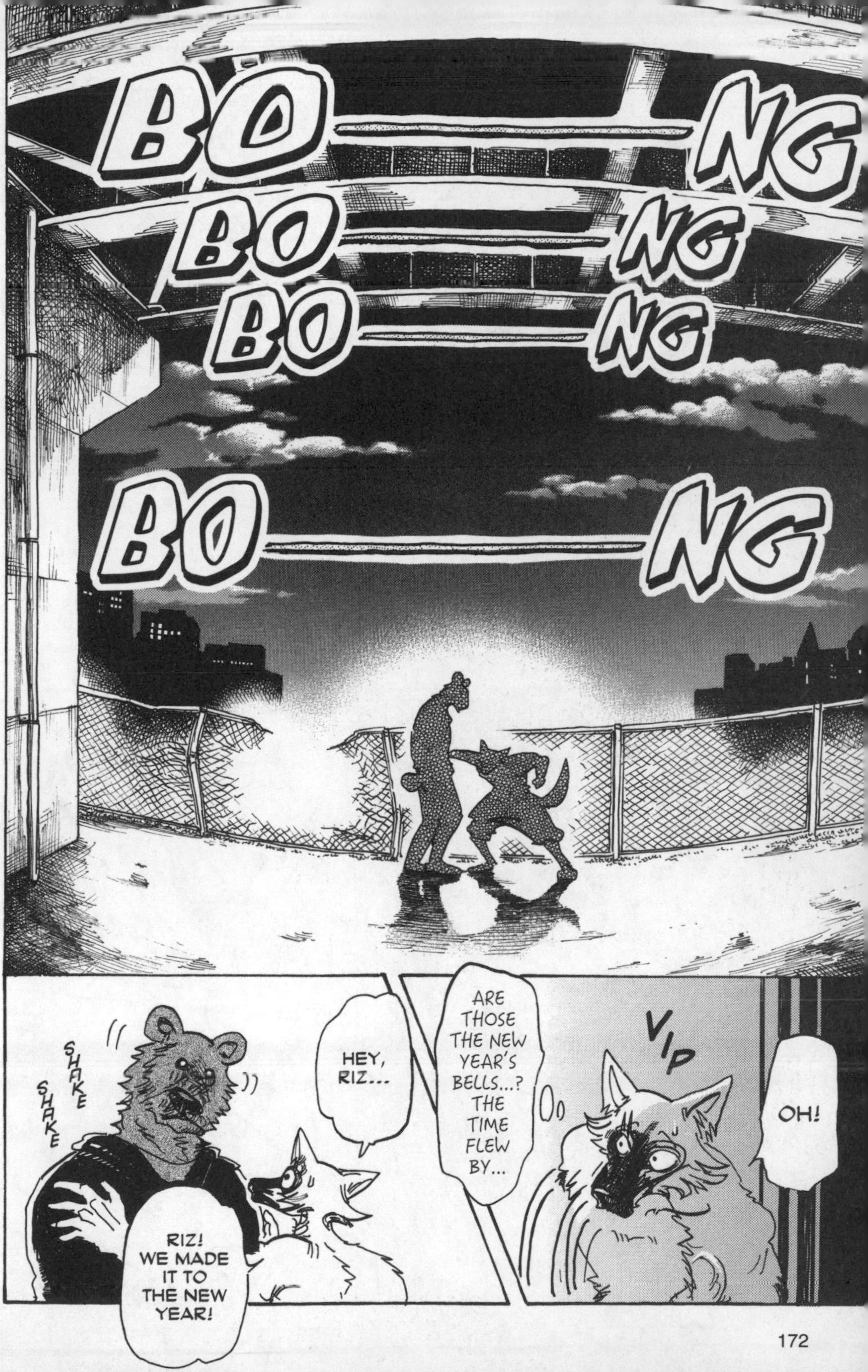
BO—NG
BO—NG
BO—NG
BO—NG
VIP
OH!
ARE THOSE THE NEW YEAR'S BELLS...? THE TIME FLEW BY...
HEY, RIZ...
SHAKE SHAKE
RIZ! WE MADE IT TO THE NEW YEAR!

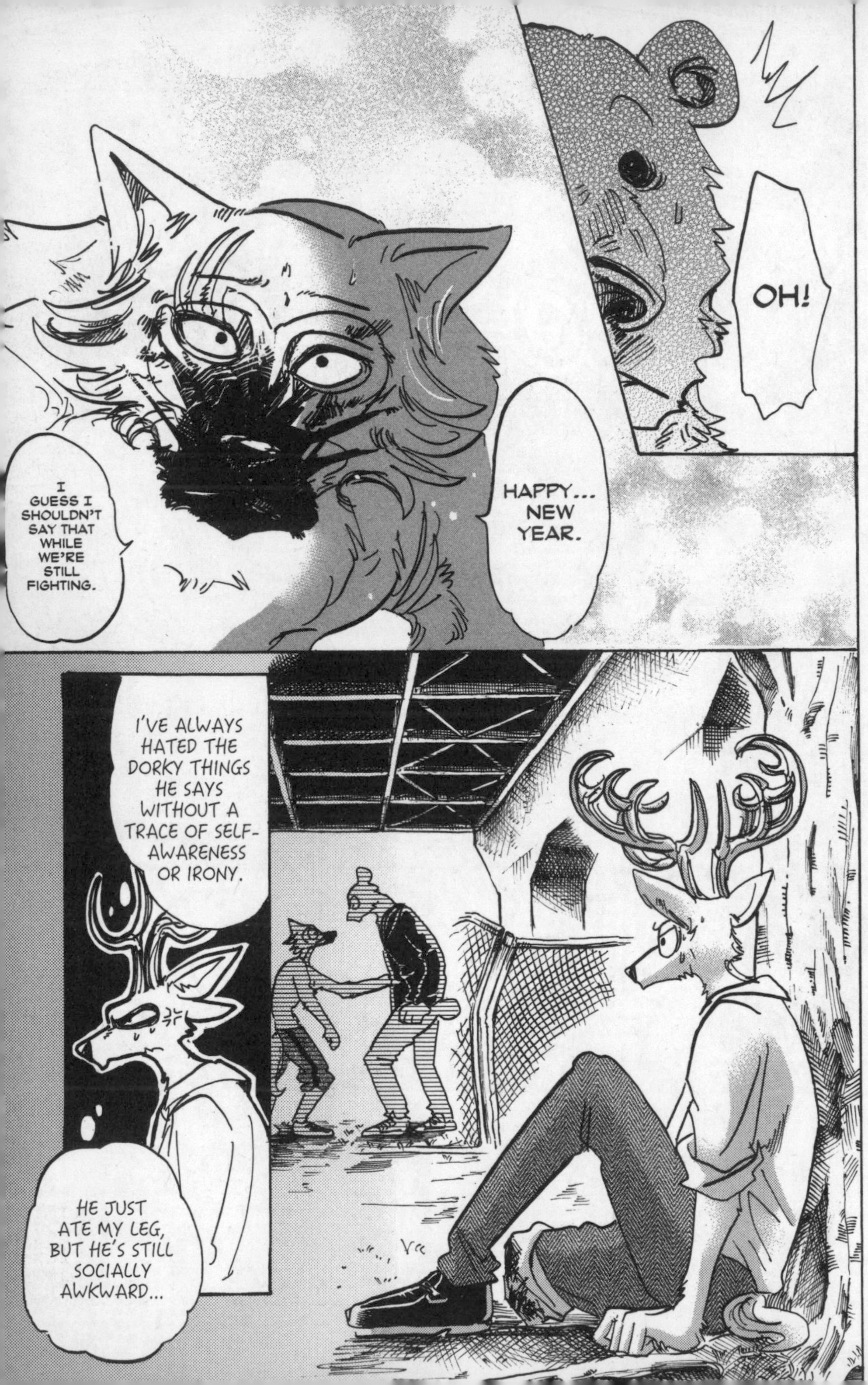
OH!
HAPPY... NEW YEAR.
I GUESS I SHOULDN'T SAY THAT WHILE WE'RE STILL FIGHTING.
I'VE ALWAYS HATED THE DORKY THINGS HE SAYS WITHOUT A TRACE OF SELF-AWARENESS OR IRONY.
HE JUST ATE MY LEG, BUT HE'S STILL SOCIALLY AWKWARD...

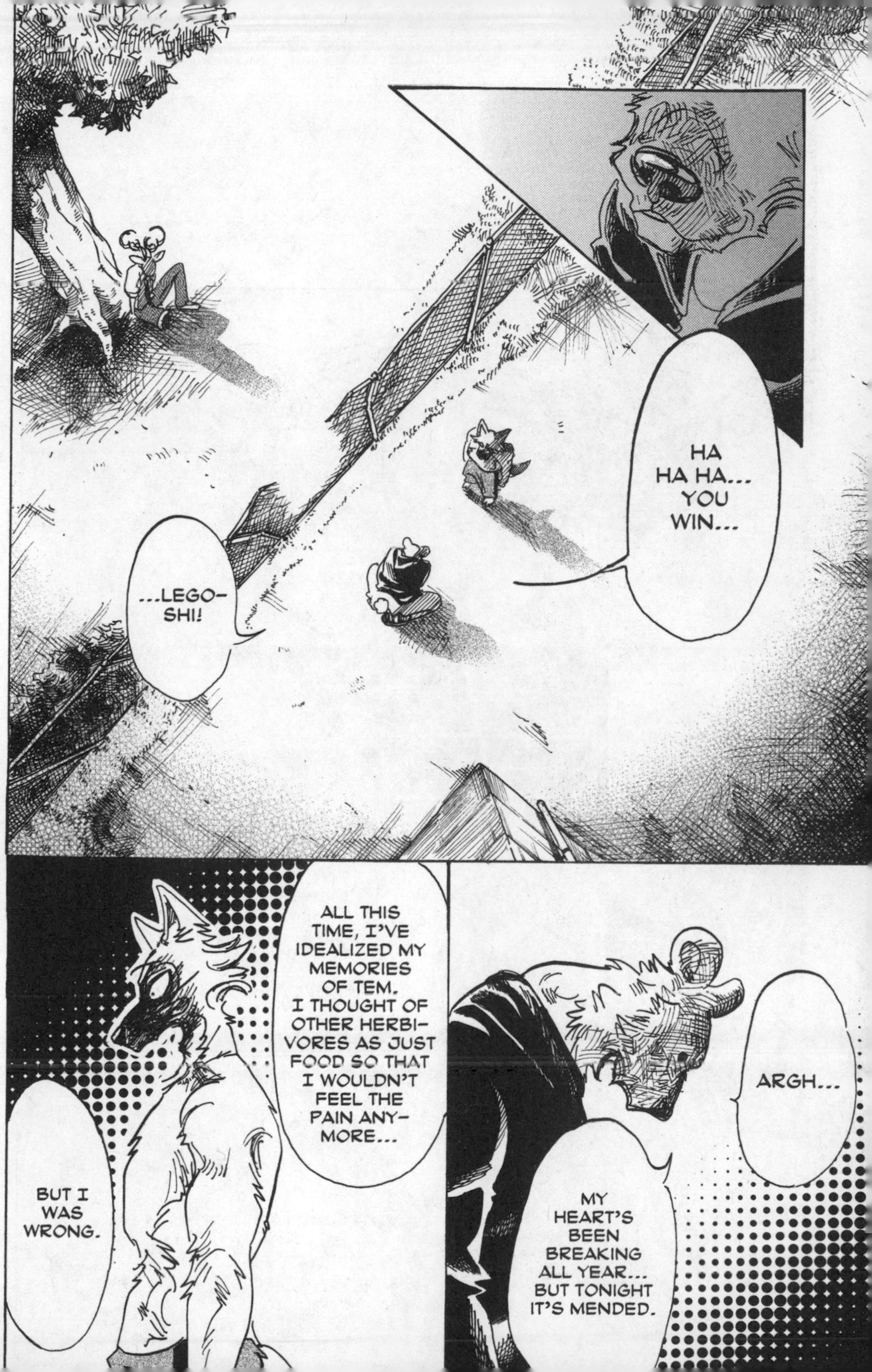
HA HA HA... YOU WIN...
...LEGOSHI!
ARGH...
MY HEART'S BEEN BREAKING ALL YEAR... BUT TONIGHT IT'S MENDED.
ALL THIS TIME, I'VE IDEALIZED MY MEMORIES OF TEM. I THOUGHT OF OTHER HERBIVORES AS JUST FOOD SO THAT I WOULDN'T FEEL THE PAIN ANYMORE...
BUT I WAS WRONG.

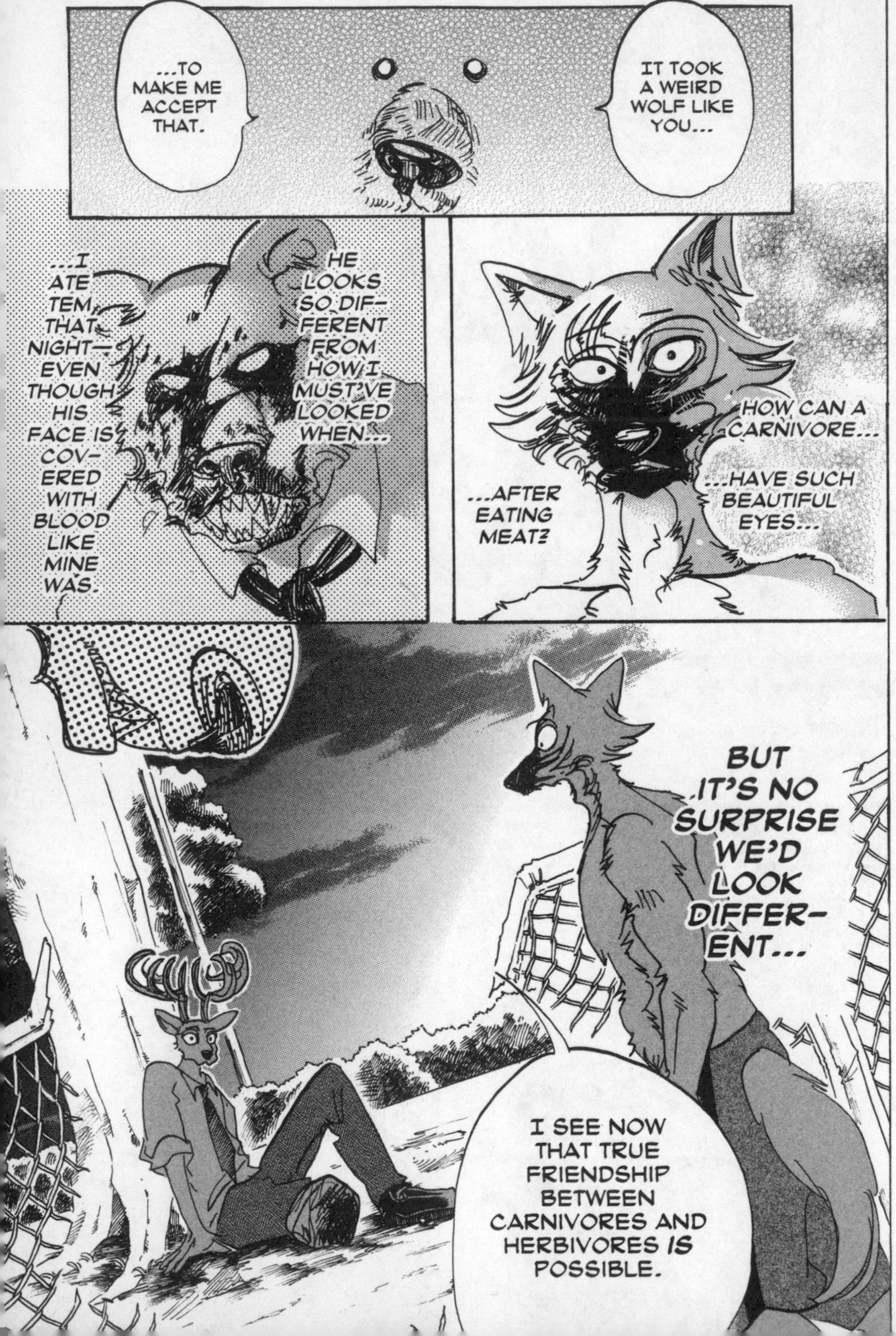
IT TOOK A WEIRD WOLF LIKE YOU...
...TO MAKE ME ACCEPT THAT.
HOW CAN A CARNIVORE...
...HAVE SUCH BEAUTIFUL EYES...
...AFTER EATING MEAT?
HE LOOKS SO DIFFERENT FROM HOW I MUST'VE LOOKED WHEN...
...I ATE TEM THAT NIGHT—EVEN THOUGH HIS FACE IS COVERED WITH BLOOD LIKE MINE WAS.
BUT IT'S NO SURPRISE WE'D LOOK DIFFERENT...
I SEE NOW THAT TRUE FRIENDSHIP BETWEEN CARNIVORES AND HERBIVORES *IS* POSSIBLE.

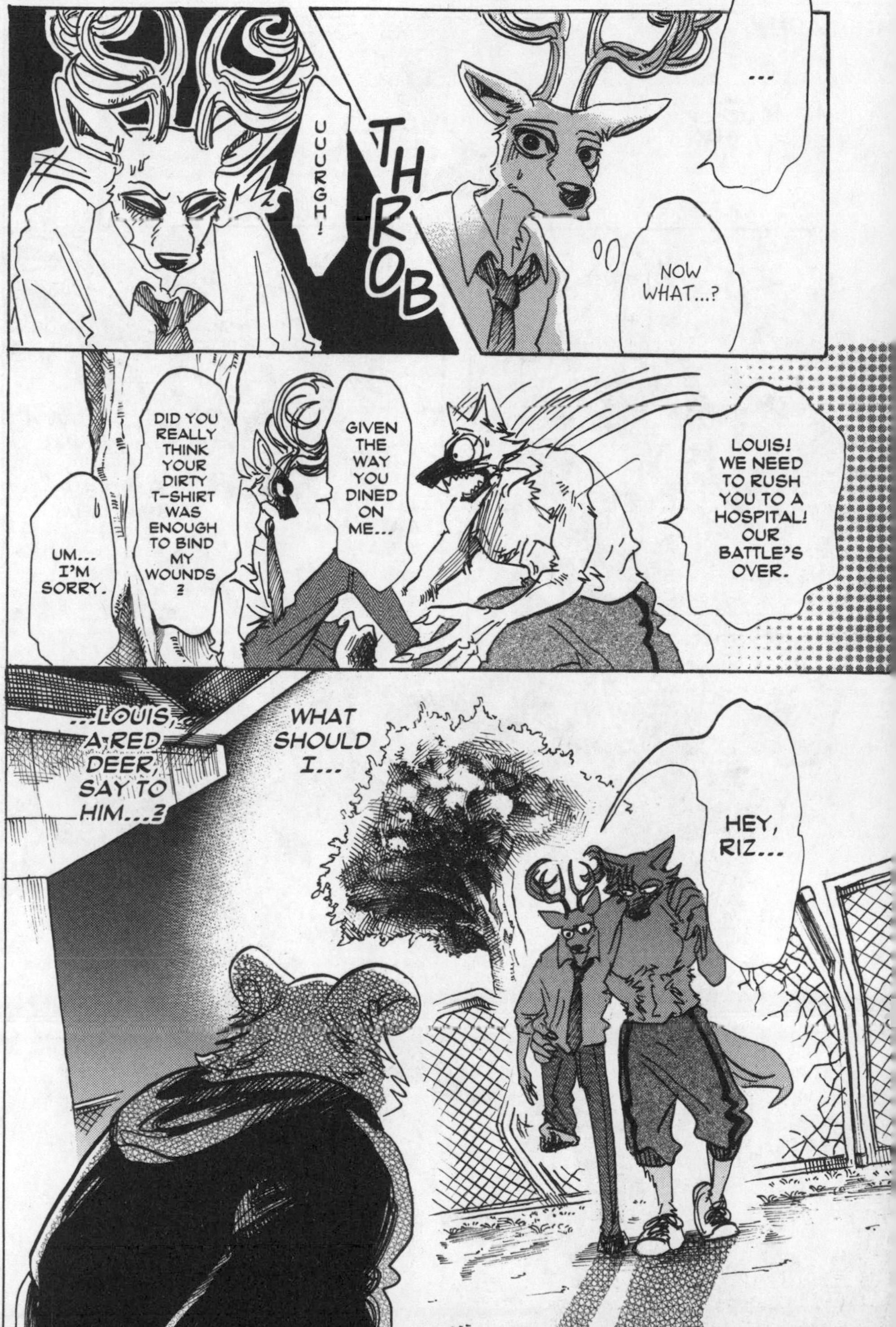
...
NOW WHAT...?
THROB
UUURGH!
LOUIS! WE NEED TO RUSH YOU TO A HOSPITAL! OUR BATTLE'S OVER.
GIVEN THE WAY YOU DINED ON ME...
DID YOU REALLY THINK YOUR DIRTY T-SHIRT WAS ENOUGH TO BIND MY WOUNDS?
UM... I'M SORRY.
HEY, RIZ...
WHAT SHOULD I...
...LOUIS, A RED DEER, SAY TO HIM...?

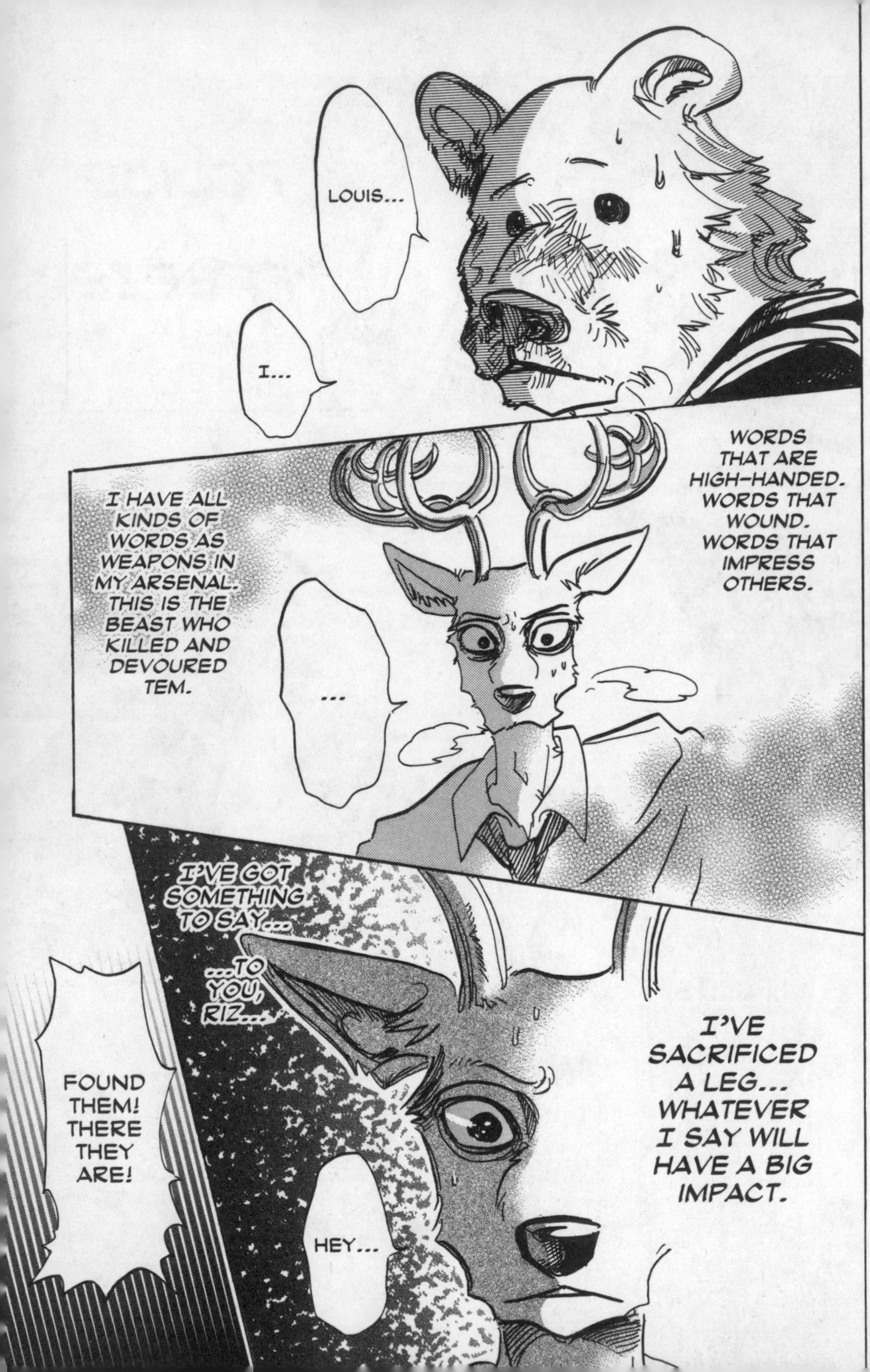
LOUIS...
I...
WORDS THAT ARE HIGH-HANDED. WORDS THAT WOUND. WORDS THAT IMPRESS OTHERS.
I HAVE ALL KINDS OF WORDS AS WEAPONS IN MY ARSENAL. THIS IS THE BEAST WHO KILLED AND DEVOURED TEM.
...
I'VE SACRIFICED A LEG... WHATEVER I SAY WILL HAVE A BIG IMPACT.
I'VE GOT SOMETHING TO SAY...
...TO YOU, RIZ...
HEY...
FOUND THEM! THERE THEY ARE!

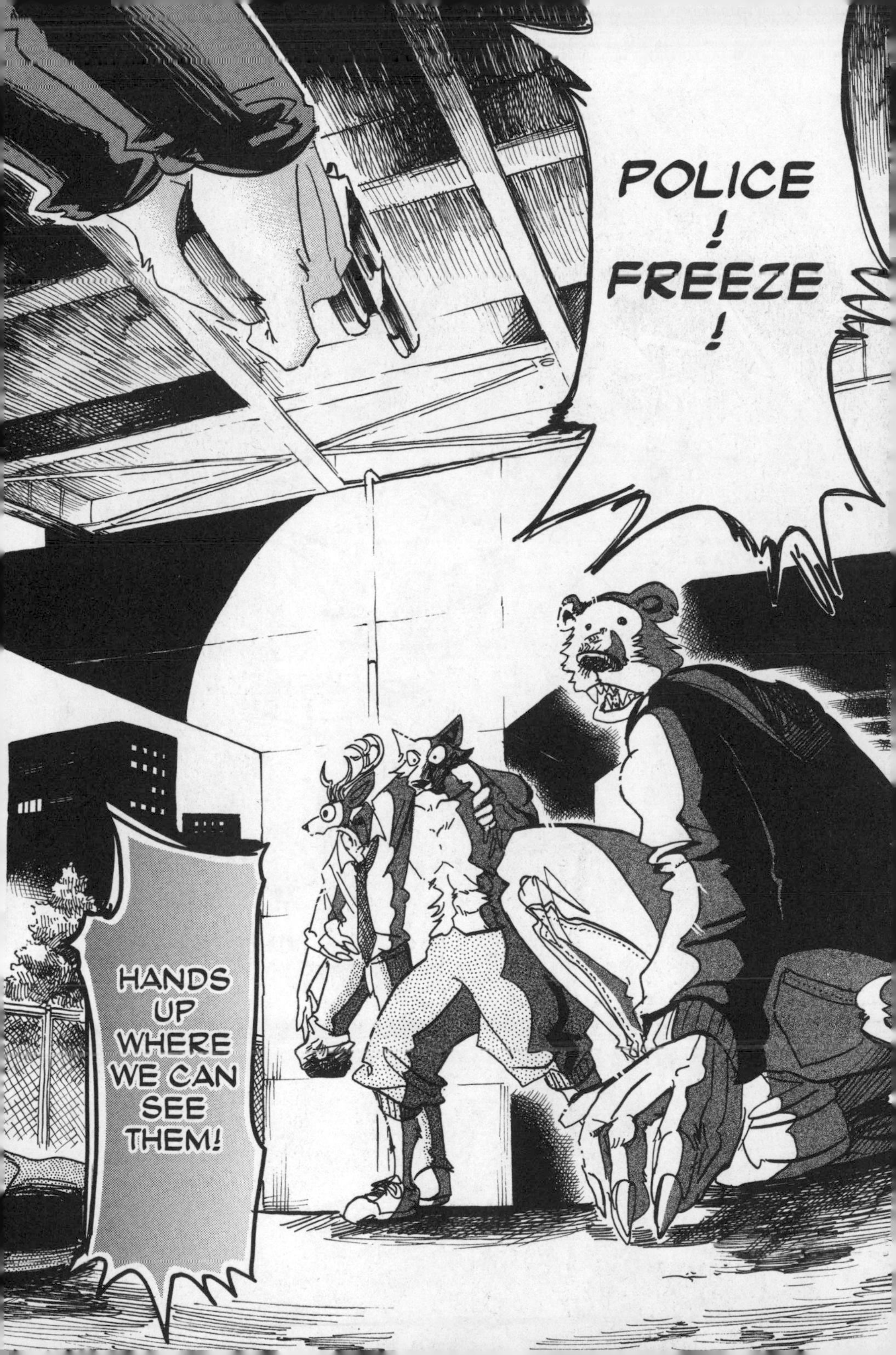
POLICE! FREEZE!
HANDS UP WHERE WE CAN SEE THEM!

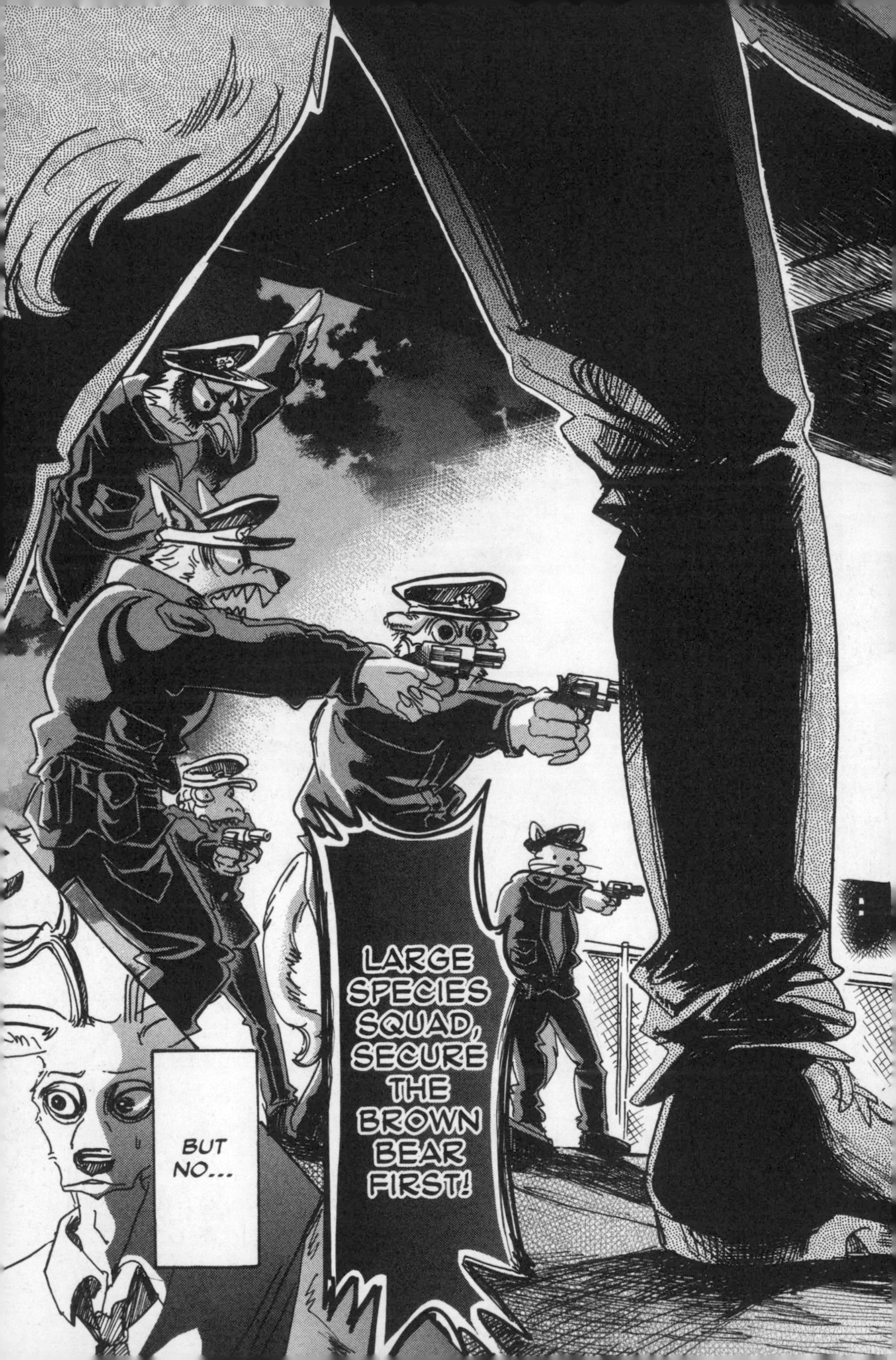
LARGE SPECIES SQUAD, SECURE THE BROWN BEAR FIRST!
BUT NO...

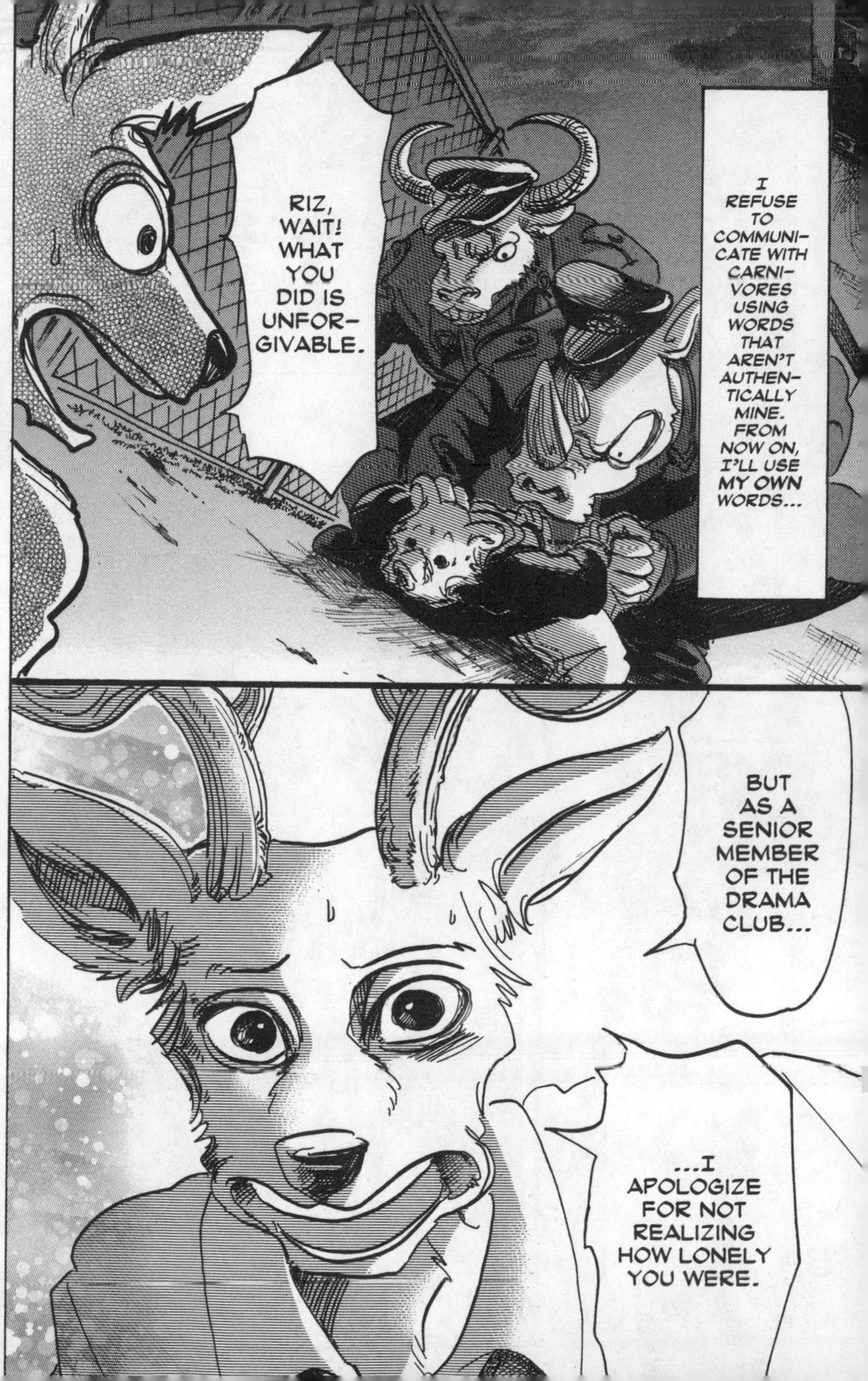
I REFUSE TO COMMUNICATE WITH CARNIVORES USING WORDS THAT AREN'T AUTHENTICALLY MINE. FROM NOW ON, I'LL USE MY OWN WORDS...
RIZ, WAIT! WHAT YOU DID IS UNFORGIVABLE.
BUT AS A SENIOR MEMBER OF THE DRAMA CLUB...
...I APOLOGIZE FOR NOT REALIZING HOW LONELY YOU WERE.

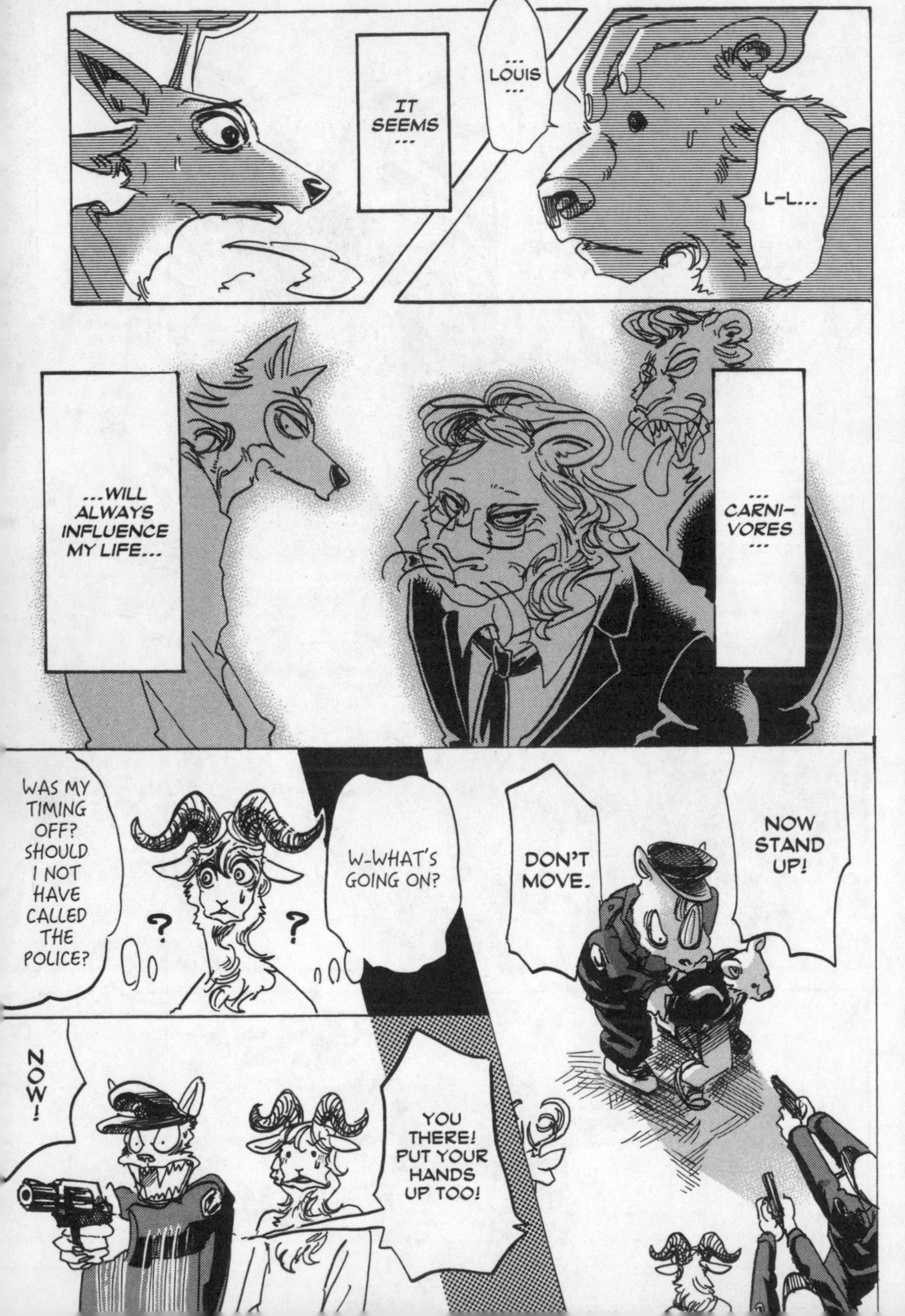
...LOUIS...
L-L...
IT SEEMS...
...CARNIVORES...
...WILL ALWAYS INFLUENCE MY LIFE...
NOW STAND UP!
DON'T MOVE.
W-WHAT'S GOING ON?
WAS MY TIMING OFF? SHOULD I NOT HAVE CALLED THE POLICE?
YOU THERE! PUT YOUR HANDS UP TOO!
NOW!

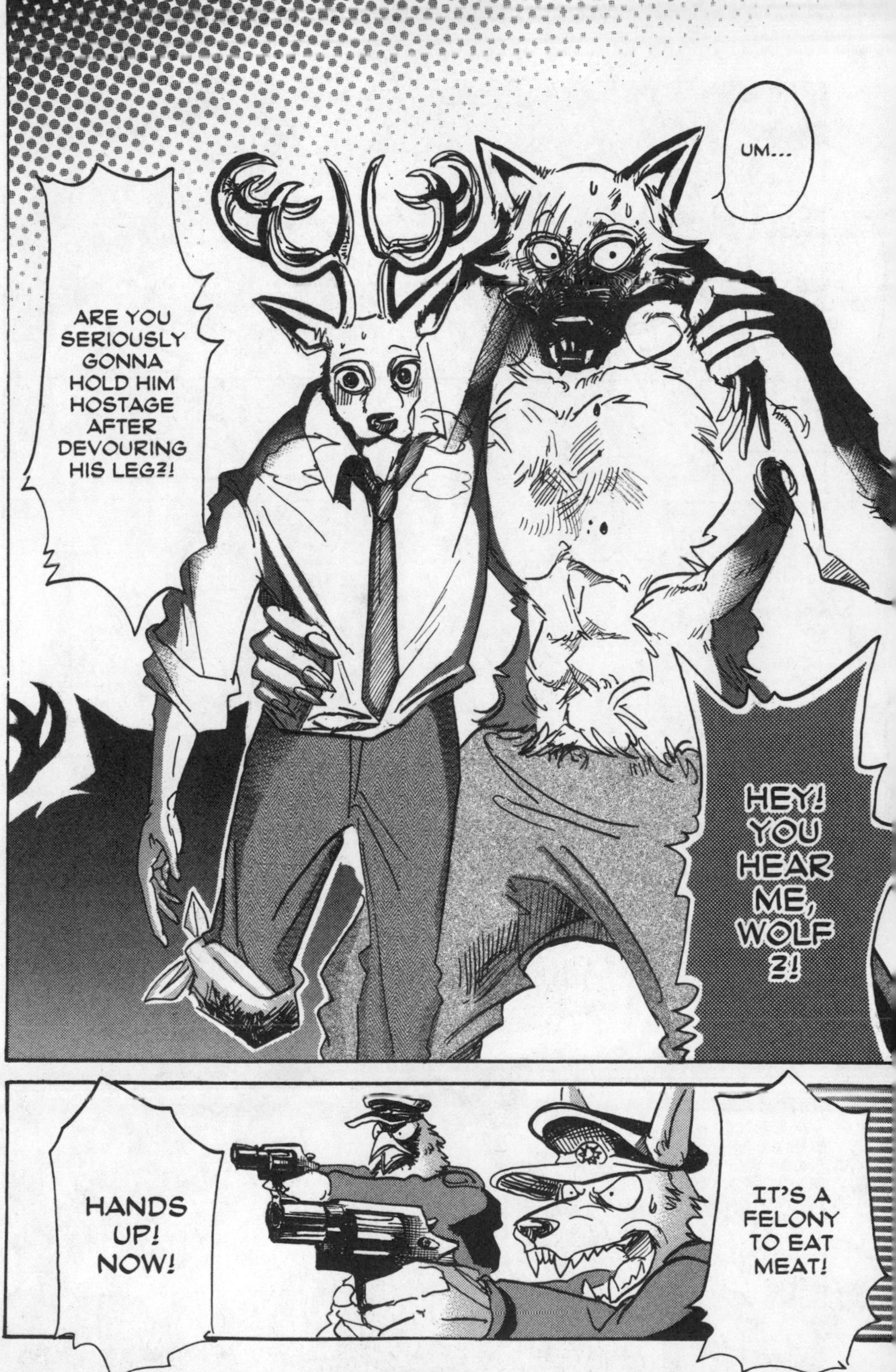
UM...
ARE YOU SERIOUSLY GONNA HOLD HIM HOSTAGE AFTER DEVOURING HIS LEG?!
HEY! YOU HEAR ME, WOLF?!
IT'S A FELONY TO EAT MEAT!
HANDS UP! NOW!

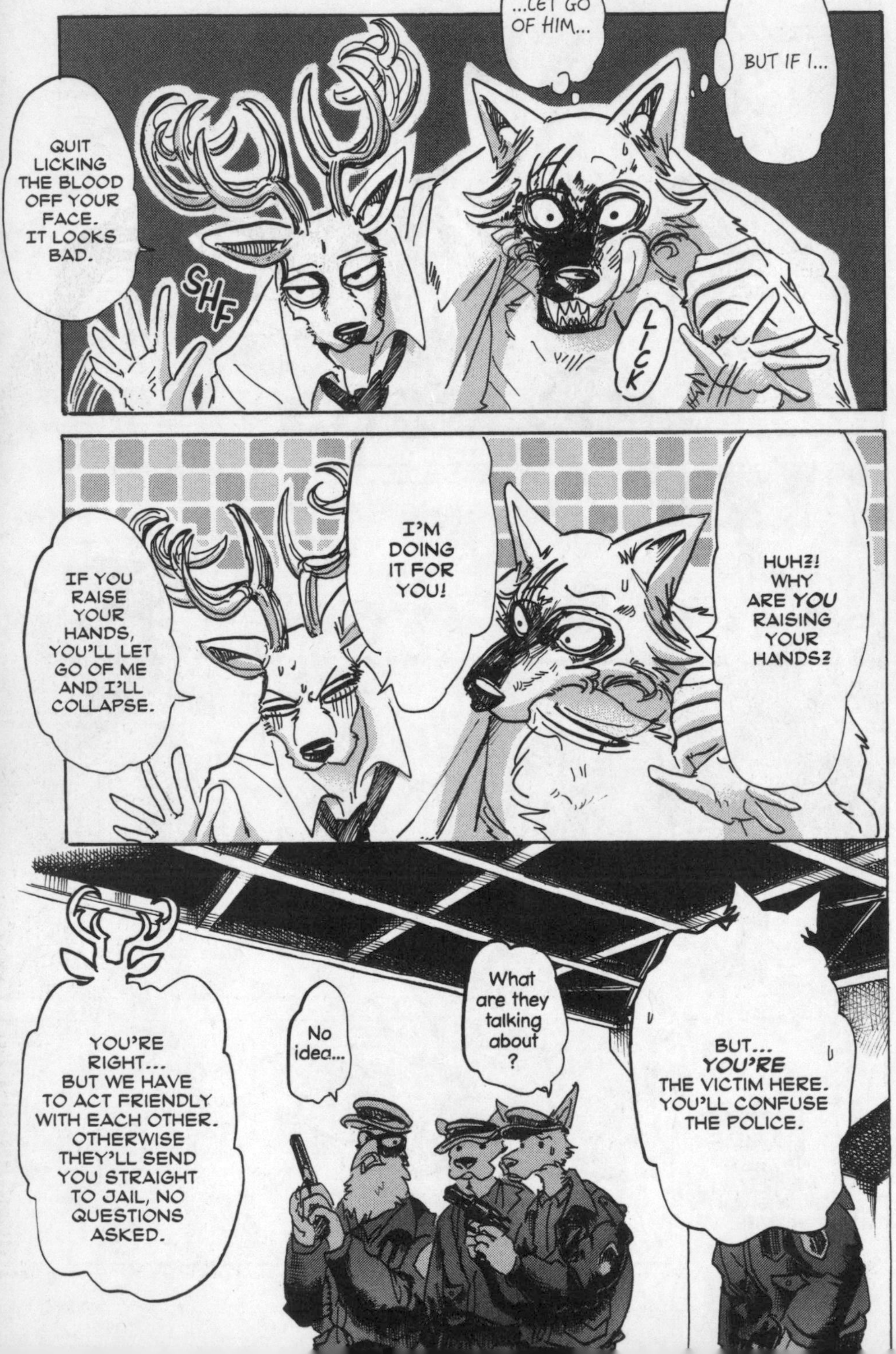
BUT IF I...
...LET GO OF HIM...
LICK
QUIT LICKING THE BLOOD OFF YOUR FACE. IT LOOKS BAD.
SHF
HUH?! WHY ARE *YOU* RAISING YOUR HANDS?
I'M DOING IT FOR YOU!
IF YOU RAISE YOUR HANDS, YOU'LL LET GO OF ME AND I'LL COLLAPSE.
BUT... *YOU'RE* THE VICTIM HERE. YOU'LL CONFUSE THE POLICE.
What are they talking about?
No idea...
YOU'RE RIGHT... BUT WE HAVE TO ACT FRIENDLY WITH EACH OTHER. OTHERWISE THEY'LL SEND YOU STRAIGHT TO JAIL, NO QUESTIONS ASKED.

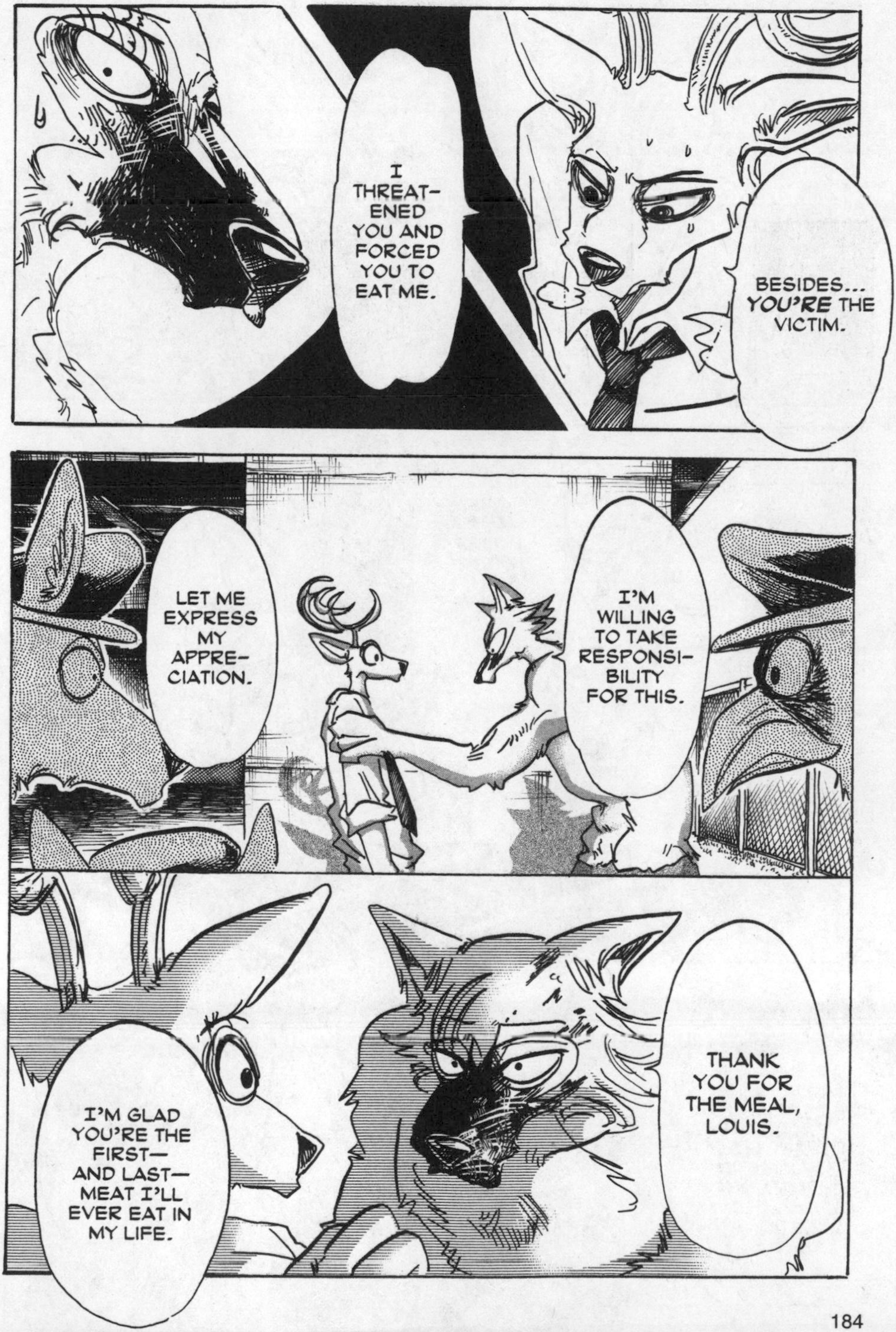
BESIDES... *YOU'RE* THE VICTIM.
I THREAT-ENED YOU AND FORCED YOU TO EAT ME.
I'M WILLING TO TAKE RESPONSI-BILITY FOR THIS.
LET ME EXPRESS MY APPRE-CIATION.
THANK YOU FOR THE MEAL, LOUIS.
I'M GLAD YOU'RE THE FIRST— AND LAST— MEAT I'LL EVER EAT IN MY LIFE.

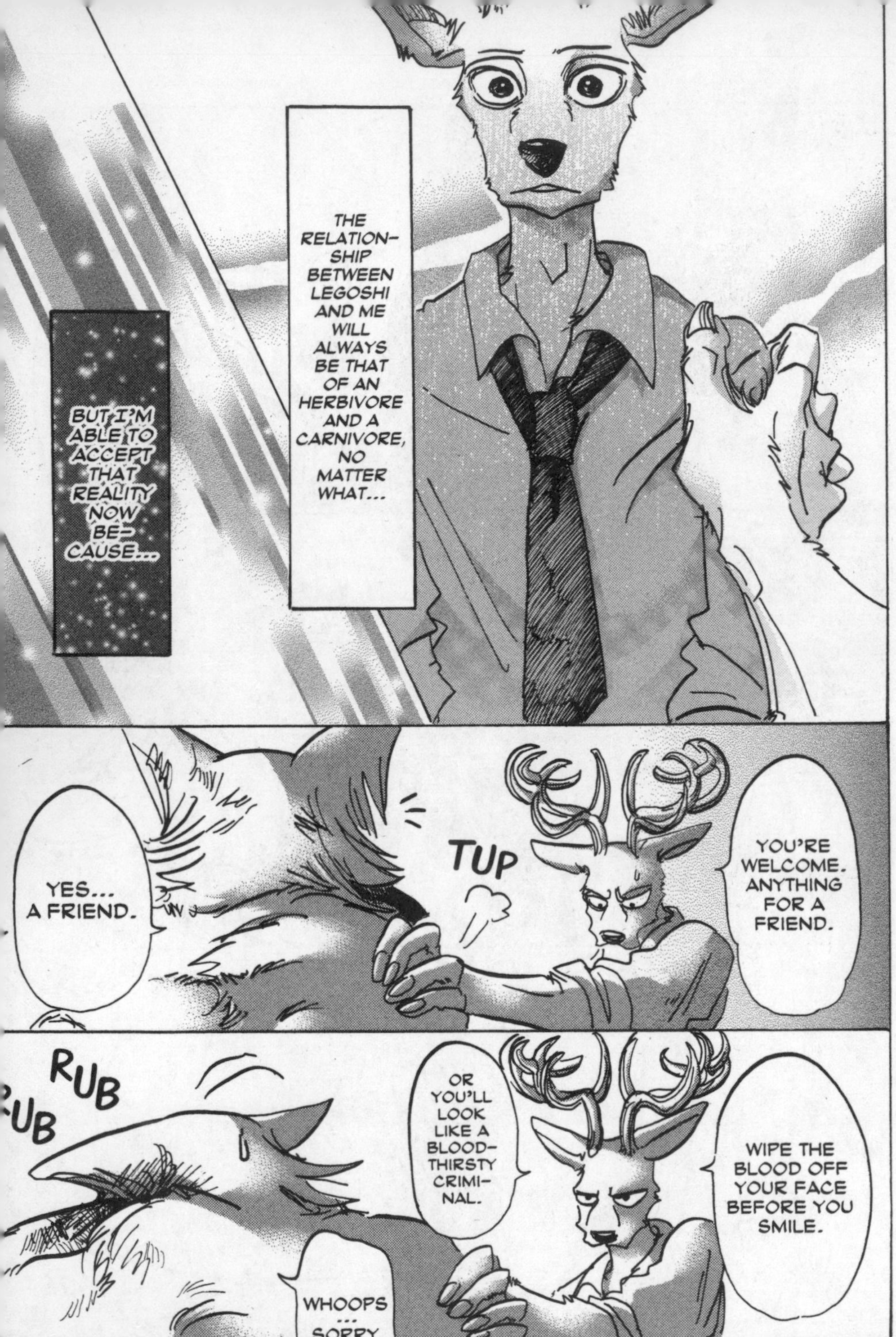
THE RELATIONSHIP BETWEEN LEGOSHI AND ME WILL ALWAYS BE THAT OF AN HERBIVORE AND A CARNIVORE, NO MATTER WHAT...
BUT I'M ABLE TO ACCEPT THAT REALITY NOW BECAUSE...
YOU'RE WELCOME. ANYTHING FOR A FRIEND.
TUP
YES... A FRIEND.
WIPE THE BLOOD OFF YOUR FACE BEFORE YOU SMILE.
OR YOU'LL LOOK LIKE A BLOODTHIRSTY CRIMINAL.
RUB
WHOOPS... SORRY.

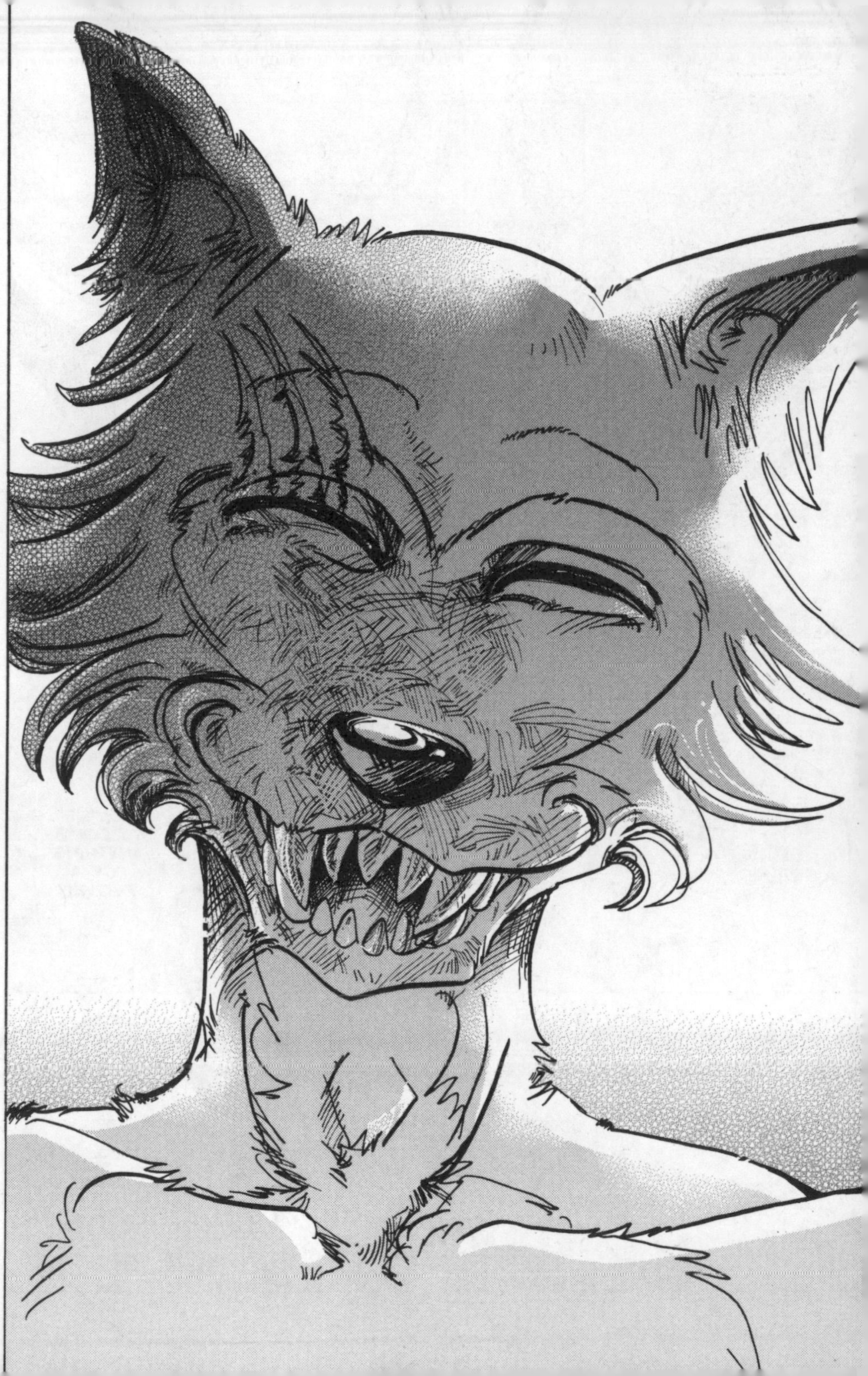

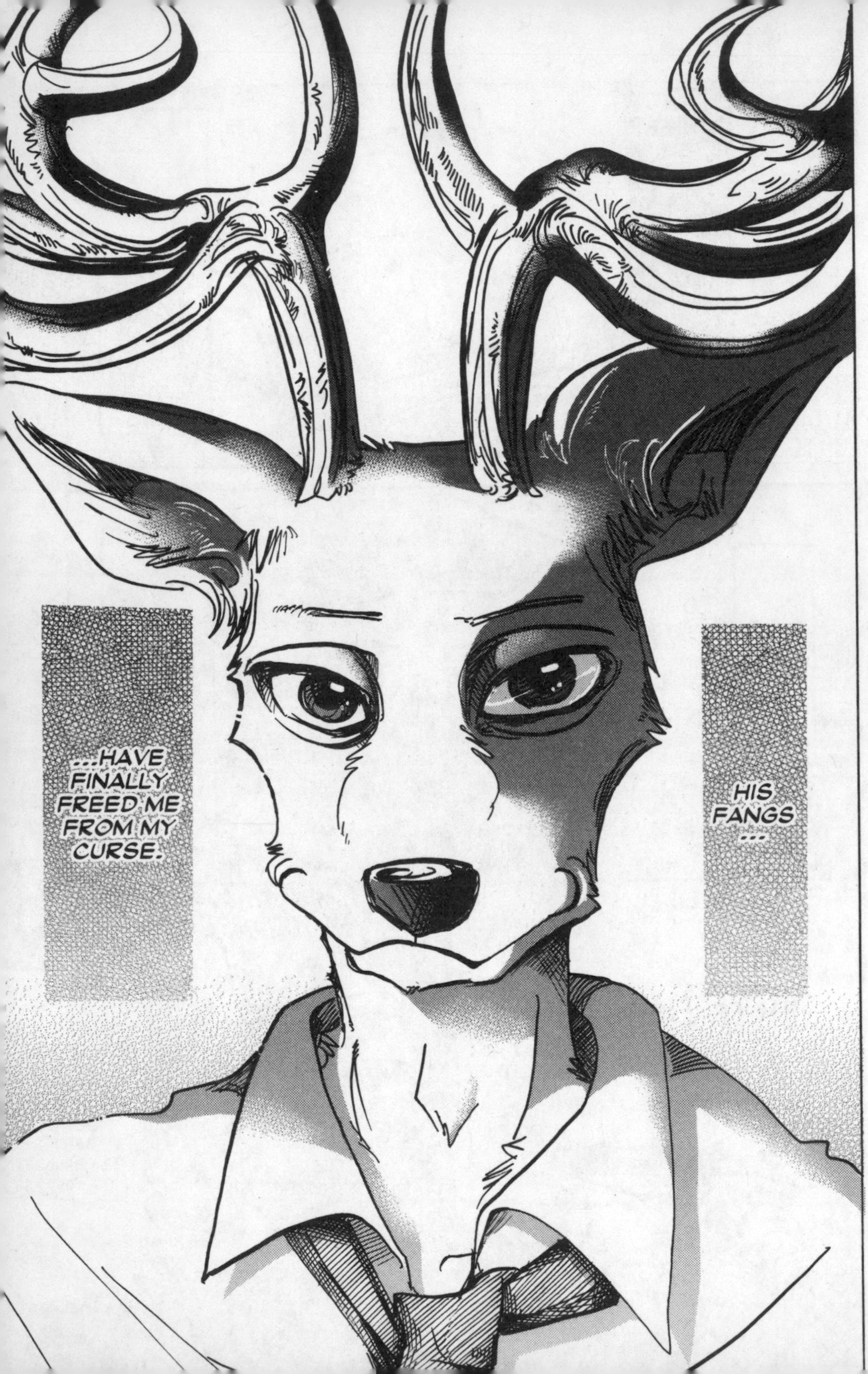
HIS FANGS...
...HAVE FINALLY FREED ME FROM MY CURSE.

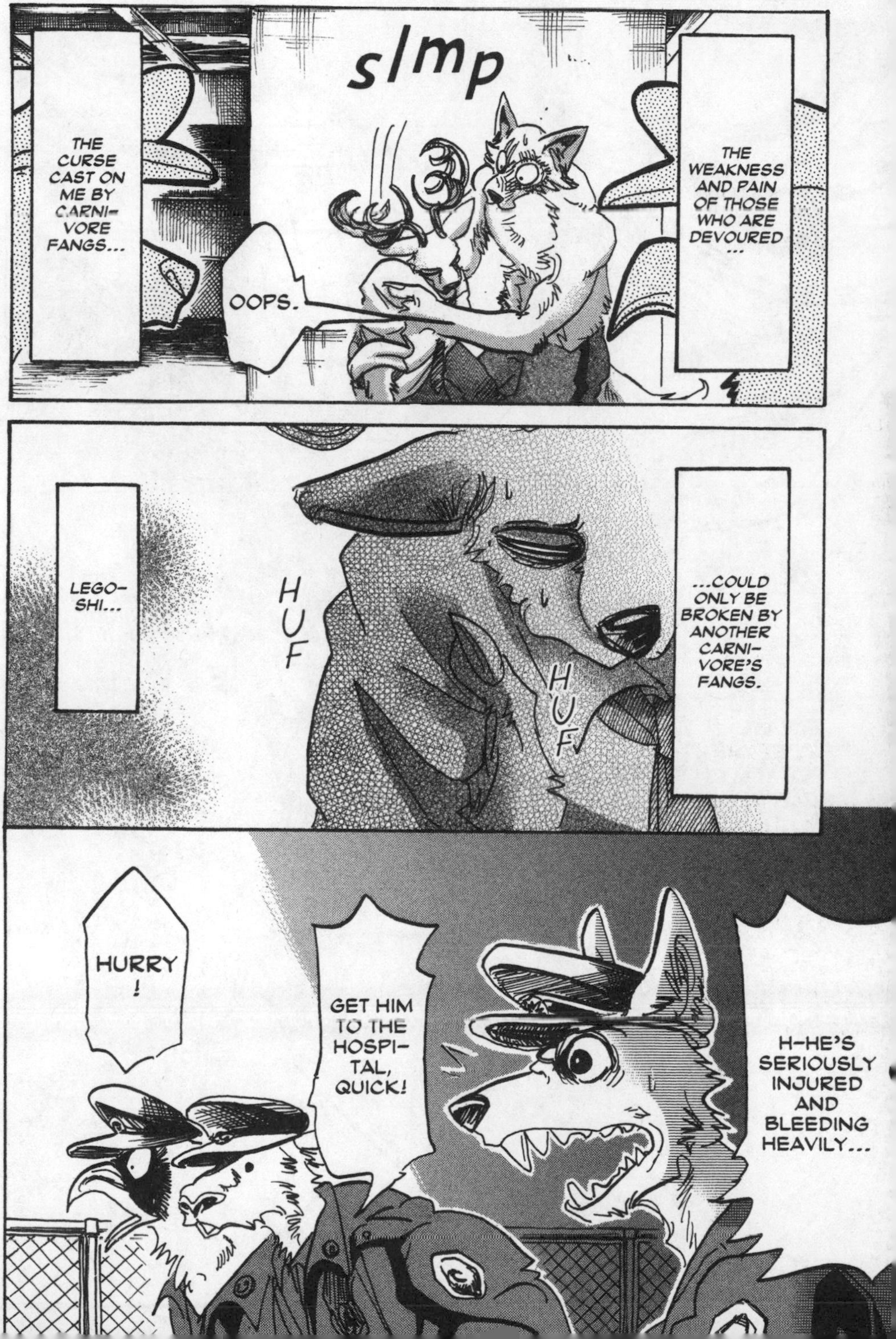
THE WEAKNESS AND PAIN OF THOSE WHO ARE DEVOURED...
slmp
OOPS.
THE CURSE CAST ON ME BY CARNIVORE FANGS...
...COULD ONLY BE BROKEN BY ANOTHER CARNIVORE'S FANGS.
HUF HUF
HUF
LEGOSHI...
H-HE'S SERIOUSLY INJURED AND BLEEDING HEAVILY...
GET HIM TO THE HOSPITAL, QUICK!
HURRY!

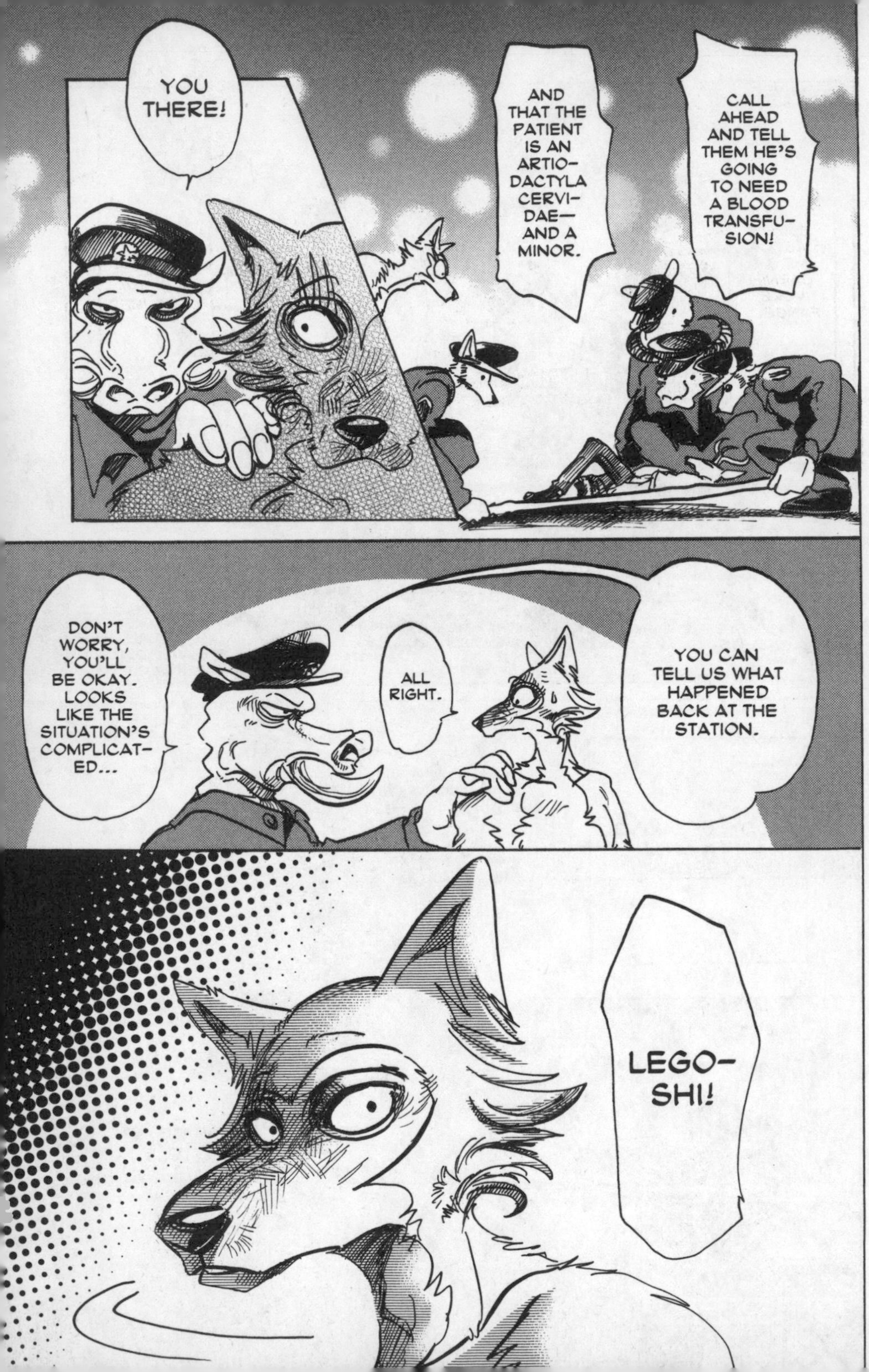
CALL AHEAD AND TELL THEM HE'S GOING TO NEED A BLOOD TRANSFU-SION!
AND THAT THE PATIENT IS AN ARTIO-DACTYLA CERVI-DAE—AND A MINOR.
YOU THERE!
YOU CAN TELL US WHAT HAPPENED BACK AT THE STATION.
ALL RIGHT.
DON'T WORRY, YOU'LL BE OKAY. LOOKS LIKE THE SITUATION'S COMPLICAT-ED...
LEGO-SHI!

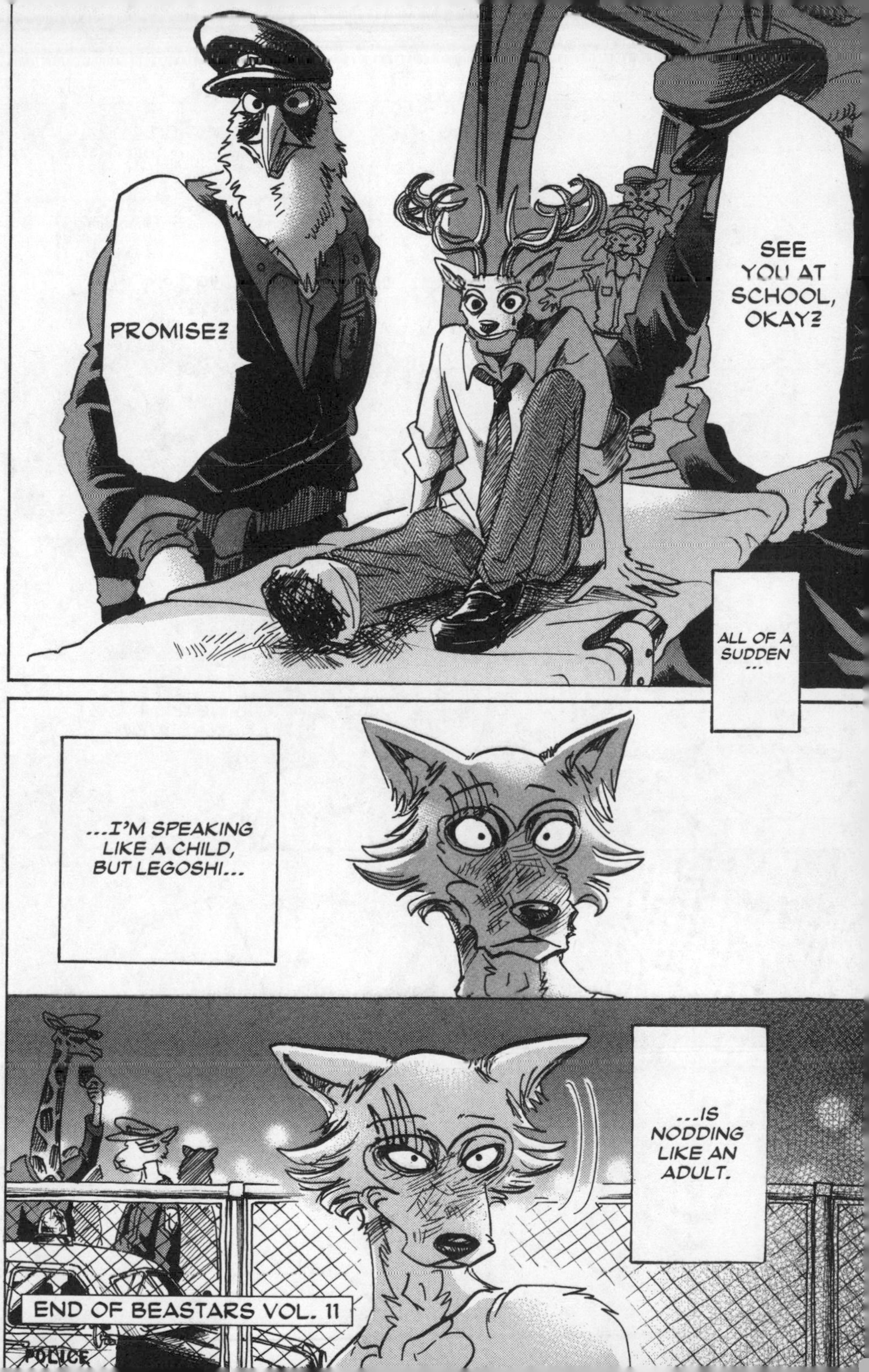
SEE YOU AT SCHOOL, OKAY?
PROMISE?
ALL OF A SUDDEN...
...I'M SPEAKING LIKE A CHILD, BUT LEGOSHI...
...IS NODDING LIKE AN ADULT.
END OF BEASTARS VOL. 11
POLICE

Shooting the frontispiece of this volume

HEY, LOOK UP! UP!

To be continued...

BEASTARS Vol. 11

Paru Itagaki

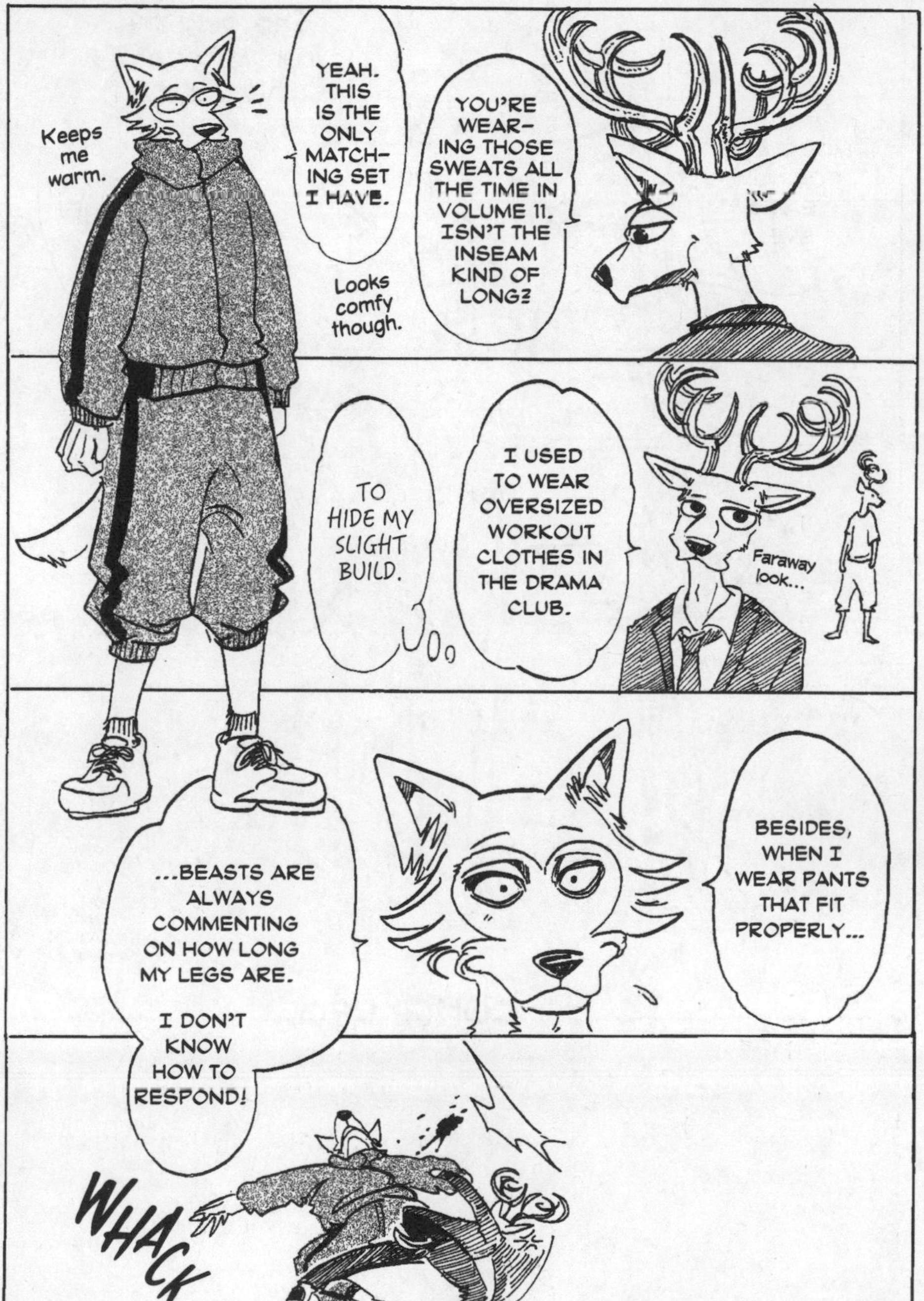

YOU'RE WEARING THOSE SWEATS ALL THE TIME IN VOLUME 11. ISN'T THE INSEAM KIND OF LONG?
YEAH. THIS IS THE ONLY MATCHING SET I HAVE.
Keeps me warm.
Looks comfy though.
I USED TO WEAR OVERSIZED WORKOUT CLOTHES IN THE DRAMA CLUB.
Faraway look...
TO HIDE MY SLIGHT BUILD.
BESIDES, WHEN I WEAR PANTS THAT FIT PROPERLY...
...BEASTS ARE ALWAYS COMMENTING ON HOW LONG MY LEGS ARE.
I DON'T KNOW HOW TO RESPOND!
WHACK

What Happened After Chapter 89

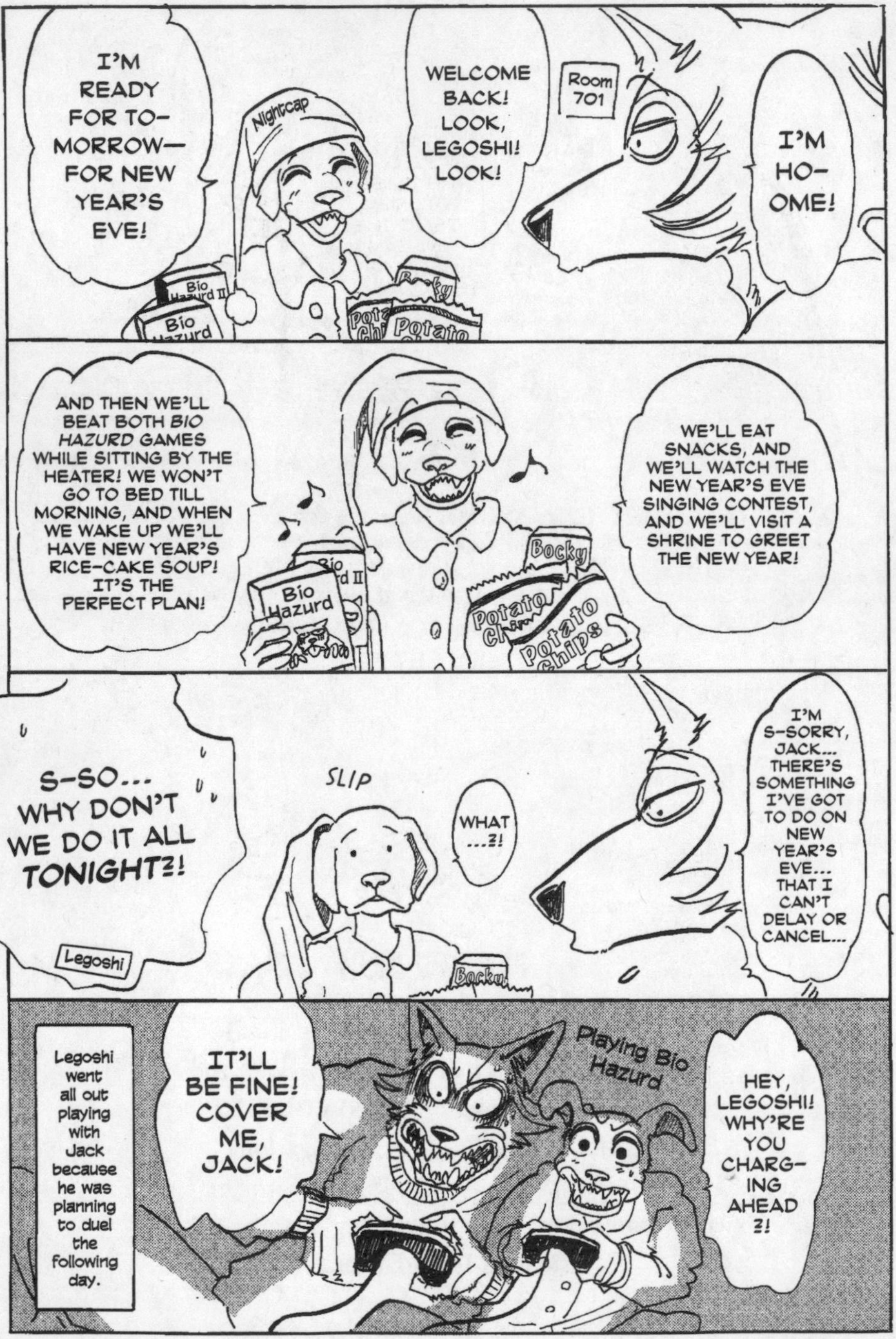
I'M HO-OME!
Room 701
WELCOME BACK! LOOK, LEGOSHI! LOOK!
Nightcap
I'M READY FOR TO-MORROW—FOR NEW YEAR'S EVE!
Bio Hazurd II
Bio Hazurd
Bocky
Potato Chips
WE'LL EAT SNACKS, AND WE'LL WATCH THE NEW YEAR'S EVE SINGING CONTEST, AND WE'LL VISIT A SHRINE TO GREET THE NEW YEAR!
AND THEN WE'LL BEAT BOTH *BIO HAZURD* GAMES WHILE SITTING BY THE HEATER! WE WON'T GO TO BED TILL MORNING, AND WHEN WE WAKE UP WE'LL HAVE NEW YEAR'S RICE-CAKE SOUP! IT'S THE PERFECT PLAN!
I'M S-SORRY, JACK... THERE'S SOMETHING I'VE GOT TO DO ON NEW YEAR'S EVE... THAT I CAN'T DELAY OR CANCEL...
WHAT ...?!
SLIP
S-SO... WHY DON'T WE DO IT ALL **TONIGHT**?!
Legoshi
HEY, LEGOSHI! WHY'RE YOU CHARG-ING AHEAD?!
Playing Bio Hazurd
IT'LL BE FINE! COVER ME, JACK!
Legoshi went all out playing with Jack because he was planning to duel the following day.

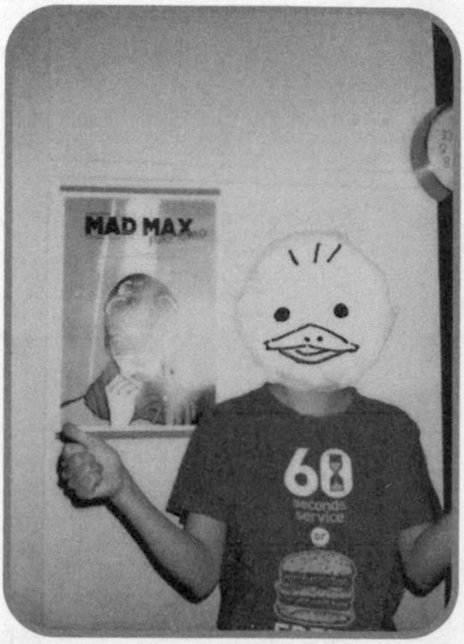
MAD MAX

I HOPE READERS CAN'T WAIT TO READ VOL. 11 THE MOMENT THEY GET IT!

PARU ITAGAKI

Paru Itagaki began her professional career as a manga author in 2016 with the short story collection **BEAST COMPLEX**. **BEASTARS** is her first serialization. **BEASTARS** has won multiple awards in Japan, including the prestigious 2018 Manga Taisho Award.

BEASTARS
VOL. 11
VIZ Signature Edition

Story & Art by
Paru Itagaki

Translation/Tomo Kimura
English Adaptation/Annette Roman
Touch-Up Art & Lettering/Susan Daigle-Leach
Cover & Interior Design/Yukiko Whitley
Editor/Annette Roman

BEASTARS Volume 11

First published in 2018 by Akita Publishing Co., Ltd., Tokyo
English translation rights arranged with Akita Publishing Co., Ltd., through Tuttle-Mori Agency, Inc., Tokyo

Printed in Canada

Published by VIZ Media, LLC
P.O. Box 77010
San Francisco, CA 94107

10 9 8 7 6 5 4 3 2 1
First printing, March 2021

viz.com

vizsignature.com

PARENTAL ADVISORY
BEASTARS is rated T+ and is recommended for ages 16 and up. It contains adult themes, sexual situations and violence.

ratings.viz.com RATED T+ OLDER TEEN

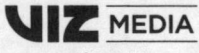

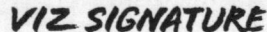

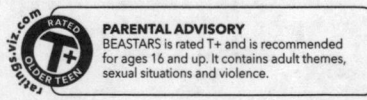

COMING IN VOLUME 12...

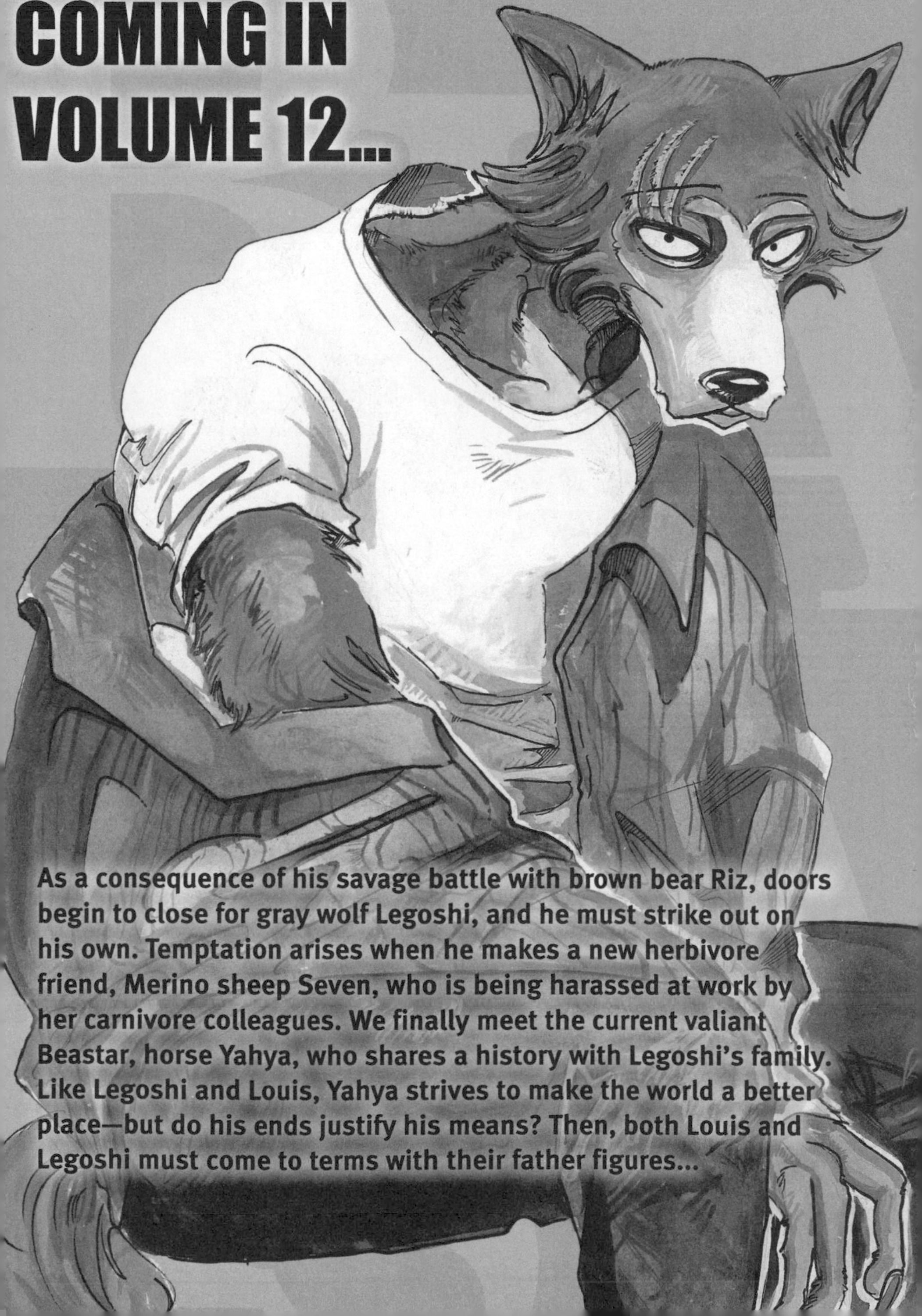

As a consequence of his savage battle with brown bear Riz, doors begin to close for gray wolf Legoshi, and he must strike out on his own. Temptation arises when he makes a new herbivore friend, Merino sheep Seven, who is being harassed at work by her carnivore colleagues. We finally meet the current valiant Beastar, horse Yahya, who shares a history with Legoshi's family. Like Legoshi and Louis, Yahya strives to make the world a better place—but do his ends justify his means? Then, both Louis and Legoshi must come to terms with their father figures...

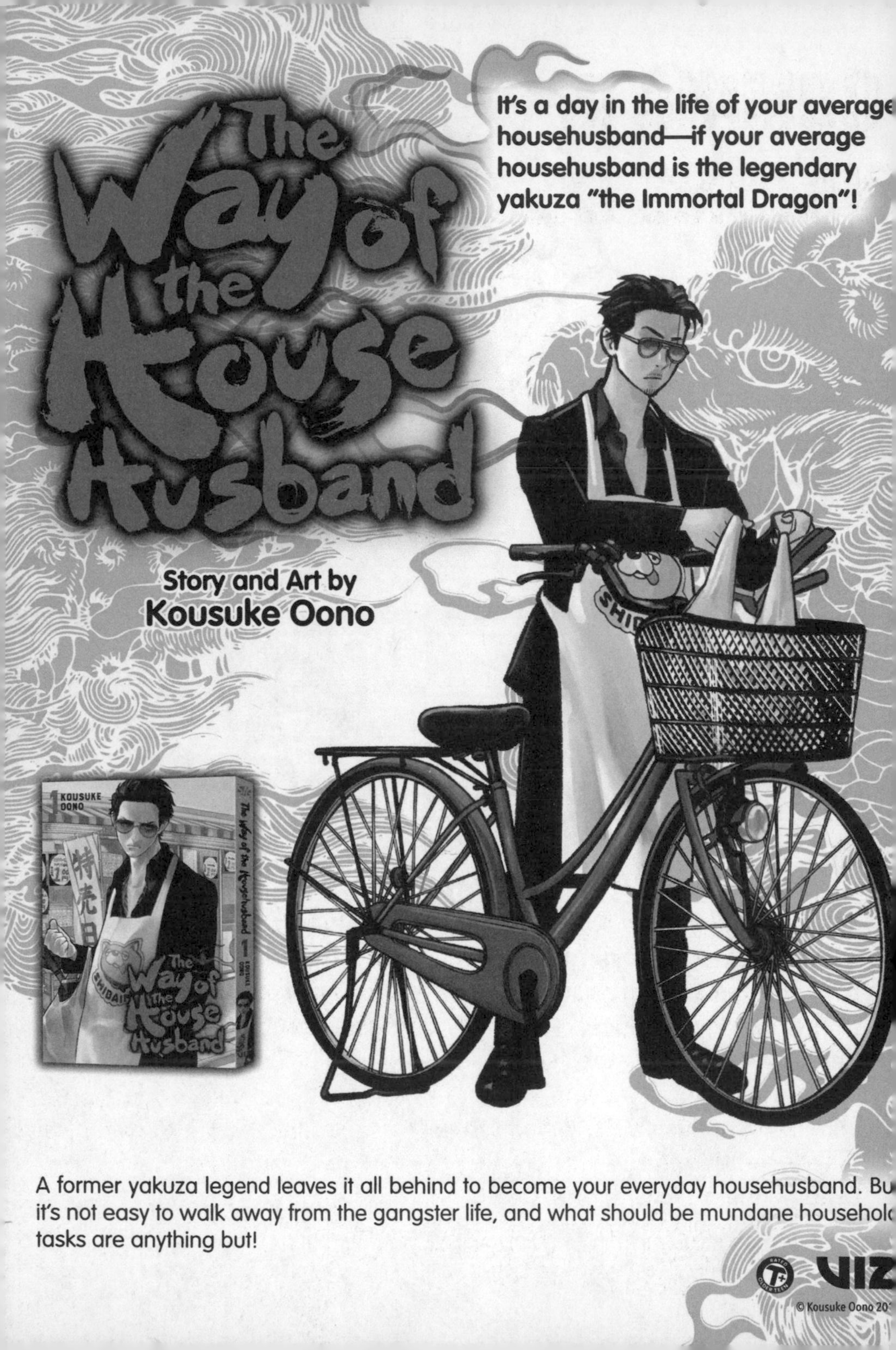
The Way of the House Husband
It's a day in the life of your averag
househusband—if your average
housebusband is the legendary
yakuza "the Immortal Dragon"!
Story and Art by
Kousuke Oono
KOUSUKE OONO
The Way of the House Husband
A former yakuza legend leaves it all behind to become your everyday househusband. Bu
it's not easy to walk away from the gangster life, and what should be mundane househol
tasks are anything but!
VIZ
© Kousuke Oono 20

CHILDREN OF THE WHALES

In this postapocalyptic fantasy, a sea of sand swallows everything but the past.

In an endless sea of sand drifts the Mud Whale, a floating island city of clay and magic. In its chambers a small community clings to survival, cut off from its own history by the shadows of the past.

This is the last page.

BEASTARS reads from right to left to preserve the orientation of the original Japanese artwork.